One of the most extraordinary players in the shadowy game of espionage, Oleg Penkovskiy could easily have defected to the West like so many of his comrades had done.

Instead, he chose to stay "in place," working for the Soviet intelligence system while transmitting valuable information to the West.

This very human and immediate book tells the whole amazing story of a man making choices in his life that would eventually result in his own execution, a man who lived on the outside of his own world.

THE PENKOVSKIY PAPERS

THE
PENKOVSKIY
PAPERS

Oleg Penkovskiy

Introduction and Commentary
by Frank Gibney

ESPIONAGE ★ INTELLIGENCE
BB
★ LIBRARY ★

BALLANTINE BOOKS • NEW YORK

ISBN 0-345-30093-9

This ediiton published by arrangement with
Doubleday & Company, Inc.

Manufactured in the United States of America

First Ballantine Books Edition: May 1982

PREFACE TO THE
BALLANTINE BOOKS EDITION

WHEN the Penkovskiy Papers were first published in 1965, they attracted controversy almost as fast as they drew readers. Doubleday's American edition almost immediately became a bestseller. Its British, French, German, Swedish, Korean, and Japanese editions were similarly successful. Before publication, the Papers gained an even wider circulation through syndication in more than 30 major American newspapers and voluminous excerpts published elsewhere around the world.

Such success was not surprising. There was intrinsic drama in the story of the highly placed colonel in Soviet Military Intelligence who chose, almost impulsively it seemed, to spy for Britain and the United States against his own government. This element of drama remains today. For all Penkovskiy's revelations about Soviet military aggression, the cynicism of Moscow's "New Class" leadership, and the power of the secret police over the Soviet peoples—the fascination of this book inheres in the story of this lonely, moody protestor against his own society and his brief, solitary attempt to bring it down.

The controversy over the book, while predictable, was extraordinarily quick in coming. The Soviet Union served up an unusually strong brew of invective. "A coarse fraud, a mixture of anti-Soviet invention and slander," "crude forgery," "CIA fake," were typical comments. As the editor, I was denounced as a "CIA hireling." When I made a statement defending the book's authenticity, *Pravda* rather picturesquely likened me to "a tired boxer, desperately throwing ineffectual punches in an effort to sustain his fraud . . ." Sterner measures than name-calling were also taken. The Soviet Ambassador in London made an official protest; an American correspondent for the *Washington Post*, which had syndicated the Papers, was expelled from the Soviet Union; and a British newsman had his visa denied for a similar reason. Rarely has the Soviet Union displayed so much agitation over an espionage case.

Although the majority of editorial comment and review of the book in the United States and other Western countries was thoughtful and favorable, a few journalists and Soviet-watchers echoed the Soviet reaction. Liberally using such words as "fraud," "fiction," and "invention," these people held that the book, as one critic put it, was the work of "some spooky committee, mischievously compiling mixtures of fact and fancy." The Papers, we were assured, could not possibly have been written by Penkovskiy because their tone didn't sound right. No "professional spy" would have taken such risks as to write a "diary," another noted, because "spies don't keep diaries." The account was too "emotional" to be true, since the cynicism it imputed to Soviet officials was excessive. Above all, the manner in which the Papers had been transmitted—i.e. how they got from Penkovskiy to me—was not stated. Hence the whole thing had to have been cooked up by the Central Intelligence Agency. Hence it had to be a fraud. Q.E.D.

Neither the source nor the logic of these attacks on the book's authenticity bothered me very much at the time. From a publishing standpoint, in fact, some were gratifying (Max Frankel's fearless excoriation of the Papers in *The New York Times* on publication day, for one thing, helped propel the book into the bestseller lists). Yet over the years the spasmodic repetition of the charges began to grate on the ears, not the least because they implied that the book's editor was either some feckless dupe or himself one of CIA's conspirators in foisting a "fraud" on an unsuspecting public (and publisher). By the late seventies, following various revelations about the CIA's alleged role in influencing everything from elections in foreign countries to the price of meat at home, a small platoon of former CIA employees with literary ambitions had gotten into the act. These gentry were quick to assert that the Penkovskiy book was just another CIA effort at self-serving propaganda. Although their authority for this view was not specified, they were duly and prominently quoted by the press. Much of what they said, I presume, was believed in the climate of a time when, by some odd inversion of what we used to call patriotism, the major danger to American institutions was supposed to come from our own intelligence agencies rather than those of the competition.[1]

Doubt about the Papers' origins was echoed in the report of the Senate Select Committee studying U.S. government intelligence activities, called the Church Committee after its then-Chairman, former Senator Frank Church. "Another CIA book, the Penkovskiy Papers," the committee report ran, "was published in the United States for operational reasons but actually became commercially viable. The book was written by witting Agency assets who drew on actual case materials. Publication rights to the manuscript were sold to a publisher through a trust fund established for the purpose. The publisher was unaware of any U.S. Government interest."

Despite its judicious-sounding bureaucratic language, the Church Committee's comment was incorrect. It gave a distorted impression of the book, how it was written, and how it was published. No one from the committee, incidentally, had even bothered to call or write me in the course of the investigations. But the statement suggested the need to write these comments, which I hope will clear up once and for all what the Penkovskiy Papers are, how they were edited, and whence they came. Sixteen years after the Papers were published, I can now write without any of the constraints on discussing them which I had felt at that time. Not least of these was the fact that even after Penkovskiy's trial in 1963, his Soviet superiors still did not know the full extent of his espionage activities.

Two basic doubts were expressed about the authenticity of the Papers. The first had to do with content. Wasn't Penkovskiy being too extreme? Few anti-Soviet protestors, before or since, had made such sweeping, violent denunciations of the Soviet leadership—or at least those leaders whom Penkovskiy had a chance to observe at close range. To the professionally "fair-minded," the very vehemence

---

[1] A distinguished exception to the run of "anti-CIA" books was Frank Snepp's *Decent Interval*, a sober but devastating account of the CIA's bungling, among others', during the final stages of the U.S. action in Vietnam. It is ironic that Snepp, an honest and constructive critic, was singled out for drastic punitive action by the CIA and the Justice Department, while others went virtually unmolested.

of Penkovskiy's expression was enough to cast doubt on its authenticity. ("Surely the Soviet leaders couldn't be all that bad.") On the other hand some Sovietologists, like the British critic Viktor Zorza, objected to Penkovskiy's statements on technical grounds. Penkovskiy, Zorza claimed, would use the word "Napoleon" or "Napoleonic" where most Soviet Russians were supposed to use the cliché word "Bonapartist." He would talk about going to "Europe," whereas all the Soviets whom Zorza knew would speak of going to the "West." Such departures from orthodox linguistics, it was held, only proved that those bumblers in CIA, who had obviously written the book, were giving themselves away by their mistakes.

The second doubt had to do with the manner in which the Papers found their way into print, not to mention how they were translated and edited. In my original introduction to the book, I had refused to say how the Papers were conveyed from Penkovskiy to the United States. Didn't this silence from the editor, some critics argued, amount to a kind of cover-up, casting doubt on the reality of the Papers themselves? Journalistic followers of the conspiratorial theory of current events, so popular in recent years, had little trouble demonstrating to their own satisfaction that any holding back of any "facts" in an intelligence matter clearly indicated a CIA plot.

Both these doubts are understandable. They deserve to be met and answered. In the first place, given the abuses of power by various U.S. governmental agencies—CIA among them—unearthed since the Watergate investigations, many Americans are rightly sensitive about the role of secret intelligence operations in a democracy. There is an inherent conflict here. At the same time, the same press that uncovered Watergate has shown itself, in many recent cases, to be as careless of the public's right to know as the bureaucrats it enjoys criticizing. Abuses of power are hardly the monopoly of governments.

When I first looked at the materials from which the Papers were selected, they were in the possession of the Central Intelligence Agency. They had indeed been smuggled out of the Soviet Union in a variety of ways, as I wrote in the original Introduction. They were indeed, as I wrote then, scanned and translated by Peter Deriabin, a former State Security (KGB) officer who had defected to the United States. He was then working for U.S. intelligence. Some of them were transcripts of debriefings with U.S. and British intelligence officers in London and Paris, in which Penkovskiy had talked not merely of military secrets; they included a wide variety of comments, animadversions, and personal observations on the Soviet system and its leaders. Others were notes written in his own handwriting or typed by the same typewriter that Soviet State Security (KGB) investigators had found in Penkovskiy's apartment and put into the trial as a primary piece of evidence. At the time I secured access to the Papers, it was felt in Washington that disclosure of their possession by the CIA would have provoked an international incident, not merely with the Russians, but with the British, many of whom were dead-against revealing the source of the papers at all. It would certainly have made matters worse for Penkovskiy, who had not yet been brought to trial by the Soviets. Even at the time *The Penkovskiy Papers* was published, no one was certain that the death sentence passed on him had been executed.

The fact that these papers were in the possession of the CIA in no way invalidated their authenticity. Deriabin, whom I trusted, had examined them thoroughly. I myself checked them to the best of my ability, as an editor and as one who knew something about the Soviet Union, Russians, and the language. I established to my own satisfaction that they were authentic. In no sense of the word were the Papers handed to me as part of some behind-the-scenes CIA publishing project or plot. Quite to the contrary, it was I who got wind of their existence and managed to pry the Papers out of the Agency for use as a book. As a journalist I was quite pleased with this achievement and remain so to this day. Since the story of how I found and edited the Papers may have some interest, I have included it below, along with some prefatory notes about the Papers' content.

There were two messages that Oleg Penkovskiy was trying to get across, principally to people in Britain and the United States. The first was his own indignation, as a career military officer and a Russian, at the cynical attitude of the Soviet leaders toward their own people, their obsession with material comforts, and the dangerous "adventurism" of their foreign policy. Penkovskiy felt strongly that the Soviet regime was about to bring on a world war.

The second thing he wanted to warn us about was the immanence of the security organizations in Soviet society. The colonel saw the Soviet Union in the grip of a police dictatorship. And this, as the Papers themselves suggest, is what impelled him to espionage—a desperate revolt of an individual against a system.

Penkovskiy wrote and dictated most of the Papers in 1961 and 1962. He was arrested in October, 1962. The events of two decades since then would seem to have proved him right. The 1962 missile crisis in Cuba came to a peak, ironically, just after he had been arrested in Moscow. The invasion of Czechoslovakia in 1968, which destroyed the liberal national Communism of Dubcek, was followed in ten years by the invasion of Afghanistan—with an assortment of African aggressions in between. As I write, the fate of Poland still hangs in the balance. Vietnam is being turned into a Soviet advanced base, and the aggressive posturings of the Soviet fleet in East Asia are worrying Asians from Singapore to Hokkaido.

Since Penkovskiy wrote, we have seen continuing purges of intellectuals and dissenters inside the Soviet Union, with concurrent glorification of the "heroic Chekists" of the KGB secret police. The latent anti-Semitism within the U.S.S.R. has over the years come to be virtually official policy, as the flood of emigrés to Israel and the West attest. Wholesale spying continues, from Soviet embassies and entire spy networks throughout the world. The crudities of Soviet persecution of dissenters has even had some effect on those moral relativists in the West, who seemed to hold that Soviet crimes against humanity are simply a matter of a "different" political system, while the real enemy is said to be in Argentina or South Korea. Finally, anyone who has read Solzhenitsyn and others on the moral bankruptcy of the Soviet regime should hardly criticize Penkovskiy for exaggeration.

It is true that many of Penkovskiy's comments were intemperate. His hatred of Khrushchev was obsessive, for reasons that I as an editor never fully understood. There were points, e.g. exact dates of one or two command changes in the Soviet Army, on which Penkovskiy's memory failed him and a few inaccuracies in his comments, e.g. he referred to a new Soviet nuclear bomb as 80-megaton, when Western experts had accurately measured it as 58. If the Papers had indeed been either fabricated or heavily edited by some CIA committee, it would have been easy to smooth over any such discrepancies. No such effort was made, although I tried in footnotes to clear up ambiguities wherever possible and state the significance of many of his cryptic comments to the general reader. When Peter Deriabin, the translator, and I started to work on them, the Papers were indeed just that—a huge mass of documents, comments, appeal, and information on which we tried to impose much selectivity and some order, but without changing a single word of what the man had said. This was no easy job, which leads me to comment on the second doubt raised about the book: how the Papers were screened, translated, and edited.

In 1958 and 1959, while a staff writer for *Life* magazine, I had written a series of articles about Deriabin, the former KGB officer, with his close collaboration. He had defected to the U.S. forces in Vienna in 1954. (The Central Intelligence Agency had asked *Life* if it was interested in publishing Deriabin's "story"; on the basis of my appraisal, *Life*'s editor agreed to do so. It was fascinating material.) Later, as part of my duties at *Life,* we developed the articles into a book, *The Secret World,* with Deriabin and I as co-authors. Doubleday was the publisher, and the book did rather well. Although CIA was obviously happy to have Deriabin's story told, no security restrictions were put on *Life* during the writing. There was no need for that kind of monitoring. The magazine's interest—and mine— was in telling the story of one man and the light his experiences shed on how the Soviet security forces controlled their country. We were not interested either in revealing or suppressing intelligence information, which had presumably been gained previously, during Deriabin's long debriefing by the CIA.

When I first met Deriabin, we had some communication problems. His English was somewhat rusty, and my command of Russian, acquired during the forties in courses at Yale College and elsewhere, was to say the least shaky. But during the months we worked on the articles and the book, we became good friends and have remained so. A tough, bright Siberian who had fought at Stalingrad, he had been drafted into the State Security. He had fled to the West in revulsion against what he had seen and learned as a member of Stalin's Guard Directorate in the Kremlin. After working for a short time in the United States as a consultant on Soviet affairs, he was asked to join the CIA as a high-level intelligence analyst and worked there for many years.

It was through Deriabin that I learned late in 1962 that another really big spy story had recently concluded. Given the public news of Penkovskiy's arrest and trial, it was no mystery whose story it was. Although I then had a demanding job in New York, as publisher of the newly founded *Show* magazine, I was intrigued by the possibility of writing another "Secret World" with wider implications. So I applied to the CIA to see if I could have access to anything Penkovskiy might have written for future publication. (In those days, at least, CIA had a regular press liaison and information office.) Deriabin had already seen some of the material on Penkovskiy and was familiar with the case. He knew Penkovskiy's background well. In Siberia, just before the outbreak of World War II, he had worked for Penkovskiy's father-in-law, General Dmitriy Gapanovich, as a political officer in the Trans-Baikal Military District. Later in Moscow he had done the same kind of Party political work as Penkovskiy had, in the early stages of his career. For a time, in the Moscow Military District, Penkovskiy had worked for one of Deriabin's old friends.

After much bureaucratic hemming and hawing, the CIA agreed that I might take a look at the Penkovskiy material, to see if I thought there was a book in it. The material, as I noted in the 1965 introduction to the book (see General Introduction), was, to put it mildly, fragmentary— "a series of hastily written notes, sketches and comments," combining much information of intelligence interest with writing of a very personal nature. Some of the material was in the form of transcriptions of interview sessions that Penkovskiy had had with British and American intelligence officers. I also heard some recordings of Penkovskiy's voice. A large portion, however, consisted of notes either typed or handwritten by Penkovskiy—much of which he had sent out on microfilm. (When excerpts of the Papers were syndicated in 1965, sample pages of the handwritten portion were released by Publishers' Newspaper Syndicate to the press; more was available for the asking. Most critics of the Papers' authenticity overlooked this fact.) I asked for and received enough documentation—pictures, personal papers, Party cards, etc.—to convince me that the Papers, if fragmentary, were authentic.

There were many in CIA, not to mention the British intelligence service, who did not want anything published on Penkovskiy at all. Ultimately, after knocking on a great many doors, I was allowed to use the Papers, which were CIA's property, select excerpts (apart from some highly classified portions), and propose them for a book. Deriabin worked on the translating and excerpting for me, but all editorial decisions about what to include or delete were mine. As I noted in the 1965 introduction, we did a great deal of cutting and splicing to turn the fragments into something resembling a connected narrative. For example, out of 700 names mentioned in the material, we kept only 200 for the excerpted Papers. The one thing we did not tamper with was Penkovskiy's words. Everything in the Papers themselves came from him. Nor did we violate his meaning or intent in our editing.

At no time did anyone from CIA even suggest what I should include or not include. The agency did insist on a final security check, which was never any secret. As I wrote in an article for Publishers' Newspaper Syndicate at the time: "At the end we showed the manuscript to intelligence agencies of the U.S. government, to make sure no violations of security were involved." As a reporter and a student of the Soviet system, I was anxious to tell the story of a man whose exploits and personality had hitherto been a mystery, except for the highly selective version given out by the Soviets at his 1963 trial.

The only constraint on me was that I not reveal directly how the Papers got to this country and not *publicly* mention that they had been held by the CIA. I thought this a reasonable restriction, which did not interfere in any way with the authenticity of the Papers. If Penkovskiy were to be the subject of a book, it had to be on the material's intrinsic merits. (Had the CIA people wished to edit and "surface" the Papers themselves, there were surely enough publishers in New York who would have printed them in those days, for one consideration or another.)

I first took the outline of the book to the New York house that had published my most recent book, *The Operators*. They turned it down on the basis of a reader's report that she would hate to publish a book about "a man who betrayed his country." I next took it to Doubleday, whose editors were somewhat more aware of the political and moral distinctions between the Soviet dictatorship and a normal "country." The late LeBaron Barker, one of Doubleday's—and American publishing's—best editors, was enthusiastic about the book's prospects. Lee Barker helped me select the title of *Penkovskiy Papers* and was of great assistance both in reducing the copious material to manageable book size and in editing the rather long explanatory sections about Penkovskiy's life. These we both had felt were needed to make the book intelligible to the average reader.

Deriabin and I agreed that the greater portion of the royalties for this book be set aside for a *Penkovskiy Foundation*, which disbursed some $74,000 in the form of grants and partial scholarships to graduate students in Soviet studies in various American universities. After this amount was disbursed, the Foundation ceased to exist.

Doubleday, as the publisher, never had any doubt that the book was being published with CIA clearance and approval. Doubleday's management knew the source of the Papers. I had made this quite clear to Lee Barker, as I had to the editor of the *Chicago Daily News*, for whom I was working in 1965, and to the head of Publishers' Newspaper Syndicate in Chicago, which distributed the excerpts. Barker at one point had asked to receive at least informal assurance from the United States government that the material in *The Penkovskiy Papers* was authentic. To this end, he and I called on an aide to McGeorge Bundy at the National Security Council, who assured Barker that the Papers were authentic and that publishing them was "in the national interest."

So much for the assertion of the Church Committee that "the publisher was unaware of any government interest."

I have yet to find the "spooky committee" that allegedly cooked up the Papers and gave them to me, neatly wrapped, to sell to a publisher. It was news to me when the Church Committee referred to me, by implication, as a "witting agency asset." I am still trying to figure out what that

Delphic phrase means. It was also news to me when various commentators later cast doubts on the authenticity of a book that "purported to be the diary of Colonel Penkovskiy." Diary was exactly what I said it was *not*. (The spelling of "Penkovskiy" rather than "Penkovsky" in the book, incidentally, was widely held by its critics to be evidence of CIA authorship, since this spelling was used by the CIA. I happened to use it because Deriabin, the translator, is a purist about transliteration of Cyrillic letters—which seemed all right to me.)

About the various "agency sources," unnamed "CIA officials," and similar ghostly authorities who told various newsmen that the Papers were somehow tainted, the kindest interpretation is that these tried and true Agency "leaks"—if such they were—did not really themselves know the circumstances under which CIA agreed to give me exclusive access to the Papers. Not many did. And it is a big agency.

One final comment on the good faith and reporting competence of the Papers' press critics may be in order: with a single exception, not one of these people ever bothered to question me about their concerns or even made any attempt to find my whereabouts. I was hardly under wraps. For ten years after publication of the Papers, I worked in Tokyo as President of TBS-Britannica, a large joint-venture publishing company. As concurrently Vice President of Encyclopaedia Britannica for the Far East area, I commuted almost constantly to Chicago and New York—not really too hard to find.

The one exception was John Crewdson of *The New York Times*. I thank him for that. Yet he got the story partly wrong, after spending two hours over the international telephone circuit, unsuccessfully trying to make me admit that my service as a Navy Intelligence POW interrogation officer in World War II was clear evidence that I had spent all the intervening time between 1945 and 1965 as a CIA agent. At least he had the honesty and sense to call me.

Not so the Church Committee or the people who reported its "findings." It is symptomatic of the looseness of so much press reporting today, with all its protective coloration of "sources revealed" or "a high official said," that reporters who expect their own unsupported words to be taken on faith apparently lack the journalistic common sense to report both sides of a controversial story.

I have no regrets for not having revealed the source of the Penkovskiy Papers at the time they were published. An element of national security was involved, which I believed and respected. It had no effect on the authenticity of the Papers themselves—unless one believes that anything involved with a government agency is automatically crooked. It is a new level of hypocrisy for people in my profession to denounce someone for protecting the source of a story, when they themselves use a variety of source-protection devices—and worse—every day in the week. These range from protecting the Watergate revelations of an anonymous Deep Throat to concealing the identity of the janitor who lets the local reporter copy down the confidential deliberations of the school board. Where important issues or principles are involved, a writer must protect his source. I did mine.

In the end, probably the most powerful vindication of the Penkovskiy Papers' authenticity keeps coming from the Soviets themselves. In the world's most spy-conscious country, the home-grown spy who stole so many secrets has become an obsessive bogeyman. I have had only one direct talk with the Soviets myself on this matter, at a Tokyo lunch in the 1970s. I had attended to listen to the then–Soviet Ambassador to Japan, Oleg Troyanovsky, an occasional friendly tennis opponent at the Tokyo Lawn Tennis Club. A Soviet Embassy man seated next to me, after making the required amount of polite conversation, suddenly asked, "Why did you write *The Penkovskiy Papers?*" I replied that I didn't write them, Penkovskiy did. I edited them and did so because I thought there was a story that should be told. "But he was a psychopath," my Soviet friend answered. "Read *Newsweek* this week and find out what *they* say about him."

Peter Deriabin, who reads such things avidly, has given me, however, a variety of clippings from the Soviet press and books written over the years about the case of Colonel Penkovskiy. It is interesting that the Russians themselves refer to Penkovskiy's material as *zapiski*—papers. As a recent book, *Military Chekists,* has it, "Penkovskiy transferred his collected espionage material to British and American intelligence centers in the form of notes and papers. When he sensed the danger of carrying such material abroad, he began secretly passing the information to British intelligence agents in Moscow . . ." In a similar book, written a few years earlier by a Lieutenant General N.F. Chistyakov, a former KGB investigator, Penkovskiy's table with the secret drawers is shown—complete with papers, code books, and the typewriter he used to pound out information and admonitions far into the night in his apartment.

This is exactly what some American critics said a "professional" spy would never do. They forget that Penkovskiy was a very unorthodox kind of fellow.

FRANK GIBNEY
OCTOBER, 1981

EDITOR'S NOTE

THIS book is primarily based on three documentary sources: the Penkovskiy Papers themselves, as they were sent out of the Soviet Union; the official Soviet record of the Penkovskiy-Wynne trial, published by the Political Literature Publishing House (Moscow, 1963); and press reports and discussions of Penkovskiy's arrest and trial which appeared in Europe, the United States, and the Soviet Union itself. I have also had long conversations with Greville Wynne. In the interests of telling a connected story, however, I have refrained from citing each source separately in the various introductory passages to the Papers themselves. In the few instances where sources outside the above-named are used, they are cited and specifically identified. At various points in the Penkovskiy narrative, I have added footnotes where some explanation of unfamiliar terms or personalities seemed necessary.

In questions of methodology, custom, and terminology used by the Soviet intelligence services, I have drawn liberally on the knowledge and experience of Peter Deriabin, the translator, who was once a Soviet intelligence officer himself. It was Deriabin who received the Penkovskiy Papers, after they had been smuggled out of the Soviet Union, and instantly recognized their importance. Not only did he translate the Papers, but his informed guidance and evaluation were instrumental in bringing them to publication. He has been of invaluable help in preparing the footnotes and other explanatory material.

To the author of the Papers this book is dedicated, in the hope that Oleg Vladimirovich Penkovskiy, reviled by Soviet propaganda as a common traitor, may be appreciated by both the American and Russian peoples for what he really was: a single-minded revolutionary who gave his life in a lonely fight against a corrupt dictatorship.

It is only fitting that the bulk of the proceeds from the sale of this book will go to a special fund set up in Oleg Penkovskiy's name to further the cause of genuine peace and friendship between the American and Russian peoples.

FRANK GIBNEY

A PERSONAL COMMENT BY
GREVILLE WYNNE

OLEG PENKOVSKIY was a most extraordinary man. I have some knowledge of the vast contribution he made to the West with his intelligence information. But I knew him not only as an intelligence officer, but first as an associate and later as a firm friend. He was an intense man. He wanted not merely to give intelligence information, but also to let the people of Britain and the United States know about his motives.

It was an unforgettable experience to accompany this man, particularly during his first visits to London and Paris, and to see the tremendous impact of our free society on a decent and, by Soviet standards, sophisticated man, but a man who had been sheltered all his life inside the Soviet system.

It was the people in the West who impressed him most. He was amazed, for example, to find that the assistants in department stores were clean, neat in dress, and well groomed, that nearly all the young ladies were attractive, smiling, and anxious to please. I had often visited the gloomy GUM department store in Moscow and the drab shops in Gorkiy street with their drab, surly attendants. So I had some idea of the mental contrast he must have been making.

Oleg was an immensely curious man. He would question me constantly about everything around him wherever we went. He was interested in religion. He had indeed been baptized himself by his pious mother. In London one day we were passing the Brompton Oratory. He asked me whether it was a church and whether he could go in to look around. He was fascinated. "This is good," he said. "Perhaps the religious doctrine is not entirely correct, but at least it gives us a principle to guide our life. At home in the Soviet Union we have nothing. There are no principles —only what the Party tells us."

It was a revelation to him to find that when he visited friends' apartments or joined groups in restaurants or clubs, in both London and Paris, he was never questioned as to why he was in Western Europe, what his background was, or any searching details whatsoever. Wherever we went he was accepted as my friend. This first amazed him, but also pleased him immensely. Such a terrific contrast from the Soviet system where it is still highly dangerous for citizens to mix socially with Westerners.

Of course his own seriousness never left him for long. He was bitter about the Soviet regime. He would weep, quite literally, when he talked about its misdeeds and the sufferings or unhappiness of his friends in the Soviet Union.

The more I knew him, the more I realized that Oleg Penkovskiy was an extraordinarily high-minded man. He was a positive man—he would keep using that phrase in English, "I know perfectly well." He did what he did because it was the one way he, as an individual, could strike back at a system that had debased his country. I never saw him waver from this basic decision from the moment we first met.

He was a man who had thought things through many months before I first made contact with him. He was willing to put up with the basic deceptions of spying and the tremendous strain of this lonely life, because he believed in a cause. He believed simply that a free society should emerge in the Soviet Union, and that it could only come by toppling the only government he knew. He was a heroic figure.

I shall never forget him.

CONTENTS

GENERAL INTRODUCTION

ON May 11, 1963 in a small but crowded hearing room of the Soviet Supreme Court in Moscow, a forty-four-year-old Soviet Army officer named Oleg Penkovskiy, a colonel of the military intelligence arm, was sentenced to be shot for treason. He was charged with the ultimate offense against the Soviet state: espionage on behalf of the United States and Great Britain. Greville Wynne, a British businessman, was sentenced with him to a long prison term, for acting as a "spy go-between."

In his trial Colonel Penkovskiy was identified as a "reserve colonel" of artillery, who had an official position as a "civilian employee" of the State Committee for the Coordination of Scientific Research Work, an organ of the U.S.S.R.'s Council of Ministers which handles all scientific and technical liaison activities with foreign countries, as part of its over-all responsibility for the technological side of Soviet economic planning. The Soviet prosecutors emphasized that the information Penkovskiy passed to the West was principally of an economic and technical nature, with only certain additional pieces of military intelligence. But the type of information, as mentioned in his indictment, gave the lie to them. It was the sort of thing that any military intelligence officer could only describe as juicy: "Top-secret information . . . reports . . . documents of great value . . . of an economic, political, and military nature and Soviet space secrets . . . [material on] Soviet troops in Germany . . . German peace treaty . . .

"List of generals and officers . . . command personnel of the antiaircraft defenses . . . photographs of passes to a military establishment . . . new Soviet war material . . . [material on] atomic energy, rocket technology, and the exploration of outer space . . ."

The open trial of Oleg Penkovskiy lasted only four days

1

and showed signs of haste in its preparation. Nonetheless it occasioned a heavy, savage burst of publicity in the Soviet press. Virtually every Soviet newspaper repeated the angry summations of Lieutenant General A. G. Gornyy, the military prosecutor: ". . . the accused Penkovskiy is an opportunist, a careerist, and a morally decayed person who took the road to treason and betrayal of his country and was employed by imperialist intelligence services. . . ." A Soviet state publishing house printed 100,000 copies of the trial transcript, for distribution to local Communist leaders, the armed services, and other interested parties. Eight British diplomats and five Americans were summarily declared *personae non gratae* in the U.S.S.R—as an alleged result of Penkovskiy's activities.

In the West the trial of Penkovskiy and Wynne attracted a brief spate of newspaper accounts and articles—principally because a British subject, Wynne, had been sentenced to a Soviet prison term. A few perceptive newsmen made a connection between Penkovskiy's vague but apparently sensitive position in the Soviet government—only the most trusted Soviet officials are allowed to deal officially with foreigners and foreign organizations—and the fact, among others, that there was an unusual number of transfers and shake-ups in the Soviet Army command at the time of the Penkovskiy disclosure, including a wholesale recall of attachés stationed abroad. "There seems to be no question," the New York *Herald Tribune* told its readers, "that Colonel Penkovskiy's exposure as a spy blew a huge hole within the entire Soviet information-gathering operation." "There have been defectees from Communism before, but never a Soviet one as high up as this," Joseph Harsch wrote in *The Christian Science Monitor*. And Charles Bartlett in the Washington *Star* suggested that "the internal significance of the trial is fully comparable to the significance attached to the Alger Hiss case in this country."

Neither press nor public received any further enlightenment from the American and British intelligence organizations with whom one must assume Penkovskiy worked. Like the wartime submariners, they are "silent services." It was to be expected, therefore, that a blasé American public, inured to fitful bursts of spy exposés almost as thoroughly as it is inured to television commercials, could go back to its daily round, preferring to take its espionage internally, in increasing dosages of James Bond or *The Spy Who Came in From the Cold*. The name of Penkovskiy quickly faded from view, as did the very fact of his existence. Even as knowledgeable a commentator on espionage matters as Rebecca West could write two years after his arrest, in *The New Meaning of Treason,* only that "Oleg Penkovskiy [was] a Soviet scientist charged with acting as a British agent. . . . As the facts of this case are not known, it is impossible to describe or discuss it."

Yet behind this long blackout of silence and unconcern lies the story of a remarkable man and a still more remarkable achievement, which it is now possible to disclose. For Colonel Penkovskiy was no mere agent, handing over moderately useful military tidbits on Soviet order of battle or economic development. On the contrary, the extent and ingenuity of his work for the West add up to the most extraordinary intelligence feat of this century.

Alone. Oleg Penkovskiy cracked the security system of the world's most security-conscious government and left it virtually in pieces after his disclosures. The gravity of his work is suggested by its immediate aftermath: one chief marshal of the Soviet Union, and in charge of tactical missile forces at that, was removed from his post and demoted; the Chief of Soviet Military Intelligence, General Ivan Serov (the "hangman" of Hungary in 1956), transferred, then publicly demoted; some three hundred Soviet intelligence officers almost immediately recalled to Moscow from foreign posts.

From April 1961 to the end of August 1962, Penkovskiy furnished the West with current, high-priority information on the innermost political and military secrets of the Soviet Union. The sixteen months during which he was, so to speak, operational, spanned a peculiarly intense time of crisis between the Khrushchev regime and the new administration of John F. Kennedy. Historians may one day term it the near-freezing point of the Cold War. Throughout this period, at a time when the invaluable U-2 surveillance of the Soviet Union had been necessarily abandoned, Penkovskiy gave information on both the current trend of Soviet political intentions and the current condition of Soviet military preparations—information which effectively canceled out the normal advantage of Soviet military secrecy and diplomatic inscrutability. 1961, we must remember, was the year of the Berlin Wall. Khrushchev's threats grew to force a military showdown, if necessary, over Berlin and the East German peace treaty. 1962 was the year of continuing crisis in Berlin and the Soviet introduction of long-range missiles into Cuba, a year of nerve-racking maneuver which ended in the successful American missile confrontation with Moscow in October 1962. A key factor in this was American ability to identify the extent and nature of the Soviet missile sites on Cuban soil. The millions who breathed their sigh of relief after that confrontation will probably never know the extent to which the disclosures of one Soviet officer made the American success possible.

The story of Colonel Penkovskiy's achievement would have remained locked in the intelligence and counter-intelligence files of three countries had it not been for the strange, arresting document which comprises most of this book. It is not a diary, nor even anything like a formal autobiography. I have called it simply the Penkovskiy Papers. The Papers are a series of hastily written notes, sketches, and comments, begun in early 1961, at a time when Penkovskiy was trying to make his first contacts with Western intelligence. What is probably the last entry (only a few of them are dated) was written on August 25, 1962, when Penkovskiy was already under heavy surveillance by the State Security forces (KGB) and barely a few weeks before he was taken into custody. (The official date of Penkovskiy's arrest was October 22.)

In the fall of 1962, about the time of Penkovskiy's arrest, the Papers were smuggled out of the Soviet Union to an Eastern European country.[1] From there they were transmitted to Peter Deriabin,[2] himself a former defector from the State Security forces, who undertook the long preliminary work of translation and selection. Their au-

[1] Like some thirty major pieces of fiction and memoirs over the last ten years—including works of Pasternak, Tertz, Tarsis, and Akhmatova—the Penkovskiy Papers were smuggled out in highly anonymous circumstances. Within a few weeks they were safe in the United States. Beyond this it is impossible to describe the details of the memoirs' transmittal. To do so, even in the scantiest outline, would serve only to incriminate some people and point a finger of suspicion, justly or unjustly, at others.

[2] Deriabin, then a major in the Soviet State Security, left Soviet headquarters in Vienna in 1954 and received asylum in the U.S.

thenticity is beyond question. The wealth of personal documentation which accompanied them—family pictures, Communist Party membership cards, copies of official orders —could have had only one source: Penkovskiy himself. They are the jottings of a lonely man playing what he knew was a lonely and desperate game, in which there was little chance of winning.

An odd combination of angry protest, exhortation, and dispassionate exposition, the Papers are arranged with little attempt at order and none at literary style. A highly personal comment on some prominent acquaintance may be followed by an almost technical observation on tactics or weapons. But they represent the political opinions, warnings, and observations of a man who, to say the least, had no one in whom he could confide. Certainly Penkovskiy hoped that they would someday be published in the West, if not the Soviet Union, to clarify his motives and, definitively, to clear his own name. They compromise a conscious testament. He obviously had no time for revision or polishing; the last entries were written when he knew he was under "observation" by the State Security, with little chance of escape.

Because the Papers are so fragmentary it seemed not only useful but necessary to add certain introductory remarks which may help fix their importance in their time and place. A man like Dag Hammarskjöld can leave behind scattered fragments of his writings[3] and they will be understood, because they are almost automatically read in context. He was a well-known figure and what he stood for was well known. Not so with Penkovskiy or his situation. Neither the importance of his position nor—still less— the significance of his personal protest will be immediately clear to most Americans. To put them in their historical setting can make a great deal of difference. If we cannot thoroughly understand the precise feelings of a Soviet citizen at a particular time in his history, we can at least appreciate them.

The Papers, furthermore, must be read in the context of the weeks and months in which they were written. Much that was important in 1961 or 1962 may be of academic

[3] In the posthumously published *Markings* (Alfred A. Knopf, New York, 1964).

interest at the moment. But we must not forget that the shape of the world we are living in today is the result in no small measure of decisions, actions, and counteractions taken then.

I have tried, therefore, to preface the Papers with some minimal editorial explanation for the following questions: 1) Who was Colonel Penkovskiy and what was his real position? 2) What actually did he tell the West? 3) What was the historical context in which he gave his information? 4) Why did he do it?

Who was Oleg Vladimirovich Penkovskiy? His own memoirs, which can be confirmed from other evidence available, paint the picture of a far different man from the "poseur" of the Soviet prosecutors. To begin with his position: he was *not* the casual "civilian employee" of the Scientific Research Committee, as the prosecution stated, but was in fact Deputy Chief of its Foreign Section, charged with the constant overseeing of delegations, missions, and other technical intelligence work with foreign countries. He was *not* a reserve colonel. As his own Soviet documents show, Oleg Penkovskiy was a regular Army colonel on active service with Soviet military intelligence and had been since his graduation from the Military Diplomatic Academy (the Army intelligence school) in 1953. His official assignment was with the Chief Intelligence Directorate (GRU) of the Soviet General Staff. As he explains amply in the Papers, his job with the Committee was a working cover.

Behind him he had a brilliant career both as a career Army officer and a faithful Communist Party servant. A former assistant military attaché in Turkey, he was a graduate of the Military Diplomatic Academy, the Frunze Academy (the Soviet General Staff College), and the Dzerzhinskiy Artillery Academy, where he had taken an intensive nine-month course in military missiles. He had been a regimental commander, as well as a staff officer and general's aide. Had he not elected to enter the intelligence arm, with its traditionally low ranks, Penkovskiy would almost unquestionably have been promoted to general officer's status himself by the early 1960s.

In the political double-entry bookkeeping of the Soviet leadership, in which Communist Party organizations and their leaders constantly check on the work of formally independent government departments and ministries, a strong Party record is indispensable for preferment. Penkovskiy became a Communist Party member in 1940, after several years in the Komsomol, the Party youth organization. Throughout his career he was a trusted political leader in the Army formations in which he served.

Adding to Penkovskiy's credentials were his associations with the great and powerful in the Soviet hierarchy. In World War II he had served as aide to Marshal Sergey S. Varentsov, then artillery commander of the First Ukrainian Front, and he continued as the Marshal's close friend, confidant, and protégé after Varentsov became a Chief Marshal of Artillery in charge of the Tactical Missile Forces. His great-uncle Valentin Antonovich Penkovskiy was by 1956, a lieutenant general and Commander of the Far Eastern Military District. Penkovskiy's wife was herself the daughter of a general with significant political connections within the Communist Party. Colonel Penkovskiy was on the friendliest terms with General Ivan Serov, who became Chief of Military Intelligence in 1958, and he maintained close relations, through Varentsov, with a number of prominent Soviet generals and political leaders. His access to secret files and information was in some respects more extensive than that of a man in charge of a Soviet ministry. Through his close connections with Varentsov, also, he had a constant pipeline into the deliberations of the Soviet Supreme Military Council, of which Varentsov as Chief Marshal of Artillery, was a member. (Khrushchev himself was Chairman.)

On the record Penkovskiy was a life-sized working model of the new, postrevolutionary Soviet official, part of the consciously established "New Class" of the Soviet Union. And out of the two-dimensional black and white of official records, orders, and citations we are able in Penkovskiy's case to reconstruct something better. Thanks to his frequent contacts with foreigners and their recollections of him, he can put together the picture of an engaging, sometimes arresting personality. A medium-sized, rather handsome man whose red hair was barely flecked with gray, Penkovskiy had a forceful but generally pleasant character. He liked good food, good wine and conversation; and thanks to his position he had grown accustomed to them—the sort of man who is used to having doors opened for him and who expects to be remembered by head waiters.

Penkovskiy had good manners. What was perhaps a natural feeling for social shadings was accentuated by his knowledge of the unending struggle for prestige and position within the Soviet hierarchy. He was almost painfully anxious to be correct, in any situation. Far more than the average Soviet official, even including those of some sophistication, Penkovskiy enjoyed small talk; he was a genuinely social man. He had a good sense of humor, if somewhat on the salty, sardonic side. Although more of an engineer than a scholar—he enjoyed tinkering and, as we shall note later, had devised several useful, patented inventions—he used the language well. He was a good family man. His occasional dalliances with ladies would be comparable to similar situations in capitalist societies, and far less frequent than the incidence of such behavior among the Soviet marshals and generals of his acquaintance.

Yet behind this good-humored façade, Oleg Penkovskiy was essentially a loner. Few men's characters can profitably be subjected to logical analysis, Penkovskiy's less than most. If he had many friends and acquaintances, he had few intimates outside of the ill-fated Marshal Varentsov (and there the official relationship was always present). His intelligence experience contributed to his reluctance to form very close or lasting friendships. That way, he could give himself one more safeguard against possible entrapment. When he decided to work for the West, this natural inner reserve needed no reinforcement.

As his Papers reveal, this outwardly convivial man possessed a powerful capacity for indignation. That quality, too, was one better concealed than exhibited in the Soviet society which he knew best. The indignation, the zeal, the scorn for injustice he kept well below the surface. Even in the prisoner's dock at his trial, he was remarkably self-possessed. He frequently corrected the prosecutor on points of fact and, although he faithfully hewed to the approved confession of guilt, he went out of his way not publicly to incriminate some Moscow acquaintances who had been summoned to testify against him.

In only one other important instance was he far from

typical—a circumstance which not only left a great many red faces in the Soviet State Security after his trial, but played no small part in Penkovskiy's own decision. His family came from the upper ranks of the czarist civil service. This fact in itself is still a damaging item in a Soviet security dossier. But his father, a young engineering student from western Russia, had also fought against the revolution as an officer of the White Army. It was a very significant matter of reflection for Oleg Penkovskiy, after he himself began to turn against the Soviet system, to note that his father had been killed fighting the Communists on the outskirts of Rostov.

Under the Soviet system any relationship to a former czarist or White officer is automatically a black mark on a citizen's record—enough to prevent him from ever traveling abroad, for example. Penkovskiy lived with this mark for the twenty-five years of his career in the Army, although it was not known, apparently, until very late in the game. It is one reason why he had so little contact with his great-uncle, the general. Each had this private matter to hide. Neither wished to call attention either to the family origins or to the family name.

The collection of intelligence information depends on two factors: access and evaluation. The most ingenious spy in history might just as well spend his time writing memoirs or selling dry goods unless he finds some access to the secrets of the government spied upon. It is equally true—and more significantly so in our time of complicated military technologies—that a man may have complete access to a government's secrets but remain of little use unless he knows what to look for and how to make an on-the-spot evaluation of what he finds.

The capacity for evaluation is high, or presumed so, among senior professional intelligence officers. But they rarely are in a position of direct access to vital security materials. Colonel Rudolf Abel, the enigmatic Soviet "Illegal" *rezident*[4] who was arrested in New York in 1957

---

4 An Illegal *rezident* is the chief of a group of two to six staff officers of the Soviet intelligence service who are serving together abroad under false, non-Soviet documentation, the better to conduct espionage, undercover political action, or sabotage and similar missions. In this book we use the exact Russian transliteration, to dis-

and ultimately exchanged for Francis Gary Powers in 1962, was manifestly a person of great political sophistication and deeply engrained intelligence training (as anyone who encountered him at his American trial can attest). Yet Abel did his work in deliberate obscurity, in a dingy Brooklyn studio, associating only with a few hack artists (for such was his cover) and cut off from the humblest of "decision-making" circles in the United States. Abel and other Soviet *rezidents* relied for their information on various agents who were more or less innocent of the Big Picture, as Soviet intelligence saw it, but could be maneuvered into sensitive locations and told to pass on specific pieces of information. A young U.S. Army technician like David Greenglass, for example, could contribute only one small if vital piece of information on the manufacture of the A-bomb to his employers, and he was used for that purpose alone. While Abel had the evaluative capacity without direct access, Greenglass had the access with only a minimal capacity for evaluation. So with the average agent, who is generally a person of relatively little prominence or position and must be given the most specific kind of instructions.

Now turn to Penkovskiy. Here by contrast is a man who decides of his own free will to become a spy for the West. He has automatic access to a great many Soviet secret and top-secret materials and he sits close to the seat of Soviet power. But he is also a trained intelligence officer, who has spent a decade of his professional life learning exactly what kind of military, economic, and political information is valuable, what kind useless, what kind merely marginal. Combine with his intelligence experience, his official position as a collector of desired scientific and economic information for the Soviets, through his Committee in Moscow.

Penkovskiy's own personal fund of information was large. Any graduate of the Soviet missile school—not to mention the Frunze Academy and the Military Diplomatic Academy—could tell Western intelligence much about the quality and quantity of Soviet missiles, their deployment, accuracy, the troops manning them, etc. A Frunze Acade-

---

tinguish this technical term from the normal English word "resident."

my officer will know a great deal about basic military doctrines and their revisions. A graduate of the intelligence school will in the first instance know the true identities and missions of great numbers of Soviet intelligence officers (who normally operate under more or less heavy cover) as well as Soviet intelligence tactics. If, for instance, the order has gone out to arrange all meetings of Soviet agents in the U.S. in movie theaters, disclosure of that fact will be of invaluable service to the FBI, which is responsible for catching them.

The range of Penkovskiy's information was literally encyclopedic. The design of a new tactical missile, the deployment pattern of Soviet missile installations—how useful this proved in Cuba—the exact planned dimensions of the Berlin Wall (see Figure 7 in photo insert), the name of the new Soviet intelligence *rezident* in London, the defects in a new military helicopter, the degree of unrest in Soviet factory towns and in the East German garrisons—thousands of pieces of information were swept up by the busy, curious mind of a man who combined the selective faculty of the intelligence officer with a capacity for memorization that can only be described as total recall. Even the most intelligent of agents will have severe inherent limitations. An infantry battalion commander will presumably know little about high-level staff planning. A scientific liaison expert will have little knowledge of military affairs. A diplomat will not be acquainted with his country's industrial potential. Penkovskiy, however, was something of a generalist. He himself combined the functions mentioned above, as well as others, and his perception had been sharpened by training in various strikingly different disciplines.

As a good intelligence officer, furthermore, Colonel Penkovskiy only trusted his recollection when he had to. Every possible bit of useful information he committed to film. The three Minox cameras in his possession received hard and constant use. His Soviet prosecutors at the trial themselves admitted that Penkovskiy had passed on to Western intelligence some 5000 separate photographed items of secret military, political, and economic intelligence!

Here again, access was important. Security officers first took little notice of Colonel Penkovskiy so frequently using the General Staff library. It hardly occurred to them that he was doing research for the United States.

In the normal course of talking military shop with his friends, Penkovskiy would run into hundreds of items of useful information about the deployment of Soviet troops, their readiness, morale, etc. He knew a good deal about specific future plans, e.g., the operation to overrun Iran in case of international trouble, the Soviet backup for an East German confrontation with Western forces over Berlin. He came to know a great deal about the whole decision-making process within the Soviet hierarchy, as well as shifts in the regime.

If the Soviet marshals are muttering angry private criticism of their political leadership, this is a piece of information well worth having in the West. If a riot over food in the industrial town of Novocherkassk has to be suppressed by troops, that is information worth having. Penkovskiy's unique pipeline into the rigorously classified meetings and decisions of the Soviet Supreme Military Council was comparable to the Soviet Union having a foreign agent in the United States, with a private pipeline into some of the National Security Council's White House meetings.

It is difficult, if not impossible, to make exact comparisons between the status of Penkovskiy in the Soviet system and that of a man similarly situated in the United States. But conjure up this sort of person: a vice president of the Rand Corporation and member of the President's advisory committee on science, a Ford Foundation consultant who was also in charge of the State Department's program for foreign visitors. A career Army officer, whose wife's father had been an assistant chief of staff of the U.S. Army, he would be a graduate of West Point, the Command and General Staff School at Fort Leavenworth, and the Military War College, and a close friend of the Air Force general in charge of SAC. The same man was secretly a division head in the Central Intelligence Agency, with important contacts in the Pentagon due to his former military activities. In addition to these official credentials, he had a wide acquaintance in Democratic Party circles.

If we object that no American could possibly do all the abovementioned jobs and keep up the associations, we are putting our finger on one difference between the Soviet system and our own. Even an Alger Hiss or a Klaus Fuchs can know only one or two segments of the complex working society of a democracy. But in Moscow few are called and fewer are chosen to join the top layer of the power structure. The lucky few grow used to doubling in brass. Accordingly, a Penkovskiy, living near the apex of a tightly centralized society, can see clearly up and down the mountain. Americans can best estimate the value of Penkovskiy's information to the West by adjusting their eyes to the perspective of the peculiarly centralized power structure in which he resided.

Penkovskiy's betrayal of the Soviet regime ranks with classic espionage cases like those of Yevno Azef, the Russian police spy who penetrated the leadership of the Social Revolutionary Party in czarist days; or Colonel Alfred Redl, the dandified Austro-Hungarian staff officer who sold his country's mobilization plans to the Russians in 1913. For Penkovskiy, like them, was linked warp and woof with the leadership he betrayed. He was a member of the club. His information was damaging, not merely because of its quality but because it was given at all. In the impact on its society the Penkovskiy affair more than equaled the Alger Hiss case in the United States.

For the sixteen months of Colonel Penkovskiy's career as an agent, the makers of United States policy were in the position of a poker player who is given fleeting glimpses of his opponent's hand and without the other fellow in the least suspecting it. That brief time of crisis underscores as nothing else the importance of Penkovskiy's disclosures to the West. The two most tantalizing questions any general or diplomat asks about a potential antagonist concern his capabilities and his intentions: what does he have and what does he plan to do with it? In 1961 and 1962 Penkovskiy enlightened the Americans and the British in both these departments with the most current information. (Thanks to his three trips to Western Europe in that period, he could respond to specific questions, as well as volunteer information on his own.) In facing down the Soviet regime over the Berlin issue and in the Cuban missile crisis, the West used Penkovskiy's information to decisive effect.

In May 1960, after the public exposure of the U-2 overflights, Nikita Khrushchev bulled his way out of the Summit Conference in Paris and set a new hard line of hostility to the United States. This was not the first time such a shift had occurred. For many years the state of Soviet-American relations had swung back and forth like an erratic pendulum or the rise and fall of tides in the Bay of Fundy. But Khrushchev found many reasons to justify a hardened line now. His public policy of "peaceful coexistence" was shaken by President Eisenhower's very public admission of personal responsibility for the U-2 overflights. Whether or not Khrushchev himself was sincere about the coexistence policy—and Penkovskiy for one believed he was not—it was already under heavy fire from the Chinese Communists, as well as influential forces within the Soviet Party. Inside the Soviet Union, Khrushchev's internal problems were multiplying, from shortages of consumer goods and failure in wheat production to rising discontent over his repression of young writers, artists, and musicians, including the malodorous episode of Boris Pasternak and *Doctor Zhivago*. Certain currents of opposition to the regime were gathering among the Soviet people. In Khrushchev's book it was a good moment for mobilizing them all against the old reliable external foe.

The first few months of John F. Kennedy's administration encouraged a new Soviet belligerence. To Khrushchev the American failure at the Bay of Pigs seemed evidence of growing weakness and indecision. Khrushchev's June 1961 conference with the new President at Vienna very evidently did not shake him in his misconception that the Kennedy administration could be both outfaced and outfoxed. The time seemed ripe, doubtless, for using threats to achieve important political victories.

In that same month of June, therefore, Khrushchev declared that he must have a settlement of the Berlin question, on Soviet terms, by the end of the year; and within the same time limit he avowed Soviet determination to sign the long-threatened treaty with East Germany, thus leaving Berlin under Walter Ulbricht's less than tender care. Soviet incidents and "provocations" increased. On August 13 the Wall was raised in Berlin, without any sharp retaliation or reaction from the Western allies.

On September 1, 1961, after continued threatening references to new high-yield bombs, the U.S.S.R. began nuclear testing in the atmosphere, deep within Soviet Asia. Khrushchev threatened to explode a fifty-megaton nuclear weapon, the largest in history to be detonated. That fall American and Soviet tanks faced each other across the barriers at the sector boundaries of Berlin.

At the last minute Khrushchev backed down from his year-end ultimatum about a Berlin "solution" and an East German treaty, but rather in the manner of a racing driver making a split-second decision not to cut a dangerous corner. Soviet aircraft, however, continued to provoke incidents in the air traffic corridors above Berlin. The disarmament conference at Geneva was virtually sabotaged by Soviet representatives, who went into their familiar slow-motion act, now refusing to discuss plans which had once seemed promising subjects for negotiation. In 1962, of course, there was the crisis over Cuba. By October 15 the White House had in its hands clear and unmistakable evidence of the emplacement of Soviet offensive missiles on the island of Cuba.

Throughout this period Penkovskiy supplied the Western allies with a running account of Soviet military preparations in East Germany, as well as the backup within the Soviet Union. As the Papers show, he was privy to the entire Soviet plan for fighting a localized war, if necessary, in Germany to enforce an effective East German control over Berlin. (We may assume that the actual intelligence reports he transmitted—quite distinct from his observations in the Papers—cited chapter and verse of the military deployment.) He continued to report the conviction of Khrushchev and the Soviet political leadership that the United States and the NATO allies would shrink from any actual military confrontation in the Berlin area. He also noted the misgivings of some Soviet generals about what would happen, in case the West called their hand. (One wonders what might have happened if some German Colonel Penkovskiy had gone over to the British at the time of Hitler's first aggressive moves in the Central Europe of the thirties.)

The strong stand taken by the West in Berlin forced Khrushchev to back off from his insistence on a 1961 treaty. Penkovskiy could in turn report the reactions to that inside the Soviet High Command. In reading the Papers it is interesting to confirm how an announced increase in the U.S. military budget or a call-up of reserves has a quick, sobering effect on "adventurist" tendencies in Moscow.

While warning about the carefully prepared Soviet trap in East Germany, Penkovskiy continued to write about Khrushchev's drive to build up the missile forces. Significantly, the Papers begin in 1961 to mention Cuba as a focus of Khrushchev's "adventurism." Few actual technical details of missiles, missile carriers, deployment sites, and their configurations are noted in the Papers—except to prove a point in passing. The Papers are a personal testament, not an intelligence report. But it is safe to conjecture that the information which Penkovskiy passed on in his regular reports was well used by the U.S. photo interpretation experts, before they called the turn so precisely on the number and types of Soviet missiles photographed moving into their sites in Cuba.

Beyond the question of technical specifications, moreover, Colonel Penkovskiy had helped educate an American President and his staff to Nikita Khrushchev's capacity for sudden and reckless chance-taking. It was an invaluable piece of political pedagogy. It is ironic that the date of Penkovskiy's arrest by the State Security was announced as October 22, just six days before Nikita Khrushchev finally told President Kennedy that he would "dismantle the arms which you described as offensive" and return them from Cuba to the U.S.S.R.

In June 1937 an eighteen-year-old higher-school graduate named Oleg Penkovskiy left his mother's house in Ordzhonikidze, in the northern Caucasus, and took the long train ride to Kiev, where he successfully passed the entrance examination at the Second Artillery School, to begin training in the officer candidates' class. For the next twenty-four years Penkovskiy lived the life of a loyal Soviet citizen, a devoted member of the Communist Party. By 1939, when he was appointed *politruk* (political officer) of an artillery battery, he was already stepping up the lowest rungs of the Soviet leadership class. His war record was distinguished—two Orders of the Red Banner, Order of Aleksandr Nevskiy, Order of the Fatherland War, Order of the Red Star, and eight other assorted medals certified him as a war hero. As his military career advanced he distinguished himself not merely by ability but also by zeal. He worked hard at the Frunze Academy, and it took no mean degree of effort to emerge first in his class at the missile school. In the intelligence service he was known as an alert Party man, quick to complain when he felt that the Party's orders or its best interests were violated.

In the sixteen months between April 1961 and August 1962, Colonel Penkovskiy coolly and carefully turned his back on these twenty-four years of Communist dedication and went to work for the two powers which he had been taught—and had himself taught others—were the Soviet Union's greatest enemies. It was no chance commitment. He had already tried to make contact with American authorities in Moscow in 1960, six months before he established communication with the British, through Greville Wynne. His first contacts with Western intelligence he had worked out in his own mind far in advance, as well as the information he first selected to show them, as a kind of *bona fides*.

As the Papers show, he transferred his allegiance to the West almost passionately. "Khrushchev and his regime," he would note, "are demagogues and liars who are advocating their love of peace as a pretense. I consider it my duty and purpose in life to be a soldier for truth and freedom to a tiny degree. . . ."

Why did he betray his government? And why at this time, not before? Although Penkovskiy devotes a great deal of space in his Papers to answering these questions, a few prefatory comments may be in order. Penkovskiy's own comments and explanations of his motives are limited by his frame of reference. He presumed in his readers a greater knowledge of the Soviet situation than most of us possess. Nor did he reckon with the curious moral relativism which leads so many professionally fair-minded products of Anglo-Saxon education to equate the motives for betraying the Soviet Union with the motives for betraying the United States or another free society, with equal disapproval of the "turncoat."

We might begin by eliminating some obvious motives attributed to spies, traitors, or defectors by people who live in comfortable homes. There was no woman in the case—and, unlike Anglo-American defectors, Penkovskiy was certainly not a homosexual. Penkovskiy was a dutiful if not exactly a loving family man. When his ultimate danger was brought home to him, his last desperate thoughts were to extricate his family, somehow, from the U.S.S.R. (In fact, his quiet co-operation at the trial, not to mention his willingness to "confess" his guilt, suggests strongly that Penkovskiy had made a deal with his State Security jailers, to save his family.) The worst the Soviet prosecution would charge him with at his trial, in this regard, was that he went out with single ladies occasionally and once, in the classic manner, drank champagne from a girl friend's slipper.

Penkovskiy could hardly have done his espionage work for money. Again, the worst his Soviet prosecutors could charge was that he once received 3000 rubles from his Western contacts for certain expenses, of which he paid 2000 back.

Nor was he a "defector" in the accepted sense of that term. Three times he was able to travel to London and Paris while he was engaged in active espionage work. On any of these occasions he could have claimed asylum and remained in the West; and on the last, as the Papers show, he thought long and hard about the possibility. Yet each time his final decision was to return and finish his work. As he wrote on October 9, 1961: "I must continue for another year or two in the General Staff of the U.S.S.R., in order to reveal all the villainous plans and plottings of our common enemy. I consider that as a soldier in this task, my place in these troubled times is on the front lines."

Strange, grandiloquent language—which to a modern American sounds as stilted as the battle exhortations in our own Civil War memoirs. But we must remember that Penkovskiy was not a modern American. He attacked the Soviet regime with the same *Pravda*-type invective with which he had once defended it. This was the only kind of language he knew. In fact, Penkovskiy's Slavic idealizations and hyperbole might have come out of an old David Zaslavskiy or Ilya Ehrenburg editorial or a passage in a propaganda play like *Kremlin Chimes,* but with the significant difference that the good guys and the bad guys are now reversed. Talleyrand's old cynical injunction of "not too much zeal" would make no more sense to Penkovskiy than it would to Mikhail Suslov if he were asked to discuss the "serious deviationist errors" of his former boss Khrushchev in the calm vocabulary of the Harvard Yard, or, for that matter, to Nikolay Gogol if it were suggested that his wild troika passage in *Dead Souls* be rewritten in the style of Walter Lippmann or Henry Adams.

Several basic reasons do underlie Penkovskiy's sudden adherence to the West. First was his sudden projection into the snake pit of Soviet intraregime politics. Until the close of World War II he was a simple professional soldier and a loyal member of the Communist Party; the Army and the Party were the only firmament he knew. But very speedily thereafter his abilities, his well-placed marriage, and his association with Marshal Varentsov brought him into close association with the Soviet power elite. Such an exposure is rarely kind to one's boyhood illusions. Penkovskiy, with his highly developed capacity for indignation, did not take easily to the constant byplay of intrigue, intimidation, and downright cheating, as generals and marshals fought their way to and from the top.

Had he stayed in a line unit, this artillery colonel would have remained reasonably well insulated from similar goings-on in the Army. But, on the advice (and with the assistance) of his father-in-law, he went into staff work, and after that, intelligence. Here he could see everything on a double level. From 1949, the year he entered the Military Diplomatic Academy, he worked for an intelligence arm dealing with sabotage, subversion, and the most secret tricks of clandestine organizations, whose own officers were under the double surveillance of their superiors and a rival, more highly regarded counterintelligence, the State Security. His official job for the Committee was itself a lie. And he was continually amazed that foreign scientists and businessmen who dealt with the Committee took its mission of liaison at face value.

Needless to say, Penkovskiy did not set out on his career with the prospect of becoming disillusioned. He was a man who liked to get ahead. He was at first fascinated by his associations with those in high places, and when he had influence he rarely hesitated to use it. He was, in a sense, a "careerist," like almost everyone else in a closed hierarchical system of government in which merit can carry one only so far without intrigue and infighting added. Yet underneath his aspirations in the Party and in the intel-

ligence apparatus, he remained first and last a professional
soldier, whose basic loyalties were formed in a period of
war, when the obvious danger to the Russian Motherland
overrode anything else. His only working tradition was a
military tradition of obedience, respect for authority, and
confidence in rank and station.

He returned to the Soviet Union from his first foreign
assignment, in Turkey, in November 1956, at a time when
the whole set of normal loyalties in Soviet society had been
shaken by Khrushchev's denunciation of Stalin in February
at the Twentieth Party Congress. The year after his return
Marshal Zhukov was removed and disgraced by the Khrushchev leadership. This was surely a blow to the simple
faith of a career military man. Zhukov's popularity among
the Soviet officer class was tremendous. Penkovskiy in his
Papers calls him "the Suvorov of our times." With his high
connections and his intelligence information, Penkovskiy
was hardly disposed to accept the conventional explanation
given the Soviet people for Zhukov's downfall. It did not
wash.

The colonel just returned from Turkey was not the only
Soviet officer who nursed a feeling of disturbance and
suspicion at the shabby treatment of his country's greatest
military hero. We must not forget how rooted in the
Soviet military establishment Penkovskiy was. His best
friends were officers of general's or colonel's rank. His
memories were military memories, his ambitions military
ambitions. It was precisely this which later led Soviet authorities, at his trial, to play down his character as a professional serving officer. For it is evident in Penkovskiy's
constant references to conversations with fellow officers
that he was not some chance freak but a well-connected,
personable man who reflected the opinions, the fears, and
the discontents of a critical segment in Soviet society. By
1960, after a decade of shake-ups, sudden changes, and
bewildering rises and falls from power, a great many officers were singing the Soviet "Ballad of a Soldier" more
than slightly off-key. As his British associate, Wynne, wrote
in his own memoirs: "Penkovskiy was like the top part of
an iceberg. There were a lot like him submerged below
the surface."

All this background might have produced a disillusioned,
cynical man, outwardly conformist but passively a member

of what the old Russians used to call the "inner emigration." What probably, more than any single factor, drove Colonel Penkovskiy to *active* rebellion against the Soviet regime was his fear of a sudden nuclear war, which might be triggered by Khrushchev's adventurism. Penkovskiy was one of a handful of Soviet citizens who knew the truth not only about Soviet preparations for nuclear warfare but about the recklessness with which Khrushchev threatened its use. This fact is absolutely key to understanding his motives.

We have grown used to crusaders against nuclear warfare in the West, to people who advocate unilateral disarmament as the only hope for some kind of survival, to prominent citizens like Lord Russell whose horror of atomic warfare warps their common-sense judgments of conflicting politics and policies. Because the Soviet security system screens the problems and inner motives of Soviet citizens from our view is no reason to suppose that a similar horror of nuclear warfare does not haunt the Soviet people, just as it does us.

Penkovskiy, to begin with, had little confidence in Khrushchev's fidelity to his policy of peaceful coexistence. He knew, from where he sat in intelligence, that the years of the public coexistence policy coincided with Khrushchev's orders to intensify Soviet intelligence and illegal espionage activity throughout the Western world. So he was understandably skeptical—and increasingly concerned—over what he felt was the gullibility of the United States and Britain in taking Khrushchev's peaceful statement at face value.

Nothing was the same for Penkovskiy from the day he first saw the secret training film showing effects of the Soviet nuclear tests. He brooded over this awesome option of the Soviet leadership. What shocked him most was the real brinkmanship which Khrushchev was apparently prepared to use, invoking threats of nuclear warfare to extract political gains. For if he conceded that Khrushchev would use nuclear warfare only as a last resort, he had no confidence that the last resort might not be reached, at Khrushchev's decision, today, tomorrow, or the next day.

Penkovskiy was aware of Soviet weaknesses as well as Soviet strength. He saw a highly risky political offensive opening over Berlin—and later developing over Cuba—at the very moment when the Soviet military forces were in a state of turmoil. The men replacing Zhukov were apt to be political generals, picked for their ability to take orders rather than to give advice—this note of worry obtrudes throughout the Papers. As a career officer Penkovskiy grew more and more worried over a policy that threatened mass destruction, without even the guarantee of strength or technical competence behind it. Khrushchev, clearly, was not much of a general. And there is nothing more unsettling to a professional military man than the prospect of amateur night at the General Staff.

As he pondered on the apparent collision course of Soviet policy over Berlin he also reflected on the helplessness of the Russian people and their ignorance of the fate that might be in store for them. It was the historic tragedy of the *narod* and the *nachalstvo*—the "people" who have traditionally felt apart, if not estranged, from their "leadership." "The people," he once wrote, "are much like soldiers. They wait. They are lied to, suppressed, abused, but they always hope for the best. I see how our Soviet leadership propagates and exploits this waiting doctrine. We wait all the time. How wonderful to wait. Die and others will wait. But in a nuclear age can a man just wait for certain death?"

In his despair the memory of his father must have come back to him. The father he had never met had not waited. He had died fighting the same regime which he himself now set out to destroy.

Casual newspaper readers, accustomed to thinking solely in terms of a steady "relaxation" or "thaw" in the U.S.S.R. since the death of Stalin, may be surprised at the story of espionage, repression, and ruthlessness in the following pages. Unfortunately Penkovskiy's story is all too true. The ultimate warrant of legitimacy within the Soviet government remains the possession of power. The elaborate mechanism of Party organization, Supreme Soviets, Republics, cultural and workers' groups remains more or less a façade. The real business of the Soviet state is conducted behind it, by the Central Committee of the Communist Party of the Soviet Union and its subordinates.

Everything about Penkovskiy was tinged with deceit or manipulation. His real occupation was not what he stated.

His real superior was not his nominal superior. His strength and position in Soviet society could not be expressed in any formal terms. Even the circumstances of his birth and ancestry were not as he had to represent them. In the fullest sense of the words he was forced to live a lie twenty-four hours a day—long before he entered into an intelligence relationship with the West. Through it all he was in a position to see the ruthlessness of the Soviet power struggle. He saw this as few men are permitted to see it, conspicuously including the average Soviet citizen.

This is not to say that the thaw and relaxation within the Soviet society are nothing but illusion. It is true that the revisionist reforms of Khrushchev loosened the ideological bonds of Soviet society and eliminated many of its doctrinaire Marxist contradictions. It is true, and demonstrably so, that the controlling police apparatus has relaxed its coercions and eased its restrictions in the twelve years since the death of Stalin. The very fact that the Soviet regime attempted to give some semblance of legality to Penkovskiy's trial argues the reality of these changes. The Soviet public is no longer docile enough to accept the shameless confessional purge trials of the Stalin period. If many Soviet "tourists" who go abroad are "co-opted" by the State Security beforehand, they are nonetheless Soviet citizens and allowed some amount of travel. If the Soviet people have little comprehension of the democratic systems of government, they are nonetheless able to exert increasing pressure on their regimes in the form of demands for consumer goods, housing, and education. These are at least the beginnings of public opinion.

Nonetheless the fact remains that Soviet society is still controlled by the security arm. The fact remains that the citizens of the Soviet Union have few personal freedoms as the West sees them. The fact remains that the entire Soviet state, and the world, can be swung into war or headed on a collision course toward war by a decision of a few men in the Central Committee. This horrendous dependence of his people on individual whim came to haunt Penkovskiy and it inspired his lonely revolt. We must never forget that the degree of his revulsion with the Soviet system increased in direct proportion to his awareness of the regime's unrestricted power and his conviction of its fundamental irresponsibility. If ignorance is bliss, it was Penkovskiy's peculiar folly to be wise. Unfortunately not many Soviet citizens are equipped to understand the premises which governed Penkovskiy's conclusions.

The Penkovskiy Papers, therefore, are not printed in any effort to worsen relations with the Soviet Union or to hinder the understanding between the two nations which our mutual nuclear knowledge makes mandatory. This book is not for those who contend that one must be either completely "understanding" toward another nation or completely hostile. It is written for those who want realistically to appreciate the greatest problem still remaining in the way of a rapprochement with the Russians, as well as the progress made toward this rapprochement. That problem is the continuing power of the security apparatus over Soviet citizens.

The State Security mechanism continues to resist all the pressures to change it within Soviet society. It continues to serve as the principal prop of the Soviet Central Committee's leadership. Over the past four years the activities of the "vigilant Chekists" of the KGB and GRU have received steadily increasing publicity in the Soviet press; and the former State Security Chief Aleksandr N. Shelepin has become one of the most powerful figures in the Soviet hierarchy.[5] As it stands, the State Security cannot be modified. It will either continue to hold its power or be destroyed.

It was Penkovskiy's thesis and his earnest conviction that the State Security forces had to be attacked at their roots before the Russian people, his people, would be capable of leading the peaceful national life he knew they deserved. And that is the thesis of this book.

---

[5] Shelepin, who bossed the KGB between 1958 and 1962, was elevated barely one month after Khrushchev's downfall in October 1964 to full membership in the Presidium of the Central Committee of the Communist Party of the Soviet Union—a necessary springboard to supreme power in the U.S.S.R. Shelepin's protégé, Vladimir Ye. Semichastnyy, the present Chief of the KGB, was promoted to full membership in the Central Committee CPSU at the same time. These promotions, rewards for KGB help in ousting Khrushchev, set the seal on the renaissance of KGB influence, which had been only slightly attenuated in Khrushchev's time. As of July, 1965 Shelepin held more prominent Party and government posts than any other prominent Soviet leader.

CHAPTER I

The System in Which I Live

MY name is *Oleg Vladimirovich Penkovskiy*. I was born on April 23, 1919 in the Caucasus, in the city of Ordzhonikidze (formerly Vladikavkaz), in the family of a salaried employee; Russian by nationality, by profession, an officer of military intelligence with the rank of colonel; I have had higher education; I have been a member of the Communist Party of the Soviet Union since March 1940; I am married; as my dependents I have my wife, one daughter,[1] and my mother; I have never been on trial for criminal or political offense; I have been awarded thirteen government decorations, five orders, and eight medals; I am a resident of the city of Moscow, and live on Maksim Gorkiy Embankment, house no. 36, apartment 59.

I am beginning the notes that follow to explain my thoughts about the system in which I live and my revolt against this system.

I would like people in the West to read what I am saying here, because they can learn much through my experience. I can expose Khrushchev's fallacies and deceits by facts and actual examples. I know more than most about his plans and his policies. I am fully aware of what I am setting out to do—I ask that you believe in my sincerity, in my dedication to the *real* struggle for peace.

I have tried to set down my thoughts in order, but I must apologize in advance for their condition. I must write hurriedly. If a fact is important, or even a name, I at least list it, in the hope that I will someday have the time to elaborate or explain it. I am unable to do this all at once —or to write all I know and feel—for the simple physical lack of time and space. When I write at home I disturb my

[1] Penkovskiy's second daughter was born on February 6, 1962.

family's sleep (our apartment is only two rooms) and typing is very noisy. During working hours I am always busy —running like a madman between the visiting delegations and military intelligence headquarters and the offices of my Committee. My evenings are generally occupied—it is part of my job. When I visit my friends in the country it is worse. Someone may always ask what I am doing. Here at home at least I have a hiding place in my desk. My family could not find it, even if they knew. And they know nothing. It is a lonely struggle. As I sit here in Moscow, in my apartment, and write down my thoughts and observations I can only hope that the persons in whose hands they eventually fall will find them of interest and use them for the truth they say.

First, let us elaborate my own personal characteristics, as our Party saying goes.

Position: Senior Officer, Special Group, Chief Intelligence Directorate, General Staff of the Soviet Army; promoted to the rank of Colonel in February 1950.

Operational Cover: Senior Expert, Deputy Chief of the Foreign Section, State Committee for the Co-ordination of Scientific Research Work.

My Parents and Relatives

Father: Penkovskiy, Vladimir Florianovich, born sometime between 1895 and 1897, Russian native of the city of Stavropol, killed in the Civil War of 1919. I never knew my father at all. According to my mother, he finished the Lyceum and the Polytechnic Institute in Warsaw and was an engineer by profession.

Mother: Penkovskaya, Taisiya Yakovlevna, born in 1900; has been living with me since 1941.

Brothers and Sisters: None.

Grandfather: Penkovskiy, Florian Antonovich, died before the Revolution of 1917; a judge in the city of Stavropol.

Grandfather's Brother: Penkovskiy, Valentin Antonovich, Lieutenant General[2] of the Soviet Army; Commander

---

[2] The literal Russian translation is colonel general (*general polkovnik*). Here and throughout the Papers, however, we have used the corresponding American or British equivalent ranks, to suggest more clearly the individual's relative position in the military hierarchy. A one-star general we designate as brigadier general, as in the U.S. Army, although he is called *general mayor* in the Soviet Army. A

of the Far East Military District. Prior to 1937 a Regimental Commander in the Antiaircraft Defense Force, Far East. In 1937–39 he was in prison, released at the beginning of World War II. He occupied the following posts during the war; Chief of Staff of the 21st Army; Chief of Staff of the Far East Military District under Malinovskiy. He was appointed Commander of the Far East Military District troops when Marshal Malinovskiy was made Minister of Defense.

Aunt: Shivtsova, Yelena Yakovlevna, prior to 1959 a housekeeper in the Afghan and Italian embassies, an informant for the State Security, resides in Moscow.

Wife: Penkovskaya (née Gapanovich), Vera Dmitriyevna, born in 1928 in Moscow, Russian, comes from a military family, knows French, does not work.

Wife's Father: Gapanovich, Dmitriy Afanasyevich, former Major General of the Soviet Army, member of the Military Council and Chief of the Political Directorate of the Moscow Military District, died in Moscow in 1952.

Wife's Mother: Lives with two grown children in Moscow. After her husband's death she received a single grant of 75,000 rubles[3] and was simultaneously awarded a monthly pension of 2500 rubles.

Education

1937: Graduated from secondary school in the city of Ordzhonikidze.

1937–39: 2nd Kiev Artillery School.

1945–48: The Frunze Military Academy (Combined Arms Department).

1949–53: The Military Diplomatic Academy.

1958–59: Higher Academic Artillery Engineering Courses on New Technology, at the Dzerzhinskiy Artillery Engineering Military Academy.

Soviet Army Service, Including Studies

1937–39: Cadet of the 2nd Kiev Artillery School in Kiev.

---

two-star general (U.S. major general) is *general leytenant*. A three-star general (U.S. lieutenant general) is *general polkovnik*.

[3] At this time the official exchange rate was four rubles to a dollar, the unofficial from ten to twenty rubles. In these Papers all amounts are given in old rubles.

1939–40: Battery Political Officer *(Politruk)*[4]: 1st Western Front (during the Polish campaign); 91st Rifle Division of the Siberian Military District and later on the Karelian front (in the war against the Finns).

1940–41: Assistant Chief of Political Section for Komsomol work at an artillery school in Moscow.

1941–42: Senior Instructor of the Political Directorate for Komsomol work in the Moscow Military District.

1942–43: Special Assignments Officer of the Military Council of the Moscow Military District.

1943–44: Chief of Training Camps and then Artillery Battalion Commander in the 27th Tank Destroyer Regiment of the 1st Ukranian Front.

1944: Wounded, in a hospital in Moscow.

1944–45: Liaison Officer for Commander of Artillery of the 1st Ukranian Front, Lieutenant General of Artillery Sergey S. Varentsov (then convalescing in Moscow).

1945: Commanding Officer of the 51st Guards Tank Destroyer Artillery Regiment, 1st Ukrainian Front.

1945–48: Student at the Frunze Military Academy.

1948: Senior Officer in the Organization and Mobilization Directorate, Moscow Military District.

1948–49: Staff Officer with Commander in Chief of Ground Forces, Ministry of Defense of the U.S.S.R., in Moscow.

1949–53: Student at the Military Diplomatic Academy in Moscow.

1953–55: Senior Officer of the 4th Directorate (Near East Desk), Chief Intelligence Directorate, General Staff of the Soviet Army.

1955–56: Assistant Military Attaché, Senior Assistant of the Military Intelligence (GRU) *Rezident* in Ankara, Turkey.

1956–58: Senior Officer of the 4th Directorate[5] of GRU in Moscow (Preparation for going overseas as GRU *Rezident* in India).

1958–59: Student at the Higher Academic Artillery Engineering Courses of the Dzerzhinskiy Military Artillery Engineering Academy in Moscow.

---

4 A person who is in charge of political work in units of the Soviet armed forces.

5 GRU area Directorate responsible for collecting intelligence in the Near and Far East in 1960.

1959–60: Senior Officer of the 4th Directorate, Chief Intelligence Directorate of the General Staff of the Soviet Army in Moscow.

1960: Member of the Mandate Commission,[6] Military Diplomatic Academy in Moscow; Senior Officer, Special Group of the 3rd Directorate,[7] Chief Intelligence Directorate (GRU), General Staff of the Soviet Army.

Party Record: Member of Komsomol from 1937 to 1939; candidate member of the CPSU from 1939 to 1940; member of CPSU since March 1940, Party Card No. 01783176.

Government Awards: Two Orders of Red Banner; Order of Aleksandr Nevskiy; Order of the Fatherland War, 1st Class; Order of Red Star; eight Medals.

Thus, one can have some idea as to who I am and what I am.

There is more to be said, of course, than the bare record. I was born in the thick of the Civil War during which my father was lost. Mother told me that my father saw me for the first and last time when I was only four months old. This occurred soon after my christening, for which purpose I was taken to Stavropol. That was in accordance with my grandfather's wish. My grandfather was a judge, but that was long ago, in the old days.

Data on my father was given to me. 1918: Ensign *(proporshchik)* in the 25th Reserve Infantry Regiment. Ensign in the 112th Infantry Regiment. 1919: Second Lieutenant *(podporuchik)* in the 1st Artillery Brigade. May 9, 1919, confirmed in the rank of lieutenant.

My father was a soldier in the White Army. My father fought against the Soviets. In reality I never had a father —that is what our Communists would say. I still do not think they know the whole truth about him. If the KGB had known all along that he was in the White Army (although I was only a few months old at the time) every door would have been closed to me: for an officer's career,

---

[6] A group of GRU directorate chiefs and medical examiners who make the final selection of the candidates for the incoming class of GRU's Military Diplomatic Academy each year.

[7] GRU area directorate responsible for collecting intelligence in the United States, Canada, South America, and Great Britain.

for membership in the Party, and especially for the intelligence service.

The Civil War ended with the Red Army's victory and I was a child without a father. My mother reared me as best she could. I was brought up in a Soviet environment. From the very beginning of my school days I showed promise, or so people say.

When I was eight years old I went to school. By 1937 I had finished ten grades of the school at Vladikavkaz. Immediately after graduating from the secondary school there, at the age of eighteen, I entered the 2nd Kiev Artillery School. I wanted to be a commander of the Soviet Army. While in the school I had joined the Komsomol. I participated actively in the Komsomol and various public activities, and was an outstanding student. I loved the artillery. While still in school I made my first contribution to the service by proposing a valuable technical improvement for which I was cited in the school's order of the day.

My future seemed quite promising; I was one of the few in my class who had finished secondary education, and the chances of my advancement seemed very good. Artillery has always been in a privileged position in Russia. From the time of Peter the Great we Russians have always been considered excellent artillerymen.

In 1939 I finished the 2nd Kiev Artillery School and was commissioned an artillery lieutenant. Shortly before graduation I was accepted as a candidate Party member. Because of my active work in the Komsomol and the fact that I had become a Party candidate, I was appointed *politruk* of an artillery battery, instead of receiving a direct assignment as a troop commander.

I remember very well how, soon after I reported to my unit, our regiment was visited by Army Commander of the First Rank (now Marshal) Timoshenko.[8] At that time he was the commanding general of the Ukrainian Military District. To us young officers he was a legendary hero of the Civil War together with Budennyy. As the saying goes,

8 Semen Konstantinovich Timoshenko, born in 1985; 1940–41 People's Commissar of Defense; commanded the troops of a front during World War II; in 1949, commanded the Belorussian Military District; in 1960 appointed to responsible work in the Ministry of Defense; candidate member of the Central Committee CPSU.

they had chopped White officers to pieces. Later Timoshenko became one of Stalin's favorites and for a short
time, before the war, he occupied the post of People's
Commissar of Defense. I remember him talking with our
army commander—I believe that it was Golikov (now a
marshal) and with another man whom I had never seen
before. Later we were told by the commissar of our regiment that he was one N. S. Khrushchev, a member of the
District Military Council. His uniform fitted him like a
saddle fits a cow.

Soon I was to participate in the Polish campaign. In
September 1939 we crossed the old Polish border and
arrived in Lvov, after meeting only negligible resistance
from the Poles. Even at that time one could notice a big
difference between life in our own country and in bourgeois Poland. We literally bought up everything we could
lay our hands on. Because we did not have enough cash,
we paid the Poles with our government bonds, thus cheating them. The Poles were quite surprised and puzzled.
They asked us: "Why are you buying up everything, do
you have nothing at home?" We answered: "Oh, yes, we
have everything, but it is just difficult to get things."

Soon after the Polish campaign I was transferred to the
91st Rifle Division of the Siberian Military District which
was being formed in the small town of Achinsk. I was
appointed a battery *politruk* in the 321st Artillery Regiment. As soon as the division had reached its full strength
we were sent to Finland, where our Red Army was trying
to break through the Mannerheim Line. We arrived at the
Karelian front, it seems to me, at the end of January
1940. Here for the first time I saw victims of the war.
Wounded and frozen soldiers and officers with blood frozen
around their wounds could be seen everywhere. Many of
them lost their fingers or toes, some of them lost ears.
Battles fought against the well-trained Finns were very
hard. We suffered heavy casualties.

Our division remained in reserve until our troops began
the assault on Vyborg.[9] It was here that both my battery

9 Vyborg was successfully defended by the Finns during the Russo-
Finnish War of 1939–40, but it was ceded to the U.S.S.R. following
Finland's defeat. It was retaken by the Finns in 1941 but captured
by the Russians in 1944 and became a permanent part of the
U.S.S.R. under terms of the peace treaty in 1947.

and I received our baptism of fire. On the very first day of battle our division lost more than half of its personnel. All three regimental commanders were killed. It was March when we finally succeeded in breaking through the Finns. Their resistance ceased, and the "short" war was over. Many of the survivors in our division were awarded decorations and medals. I received thanks and a cigarette case. The division was sent back to Achinsk to re-form.

I did not go with my division. As one of the best and youngest political workers, I was placed at the disposal of the Moscow Military District's Political Directorate for further assignment in the service.

Now a new era in my life began. Upon arriving in Moscow, I was assigned as Assistant Chief of the Political Section for Komsomol Work at the Krasin Artillery School. In 1940, life in Moscow, as compared to life in Siberia or at the Karelian front, was rather pleasant. In spite of being quite busy, I often found time for personal amusements, and made new acquaintances in Moscow. For the students at the school I organized cultural trips to the movies and theaters of Moscow. Still, the largest part of my time was consumed organizing propaganda and agitation among the students: lectures, political information, discussions, reading of newspapers and journals, etc. So much that I became sick of it myself. I knew the *Short History of the Communist Party (Bolshevik)* almost by heart, and yet regardless of this, I continued to study, study, and study. Such is the fact of being a political worker in the Soviet Army.

All my efforts to make my lectures and political information interesting were unsuccessful. The students quite often dozed and in some cases actually slept during their political studies. Having actively developed Komsomol work at the school, I achieved certain positive results, but my ardor soon disappeared. Quite often students visited me with various complaints about poor conditions at home. One complained about his parents being heavily taxed; another complained that his family's only cow was taken away for back taxes; a third said his old father had been imprisoned because he had not gone to work, and so on.

On the one hand, I sympathized with the students and helped them as much as I could. Yet at the same time I had to write reports to the District Political Directorate on unhealthy attitudes among the students, and combat these attitudes myself. My basic duty as a Komsomol worker was to raise the quality of studies and strengthen Communist discipline. While inwardly disagreeing with many rules and regulations of the military service, I nevertheless continued to put the Party line into practice. I had no other choice. I did not think of quitting the Army because there was no other place for me to go. The life of a Soviet officer is better than that of an engineer. Everybody knows that. I had no other specialty.

While still in the artillery school, I was accepted as a Communist Party member. My only desire at that time was to switch from political work to a command assignment in the field, but this would entail great difficulties. Although I had the advantage over other political workers because I had finished an artillery school, it was not until much later, during the war, that my wish to get a command assignment was finally realized.

The news about the German attack on the Soviet Union in June 1941 came as a shock to me, as it did to the majority of those serving in the Red Army. We simply refused to believe the news about the crushing defeats inflicted upon our troops at the border. When Stalin on July 3 began his radio address to the Soviet troops with the words "brothers and sisters," we all realized that something extremely serious had happened. Stalin had never addressed the people like this before.

At approximately the same time, I was transferred from the Artillery School to the Political Directorate of the Moscow Military District as instructor to the members of Komsomol. One of the first documents which came to my attention in my new position was the order for the arrest and execution of General Pavlov, Commander of the Western Front, and his Chief of Staff, General Klimovskikh, as well as some others who failed to stop the German advance on their sectors of the front.

Soon the rumors about the mass surrender of Soviet officers and men reached Moscow. Moscow had also learned about the German encirclement of two of our armies in Belorussia, the retreat in the Ukraine, the heavy fighting in the Smolensk area, etc. Wounded men began to appear in the hospitals in Moscow, and they related frightful stories about German invincibility, especially about their ceaseless air raids and aerial bombardment, carried out almost unpunished because our own Air Force had been destroyed on the ground during the very first days of the war. Whatever little remained of it was paralyzed by the Germans. Our ground forces were left without any cover or support.

As the fall of 1941 came, the news from the front became worse and worse. In October the Germans broke through our defensive lines east of Smolensk and Bryansk and encircled six or seven of our armies, taking about half a million prisoners. After this, the road to Moscow was open.

General Zhukov was hastily summoned from Leningrad to assume command of the Western Front. At the same time, Major General Artemyev, Commander of the Moscow Military District, was appointed Commander of the capital's defense. Artemyev was an NKVD general; he first commanded an NKVD[10] division in Moscow and then, in 1941, had become the District Commander. At that time most of the commanding generals assigned by Stalin to various posts in the defense of Moscow were NKVD generals. Artemyev's political commissar was Konstantin Fedorovich Telegin, the Commandant of Moscow, General Sinilov, and the Commandant of the Kremlin, General Spiridonov. Army commanders such as Ivan Ivanovich Maslennikov and Khomenko also were NKVD generals. Later all these commanding generals from the NKVD pretended to be real Red Army generals, but only one of them, Khomenko, has proven himself as a good combat general. However, Maslennikov later became the commander of a front.

It remains a fact, however, that all these NKVD generals were assigned to various posts in Moscow by Stalin in 1941; they proved very valuable to Stalin during the panic which enveloped the city during the period of

10 The initials NKVD stood for the People's Commissariat for Internal Affairs, a forerunner or predecessor of the present KGB— the Committee for State Security. NKVD troops were most trusted by Stalin and were used during the war to prevent, by force if necessary, the retreat of Red Army units and to set examples of courage in the face of enemy attacks. NKVD officers were ranked in military fashion, as are KGB officers today.

October 16 to 19. By that time the Party leadership and NKVD and militia officials had begun to flee to the East. Looting was taking place everywhere. The government declared the city in a state of siege, and began to mobilize the population to dig trenches and build fortifications. The local population was also used to form "volunteer" divisions and "people's militia" which were sent to the front untrained and half-armed in order to stem the German advance and give Zhukov time to regroup his depleted troops.

The struggle for Moscow reached its highest point in early December 1941. Zhukov had nerves of steel. He would not commit his reserves to battle until the Germans advanced too far, stretching their communication lines, and got stuck in deep snow only a few kilometers from Moscow. Tanks without fuel and with their tracks frozen found themselves buried in snow, while their air forces were grounded by terrible blizzards. Then our entire force was thrown at the Germans, inflicting a great defeat upon them. Zhukov, Konev, and Rokossovskiy led their armies skillfully, and the spirit of the troops rose considerably when they realized that they could defeat the Germans. By the end of the winter of 1941–42, our troops had driven the Germans back almost as far as Smolensk.

In the summer of 1942, when our troops were retreating on the Southern Front in the direction of Stalingrad and the Caucasus, I was assigned to the War Council of the Moscow Military District, again to do political work. My superior at that time was Division Commissar [i.e., a political major general] Dmitriy Afanasyevich Gapanovich, Chief of the District Political Directorate. Dmitriy Afanasyevich became quite fond of me and treated me very well. Once he invited me to his home and introduced me to his family, including his daughter Vera, a very attractive girl about fourteen years old, with dark hair, whom I happened to see quite often later during my stay in Moscow.

At that time, however, all our thoughts were riveted on the South, where our exhausted troops had already begun to entrench themselves in the ruins of Stalingrad on the Volga. The summer and the fall for us in Moscow were a period of endless, agonizing waiting. We were aware of the daily bombardment to which the city was subjected by

German bombers and heavy artillery, of the way our soldiers fought the Germans in ruined buildings of the city, crawling toward each other among fires and through the smoke and dust which constantly hung over the city.

Finally, in the middle of November, it became known to us that our army had gone on the offensive, encircling the 6th German Army and part of the 4th Armored Army. Two and a half months later, in February 1943, the resistance of the besieged German garrison was broken and more than 300,000 prisoners were taken.

I heard from my colleagues in the district headquarters that my grandfather's brother, then Brigadier General Penkovskiy, participated in this battle as Chief of Staff of the 21st Army commanded by General Chistyakov. He distinguished himself and was awarded a decoration.

Several months later our armies met the German armies in a large battle between Orel and Kharkov. This was the third decisive battle of the war. The special feature of this battle was the mass employment of tanks by both sides. We used about five tank armies in this battle. The battle ended in August with the complete victory of Soviet arms. The Germans began a general retreat along the entire Dnepr River line. Our troops displayed great skill, combat proficiency, and heroism. Later I heard from General Gapanovich, who had friends in the Political Directorate of the Voronezh front (one of the four fronts which participated in the battle), that a serious argument took place between General Zhadov, Commander of the 5th Guards Army, and General Rotmistrov, Commander of the 5th Guards Armored Army, in regard to their respective actions during the battle. Each accused the other of having exposed the other's flank to the Germans by his premature retreat. Some members of the staff compared it to the well-known argument between General Rennenkampf and General Samsonov during World War I.

Coming up to the Dnepr, our troops crossed the river under heavy enemy fire and in November 1943 took Kiev. I tried constantly to be sent to the front; after all, I was a skilled artilleryman with combat experience acquired in the Finnish War. At long last my request was granted, and in November 1943 I was placed at the disposal of the artillery commander of the 1st Ukrainian Front in the Kiev area.

So ended my life in Moscow, the life of a rear-echelon drudge, and my political work. I said good-by to it without regret and was impatiently waiting for the chance to measure swords personally with the Germans. After all, at that time there were already several hundred decorated heroes of the Soviet Union, but all I had was a cigarette case which I got for fighting the Finns. I expected to be assigned as a battalion commander; I was already visualizing myself as a commander of an artillery regiment.

I must confess that when I arrived at the front my new comrades greeted me with a certain amount of mistrust. They were battle-seasoned veterans who had fought in the Ukraine and at Stalingrad, who more than once had looked death in the eye, and who had earned many combat decorations. Their tanned, wrinkled, stern faces spoke of heated skirmishes with the Germans. And then there was I, a major, an officer since 1939 who quietly sat out almost the entire war in Moscow without any combat experience against the Germans. The reception given me made my desire to get to the front lines as soon as possible even stronger. I was quite disappointed, therefore, to find out that I was being appointed chief of training units in which new replacements for the Antitank Artillery of the 1st Ukrainian Front were received and trained. These units were furnishing replacements to the antitank artillery regiments, which had suffered considerable losses at the front. At that time we had twenty-seven such regiments. I received partly trained recruits as well as old artillerymen returning from hospitals, sorted them out, and sent them to the units where they were most needed, according to instructions.

While occupying this position I had the opportunity to meet Lieutenant General of Artillery Sergey Sergeyevich Varentsov, Commander of Artillery of the 1st Ukrainian Front. From the very start I became very fond of this veteran artilleryman and patriot. He had been at the front since 1941, had been wounded, and after a succession of combat commands had reached the post of Artillery Commander, first of an army and then of a front. Sergey Sergeyevich was a powerfully built man with broad shoulders and a shock of white hair on his head—he could be recognized half a kilometer away when he was without his cap. I think he was taken with me. When I complained to him that I was once more given an administrative rear-area job, instead of bawling me out as most of the generals would have done, he took me aside and told me that he liked my enthusiasm but that I had spent too much time in the rear. Therefore I needed some time to become adjusted to field conditions prior to taking a combat command assignment.

Such an opportunity presented itself in February 1944. I was sent to the 8th Guards Antitank Artillery Brigade. The brigade consisted of three Guards regiments (the 322nd, the 323rd, and the 324th), each having six batteries (57-mm and 76-mm antitank guns and a certain amount of 100-mm guns), and approximately five hundred men in each regiment (when at full strength, which never happened). The Commander of our brigade was Lieutenant Colonel Chevola, a strict, skillful, and experienced artilleryman who liked to be under enemy fire together with his soldiers. The regiment to which I was assigned was commanded by Hero of the Soviet Union Major Tikvich, a gay, cheerful, happy-go-lucky man who liked his drink. Soldiers loved him for his personal bravery in battle. Soon after my arrival in the regiment, Tikvich got into serious trouble because of a woman and he was removed from his post. In March, upon General Varentsov's recommendation, I was appointed regiment commander.

After we took Kiev and defended successfully the fortified bridgeheads on the western bank of the Dnepr, our Supreme High Commander organized a large concentration of forces, which were to push beyond the Dnepr and the 4th German Panzer Army, which was located between the Dnepr and the Carpathians. During the preparation for this new advance our brigade was visited by Commander of the Front General Nikolay Fedorovich Vatutin, Khrushchev, a member of the War Council of the front, and General Varentsov.

On February 28, however, the jeep in which General Vatutin was riding was ambushed by Ukrainian nationalists who were operating in this area as guerrillas, and General Vatutin was mortally wounded. He soon died in one of the hospitals in Kiev. Marshal Zhukov was appointed the new commander of the 1st Ukrainian Front. Despite the fact that he was considered an outstanding military commander, veteran officers said that this change just before the start of the offensive operation had a negative effect on its course.

Some people feel that Zhukov failed to take sufficiently decisive measures to strengthen the weak spots, whereas he himself maintains that certain army commanders (including Grechko and Badanov) let him down. At any rate, the Germans escaped full encirclement, going south and west, and we thus missed a chance to set up another Stalingrad for them in the Dnestr area. Later, in the middle of April, our 60th Army, which was then commanded by General Kurochkin (at present he is the Chief of the Frunze Military Academy in Moscow) took Ternopol, where my regiment participated in defending the city from German counterattacks.

By the end of the month both sides went over to the defense; Marshal Zhukov was taken away from us and appointed to the General Headquarters of the Supreme High Command. Assigned in his place was Konev, who had just been promoted to the rank of marshal for his successful operations in the Ukraine. Sergey Sergeyevich Varentsov told me later that there was no better soldier in the Red Army than Marshal Zhukov; he never hesitated using strong language to display his authority. Marshal Zhukov was always popular among ordinary soldiers and junior officers, with whom he tried to be on even terms. They saw him as a legendary Russian warrior-hero. At the very same time, he was extremely strict with his generals, bawling them out and using the roughest kind of language in the presence of their officers. Some of these generals, General Batov[11] for example, have not forgotten this. For this reason, when Khrushchev decided to remove the Marshal in 1957, he had no trouble finding enough senior commanders who were willing to help him in this matter.

A lull set in on the 1st Ukrainian Front, lasting until June, after which preparations started for a new offensive, in the direction of Lvov and southern Poland. In this

11 Pavel Ivanovich Batov, born in 1897; joined the Red Army in 1918; during World War II he commanded first a corps and then an army; in 1954–55 he was the first Deputy Commander of Soviet Forces in Germany; from 1955–60 he was the Commander of the Carpathian and Baltic Military Districts; at the present time he is the First Deputy Chief of the General Staff of the Soviet Armed Forces and Chief of Staff of the Combined Armed Forces of the Warsaw Pact countries.

period of preparation, during a reconnaissance operation, I was wounded in the head. It was a serious wound. I received a concussion, and both my upper and lower jaw on the right side of my face were damaged. I was sent to a hospital. It was only after a two-month period of treatment that I began to get ready for my return to the front.

During a short stay in Moscow I visited General Gapanovich and again met his daughter Vera. Right then and there I fell in love with her. She was now sixteen years old, a real beauty.

General Gapanovich told me that General Varentsov was in a hospital in Moscow where he was being treated after an accident which happened to him at the front. It seems that he was riding in a car to see Marshal Konev when, due to the driver's carelessness, the car collided with a tank. Sergey Sergeyevich suffered a broken hip. Doctors told him that he would have a limp for the rest of his life. He was a patient in the Generals' Hospital on Serebryannyy Lane in Moscow.

When I visited him I found his spirits very low. Not only was he suffering from physical pain, but he was also depressed by rumors about a tragedy that had occurred in his own family, who were living at that time in Lvov, then the headquarters of our front. Sergey Sergeyevich appointed me his personal liaison officer with the Artillery Staff Headquarters of the 1st Ukrainian Front. When he sent me to Lvov, he asked me to find out exactly what happened to his mother and two daughters and, if necessary, to take care of them. My assignment to Varentsov's staff made it possible for me to travel freely to Moscow.

So I went to Lvov. There I really found a tragedy. Sergey Sergeyevich had been married twice. His first wife, Anya, died of tuberculosis in Leningrad, and after this Varentsov married Yekaterina Pavlovna, who was the wife of a venereologist. (They fell in love and she got a divorce from the doctor.) From his first marriage Varentsov had one daughter, Nina, who was working in a hospital near Lvov. She was married to a major whose name was Loshak. He was a Jew. He and two other officers were caught stealing "socialist property," tried by a military tribunal, and shot. Actually, they had been selling cars and spare parts on the black market.

Nina loved her husband very much. After he was shot,

nobody wanted to talk to her, nobody wanted to have anything to do with the wife of a man who had been executed.
She could not bear this, and once when a wounded lieutenant was passing her in the hospital corridor, she grabbed
his pistol and shot herself. At that time Varentsov's old
mother was in Lvov. She was unable to handle the arrangements for Nina's burial, and no one wanted to help her.
As soon as I saw this situation, I quickly made my decision. I sold my watch, bought a coffin and a black dress,
and had Nina buried. I also helped Varentsov's mother
to get some coal and firewood—she was sitting home
freezing.

Major Loshak had been arrested by "Smersh";[12] at the
trial he was accused not only of stealing socialist property,
but also of sabotage and undermining the power of the
Red Army.

This is the way things have always been done in our
country, and that is how they are done today. A person
is arrested for speculation, but then some political significance must always be attached to it.

Upon my return to Moscow I gave Sergey Sergeyevich
a detailed account of everything that had taken place in
Lvov and what I had done. He embraced me, kissed me,
and said, "You are now like my own son." My friendship
with Varentsov and his family has continued since then.
He calls me his boy and son, and frankly he has taken my
father's place. When talking about Smersh and Nina,
Sergey Sergeyevich has often mentioned that he now understands what the families of those whose husbands and
relatives were arrested by the NKVD had to live through.
He did not believe Rokossovskiy[13] and others before, but

---

[12] Smersh (literally "death to spies") was in fact the Chief Directorate of Counterintelligence of the Soviet armed forces. It became a
part of the MGB in 1946 and remained so until February 1947, at
which time the name disappeared. Today it is known merely as the
Chief Counterintelligence Directorate of the KGB for the Soviet
Armed Forces (3rd Chief Directorate).

[13] In 1937 Marshal Konstantin Konstantinovich Rokossovskiy was
imprisoned and brutally tortured for allegedly participating in a
clique which had supported Marshal M. N. Tukhachevskiy, who was
liquidated in 1937 for "treason." Later Rokossovskiy was released
and reinstated, minus his teeth. During the period of the Great
Purge of 1936–38, by conservative estimates, from 20,000 to 35,000
officers were purged. This was 35 to 50 percent of the Soviet officer
corps.

now after Nina's death nothing will make him forgive those who are responsible for her death. This incident that occurred in Varentsov's family made a deep impression on me.

I continued traveling between Moscow and the Front Headquarters with instructions from General Varentsov to his deputy, General Semenov, the Commander of the 7th Artillery Corps Korolkov; and the Divisional Artillery commanders Sanko (who at present is serving under Sergey Sergeyevich in the Chief Artillery Directorate), Kafanov, and others. At the end of 1944 I returned to the front, where I was assigned Commander of the 51st Guards Tank Destroyer Regiment. It was just at the right moment; preparations were starting for a new offensive whose purpose was the final liberation of southern Poland and a direct assault against southeastern Germany.

Our offensive began in the middle of January. Despite snow and severe weather our assault units broke through the German lines, our armored units advanced and took Krakow, and the very same month we crossed the old German border and captured our first German city, whose name, as far as I can remember, was Kreuzburg.

The entire Army rejoiced. The day of the capture I happened to be at the Artillery Headquarters. Sergey Sergeyevich, in high spirits, introduced me to Marshal Konev, Commander of the Front, telling him that I had recently come up with an excellent idea on how to decrease the amount of time spent in training antitank guns.

It must be mentioned here that we were having difficulties turning the guns from one direction to another when German tanks broke into our defense zones, especially when only one or two men were left to man a gun because of losses among gun crews. It occurred to me that a steel plate with a spindle in the center could be installed on the ground, covered with heavy gun grease, and then another plate put on top of it with the wheels of the gun secured to it. The crew could then turn the gun quickly in any direction to fire at the advancing tanks. My invention had already been adopted by Sergey Sergeyevich; Marshal Konev, after pondering the idea for a while, commended me for initiative and inventiveness. "Here is a good candidate for the Military Academy, Sergey Sergeyevich," said Konev before leaving, pointing at me. Later, for this invention and for a combat operation that had been conducted well, I was awarded the Order of Aleksandr Nevskiy. All this lifted my spirits considerably, and I went back to my regiment anticipating a brilliant military career.

The struggle against the Germans continued to be extremely savage, especially in the thickly populated region of Silesia, where for the first time I experienced the charms of street fighting. The German tanks appeared unexpectedly from side streets and alleys, in front and behind us; sometimes we had to fire at them point blank, turning the guns around and training them on the target at the last moment. Men choked from the dust rising above the heaps of broken stone and brick of the demolished buildings, while ashes from the burning lumber settled on the snow, turning its color from white to dirty gray or black.

In February we emerged from the industrial regions, pursuing the Germans across the Oder. We advanced as far as the Neisse, where we stopped for a respite before the final offensive against Berlin. I was pleased to see my old brigade, the 8th Guards Tank Destroyer Artillery Brigade, mentioned several times in Stalin's orders, as well as the 32nd Brigade, whose commander, Colonel Ivan Vladimirovich Kupin, was a good friend of mine. At the present time he is a general and is in command of artillery of the Moscow Military District. Kupin is also a good friend of Varentsov's and is indebted for many things to Sergey Sergeyevich, who got him out of trouble many times. (Kupin's nephew is married to one of Varentsov's daughters by his second marriage.)

April 1945 came, and the war was almost over. My regiment was providing support for the southern group of the front which was advancing through Dresden and Prague and then through Czechoslovakia into Austria, where we replaced the 3rd Ukrainian Front. The headquarters of our Central Army Group, under the command of Marshal Konev, were in Baden. I took the opportunity to remind Sergey Sergeyevich of Konev's remark about my attending the Military Academy. At that time I was already a lieutenant colonel with five decorations and six medals—and besides I wanted to marry Gapanovich's daughter Vera and live in Moscow.

Sergey Sergeyevich immediately agreed. At the end of

August 1945 he wrote an official recommendation for my acceptance at the Frunze Academy. I passed the entrance exams and began my studies in the academy. In the fall Vera and I, with the blessing of her parents and my mother, were married.

My studies at the Frunze Military Academy continued for three years. For me this was a period of intensive study and of a happy family life. Our first child was born in 1946. It was a girl whom we named Galina. In the same year, with the help of my father-in-law, General Ganapovich, I was able to get an apartment in a new nine-story house built on Maksim Gorkiy Embankment with a view of the Moscow River, where I am still living at the present time.

Then studying at the academy were a number of promising officers, some of whom are generals now. I remember two of them particularly well: Lieutenant General Yaglenko and Hero of the Soviet Union Lieutenant Colonel Vasiliy Illarionovich Shcherbina, who is now serving in the Volga Military District in Kuybyshev. The Commandant of the academy was an old man, Lieutenant General Tsvetayev, an army commander during the war, chronically ill, which was the reason why we very seldom saw him. He died, I think, in 1950.

My father-in-law, as a well-placed political general, was a man of some influence. I was often present in his apartment when he was visited by his friends and acquaintances and there I became acquainted with many senior officers of the Moscow Military District Staff, the Moscow Garrison, and the General Staff.

After 1946 I temporarily lost contact with Varentsov. He was assigned to the Transcaucasian Military District. I did not see him until he came to Moscow to attend some courses at the Voroshilov General Staff Academy and the Dzerzhinskiy Engineering Artillery Academy.

My acquaintanceship with representatives of the higher circles of command, acquired through my father-in-law and Varentsov, aroused a certain amount of envy among my colleagues at the academy. I am almost sure that it was one of them who denounced me to organs of the MGB[14]

---

14 One of the responsibilities of the MGB (Ministry of State Security) and its successors was that of counterintelligence and security within the Soviet armed forces. The component of the MGB

as an alleged black-market speculator, a charge of which I was absolutely innocent. I was summoned to the Smersh Counterintelligence Directorate of the MGB, which, I must confess, scared me very much, but the whole thing was happily resolved.

At that time Soviet Army officers had to watch themselves very carefully because many high posts in the Moscow Garrison were occupied by MVD and MGB generals. Understandably, a great deal of enmity existed between them and the regular Soviet Army officers. Some of the latter, such as General Yegorov, who was then my father-in-law's deputy in the District Political Directorate, openly talked of the "Chekists" occupying posts in the district headquarters. But there were also others, like General Zolotukhin, who had a reputation for licking the boots of the MGB. Some of my father-in-law's colleagues even accused him of being too friendly with the MGB.

In 1948 I completed the course in the Frunze Academy and pinned on my chest the diamond-shaped insignia of a graduate. Now I had to decide what to do next. I had an offer to enter the Military Diplomatic Academy, which would open the way for a career of a military intelligence officer and a chance to be a military attaché abroad. This idea appealed to Vera, but her father advised me to pass this offer up for the time being. He maintained that it would not be wise for me, a young and highly qualified artillery officer, to give up a career which had started well in this field and to change for work in the GRU, which would prove to be a dead end for me. Instead, he advised me to get an assignment in the Moscow Military District. I agreed with my father-in-law's arguments and got an assignment in the Organization and Mobilization Directorate of Lieutenant General Sandalov, the District Chief of Staff. Unfortunately, General Sandalov, a fair and sympathetic person, was later badly maimed in an airplane accident. He is now living as an invalid with his legs paralyzed.

I served in the District Staff a total of six months. Shortly before my arrival, sudden changes had taken place in

---

responsible for this function was, and still is, known commonly as the Special Section [*Osobyy Otdel*]. The MGB was a successor of the NKVD and a predecessor of the KGB.

the district. General of NKVD Artemyev was replaced by Marshal Meretskov, and my father-in-law was assigned to one of the remote military districts in the Urals. Some people said that the one behind it was Marshal Bulganin, then Minister of Defense, who was trying to gain the favor of Army officers—many of whom, General Yegorov and General of Armored Troops Butkov, for example, were openly expressing their satisfaction on this score. Their joy, however, was short-lived.

In 1949 General Artemyev returned, and what was even worse, especially for the Air Force officers, Stalin appointed his son Vasiliy Commander of the Air Forces of the district. Vasiliy Stalin was a drunk and a rowdy. Everybody hated him. He was especially rude toward Lieutenant General (now Marshal) Moskalenko, Commander of the Antiaircraft Defense of the city of Moscow, deriding him for always being sick. He said he ought to be riding in a wheel chair instead of a staff car. I was not at all surprised by the fact that "Vaska" (as many called Stalin's son) was getting along so well with the NKVD generals. But as soon as his father died he was removed from his post —in fact, removed altogether from the Air Force.

After serving six months in the Moscow Military District, I succeeded in getting transferred to the Staff of the Ground Forces. The Commander in Chief was then Marshal Konev and his Chief of Staff was General Malandin. Among the officers I met here I became most friendly with Major General Baklanov, Chief of the Physical Training Directorate. Baklanov, who at the present time holds the post of Commander of the Siberian Military District, was a tall, well-built man with excellent military bearing. He distinguished himself during the war when commanding one of the Guards divisions of the 5th Guards Army of General Zhadov, which was included in the 1st Ukrainian Front. Baklanov and Zhadov were great friends. I foresee that Baklanov[15] will advance far in the service. In the past he owed much to Zhadov, but I would not be sur-

---

15 Gleb Vladimirovich Baklanov, born in 1910; joined the Soviet Army in 1932; held various command positions during World War II; 1960–64 was the Commander of the Siberian Military District; at present commands the Northern Group of Forces, a lieutenant general.

prised if in the future Baklanov will be in a position to protect Zhadov.[16]

At the end of 1949 the question again arose of my transfer to the military intelligence service and study at the Military Diplomatic Academy. I finally gave my consent and entered the regular course of the academy, with the idea of becoming a professional military intelligence officer. Soon after that, on February 6, 1950, I was promoted to the rank of colonel.

At this point it will be enough to mention only that at the academy I learned how to conduct military espionage and completed a three-year course in the English language, which I mastered, I believe, fairly well. On July 22, 1953, I was graduated from the academy and assigned to the Chief Intelligence Directorate [GRU] of the General Staff of the Soviet Army. I was made Senior Officer of the 4th Directorate responsible for the Near East.

In March Stalin had died. Soon thereafter came Beriya's arrest and there began the rule of the so-called "collective leadership," which consisted of Malenkov, Molotov, Bulganin, and Khrushchev. The new leadership undertook formulation of a new policy: economic and political penetration of the Near East. Soviet military intelligence was interested not only in the strength of the British and their intentions in the Suez Canal zone, but also in the potential of Egypt as an anticapitalist military power in the Near East. My work was directed against Egypt.

In August 1954 I was transferred to the Pakistan Desk and began to prepare myself for the post of assistant military attaché in Karachi. However, the Pakistani refused to give their approval to the expansion of the Soviet military attaché's staff in their country. Soon after that I prepared to go to Turkey, to be an assistant military attaché there.

In the summer of 1955 I arrived at my new post in Ankara. My wife Vera also came with me. At the beginning, when I was acting military attaché, we had to attend all the official receptions and pay various visits.

---

[16] Aleksey Semenovich Zhadov, born in 1900; in 1953 he was the Commandant of the Frunze Military Academy; in 1954 the Commander of Soviet troops in Austria; in 1957 the Deputy Commander in Chief of Ground Forces; in 1959 he became First Deputy Commander in Chief of Ground Forces.

In January 1956, the newly assigned Soviet military
attaché, Brigadier General of GRU Nikolay Petrovich
Rubenko, arrived in Turkey. My relations with him gradually became quite strained, and as a result, in November
1956, I was recalled to answer various charges. The circumstances leading to my recall bear retelling because they
had an important effect on my career. Rubenko, whose real
name is Savchenko (Rubenko was used as an operational
"cover"), had once worked as military attaché in Kabul.
He was an older man, about sixty, and rather crude in his
approach to our work. One of his assistants, named Ionchenko, tried to recruit some agents in Turkey by brazenly
propositioning them. He would meet a Turk in the street,
invite him to a restaurant, and almost immediately propose
that he become a Soviet agent, for good pay. "You love
me, and I will take care of you," he would say. "Now get
me a military manual. Here is the money. Take it!"

This sort of thing was soon noticed by Turkish counterintelligence. So it was no surprise that another time, Ionchenko[17] was apprehended at a meeting by Turkish police.
I had to go get him out. He had gone to the meeting with
Savchenko's permission, at a particularly ticklish period,
during a visit of the Shah of Iran to Turkey, when Moscow
had forbidden any meetings with agents. When I gave
Savchenko my opinion about his violating Moscow's orders, he became angry and told me to mind my own business. To straighten out this matter, I sent a cable to Moscow
through the channels of our other intelligence organization
in Turkey, the *rezidentura* of the KGB. When GRU
headquarters discovered this, I was recalled, accused of
writing a report about my chief and sending it through
channels of our bitter rival—this interservice jealousy between the GRU and KGB runs through most Soviet intelligence activities.

The matter did not end with my recall. The disagreement was finally reported to Khrushchev, who keeps a
close watch on intelligence activities. Khrushchev gave
orders to have the matter thoroughly investigated, to find
out who was right and who was wrong. I was spoken to

[17] Ionchenko was nearly discharged as a result of this action but
was assigned finally to the Military Diplomatic Academy as an instructor and then to Vietnam as an advisor to Ho Chi Minh on
intelligence matters.

rather sternly for not having treated my superiors with proper respect; at the same time, I was told that my action itself in alerting Moscow was correct. After the investigation Savchenko was punished by the Party and dismissed from the GRU. At the present time he is a department head in the Institute for Oriental Studies.

Despite this vindication, my stay in the reserve dragged on. As Smolikov, Chief of Personnel, told me: "In principle you were right to denounce Savchenko, but you must remember that Savchenko is a general, and not many generals will accept you after this incident." After this, I decided to see Sergey Sergeyevich Varentsov. I told him about my differences with the GRU, and I expressed the desire to go back to a command assignment in the artillery. Sergey Sergeyevich promised to do all he could to help me.

After a long wait, in September 1958, I was sent to the Dzerzhinskiy Military Artillery Engineering Academy to attend a nine-month academic course for the study of missile weapons. I happened to be the senior colonel among the sixty officers in my course and was appointed sergeant major of the course. I thought that in this way I had finally finished with my work in the GRU. However, when I finished the course (with an excellent rating) in May 1959, I was not permitted to return to a line unit. Instead, I was again placed at the disposal of the GRU. In November 1960 I was given a new assignment, the one I am working on now while writing these lines. As a serving officer in military intelligence, I was detailed to the State Committee for the Co-ordination of Scientific Research Work of the U.S.S.R.

That is the outline of my life in this system. I began as a good Komsomol. From the beginning I had showed promise, or so people said, for becoming a builder for Communist society—as A. Bezymenskiy has written, "a Komsomol to the nth degree." As a *politruk* I worked as a guide and educator of the soldier masses. I believed in the Soviet system and was ready to fight anyone who even talked against it.

It was first during the struggles of World War II that I became convinced that it was not the Communist Party which moved and inspired us all to walk the fighting road from Stalingrad to Berlin. There was something else behind us: Russia. We believed in the end that we were fighting for the Russia of Suvorov and Kutuzov, of Minin and Pozharskiy, not for Soviet Russia but for Mother Russia.

Even more than by the war itself, my eyes were opened by the work with the higher authorities and general officers of the Soviet Army. I happened to marry a general's daughter, and I quickly found myself in a society of the Soviet upper classes. I realized that their praise of the Party and Communism was only in words. In their private lives they lie, deceive, scheme against each other, intrigue, inform, cut each other's throats. In their pursuit of more money and advancement for themselves they become informants for the KGB on their friends and fellow workers. Their children despise everything Soviet, watch only foreign movie films, and look down on ordinary people.

Our Communism, which we now have been building for almost forty-five years, is a fraud. I myself am a part of this fraud; after all, I have been one of the privileged. Years ago I began to feel disgusted with myself, not to mention with our beloved leaders and guides. I felt before, and I feel now, that I must find some justification for my existence which would give me inner satisfaction. I argued with myself. I swore at myself. Finally I became certain that what we call "our Communist society" was only a façade. One cannot help agreeing with Molotov, who after Stalin's death stated "by mistake" that we were still far from having built socialism, to say nothing of Communism.

Inwardly I have not grown one bit, and I have the feeling that every day our "Communism" is pulling me back instead of moving me forward. Some disease or infection is gnawing and eating at our country from within, and we must do something to stop it. I do not see any other choice, and this is the main reason why I am joining the ranks of active fighters for a better future for my people.

The Communist system is harmful to our people. I cannot serve a harmful system. There are many people who think and feel as I do, but they are afraid to unite for action. So we all work separately. Each man here is alone.

I feel contempt for myself, because I am part of this system and I live a lie. The ideals which so many of our fathers and brothers died for have turned out to be nothing more than a bluff and a deceit. I know the Army and there are many of us in the officer corps who feel the same way.

I praise our leaders, but inside me I wish them death. I associate with highly placed, important people: ministers and marshals, generals and senior officers, members of the Central Committee of the Communist Party of the Soviet Union. These people have not done me any harm personally; on the contrary, some of them have helped me to obtain my present position. Several still help me today. Nonetheless I can no longer abide this two-faced existence.

Khrushchev's is a government of adventurers. They are demagogues and liars, covering themselves with the banner of the struggle for peace. Khrushchev has not renounced war. He is quite prepared to begin a war, if circumstances turn favorable to him. This he must not be permitted to do.

In the past, our General Staff and our foreign representatives condemned the concept of surprise attack such as Hitler used. Now they have come around to the viewpoint that there is a great advantage to the side that makes a sudden massive attack first. They prepare themselves to be in a position to do so. Since he cannot muster enough strength to strike at all potential enemy countries simultaneously, Khrushchev singles out the U.S. and Britain as his attack targets. He estimates that the other Western allies would disintegrate due to differences among themselves. They would be happy to be alive.

From what I have learned and what I have heard, I know that the leaders of our Soviet state are the willing provocateurs of an atomic war. At one time or another they may lose their heads entirely and start an atomic war. See what Khrushchev has done over Berlin.

The Soviet leaders know exactly that the Western world and especially the Americans do not wish an atomic war. This desire of my Western friends for peace is what the Soviet leaders try to use to their own advantage. It is they who wish to provoke a new war. This would open the road to the subjugation of the entire world. I fear this more every day. And my fears confirm my choice to make this invisible fight.

In Moscow I have lived in a nuclear nightmare. I know the extent of their preparedness. I know the poison of the new military doctrine, as outlined in the top-secret "Special

Collection"—the plan to strike first, at any costs. I know their new missiles and their warheads. I have described them to my friends. Imagine the horror of a fifty-megaton bomb with an explosive force twice what one expects. *They* congratulated themselves on this.

I must defeat these men. They are destroying the Russian people. I will defeat them with my allies, my new friends. God will help us in this great and important work.

It is necessary somehow to drain the energy and to divert the great material and living strength of the Soviet Union to peaceful purposes—not to bring about a great world conflict. I think it is necessary to have meetings, secretly conducted. Not summit meetings. Those Khrushchev welcomes. He will use the decisions reached at summit meetings to increase his own prestige *vis-à-vis* the U.S. and England. This you in the West must understand.

This is why I write these observations of mine to the people of the United States and Great Britain.

Many things have contributed to this my new dedication. The last three years of my life have been very critical, both to my way of thinking and in other matters, about which I will report later.

I have thought long and hard about the course I am to follow. I ask only that you believe the sincerity of my thoughts. I wish to make my contribution, perhaps a modest one but in my view an important one, to our mutual cause. Henceforth I am your soldier, pledged to carry out everything which is entrusted to me. I will give all my strength, knowledge, and my life to this new obligation.

In presenting the above, I want to say that I have not begun work for my new cause with empty hands. I understand perfectly well that to correct words and thoughts one must add concrete proof confirming these words. I have had, and do have now, a definite capability for doing this.

CHAPTER II

The Dark World of the GRU

INTRODUCTION

IT was natural for Penkovskiy to begin with the bare facts of his life. There is no dispute about them. Even the prosecutor at his 1963 trial conceded that "Penkovskiy looked like quite a good worker. He rose rapidly up the ladder in his career. . . ." The biography is one of the few well connected segments in the entire Papers. Until the year 1949 it presents the normal record of a better than average artillery officer in the Soviet Army, who could attain colonel's rank at thirty-one. That year Penkovskiy entered the Military Diplomatic Academy. It was the turning point. In the months that followed, the newly created Soviet colonel took leave of what had been a relatively simple, uncluttered life as a professional soldier to enter the intelligence arm.

The Soviet intelligence service is not like the American or British or French, a body organized on more or less confidential lines for the purpose of seeking out the military secrets of foreign nations and preventing the detection or theft of one's own. In the Soviet system the intelligence services constitute a weird fourth dimension of the national society, immanent and indispensable—as that society is now organized. The Committee of State Security (KGB) and the Chief Intelligence Directorate (GRU) of the Soviet General Staff divide the intelligence mission between them; and as Penkovskiy frequently notes, the KGB is the larger, more pervasive, and more powerful of the two. But the GRU itself is far more than a military intelligence organ. Its functions include political espionage and subversion to an almost unlimited degree.

53

Penkovskiy set his usual high standard during his three years at the Military Diplomatic Academy and he did well in the attaché's office at Ankara. He appeared there as a rather better edition of the Soviet attaché than is normally encountered. He was personable and spoke English well enough to get along. His wife, who spoke French, was a pretty, demure lady who rarely projected herself into conversations, but struck people as well mannered and rather pleasant.

In Ankara, Penkovskiy on his own developed a regard and a sort of envious affinity for the Western military men which they did not at the time perceive. As far as the Turks were concerned, he was a standard Soviet attaché who bore watching. Aside from one trip to Trebizond, to look after the remains of a crashed Soviet military aircraft, he stayed in the capital and stuck to the normal routine of diplomatic association. For the first few months of his stay, Penkovskiy served as acting *rezident,* a position of authority which he extremely enjoyed. He made the usual military intelligence rounds and supervised what agent work the GRU controlled.

Beneath the surface, however, the activities of the Soviet intelligence missions in Ankara had more than their share of backbiting and internal bitterness. (Penkovskiy's own wife was propositioned by Vavilov, the KGB Chief—a matter which he did not take lightly.) When the new resident, Rubenko (*né* Savchenko), arrived, things did not go smoothly. He was rude, overbearing, and a general. When he overrode Penkovskiy's advice once too often, on the matter of his agent handling, Penkovskiy reported him to Moscow, as he notes in the first chapter.

Penkovskiy's trouble with his chief was hardly a unique occurrence in the Soviet system, in which conflicts between rival bureaucrats are more the rule than the exception. Yet for a General Staff colonel, however justified and however well connected, to challenge the authority of his superior, a general, was somewhat like the case of the obstinate motorist who "died defending his right of way." The GRU is a military organization, and no general likes to have a subordinate go over his head to the leaders of the Party.

When Penkovskiy returned to Moscow he received something less than a hero's reception at GRU headquarters on the Arbat. His wife, Vera, was upset and disappointed that her long-awaited tour overseas had been cut short, after little more than a year; she missed the foreign colony's parties and the chance to use her French. And one ex-artillery colonel was up on the shelf, indefinitely, awaiting reassignment. It took Marshal Varentsov's intervention, as Penkovskiy admits, to have him posted to the Dzerzhinskiy Artillery Engineering School, for the nine-month course in missiles.

Although Penkovskiy was graduated first in his class from the Dzerzhinskiy School, he did not receive a field command. Instead, he was returned to the Fourth (Asia) Directorate of the GRU. Soviet intelligence is somewhat like the priesthood. Once ordained, one finds it highly difficult to leave. Penkovskiy was ticketed for the military attaché's job in India, however, a responsible post which probably promised a promotion to general's rank.

It was then, after twenty-three years of constant security checks, that someone in the KGB apparently unearthed the information that his father had been a White Army officer. When the GRU personnel chief, Major General Shumskiy, confronted him with this fact, Penkovskiy produced a statement by his mother explaining the circumstances, which was then put in his file. Penkovskiy himself did not believe that his father's story was accurately known or widely circulated. But the suspicion was disturbing enough to knock out his assignment to India.

He spent another uneasy two months in the reserves while the implications of this "counterrevolutionary ancestry" were considered. For a Soviet intelligence agency it was a serious matter. In the end the powers-that-be decided that Penkovskiy's experience was too valuable to be canceled out by his heritage. He was returned to active duty as a senior desk officer in the Fourth Directorate.

In June 1960, Penkovskiy was assigned to the Mandate Commission *(Mandatnaya Komissiya)*, the selection board which presided over the entrance of students to the Military Diplomatic Academy, the GRU training school. He was designated chief of the incoming class, a sort of military senior tutorship and a post which was usually given to a general. He did not, however, get any inkling that he would be promoted to general's rank.

After ten years in grade and five years in higher staff schools, Penkovskiy did not take kindly to this new distinction. A restless man, he preferred to work in the field. At length he persuaded General Shumskiy to rescind this appointment in favor of an operational assignment. On November 15, 1960 Penkovskiy was assigned to a special group of GRU officers slated for work in various Soviet government organizations which had official dealings with foreign countries. Penkovskiy's general assignment here was the State Committee for Science and Technology[1] (GNTK). It was a coveted assignment, with a promise of extensive foreign travel.

Penkovskiy's intelligence experience was thus as an attaché, an instructor, scientific and technical expert, and foreign liaison specialist. So in the following portion of the Papers, describing the GRU, he has been able to supply a peculiar insight into Soviet intelligence operations in foreign countries, as well as measures taken against foreigners inside the U.S.S.R. As he wrote this section barely four years ago, the people he writes about are for the most part still on active service and the numbers he uses are reasonably accurate. It is sobering to contemplate the total he gives of 3000 staff intelligence officers out of the 5200 Soviet representatives in the Soviet embassies and consulates in some seventy-two non-Communist countries. Add to this Penkovskiy's calculations about the number of Soviet representatives "co-opted" for work with intelligence organs and the number of "pure" Soviet diplomats shrinks to something less than 20 per cent of the total. One is tempted to ask, with Penkovskiy, "Where have the legitimate Soviet diplomats gone?"

Penkovskiy himself was of course accustomed to the ubiquitous nature of Soviet "intelligence organs." He could not understand why people in the West did not more generally realize this fact. In the comments that follow, and in most of the Papers, he is constantly warning his "friends" that they have little concept of the real scope of the Soviet intelligence effort. These pages are often fragmentary, as he tries to jot down names of people and functions while he remembers them. They add up, how-

---

[1] The predecessor of the State Committee for Co-ordination of Scientific Research Work (GKKNR). The GNTK was abolished in April 1961 when the GKKNR was established.

ever, to a Brobdingnagian apparatus of Soviet espionage and subversion operating under the guise of diplomacy, press, tourism, scientific exchanges, and trade.

If the tone of his jottings about the intelligence apparatus is somewhat stilted and professorial, it is the tone of a Soviet military instructor who was, in a sense, addressing his class. There is no doubt that Penkovskiy felt a double mission: 1) to give the West immediate information of the Soviet leadership's plans; and 2) to sketch as best he could the rationale and the mystique behind those plans.

What makes Penkovskiy's explanations about the Soviet intelligence so peculiarly effective, also, is that he wrote it all down not from recollection after the fact, but while he was working in the midst of the Moscow "Center."[2]

The passages on the GRU were probably begun in the first months of 1961. At that time Penkovskiy had yet to make actual contact with anyone on the Western side. It is a known fact that he had approached several American students in Moscow late in 1960 with a letter offering his services to the United States. The letters were forwarded to the U. S. Embassy, but the officials there were apparently too cautious to open discussions. Similar offers are often made to Americans by Soviet counterintelligence agents in the time-honored device of "provocation," with the hope that the American officer responding can then be accused of espionage on a trumped-up charge, deported or even imprisoned for propaganda purposes. The time for making such an overture, too, was particularly unfortunate, coming so soon after the highly publicized trial of Gary Powers and the high tide of anti-American sentiment then running in Moscow. And it was probably inconceivable to the Americans who received the message that a man as high up as Penkovskiy would have become so openly disenchanted with his system.

It was certainly inconceivable to the Soviets, and it has remained so. As for the GRU's effect on Penkovskiy and his personal reaction against it, he best describes this himself.

---

[2] The Center is the name traditionally given to Soviet intelligence headquarters in Moscow.

PENKOVSKIY'S TEXT

I have been collecting material on the GRU for two years. I already have over five hundred pages of notes and over seven hundred names of officers and civilians who either work directly in the GRU or are connected with the GRU as collaborators—"co-opted," as they say.

The Soviet government goes in for espionage on a gigantic scale. That is what "peaceful coexistence" and Khrushchev's "struggle for peace" really mean. We are collecting intelligence always and everywhere. Daily we are improving and expanding our already swollen spy apparatus. I speak basically of military espionage. When I say "military" it does not mean that we are engaged only in military espionage. We conduct technical, scientific, and economic espionage as much as military—we operate in all directions. By saying "military" I mean the espionage conducted by the GRU.

I know less about the specific activities of our "neighbors," the KGB.[1] The number of people working there is several times larger than in the GRU. They are trusted more and they get more money. They are always assigned more positions in the embassies and in all our representation abroad.

Besides the GRU and KGB, the Ministry of Foreign Affairs and the Ministry of Foreign Trade each has its own intelligence department. Everybody is involved in spying —all Soviet ministries, committees, the Academy of Sciences, etc. Anyone who has anything at all to do with the work of foreign countries, or who is connected with foreigners in the course of his work, is perforce engaged in intelligence work. We are all spies. If a committee or a ministry has no intelligence section of its own, the GRU or KGB, upon approval by the Central Committee CPSU, will organize our own intelligence sections there or else assign our intelligence officers to them.

Here is a list of some of the Soviet ministries and various committees through which we conduct intelligence and where we [i.e., the GRU and the KGB] have our represen-

---

[1] In Soviet military intelligence parlance, *sosedi* ("neighbors") always refers to the KGB, who in turn call the GRU "our military neighbors."

tatives; some of these state institutions are completely staffed with KGB or GRU personnel:

Ministry of Foreign Affairs

Byurobin (now the UPDK)—the office providing services for the Diplomatic Corps in Moscow

Ministry of Foreign Trade

Inturist (almost 100 per cent KGB, only a few GRU officers)

All-Union "International Book" Association (almost 100 per cent KGB)

All-Union Chamber of Commerce

State Committee for the Co-ordination of Scientific Research Work (my own Committee—I shall speak about it separately)

State Committee for Foreign Economic Relations

State Committee for Cultural Relations with Foreign Countries

Council for the Affairs of Religious Sects, under the Council of Ministries, U.S.S.R.

Council for the Affairs of the Russian Orthodox Church

TASS (The Soviet Union Telegraph Agency)

Union of the Red Cross and the Red Crescent Societies

Committee of Soviet Women

Ministry of Culture, U.S.S.R.

Soviet Committee for the Defense of Peace

Committee of Youth Organizations, U.S.S.R.

The Patrice Lumumba Peoples' Friendship University (The Pro-rector is Colonel Yerzin, a KGB officer who formerly was the KGB Chief in Turkey and India)

Union of Soviet Societies of Friendship and Cultural Relations with Foreign Countries (Anglo-Soviet Friendship, Soviet-Indian Friendship, etc. Over forty such societies)

Soviet Committee of the World Federation of Trade Unions

Soveksportfilm

Sovimportfilm

The Moscow Post Office, 26 Kirov Street

Central Telegraph, 7 Gorkiy Street

The Academy of Sciences, U.S.S.R.

Lomonosov State University

This list is not complete—it could be made much longer. *In short, there is no institution in the U.S.S.R. that does not have in it an intelligence officer or agent of either the GRU or KGB. Furthermore, the majority of the personnel in Soviet embassies abroad are KGB and GRU employees.* The proportion of KGB staff officers to the rest of Soviet embassy personnel is usually two men out of five. GRU staff officers number one man in five. There are generally fewer GRU men, but we must be counted separately because our "neighbors" and we rarely work together. In most embassies it can be stated without error that 60 per cent of the embassy personnel are serving officers in intelligence, either KGB or GRU. Obviously most of the other embassy employees are regularly co-opted for intelligence purposes.

The Ministry of Foreign Affairs and the Ministry of Foreign Trade exist as such only in Moscow. Abroad everything is controlled by the KGB and us, the GRU. The West is trying to accomplish some improvement of relations with the Soviet Union by diplomatic means. We do not even have diplomats, such as the West understands the term. We do all kinds of work except diplomatic.

An ambassador is an employee first of all of the Central Committee CPSU, only secondly of the Ministry of Foreign Affairs; often he himself is part of either the GRU or the KGB. Now a great many of the Soviet ambassadors stationed in non-Communist countries are former intelligence officers from the GRU or KGB.

The KGB and GRU *rezidents* invariably have high diplomatic rank—counselor of embassy is a favorite cover. The other big jobs in the embassy, according to a decision of the Central Committee CPSU, are divided among GRU and KGB intelligence personnel. And if there are a few literate people in the embassy who work solely for the Ministry of Foreign Affairs, they are there only because they know protocol procedures and know how to write notes. They do nothing else. Even such "real" diplomats are co-opted into intelligence work either by the KGB or GRU, whoever gets them first.

Prior to my trip to Turkey I thought that the Ministry of Foreign Affairs and the embassies were important organizations with authority. But now I know there is only the Central Committee CPSU, and in the embassy two intelligence *rezidenturas:* GRU and KGB. They are the ones who handle everything. The Ministry of Foreign Affairs stays in the background.

The GRU is of course part of the Soviet General Staff. The entire work of the General Staff, especially of the GRU, is supervised by the Central Committee CPSU, which has for this purpose certain special sections.

The Central Committee sections most closely connected with the GRU are:

Administrative Section: Head of the section is Nikolay Romanovich Mironov,[2] Major General of the KGB.

Foreign Political Personnel Section: Head of the section is Aleksandr Semenovich Panyushkin, former chief of KGB Foreign Intelligence, ambassador to China and the U.S.A.[3]

Political Section: This is the Chief Political Directorate of the Ministry of Defense, but it has the status of a section of the Central Committee CPSU. See how they lock together. Chief of the section is Marshal of the Soviet Union Filipp Ivanovich Golikov.[4] He is a member of the Central Committee CPSU and a Deputy of the Supreme Soviet, U.S.S.R. As Minister of Defense, Marshal of the Soviet Union Rodion Yakovlevich Malinovskiy is also responsible for the activities of the GRU. He is also a member of the Central Committee CPSU and a Deputy of the Supreme Soviet, U.S.S.R.

Next in line is Chief of the General Staff, Marshal of the Soviet Union Matvey Vasilyevich Zakharov,[5] who at

[2] Mironov was killed in an airplane accident in Yugoslavia on October 19, 1964, along with Marshal Biryuzov.

[3] Aleksandr Semenovich Panyushkin, born in 1905, was graduated from the Frunze Military Academy in 1935; 1939–44 served as ambassador to China; 1947–52 ambassador to the U.S.A.; 1952–53 ambassador to Communist China; in 1953 he was a general in the MVD, Chief of the Foreign Intelligence. In 1962 he was named head of the Central Committee CPSU Section and identified as a major general.

[4] Golikov was released from his position in May 1962 for "reasons of health." He was succeeded by General Aleksey Yepishev, who was ambassador to Yugoslavia at the time of his appointment.

[5] In February 1963, following the Cuban crisis, Zakharov was relieved of this position and replaced by Marshal Biryuzov, a rocket expert. Zakharov was reappointed as Chief of the General Staff in October 1964, after Biryuzov was killed in an airplane accident and, coincidentally, after the fall of N. S. Khrushchev.

the same time is First Deputy Minister of Defense of the U.S.S.R., Deputy of the Supreme Soviet, U.S.S.R., and member of the Central Committee CPSU. During the period of 1950–51, he was briefly Chief of the GRU. He was not a marshal then, but only a general. Zakharov was not an experienced intelligence officer at that time, but since he became Chief of the General Staff he has been following GRU activities with interest. He has established good mutual relations with Serov. Thus, two intelligence officers are directing the work of the GRU: Zakharov, the military man, and Serov, originally from the KGB.

Following Zakharov, during the period approximately from 1951 to 1956 and again from 1957 to 1958, the Chief of the GRU was Lieutenant General Mikhail Alekseyevich Shalin. He is considered a good, experienced intelligence officer. He has been working in intelligence since the war. He is a friend of Generals Kislenko and Starchenko. They drink together and divide between them the presents which their officers bring them from abroad.

During the period of 1956 to 1957, the Chief of the GRU was Lieutenant General Sergey Matveyevich Shtemenko. At one time he was also the Chief of the General Staff.

Since January 1959, General Ivan Aleksandrovich Serov has been Chief of the GRU. He used to be Beriya's Deputy. After the latter's execution and until 1959, he was Chairman of the State Security Committee (KGB).

The GRU is one of the largest Chief Directorates of the General Staff and of the entire Ministry of Defense. It is the Second Chief Intelligence Directorate of the General Staff. The GRU is subdivided into Desks and Groups.

The Chief of the GRU, General I. A. Serov, has two Deputies: Major General Aleksandr Semenovich Rogov, for operational matters, and Major General Khadzhi D. Mamsurov, for general, i.e., administrative, matters.

An important role in the work of the GRU belongs to the GRU Party Committee, whose Secretary is Colonel Alikin. Colonel Vasinin is an aide to Serov.

GRU intelligence work is divided into three main parts: (1) Strategic Intelligence, (2) Operational Intelligence, (3) Combat Intelligence.

Organizationally, the GRU breaks down as follows:

The *1st Directorate*—Illegals; Chief, Rear Admiral L. K. Bekrenev.[6]

The *2nd Directorate*—Strategic Intelligence for European Countries; Chief, Major General Aleksey Andreyevich Konovalov.

The *3rd Directorate*—Strategic Intelligence (Anglo-American); Chief, Brigadier General V. S. Sokolov. All Central and South American countries are included in the 3rd Directorate, which has an individual Desk for each American country. Countries friendly to Great Britain, former dominions, and others also are included in the 3rd Directorate.

The *4th Directorate*—Strategic Intelligence for the Countries of the Middle and Far East; Chief, Major General P. P. Melkishev.

The *5th Directorate*—Diversion and Sabotage; Chief, Major General Mikhail Andrianovich Kochetkov.

The *6th Directorate*—Operations Directorate—Intelligence Posts (RP) in military districts bordering on foreign countries.

Information Directorate—Evaluates, processes, and publishes intelligence sent back from stations abroad; also in charge of the Classified Library; Chief, Major General N. A. Korenevskiy.

Naval Intelligence Directorate—No longer exists; a small section or group remains for the co-ordination of intelligence on the naval forces.

Recently an African Section of Strategic Intelligence has been organized, whose Chief is Naval Captain Ivliyev.

Next, within the GRU there are so-called Operations Sections:

Scientific-Technical Intelligence Section: Chief, Brigadier General Sheliganov.

Communications Section (Coding and Decoding): Chief of this section is Colonel Silin. The Communications Section has in it a group for receiving and dispatch-

---

[6] Rear Admiral Leonid Konstantinovich Bekrenev was Chief of the Illegals Directorate of the GRU until his assignment to the U.S. in 1962 as the Soviet naval attaché. He departed for the U.S.S.R. early in 1963 probably as a result of Penkovskiy's arrest and disclosures to the Soviet interrogators.

ing diplomatic mail. The Chief of the group is Major Serebryakov.

Section for the Countries of the People's Democracies. In the past this was a directorate, which included all the countries of the people's democracies as well as China and Korea. Presently China and Korea have been transferred to the Far East Directorate. There has been talk about transferring the entire directorate for the people's democracies to the 10th Directorate of the General Staff, of course only as far as the subordination is concerned. The personnel will remain ours.

Foreign Relations Section: Chief, Brigadier General Mikhail Stepanovich Maslov. This is an operational section which under the cover of Ministry of Defense directs all dealings with foreigners in the so-called official manner.

After this come the normal service sections:

Communications and Radio Intelligence
Organizational Section (selection of cover)
Archives Section
Administration and Supply Directorates and Sections
Personnel Directorate, etc.

There is an important *Training School Section,* in charge of the following schools: Military Diplomatic Academy (head of the academy is Major General of Armored Troops Vasiliy Yefimovich Khlopov); Military Institute of Foreign Languages; Institute of Communications; Intelligence School in Fili, for junior officers; Training School for Illegals, part of the 1st Directorate (Illegals) —head of the school is Colonel Dubovik; School for Saboteurs, part of the 5th Directorate (Diversion and Sabotage).

In addition to the schools I have noted, six- or nine-month refresher courses are periodically conducted under the Military Diplomatic Academy. There are probably other schools and courses of the GRU which are unknown to me. At one time the Military Institute of Foreign Languages was part of the Academy, but it later became an independent institute again.

There are many different technical laboratories and even some small plants and shops in and around Moscow which do work for the GRU.

Even this brief enumeration of our directorates, sections, and groups should give one a fairly good idea of the GRU's scope. We are engaged in espionage against every country in the world. And this includes our friends, the countries of the people's democracies. For, who knows, some fine day they may become our enemies. Look what happened with China! Months before the break with China became clear, we had already transferred all our workers from the 10th Directorate for the Countries of the People's Democracies[7] to the Far East Desk. Instructions came direct from the Central Committee CPSU to begin intensive intelligence activity against China.

Not only do we of the GRU conduct military, political, economic, and scientific intelligence, but we are engaged in propaganda activities, provocations, blackmailing, terroristic acts, and sabotage. These are the basic methods of our work. The difference between us and the KGB is only that we do not work against the Soviet people, we do not spy on them; but as far as foreign intelligence work is concerned, we do the same as the KGB. It is true that we pay more attention to collecting information on the armed forces and military installations of the Western countries. But directives come to both of us from one and the same center, the Central Committee CPSU. By directive of the Central Committee, we maintain close contact with "our neighbors" of the KGB. We constantly compete with each other in espionage. We try to prove that we work better and they try to prove the opposite.

We do not like them, and they know it. The KGB Special Section has its informants and co-optees among GRU officers. But we are not in a position to complain. We just have to live with them, especially now that Serov has come over from the KGB to become our Chief. The KGB is in the dominant position. They are the ones who investigate us and run clearances on us. It is they on whose

---

[7] As noted earlier, this directorate was downgraded to a section in the GRU, but in the General Staff the 10th Directorate remains as the directorate for the countries of the people's democracies and works actively with the Warsaw Pact nations in all matters pertaining to military subjects.

recommendations officers are ousted from the GRU. It is they who rummage through our personal affairs, like policemen searching a suspect's hotel room. Even for a GRU officer to go abroad, KGB approval is necessary.

The 1st Directorate, or the Illegals Directorate, is responsible for the establishment of deep-cover agent networks in Western states. An agent being sent to another country as an Illegal,[8] i.e., a deep-cover agent, does not necessarily have to be a Soviet citizen or an officer of the GRU; he may be a citizen of any country. Prior to the war, the majority of our Illegals were foreigners. At the present time several precautionary measures have been taken, and in most cases only Soviet citizens trained and documented in the U.S.S.R. are used. An Illegal agent who is not a Soviet citizen and who has no relatives in the U.S.S.R. is much more difficult to control.

For the past few years the GRU has been engaged in training Soviet Army officers and civilians to be sent to other countries as Illegal *rezidents*[9] or principal agents outside the U.S.S.R. These Illegals leave the country under deep cover, equipped with thoroughly prepared documentation that is beyond any suspicion.

Great importance is attached to the selection of Illegals. The GRU has a special school for training them, but most Illegals must pass a lengthy individual training course as well. Sometimes this training course lasts several years.

Assignments are distributed among the new graduates of the Military Diplomatic Academy in the presence of the chiefs of all the directorates, the Communist Party Chief of the GRU, and some senior officials of the GRU. These people do more than look at the students' final grades. They also consider their personal moods, hobbies, and temperament, the color of hair, eyes, etc. On the basis of this scrutiny some of the graduates are later as-

---

8 Richard Sorge, in Japan prior to the outbreak of World War II, was a GRU Illegal. Colonel Abel in the U.S., mentioned in the Introduction, was an example of a KGB Illegal.

9 An Illegal *rezident* is the head of the network and has his own communication channels to Moscow, separate from the communication channels of any other Illegals' network in the same country and separate from the communications used by officers of the *rezidentura* under cover of the Soviet Embassy or other official Soviet representation, as in the United Nations in New York.

signed to Illegal work, while the rest go into legal operational work.

Young and unmarried graduates are usually assigned to Illegal work and then only a few carefully selected officers. For example, one year eighteen persons were chosen for the 1st Directorate. At the most, only four or five of them will actually become Illegals. Thus, for instance, Boris Putilin was being prepared to go to Spain, but they found something wrong while investigating his relatives, so now he is working in the Military Publishing House. He was even discharged from the GRU.

My friend Shcherbakov was an Illegal for eight years. By the time he returned to the Soviet Union he had almost forgotten Russian. For eight years he never spoke one word of Russian, and they had to assign an interpreter to him.

Myasoyedov is also an Illegal. The "safe" apartment house for Illegals is on the outskirts of Moscow. There are many such apartments there.

Besides the Illegals Directorate, each national or area Desk has its own groups of Illegals. Illegal *rezidenturas* and Illegal agents exist in almost every country and in rather large numbers. In recent years the General Staff, Serov, and Khrushchev himself have begun to show particular interests in Illegals. They say that only with the help of Illegals can one establish exactly what our enemies are doing and what their potential and their capabilities are.

Bekrenev has done a fairly good job of organizing the Illegals' work, but apparently the results are not too good because he is constantly scolded and criticized by Serov. At a Party meeting of the 1st Directorate, Serov tore Bekrenev to pieces. He said that Bekrenev did not work hard enough, hence the Illegals' network was weak. Special emphasis in that respect was placed upon our "principal enemy"—the U.S.A. Serov claimed that all our attachés were doing was collecting newspapers and rubbish; everything that was of value came from the Illegals. Therefore special emphasis must be placed on intensifying the work of Illegals in the future.

All foreigners recruited by Soviet intelligence must sign an agreement that in case they are exposed or arrested, they will never reveal their connection with Soviet intelligence.

All Illegals are instructed not to admit that they are Soviet agents or Soviet citizens in case they are caught. It is preferable that they should commit suicide, take poison, shoot themselves, jump out the window. One of the tasks of the intelligence service is to remove agents who are not needed any more by murdering them, poisoning them, or by some other means. A GRU agent may be shot or poisoned if it is feared that he is breaking down or is telling what he knows, or, simply, if he knows too much. Or a warning may be received that a given agent is a foreign provocateur or that he may commit a provocation. Then orders are given to kill him and he is eliminated by any means.

Illegals in the U.S. are of the greatest significance. There is a special room in the 3rd Directorate of the GRU in Moscow where communications with the Illegals in the U.S. are maintained day and night by three operators.

Illegals use radio receivers. Sometimes it is done this way: A radio receiver is purchased in the country to which the Illegal is going. This radio receiver is brought to Moscow, altered in the necessary manner, and then it is sent back to the country where the Illegal is waiting for it, and turned over to him. Thus, the radio receiver has the appearance of a locally produced set which will not arouse anybody's suspicion.

Denis Polyakov,[10] who works with me in the Committee, was sent to the U.S. in 1960 with a delegation. His primary task on behalf of the 1st Directorate was to collect the addresses of some of the buildings in Washington and New York that have been torn down, so that we might use these addresses in the future for Illegals—i.e., if a citizen of that particular country had lived in a building which was later demolished, it would be quite difficult to establish his exact identity. Polyakov did get several such addresses in Washington, one in New York, and one somewhere else. These addresses will be used someday in the activities of Illegals.

As a rule, Illegals are given the task of joining some club, perhaps even two clubs; money for their activities is deposited in some particular bank. But all this must still be backed up by a good solid cover story. Where does this

[10] Also a GRU officer.

money come from? It could of course be inherited. In practice it is often transferred from one bank to another, or sent from some other country, from a foreign bank for deposit to the Illegal's checking account. For example, if an Illegal had a barber shop and has saved, let us say, 10,000 pounds sterling or dollars (of course, with the help of the GRU) and is moving from London to Birmingham or vice versa, or from one country to another, for instance, from England to Canada, or to the United States, or Australia, or France, it will look natural if he brings his own savings with him. He must not appear to have received money from some unknown place in some unknown way.

It is felt that small financial companies and small banks, i.e., branches of large banks, are best to deal with because they do not investigate their clients so thoroughly. It is also believed that it is much more convenient to keep a small account in a small bank, transferring it later to another bank.

Good cover activities: barber shops, tailor shops, shoe repair shops, small companies and small stores, watch repair shops, photo studios, etc.

Communications with the agent network operating in foreign countries, as well as other types of intelligence work against neighboring countries, are carried on from various points—from merchant ships, warships, various coastal stations. When a Soviet ship sails to a foreign country, there are always three or four intelligence employees among its crew—sometimes a whole group. They carry with them radios and other technical equipment, to establish communications with the agents in that country. For example, in the Black Sea area, where intensive intelligence work is conducted against Turkey, there are special posts in Batumi, Sukhumi, Leninakan, Sevastopol, and other cities, from which radio communications with the agent network are maintained and other operational activities are conducted.

In all the cities mentioned above there are intelligence posts [in Russian: *razvedyvatel'nyy punkt*] from which intelligence work against neighboring countries and especially against Turkey is carried out day and night. Even on board the Soviet ship that brought Khrushchev to New York there were some GRU and KGB intelligence officers with specific tasks to perform. When Khrushchev visited

England in 1956, he brought Serov with him on the ship, with a large group of Serov's people.

There are well-organized large Illegal *rezidenturas* in Spain. The work of the Illegals there is aided by Dolores Ibarruri, Secretary-General of the Communist Party in Spain. She now lives in France. That organization exists solely on money from the Soviet Union.

The creation of Illegal *rezidenturas* in Spain is facilitated by the fact that many Spaniards went to live in the Soviet Union after the Spanish Civil War. They speak both Spanish and Russian well. Some of them are recruited by Soviet intelligence as Illegals and then sent to Spain. It should be added here that these people not only conduct intelligence work against the Franco government but also spy on the American bases in that country. Because there is no legal *rezidentura*[11] in Spain, all espionage work there is based on Illegal *rezidenturas*.

While I was still in Turkey, preparations had begun for creating one or two Illegal *rezidenturas* in Egypt, Pakistan, and Afghanistan. It is possible that by now they are in operation. It was contemplated to use Turks from Bulgaria as well as Bulgarians who had settled in Turkey and had been living there for a long time. The agent network operating in Turkey at present is of little value. It is trivial. Turks are very difficult to recruit; they immediately run to the police and report.

The counselor of our embassy in India, whose name is Sergey S. Veshchunov, once revealed to me that there was one Illegal *rezidentura* of the GRU in New York, consisting of Soviet agents who had been infiltrated through third countries, while a second, small Illegal *rezidentura* also existed there, consisting of operational employees of the GRU. There probably is an Illegal *rezidentura* in Washington, but I have heard from the members of the 3rd Directorate[12] that in Washington the agents are old and their capabilities limited.

From the viewpoint of the GRU, the tactics of the agent network include the following: recruitment of an agent, training of an agent, organization of the *rezidentura*, and

11 The U.S.S.R. does not have diplomatic relations with Spain so it has no official representation to provide legal cover in Spain.

12 Area Directorate of the GRU responsible for intelligence operations in the United States.

operations. The recruitment procedure includes spotting a prospective agent, establishing his motivation, studying all the facts about him. When the operations officer is certain that the candidate can be recruited, he must obtain permission from Moscow to do so. The whole recruitment process lasts several months, sometimes several years, before the new agent is ready to operate.

Spotting is considered a very important, if not the most difficult, part of agent recruitment. Often months, and sometimes years, are spent in finding a candidate. A special course on the mechanics of recruitment is taught in the Military Diplomatic Academy. Instructors and senior instructors teaching this course are usually experienced operations officers who themselves served abroad as legal or Illegal *rezidents*.

Sometimes, for special reasons, a specialist in agent spotting may be sent from Moscow to the local *rezidentura*. The GRU devotes much of its time and attention to the selection of such specialists. First of all, a recruitment specialist must be a cosmopolite, know foreign languages, know the outside world and many other things not always known by an ordinary officer. He must be able to discuss Western literature, art, sports, etc. The officer's own character is extremely important. He must be able to get along with people and enjoy their confidence. Naturally, a man who shows antagonism toward others cannot be a successful agent spotter, because personal contact is one of the means used by an Illegal *rezident* in looking for candidates. Information for spotting may be obtained by a *rezident* during parties, card games (bridge, poker), and from various kinds of conversations. Various types of foreign artists (actors, musicians, dancers, etc.) are often used for spotting because they usually have easy access to highly placed circles in government, finance, science, etc. At the present time there is quite a large number of such artists, who had or still maintain contact with Soviet agents as well as with prominent physicists or other scientists.

The intelligence service has four sources from which to select agent candidates: first, candidates who are already being processed by intelligence officers for one purpose or another; second, candidates recommended by the local

Communist Party;[13] third, persons who can be used under their official cover; fourth, persons with important social connections.

Sometimes a candidate who is being processed by an intelligence officer in turn becomes a valuable source of other possible candidates. In the process of submitting information concerning himself, he mentions his friends and acquaintances, who may prove to be valuable intelligence material.

Intelligence officers of legal *rezidenturas* always use their official cover, such as assistant attaché, TASS correspondent, member of a trade mission, etc. They use this cover for spotting. In accordance with their official positions, they visit the appropriate ministries and agencies of the country to which they were sent. These visits are made ostensibly in the line of official duty. In reality, however, these officers are seeking persons suitable for recruitment. The GRU is constantly in need of agents among the employees of all different kinds of foreign governmental institutions, especially in the field of atomic energy, industry, armed forces, and in political circles. For this purpose intelligence officers use the so-called "social approach" method. Recently, secret directives have been sent out to all *rezidenturas* ordering establishment of social contacts with as many Americans as possible.

The entire purpose of developing social "friendships" is to seek out new agents. In conducting these meetings and contacts, the GRU's special attention is directed toward persons in interesting official positions or with access to needed information, as well as people with "democratic leanings" who because of their political naïveté are easy prey for Communist propaganda and can be easily recruited. Both the GRU and the KGB are always looking for persons who are easy subjects for blackmail because of their sexual inclinations, people who have relatives in the U.S.S.R., etc.

Official receptions at Soviet embassies, consulates, for-

---

13 In 1960 a directive of the Central Committee CPSU was circulated to all GRU overseas installations stating that postwar restrictions on the use of foreign Communist Parties for espionage purposes no longer applied. From that date on, they were free to recruit foreign Communist Party members as agents without prior approval.

eign missions, etc., are carefully planned, with invitations sent to all those of interest to the intelligence service. Employees of the embassy, consulate, or mission are chosen in advance to establish contact with the target. As soon as the intelligence officer becomes acquainted with the candidate, he begins to pay much attention to him. During the time he is making the acquaintance, the intelligence officer may express regret that they cannot continue their talk, suggesting another meeting under more convenient circumstances, i.e., dinner, the theater, or a meeting at some Soviet institution in order to see a Soviet film.

In some areas and cities the GRU gets some information on prospective agent candidates from monitored telephone conversations. Information obtained in this manner from conversations carried on between government institutions is of considerable interest for the intelligence service.

Once a person appears to be a suitable candidate, the intelligence officer prepares his preliminary appraisal of the candidate and starts his processing. He must obtain complete information about the candidate's personal life, which in some cases is quite difficult to do. This type of information includes details on the candidate's family, his personal habits, interests, leanings, etc. All this must be reported in writing.

A candidate may be transferred from one operations officer to another during processing. Sometimes spotting is done from Moscow. Moscow extracts data from official documents (on scientists, engineers, etc.) which are documented in reports registered in card files.

In recruiting, the GRU tries first of all to use material inducements, blackmail, and all sorts of pressures and threats. Of course, agents are recruited also on an ideological basis; but these represent the smallest percentage of agents recruited.

When processing a candidate, the operations officer proceeds on the basis of two principles: first, establish friendly relations; second, create conditions which will make the candidate feel indebted to the intelligence service.

In doing this work, the operations officer must put the candidate in such a position that the latter would not be able under any circumstances to turn down recruitment.

To accomplish this, the operations officer must see to it that the candidate, by being given various small assignments and errands to run, becomes involved in some kind of intelligence work even prior to his actual recruitment.

Upon completing a candidate's processing, when the operations officer becomes certain that the candidate is capable of carrying out intelligence work and that he cannot refuse being recruited, he must obtain permission to recruit the candidate. The length of time it takes to receive the permission varies. Usually it takes two to three weeks.

After receiving permission the operations officer carries out the recruitment and makes it formal by obtaining the candidate's signature and giving him a pseudonym. When an agent is recruited, however, he is not told for which particular intelligence service he is going to work; he is simply told that he is going to work for the Soviet Union.

Upon completion of his recruitment, the agent is registered in the central operations file in Moscow. After several meetings with the newly recruited agent, final confirmation of his recruitment takes place.

At the beginning I thought I would put down on paper everything that is known to me about the GRU and the entire Soviet espionage network, but I can see now that I have not time to accomplish this. The amount of material is too great to digest. And my writing conditions are far from ideal. I am pressed on every side. I will try to be brief, because there is so much to cover. It is not my own life that I want to describe. I am writing the biography of a system. A bad system.

Each person living in the West must fully understand one thing: espionage is conducted by the Soviet government on such a gigantic scale that an outsider has difficulty in fully comprehending it. To be naïve and to underestimate it is a grave mistake. The Soviet Union has many more representatives in countries such as, for instance, England, the United States, or France, than these countries have in the Soviet Union. In England alone, we have a whole battalion of them. Western countries must reduce the allowed number of Soviet representatives. As soon as another Soviet agent is caught, send a note proposing that the personnel in Soviet embassies, trade missions, consulates be cut. This will create confusion. It will, in turn, reduce Soviet espionage.

KGB and GRU personnel in Soviet embassies: I have noted already the ratio of KGB officers in an embassy. In a Soviet consulate, almost 100 per cent of the personnel are KGB, with one or two GRU officers included. Even the GRU has always had a hard time trying to use consular cover for its people; every opening is taken by the KGB.

In an embassy the KGB spies on all personnel, including us in the GRU. The KGB men watch absolutely everything that goes on: the purchases people make, how they live and whether it accords with their salary, where they go, which doctors they visit, whom they meet, how much drinking they do, their morals. The KGB listens constantly to what the people say. In short, almost every move in an embassy employee's life is known to the KGB. Meanwhile we in the GRU watch the KGB in turn. We want to establish which of our GRU men are connected with the KGB or work as their informants or co-optees.

The GRU and KGB have people in every Soviet representation abroad: the UN, the trade missions, TASS, Aeroflot, Merchant Marine, newspaper correspondents, etc. Not all our GRU officers are highly learned people, but the majority of them have had engineering or enough scientific training to carry on discussions with representatives of the scientific world. Because of the shortage of scientific personnel in the GRU, we co-opt our scientists for work with us, and these scientists carry out intelligence assignments in accordance with our instructions. This is done upon instructions from the Central Committee CPSU.

Even the head of the Soviet hospital in Iran, Colonel Makarov, was an intelligence officer. He is a graduate of the Kirov Medical Academy. Another friend of mine, Colonel Yanchenko, went to Guinea as a news correspondent. He is an officer of strategic intelligence of the GRU and always works under TASS cover.

One more thing. In the past the senior military attachés were automatically also the GRU *rezidents* in their respective embassies. This is not true any more; they were too easy to expose. Now the job of *rezident* is assigned to another man who usually operates under a civilian cover in the embassy. He may be an ambassador, counselor, first or second secretary. Of course, a military attaché is also a GRU intelligence officer, but never the *rezident*. This reorganization also provided the GRU with the opportunity to have an extra GRU officer in the embassy. The *rezident* usually is a colonel or a general.

The military attachés were relieved of their duties as *rezidents* by a special decree of the Central Committee CPSU dated January 22, 1961.

Personal letters of all embassy personnel, including the GRU and KGB, are read by special persons prior to being mailed—especially letters written by the wives—to see that nothing out of order appears in them. Even the most simple things are frowned on. For example, to say that we eat well here and have plenty of meat and milk, we drink milk every day, etc., is considered bad, because it should not be revealed in letters back home that there is plenty of everything outside the U.S.S.R. "Why write about things like that? One can get along without writing such drivel." In these cases the person responsible is given a warning that in the future he must be more discreet; he should warn his wife, too.

All drivers of GRU officers' cars abroad are GRU intelligence officers themselves. Some of them even have the rank of major and higher. Senior Lieutenant Fokin is the driver for a military attaché. In the U.S. a lieutenant commander in the Soviet Navy also was a driver.

Women work in the GRU only as secretaries and typists, or do some other type of nonoperational work. There are several who work in the Illegals Directorate and in the Directorate for Sabotage and Diversion. There was a woman who lectured at the Military Diplomatic Academy, but later it was discovered that her brother had been executed, which she had concealed from the GRU, and she was fired immediately.

At the present time intelligence work is conducted in India with great care. However, recruitment of agents and contact with the agent network continue. Operations will remain frozen until a given time, but when the signal comes to start again, our agents will go to work immediately. Meanwhile the agents are being supplied money and equipment, and new candidates for recruitment are being selected. Both the GRU and KGB have good agent facilities in India. Both are constantly watching Nehru, his government, and its policies, as well as all its diplomatic actions.

In Pakistan there are more agents intended for subversion and sabotage, because it is not considered so friendly a country as India. When I was working on the Pakistani Desk, even then the plans for sabotage activities and their objectives in Pakistan were completed. They included damaging the sources of water supplies, dams, poisoning of drinking water, and so forth, in order to spread panic among the population. At the same time there already exists printed propaganda material and material misinforming the population that all these acts of sabotage were perpetrated by Indians and Americans. This is to intensify the ill feeling between Pakistan and India. The KGB has more representatives in Pakistan than the GRU.

Here is an example of how Khrushchev, by using Afghanistan, wants to spoil relations between Pakistan and India. Marshal Sokolovskiy was on a trip to Afghanistan in September and October 1961 with a large group of senior officers. The purpose of the trip was to study the combat readiness of the Afghan armed forces, so that we might draw up plans to improve the military skill of these forces and increase their fire power. Plans are being made, also, for extensive training of Afghan officers in Soviet military schools as well as the dispatch of large numbers of Soviet military instructors to Afghanistan. Under discussion is the possibility of sending Soviet troops into Afghanistan at the appropriate time for joint operations against Pakistan. Sokolovskiy also had orders to reconnoiter certain specific areas of Afghanistan, for selection as possible missile sites. These areas will later have the necessary geodetic and engineering work carried out in them. The Afghan Army will be partially rearmed and will receive new armament.

At the same time, a group of GRU officers was busy preparing to dispatch agents to Pakistan from the territory of Afghanistan. These agents are to work ostensibly as agents of India, but of course actually for Soviet intelligence. Thus the GRU can create the impression of India spying against Pakistan.

India was, of course, the biggest target of all in this area. I very nearly went there myself. Immediately after my graduation from the Dzerzhinsky Military Academy in 1959, Serov, who had been informed of my progress, suggested that I go to India. India is considered to be our territory—that is, we might conduct extensive operations in that territory in the future. It would be useful if an officer with my background in missiles were sent there because it is possible that in the not too distant future missiles may be given to India.

I was almost completely processed for my departure. Pavlov had been the military attaché there—he has since been removed—and now there is a brigadier general, a troop commander. There is a new tendency not to have career intelligence officers occupy the military attaché's slot. Because the new military attachés do not need to have any intelligence background to fulfill their functions, the GRU can take people from the troops—just run-of-the-mill people who have no language or area knowledge—just a general to represent the armed forces of the Soviet Union. So a general was sent there. Now his assistant is a classmate of mine. Just as I was all set to go as his assistant, my trip was postponed and then canceled.

I heard something of conditions there from my friend Shapovalov from the London GRU office. He was in India, a secretary in the military attaché's office. He was an assistant to the military attaché—he knows English badly ["*badly*" was written in English]. He is working in the scientific group which is like the one subordinated to me. His chief is Pavlov, who is married to Voroshilov's daughter.

The military *rezidentura* in India has its agent net on ice. There is a radio operator with everything cached away. There are two brothers in the agent network. They get money; we feed and support them; we check their health, etc., so that they are always available to put the radio in operation. Mr. Nehru should be told all this. All is held in reserve. Everything is cached in zinc boxes which are soldered and are airtight. There we are waiting.

This is the way we operate everywhere, making our

provocations while we scream in public about "peaceful coexistence."

The 5th GRU Directorate, which engages in diversion and terroristic activity, has plans not only for immediate crisis points like Berlin. It has complete plans on what buildings should be blown up, who must be assassinated, what must be destroyed in New York, Washington, London, etc. Of course, this is not to be done now, but if and when it becomes necessary, the signals will be given.

This directorate assigns tasks to all Army, Air Force, and Navy attachés to gather information on the objectives which must be sabotaged or destroyed in case of general war or a specific local crisis. In addition, attachés are also directed to gather information on areas best suited to land airborne forces, etc., while they travel around the countries to which they are assigned. This is done to prevent such mistakes as, for example, dropping paratroopers in a swamp where they may all be annihilated. This 5th Directorate has very broad tasks to fulfill in peacetime, as well as in case of war.

The 5th Directorate is responsible for so-called misinformation activity to confuse the population. Plans have already been made about broadcasts which will go on the air; the leaflets and other types of propaganda materials have already been printed for use in disorienting the populations in the areas where a war or an incident might take place.

At the present time the chief of the 5th Directorate is Major General Kochetkov, former head of the Military Diplomatic Academy. The 5th Directorate is also engaged in establishing *rezidenturas* in all countries, including the countries of the democratic bloc. The *rezidenturas* and separate agents prepare staging areas for future landings of airborne forces in accordance with the plans of the General Staff, and they train small groups of agents for the destruction of specific objectives. At the present time they are not engaged in any active sabotage activity, but they are ready for it.

The 5th Directorate also directs a school for training saboteurs and terrorists, in which approximately two hundred inveterate cutthroats are periodically undergoing training. If time will allow, I shall speak about this activity in more detail later.

A few more words about the GRU leadership. When Lieutenant General Shtemenko was Chief of the GRU, he worked very hard and introduced many wise reforms. As I have said before, during Stalin's time he was a general and Chief of the General Staff. After Stalin's death he fell into disfavor and he was reduced to a major general. Then, when Khrushchev took over, Shtemenko was made Chief of the GRU and was promoted to lieutenant general. He was a good chief, mainly because of his administrative abilities, but was disliked by the generals of the General Staff.

The present Chief of the GRU, Serov, is not the most brilliant of men. He knows how to interrogate people, imprison them, and shoot them. In more sophisticated intelligence work he is not so skillful. Serov was a Beriya man. Beriya took a liking to him and shot him up to the top quickly.

As Chairman of the KGB, Serov was a minister, because that position automatically confers ministerial rank; when he was transferred over to the GRU, he became a Deputy Chief of the General Staff, but lost his ministerial rank. At the GRU, Serov studies the intelligence situation, but his deputy, Major General Rogov, does most of the work. Another deputy, Major General Mamsurov, an Armenian, handles housekeeping and administrative affairs only. The GRU people respect Serov because he did not interfere with the normal chain of command.

There were no official orders about closer co-operation between the GRU and the KGB after Serov's transfer. But when the GRU sent the KGB any inquiries regarding foreigners, new Soviet Illegals, etc., it was noticed that the KGB now sent prompt replies. After all, Serov's former subordinates among the "neighbors" respected his signature. Fundamentally, however, there were no real changes in the KGB relationship.

Serov expects to be promoted to marshal, but it is doubtful he will get it. He knows absolutely nothing as far as military affairs are concerned.

Ivan Aleksandrovich Serov. My first acquaintance with Serov came through the Turkish assignment, when I sent the cable through KGB channels to the Central Committee CPSU about the incorrect action of our GRU *rezident*, Rubenko. The cable got into Serov's hands (he was then the KGB Chairman) and only then was forwarded to the Central Committee. Since that time Serov has remembered my name, and after his appointment as Chief of the GRU, he became personally interested in my work. Eventually a certain degree of friendship developed between us, and I visited him several times at his apartment and at his country house. Although I had no personal desire to cultivate him, I was one of his subordinates. As such I did everything Serov ordered me to do and tried to curry favor with him, for my own advancement. When other senior officers and chiefs of GRU directorates found out about my good relations with Serov, their attitude toward me changed noticeably, for the better. My personal relationship with Serov placed me in the forefront of GRU officers.

Serov lives on Granovskiy Street. Many ministers, members of the Central Committee, and marshals also live there. Rudenko, the Procurator of the U.S.S.R., lives on the same floor as Serov. When Serov was the KGB Chairman, he arrested people, and Rudenko signed the death sentences. One would drop in at the other's place in the evening for a drink, and they together would decide who should be put in jail and who should be shot. Very convenient. Below Serov is Marshal Zhukov's apartment. One floor up lives Suslov, member of the Central Committee CPSU, and above Suslov lives Furtseva.[14]

ADDITIONAL NOTES

Major General Fedenko was Deputy Chief of the GRU. He is now in Moscow.

Brigadier General Fedorov is Chief of the 10th Directorate of the GRU for the People's Democracies.

Brigadier General Tyulenev also works in the 10th Directorate.

[14] This building is occupied by a large number of Soviet hierarchy. It has been reported that Khrushchev himself now has an apartment there.

Colonel Kondrashev, the military attaché in Turkey, an engineer, is now an instructor at the Military Diplomatic Academy in the Area Studies Department. He spent five years in Turkey. His work was poor.

One Turk, while on business in Afghanistan, was recruited by Soviet intelligence. His father is a Kurd, but he conceals this fact.

All Africans, as well as representatives of Afghanistan, Turkey, and Iran, are called by us simply colored (blackskinned). This is the usual name used in all Soviet directorates and sections.

The 1st Chief Directorate of the General Staff is Operations. The 2nd Chief Directorate of the General Staff is us (GRU).

Major General Konovalov's deputy for a long time was Brigadier General Melkishev. At the present time Brigadier General Melkishev is Chief of the 4th Eastern Directorate in place of Brigadier General Zotov. Zotov was military attaché in Italy and in France. He is now going as military attaché to Hungary.

Chiefs of the Military Diplomatic Academy: Slavin, formerly was ambassador to Sweden; Major General Dratvin; Major General Kochetkov.

There are ninety-eight to a hundred students in each Academy class.

The military attaché in Pakistan is Colonel Dubrovin, a Strategic Intelligence officer.

Our agent "Kapral" in Ceylon has given us very valuable information.

Colonel Vasiliy Maksimovich Rogov, who is short, should not be confused with Major General Rogov, Serov's deputy.

The head of the First Section of the GRU is Brigadier General of Aviation Sheliganov. The section has a photographic section, secret writing section, etc.

Acting *rezident* in London is Karpekov, a Tartar.

The GRU *rezident* in India, Sergey S. Veshchunov, and the *rezident* in Egypt, Postnikov, were present at the conference of *rezidents* at the Central Committee which was held during the second half of June 1961.

In Japan the ambassador's advisor for scientific and

technical matters is Colonel Sergeyev, a GRU officer. Sergeyev is not his true name.

Major Nikolay Kishilov works for Konovalov; Colonel Fukovskiy is in Iran; Colonel Bokarev is Smolikov's deputy; Colonel Bychko works in the 3rd Directorate (previously he was in Canada recruiting agents).

CHAPTER III

Penkovskiy's Committee

INTRODUCTION

THE Mount Royal Hotel in London is a squat, unprepossessing beehive of commercial travelers and middle-priced tourists, which occupies its own block on Oxford Street, within sight of Marble Arch. Traffic around it is generally busy and people rush in and out of its entrances with an air of serious if transient purpose. At 11 P.M. on the night of April 20, after a rather hectic bilingual dinner, a trimly dressed visitor, whose accented English marked him as probably a foreign businessman, left his own party, passed through the crowded lobby, and went upstairs to an inconspicuous suite. There his knock was answered by an Englishman of his acquaintance, who quickly opened the door and let him in. There were four other gentlemen in the room, two of them British and two American. It was Oleg Penkovskiy's first encounter with Western intelligence.

For hours he talked. He had first handed over two packets of closely handwritten notes and documents, materials which he had been preparing for some time on Soviet military missiles and other matters, by way of showing his credentials. They were eagerly scanned. There was understandably an air of intense interest in the room as he went through the facts of his background and position. For it must have been quickly apparent that Colonel Penkovskiy represented a major intelligence breakthrough, better even than his advance billing had suggested.

The meeting in the Mount Royal was the fruit of a contact which Penkovskiy had established with a visiting Englishman in Moscow, and sedulously cultivated. Greville Wynne was a sort of commercial traveler on an international scale, specializing in the import and export of heavy industrial equipment between Soviet-bloc countries and the West.

In 1960 Wynne had organized the visit to Moscow of a British trade delegation. He arrived there in December, almost a week ahead of the delegation, and perforce spent a great deal of time with Penkovskiy, who represented the Soviet authorities in this matter, arranging the delegation's meetings and itinerary. Penkovskiy had "studied" Wynne. His earlier efforts to establish contact with U.S. intelligence having failed—intelligence agencies seem to display their excessive boldness or excessive caution when faced with the main chance—Penkovskiy now saw the opportunity to state his case to the British. As he said later during his questioning at the Moscow trial: "Having become acquainted with Mr. Wynne, I decided to try to make contact with British intelligence through him, but I did not do this at once. I wanted to study him first in order to discuss this question at subsequent meetings."

In their talks during Wynne's December visit, he and Penkovskiy had arranged for a Soviet delegation to fly to London early in 1961, in order to visit various British firms interested in Soviet trade. When the promised delegation did not appear, Wynne went back to Moscow to find out what was wrong. Again, Penkovskiy was the man he had to see. By this time the two were on a first-name basis. Penkovskiy—quite unknown to Wynne—seized the opportunity of Wynne's second visit as his chance to make contact with the West. This happened in the first week of April 1961.

To the Soviet mind, anyone in Wynne's position would have had to be some sort of intelligence agent. So to Penkovskiy, who despite his exposure to foreigners inevitably retained the tactical outlook and limitations of a Soviet educational product.

By this time Penkovskiy had made up his mind to go over to the Western side. The uncertainties of his life within the GRU must have been a catalyzing factor, given the steady dissatisfaction which had been building up within him over the dangerous "adventurism" of the Soviet regime and the nostalgia he continued to feel for the freer life of Westerners, even the bit he had glimpsed in his year's service in Turkey. As he wrote later, in the Papers: "Years ago I began to feel disgusted with myself, not to mention with our 'beloved' leaders and guides. I felt before, as I feel now, that I must find some justification for my existence which would give me inner satisfaction." It is the voice of a man seeking new roots, of a soldier who was looking for a new flag.

Not the least of the factors spurring Penkovskiy's search was the State Security's discovery of his father's identity as a White officer. Twenty-three years of hard work and initiative in the Soviet service were now clouded by another man's decision, taken in 1918, to fight the Bolshevik Revolution. Why, Penkovskiy might ask himself, had the ubiquitous KGB not known of his father before this? Why had the information suddenly been used as a club over him? He had secretly been proud of his father's memory, despite their difference of allegiance. More and more, his own experience now suggested to him that Vladimir Penkovskiy had made the right choice in 1918.

When Penkovskiy saw Wynne in his room at the Hotel National in Moscow, he was able to assure Wynne that the promised Soviet delegation was already selected. As he had before, he talked a great deal about himself, in the course of discussing plans for the delegation's visit. Wynne was quick to detect a certain agitation in the behavior of his official Soviet contact. As they walked through the Moscow streets, safe from the danger of being overheard, Penkovskiy's comments about the Soviet scene became less circumspect. The Russian began to deride the official explanations for Soviet economic shortages and he made some fairly critical remarks about the regime. The life of the ordinary Soviet citizen, Penkovskiy implied, was far from a happy one.

Things came to a head when Wynne finally saw a list of the Soviet delegates. He objected that the distinguished delegates, principally professors and technical research experts, were people who had little if anything to do with commercial negotiations. They hardly constituted the businesslike trade delegation that his companies expected. It was clear to Wynne that the Russians were interested in obtaining information, not in purchasing goods.

Penkovskiy admitted that Wynne's objections were sound. But he pleaded with Wynne to accept the delegation,

as constituted. "Please don't object to the delegation,
Grev," he said. "I must come to England. If you make
trouble, I cannot come. For if you do not accept this
delegation, there will be no chance of my going to London
at all—since I am scheduled to lead these delegates."

With this, for the first time Penkovskiy told Wynne
bluntly about his fears for the Russian people. The situation in the Soviet Union, he said, was intolerable and its
leadership dangerously unstable. He possessed certain facts
about Soviet conditions which he must convey to "interested parties" in the West. Above all, he must talk himself
to people in the West, "to tell them what conditions in
the Soviet Union are really like."

Wynne was aware that the Soviet regime specialized in
having secret police provocateurs tell similar stories of
disenchantment with their own government, in the hope
of entrapping Western visitors. But he was a shrewd judge
of character. He had never met anyone quite like Penkovskiy. Not only had he come to believe in the man's
sincerity, but he was able to appreciate the value of a
man like Penkovskiy to the Western intelligence contacts
whom Penkovskiy was obviously seeking. From his extensive travels in Eastern Europe, Wynne knew the conditions which Penkovskiy was endeavoring to describe.

He agreed, therefore, not to question the suitability of
the Soviet delegates to London, so that Penkovskiy might
have his chance to go there himself and tell his story to
the "interested parties" he sought. Before he left Moscow,
on April 12, 1961, Wynne had been given a double-
wrapped, double-sealed envelope containing a letter from
Penkovskiy addressed to British intelligence. Penkovskiy
gave Wynne the further information that he planned to
arrive in London, in about a week's time.

It was a sign of the GRU's trust in Penkovskiy, and his
value as an intelligence officer, that he was sent to London, in charge of a delegation (with nothing more said in
the Arbat offices about his damaging ancestry). He was
shepherding a large group of Soviet technical and trade
experts, for the ostensible purpose of making contact with
British firms and discussing certain trade prospects and
technical exchanges. He did this in his official capacity as
deputy head of the foreign department, in the State Committee for the Co-ordination of Scientific Research Work.

As a colonel in the GRU, his real mission was of course an intelligence one: to conduct what industrial and technical espionage he could, and if possible develop some British contacts in the companies visited—all the while keeping an eye on the members of his own Soviet delegation. The visit of the delegation had been arranged through the office of Anatoliy Pavlov, counselor of the Soviet Embassy and the Committee's representative in London—actually himself also a GRU colonel and deputy chief of GRU activities in the U.K. (If nothing else, both the Soviet delegation and the British firms it visited enjoyed more than their quota of security supervision.)

Penkovskiy's visit to London lasted until May 6. For those sixteen days he led an extraordinarily triple life. His delegation from Moscow obediently respected him as a trusted state and Party official. Less obviously, he was greeted by the GRU *rezidency* in London as a working senior intelligence officer, with good political connections. The brand-new third layer of his existence was happily unsuspected by either of his two sets of Soviet colleagues. He continued to hold night meetings with Western intelligence officers, after he had arranged the affairs of his delegation during the day, and with them planned the pattern of his future work in Moscow. Wynne continued to be useful here, as an intermediary. Since he represented some of the firms the Russians contemplated doing business with, his presence was plausible.

Penkovskiy boldly ordered his official work to fit his new intelligence mission. When he was hard put to arrange enough secret meetings—because the delegation had to visit a succession of British factories outside of London —Penkovskiy asked the Soviet ambassador for permission to stay an extra four days. He wished, he said, to show the delegation the British Industrial Fair then about to open in London. Permission was granted, and Penkovskiy was thus enabled to have two additional sessions with the four Western intelligence officers, known to him only, in the words of his 1963 Soviet trial, as "the British intelligence officers named Grille and Miles and the representatives of the American intelligence service, who called themselves Alexander and Oslaf." For the sake of convenience and to avoid suspicion, they continued to meet in the Mount Royal Hotel, where members of the visiting delegation were housed.

Penkovskiy's energy was prodigious. While continuing to do his duty by the Soviet technical delegation, politically and socially (Penkovskiy had charge of their money, in the best Soviet tradition, so he supervised their shopping trips in the London stores), he received an intensive short course in intelligence communications. As he later admitted at his 1963 trial, he was given a Minox miniature camera and instructed in its use, as well as a transistor radio receiver for keeping up one-way communications with the West. It was arranged to maintain contact with him through Wynne, or another Western emissary, if he proved unable to return to Western Europe in the near future. He drilled himself in radio procedures and all the technical but vital minutiae of the spy in action.

His Soviet trial soberly records: "The foreign intelligence officers recommended to Penkovskiy that he keep this spy equipment in a secret hiding place that was specially equipped in his apartment. Alexander and Oslaf warned Penkovskiy that Wynne would soon be arriving in Moscow and would bring him a letter from them, but if necessary, appropriate instructions would be transmitted to him by radio.

"At the same time Penkovskiy . . . received the assignment to photograph secret documents for the foreign intelligence services."

Penkovskiy asked in return that he be granted U.S. or British citizenship and work commensurate with his experience, in case events ever forced him to flee the Soviet Union.

Having thus crossed his Rubicon, Penkovskiy returned to Moscow, laden with presents for some of his high-placed Soviet friends, a full report of the trade and technical mission (which Moscow judged a great success), and an unobtrusive Minox camera with a great quantity of film.

The next entry in the Papers was written with new confidence. It was begun, evidently, on May 16, just ten days after Penkovskiy's return from London. In it he outlines the real work of his Committee—as yet far from appreciated by the West—and continues his rundown on Soviet personalities and their problems.

Penkovskiy's Committee was, and is, virtually a ministry in size and importance.[1] It represents the greatest national effort ever made for the systematic collection of industrial, scientific, and technological intelligence.

The research and development activities of modern science and industry have swelled to vast proportions. In the decade between 1953 and 1963, for example, the yearly bill for industrial research and development in the United States alone had jumped from $4.3 to $13 billion. The Soviet Union, for all its *sputniks,* steel mills, and scientific advances, remains far from the advanced industrial society which it would like to be (and generally claims it is). And in their desperate rush to accelerate development both in heavy industry and in consumer goods areas, Soviet economic planners—to put it charitably—often lack the luxury of time to do their own research.

The State Committee for the Co-ordination of Scientific Research Work, accordingly, works like a surreptitiously operated clearinghouse for new developments in virtually every area of modern industry and technology. Few industrial countries escape its notice. A Committee directive to its agents in Canada, for example, asks for information on everything from diagrams of Raytheon's ultrasonic saws to the Ministry of Agriculture's plans for exploiting subsurface peat deposits and drawings of an "installation for the continuous production flow of margarine" at Lever Brothers. Soviet trade missions, members of the Academy of Sciences, and almost every delegation sent overseas on technical business work under the Committee's aegis. Its key personnel are drawn equally from the Soviet Academy of Sciences and those two scientifically oriented organizations, the KGB and the GRU.

The Committee's activities are world-wide. Its representative in Germany will be praised for sending in information about the production of semiconductor rectifiers by the Siemens firm—the techniques were immediately utilized by Moscow's "Dynamo" electrical equipment plant in Kirov. The Committee's English representative proposes a liaison plan for work with the huge British

[1] Typically, the Soviet leadership altered the Committee's organization slightly, after Penkovskiy's arrest, but its size, its functions, and its personnel remained the same.

chemical complex, ICI. Moscow takes it under consideration.

At the top of the Committee sits a fifteen-man presidium, a sort of "scientists' soviet," as Penkovskiy called it. Under its direction a large staff of highly trained experts (447 in Penkovskiy's time) continually maps out targets, assigns information-collecting duties to its men in the field, then processes the results—to be distributed to Soviet science and industry. Overt exchanges of technical information are part of the Committee's job—its "receivers" in foreign countries do nothing but collect technical books, pamphlets, and manuals; but where espionage methods work more quickly, they are used. Hence the heavy percentage of Committee employees who are co-opted by the GRU and KGB, if not actually on their staffs.

Other countries have their collections or exchanges of technical information, but nowhere on such a methodical and clandestine level. And the exchanges are apt to be one way. As Penkovskiy writes: "In the Soviet Union we were very careful to give our exchange visitors generally worthless information. We show them only what they know already."

Until Penkovskiy's disclosures very little was known about the real scope of the Committee's activities, to say nothing of its incorporation in the Soviet intelligence effort.

PENKOVSKIY'S TEXT

During our sixteen-day period of work, a new Alliance was created, an Alliance of friendship and struggle for our common goal. I believe that this Alliance will be eternal. G O D will help us in this great and important work.

May 16, 1961.

Our Committee was formerly called the Scientific-Technical Committee. In 1961 it was completely reorganized and was given its present name: State Committee for Coordination of Scientific Research Work [GKKNR] of the Council of Ministers U.S.S.R. Address: 11 Gorkiy Street, Moscow. The number of employees was considerably increased, the largest expansion taking place in the Directorate for Foreign Relations (in the past this was just a section). This was done to improve the collection of scientific and technical intelligence information from the West by working with delegations from Western states, as well as by sending our own delegations to scientific specialists abroad and organizing various exhibitions in foreign countries. Our Committee conducts this work jointly with the Ministry of Foreign Trade and the All-Union Chamber of Commerce.

To make it easier for a foreign reader to understand how scientific research work is "co-ordinated" in the U.S.S.R., I have drawn an organizational chart of the Committee which is enclosed with these notes.[1] One can see from this chart which are the questions in which Soviet intelligence is most interested and how the entire work is co-ordinated. The Committee, in short, is now like a ministry. Its Chairman, Rudnev, enjoys all the privileges of a minister.

All these directorates are subdivided into sections and groups. The directorate for collaboration with Socialist countries is specially organized into twelve joint commissions: for Czechoslovakia, East Germany, Poland, Hungary, Rumania, Yugoslavia, Bulgaria, Albania, China, Mongolia, North Korea, and North Vietnam. This directorate has its own section for sending Soviet specialists abroad to the countries of the so-called socialist camp only.

In addition to the directorates and sections mentioned above, there are many organizations and institutions under the jurisdiction of the Committee, e.g., the Consortium of Publishing Houses of Scientific Research Material (ONTIZ); State Energy Publishing House (GOSENERGOIZDAT); the All-Union Institute of Scientific-Technical Information; other institutes of scientific-technical information; the Exhibition of the Achievements of the National Economy of the U.S.S.R. Various libraries also fall under the Committee's jurisdiction.

There are Committees for the Co-ordination of Scientific Research Work in each union republic. Thus, the Chairman of the Committee for Co-ordination in the R.S.F.S.R. is Pavel Ivanovich Abroskin; in the Georgian

1 See Appendix I.

S.S.R., G. Sh. Mikeladze; in the Moldavian S.S.R., Nikolay Dmitriyevich Chernyavskiy.

Rudnev's appointment as Chairman of the Committee was not an accident. His appointment throws even more light upon the activities of our Committee, i.e., what type of scientific research work we co-ordinate. Previously, Rudnev worked for a long time in the Ministry of Armament; he was later Chairman of the State Committee for Defense Technology. He is a member of the Central Committee CPSU and at the same time is one of Khrushchev's deputies in the Council of Ministers.

Therefore it is no surprise that Rudnev always emphasizes collection of information and technical inventions which are primarily suited for military use. Some of the people in our Committee say that we are merely an appendage of the Ministry of Defense and the State Committee for Defense Technology. I know this to be the case, as do the other military intelligence officers attached to the Committee; but the Committee's ordinary engineers and scientists talk about it secretly, as if it were some hidden discovery.

Rudnev's predecessor Khrunichev (now deceased) also had worked almost exclusively in war industry prior to becoming the Chairman of the Committee. At one time he was Minister of the Aviation Industry.

I do not mean to convey that we work for military purposes only. The Committee has many different sections and directorates which work strictly in the field of the national economy. The direction of all our so-called co-ordination of scientific research work, however, is undoubtedly of a military nature.

This also makes it clear why there are so many GRU and KGB intelligence officers in our Committee. I landed in the Committee as a result of Khrushchev's policy of "peace." The Committee is used as a good cover to collect espionage information abroad through our delegations, as well as inside the U.S.S.R. by the friendly receptions and "services" we render foreign delegations. Such friendly contact and exchange we might better call "friendly deceit." Often we officers of the GRU and KGB in the Committee cannot understand how the foreigners believe us. Do they not understand that we show them in the U.S.S.R. only those things which are well known to everybody and do not represent any technical improvements? If there is something new under way at a plant being shown to foreigners, we simply give orders to its director: "Show them everything . . . but have Shops 1 and 5 closed for repairs." That is all; short and clear.

I have on my desk a list called "Cities and Areas of the U.S.S.R. Closed to Foreigners." This list is the basis for our planning of receptions and trips for foreign delegations in the U.S.S.R. For example: a delegation of four Canadians received permission to visit Krivoy Rog. There are some large plants there, but not too much work is done for defense. For the sake of speed, they had asked to be allowed to go there by air with a stop in Dnepropetrovsk, which is very close to Krivoy Rog. This request, however, was categorically refused. They had to go by train, thus taking twenty-two hours before reaching Krivoy Rog. For the Committee has categorical orders not to allow any foreigners to visit the Dnepropetrovsk area. The reason is that in Dnepropetrovsk there are many metallurgical and defence production plants, including one of our largest missile plants.

The city of Gorkiy is also closed to all foreigners, including representatives of the satellite countries. Gorkiy is closed because of its closeness to the city of Sormovo, where all kinds of secret things are built, including submarines. In addition to the large automobile plants in Gorkiy, one of the largest aviation plants is also located there.

I shall say a few words about the Directorate of Foreign Relations, in which I "work" under the cover title of Deputy Chief of the Foreign Section. To make every fool believe that I am a legitimate employee of the State Committee for the Co-ordination of Scientific Research Work (GKKNR), I was issued an ID card No. 0460, Registration No. 79. (We are still using the old ID application blanks of the State Scientific-Technical Committee; their replacement by new ones is being prepared.) A photostatic copy of the same is enclosed herewith, as well as two "real" calling cards in Russian and English, which I use as part of my cover when dealing with foreign delegations and "exchanging" scientific information with them. [See photographs.]

The Chief of our Foreign Directorate, Dzherman Mikhaylovich Gvishiani, seemingly does not belong to any intelligence service. However, if one recalls the fact that Gvishiani's father was a distant relative of Stalin's and a KGB general, one can assume that our Gvishiani is also connected with the KGB. Unfortunately, I cannot be positive about it. Many of our KGB neighbors brag about their true status, but Gvishiani is more careful about this.

Gvishiani is married to Kosygin's daughter. Many times in discussions with his son-in-law, Kosygin openly criticized Khrushchev and bluntly stated that Khrushchev was completely messing up our industry and economy. One day, when he was drunk, Gvishiani told me, "Oleg Vladimirovich, our day will come." Because of this even Rudnev is rather afraid of him. He always greets him with a handshake like an old friend.

Gvishiani has two deputies: Yevgeniy Ilich Levin, a colonel in the KGB and the KGB *rezident* on the Committee, has been abroad many times on intelligence assignments. Viktor Nikolayevich Andrianov, lieutenant colonel and the GRU *rezident* on the Committee, worked as a GRU intelligence officer in Austria and Germany. Andrianov often bragged to me about his good connections among the Americans in Austria, adding that he even had intimate relations with an American woman when his wife was in Moscow. There is talk that Andrianov will go to Switzerland as a Soviet consul.

Valentina Ivanovna Chumakova, a KGB employee, is Gvishiani's secretary.

Our directorate has several sections:

Department for Relations with Foreign Countries. The Chief is Boris Georgiyevich Lopatenko, who is also an intelligence officer in the KGB. He works in close contact with Levin.

The Deputy Chief is Denis Nikolayevich Polyakov, a lieutenant colonel in the GRU. He works with me; we share the same office. He served in India as First Secretary of the Soviet Embassy. He was quite successful and recruited several agents. He was ordered to leave India within twenty-four hours when it was discovered that his wife had had intimate relations with one of the embassy employees. Twice in 1960 and again in 1961, Polyakov went to the U.S.A. with Soviet delegations to carry out intelligence assignments. Early in 1962 he went on temporary duty to Cuba to train deep-cover Illegal agents for work in the U.S. and Latin American countries. His comments about the Cuban people were, to say the least, uncomplimentary; he called them "stupid half-breeds, dirty and uneducated." He complained about not being able to find a single decent woman with whom to have a pleasant time. Polyakov is an artilleryman by profession; he is a graduate of the Dzerzhinskiy Artillery Military Academy, and in 1953 he finished the Military Diplomatic Academy.

In the Committee, Polyakov, using the cover of Deputy Chief of the section, is actually the Chief of the American Desk and sometimes substitutes for Andrianov as the GRU *rezident*.

GRU as well as KGB intelligence officers occupy all the key positions in foreign relations sections of those Soviet ministries which contain them. They conduct intelligence work among foreign delegations, tourists, etc., visiting the U.S.S.R. Our section of the GRU which operates in Moscow under the cover of foreign relations sections of the GKKNR has in it about eighty or ninety senior officers from strategic intelligence.

The question of how many GRU and KGB intelligence officers should be assigned to what organization, for example, to our Committee, is decided jointly by representatives of the GRU, the KGB, and the Central Committee CPSU. Each representative has to explain why he needs the number of officers requested and for which particular assignments. The final decision is made by the Central Committee CPSU through its Administrative Section. It should be mentioned, speaking of our Committee, that a special top-secret decree of the Central Committee CPSU and the Council of Ministers U.S.S.R. was issued plainly stating that "the State Committee for the Co-ordination of Scientific Research Work of the Council of Ministers U.S.S.R. is to have within its ranks twenty-five to thirty men from the Chief Intelligence Directorate (GRU) of the General Staff." That is how closely Khrushchev and the Central Committee direct Soviet intelligence work and manipulate our "covers."

The Committee and the Council of Ministers pay us our salaries in accordance with the positions occupied by us in the Committee, but the financial details are handled

jointly by the finance section chiefs of the GRU and the
Committee. The money we spend in conjunction with our
work on the Committee is reimbursed from the funds of
the GRU or the Ministry of Defense.

A decree similar to the one regulating the number of
GRU intelligence officers in the Committee exists also in
regard to the number of KGB officers in the Committee.
I do not know the exact number, but as usual there are
more of them than of our officers. The KGB has many
more co-opted civilian specialists who have signed an
agreement to work as KGB informants. They are especially useful in technical and scientific situations, such as we
have at the Committee.

Our existence as intelligence officers in the Committee
—KGB or GRU—is known only to the Chairman of the
Committee and his deputy, in my particular case to the
Chief of the Directorate for Foreign Relations, Gvishiani.
The others can only guess. Those working in the Committee, however, often notice that we are busy doing some
other kind of work. For example, I am absent from the
Committee quite often. Sometimes I say that I have to
go to the post office or to the bank; sometimes I use some
other excuse for leaving the office. But people are not
fools. They come to know that some other activity besides
routine work is being done. The nonintelligence employees
notice that none of us is ever punished for long absences
or even given warnings. They naturally surmise that we are
carrying out some other type of work.

After a visiting Soviet delegation has been formed and
each of its members has been given permission to go
abroad by the Central Committee CPSU, we select certain
scientists, engineers, or any other suitable members of the
delegation, summon them to the GRU, and instruct them
individually on the type of information we need and
what they should direct their attention to while abroad.
Such co-optees sign a special document stating that they
must not make known their connection with the GRU.
Divulging any connection with the GRU is a punishable
offense—this is stated in the document.

Co-opted specialists are very useful (especially when a
delegation does not have enough regular GRU officers
assigned to it). They are given extra money while abroad
and upon their return they get some kind of a bonus, say

1000 or 500 rubles, an expression of gratitude. We tell a successful co-optee: "You do good work. If there is a war, we will take you into the Army and give you senior officer's rank."

Aside from this basic type of work in the Committee, we have a direct order to screen the civilian personnel for young specialists, engineers, scientists, etc., whom we could recommend for assignment to the Illegals Directorate under Bekrenev. When such a specialist is spotted, his name is submitted to Bekrenev. After the proper investigation, the person is given specific training and becomes an Illegal.

Our main task as GRU intelligence officers in the Committee is recruitment of agents among the foreigners visiting the U.S.S.R. Of course, it does not often happen that a foreigner is recruited. We also collect information through personal contacts and conversations, by eavesdropping, by stealing secrets from the visitors' pockets, examining baggage, etc.

To maintain our cover effectively, we are well documented and well versed in technical matters. Naturally we wear civilian clothes.

Thus while I am a colonel on active duty in the GRU (as my real identity card states) here in the Committee and as far as our "neighbors" are concerned, I am merely a "colonel in the reserve."

The reception of each foreign delegation in Moscow requires very careful preparations on our part. We prepare quarterly, monthly, and daily plans in which our experts describe in minute detail how the members of the delegation should be treated and cultivated.

The operations of GRU officers serving abroad as members of delegations of Soviet scientists and specialists are covered by another separate plan. There is a separate set of operating instructions covering the work done with Soviet delegations going abroad, e.g., co-opting their members to carry out various intelligence tasks, organizing co-optee nets, selecting candidates for Illegal work.[2]

Each Soviet specialist who goes abroad has to submit a detailed report of his trip, and if this report contains

[2] A photostatic copy of one of these plans, covering the third and fourth quarters of 1962, appears in Appendix II.

nothing valuable, he is reprimanded, criticized, and, as a
rule, is never sent abroad again. When some valuable information is obtained by a member of a delegation, it is
immediately reported to the GRU *rezident* or sometimes
to the ambassador himself, and the material is immediately dispatched to Moscow either by diplomatic pouch or by
cable.

All members of Soviet delegations traveling abroad are
carefully instructed as to what types of conversations they
should engage in and how to answer various questions. I
can say in all honesty that there is nothing new that the
Western scientists and specialists could learn from the
Soviet specialists; neither will they get any valuable information when visiting Soviet exhibitions abroad. Thus,
for example, the exhibits prior to being shipped to the
London Exhibition of 1961 were carefully checked by
KGB technical specialists to make sure that there was
nothing new which the foreign scientists could see or steal.
Some exhibits in fact, are purposely put together in a distorted form, e.g., the cone of the *sputnik* on exhibit was
not built that way, the spheres were of another type. This
was done to confuse the viewer, technically speaking,
while making a strong impression in a propaganda way.
Almost all the exhibits in London connected with the
sputnik were experimental or distorted. They did not represent the real *sputnik* that was launched by the Soviet
Union.

As a rule, Soviet scientists, engineers, and technicians
who work directly in the production of missiles and missile
armament are not allowed to go abroad. But lately, because these scientists must know something about U.S.
missiles and about those of other countries, they have been
given permission to travel abroad, provided they have not
participated in any production work connected with the
Soviet missile program for the past two years—and, of
course, only if they have been carefully checked. The
Central Committee CPSU exercises extreme caution in
this matter. It is very careful about letting these people go
abroad. These people are high-ranking scientific and
specialist personnel of the Central Committee CPSU. The
two-year waiting period was established because it was
figured that during the two years the techniques would
advance to the point where what was known to these

people two years before would have lost its importance. Therefore, if they defected to the West, they would not be able to talk about these techniques in such detail as they could have done two years earlier; and they would not know about the latest innovations.

The Western countries, specifically the United States, Great Britain, France, and Canada, must maintain maximum vigilance in conducting the exchange of scientific research delegations and various exhibits. They should introduce the same kind of strict procedure and control that is used in the U.S.S.R. The way things stand now, when visiting the U.S., Canada, or any European country, we travel freely around these countries, see everything we wish to see, and steal all the secrets needed by us. But when foreign delegations visit the U.S.S.R., they encounter all sorts of restrictions and are sent only to those places where we want them to go. What do we let them see? Only that which is of no value. When foreigners express a desire to see something that is new and really valuable in regard to science, we find all sorts of excuses to refuse their requests. On my desk I have a list of pretexts and alternate proposals which we use to keep foreigners out of certain areas of the U.S.S.R.

1. The plant is under repair.
2. A bridge is closed.
3. There is no airport, and the railroad tracks have been damaged by recent frost; therefore, temporarily, there are no trains running.
4. The weather is unfavorable at the particular time of the year (rains, snowstorms, etc.).
5. The local hotel is not ready for guests.
6. There has been a case of plague in the area; therefore it is inadvisable to go there.
7. All hotels are completely filled with tourists, etc.

There are also cases when we take a delegation through museums and parks in Moscow until its members are so tired that they themselves call off the trip to a plant or a factory, preferring to go to their hotel to rest. Or, instead of taking the delegation by plane, we put it on a train. As a result, the delegation has enough time to see only one or two installations in which they are interested instead of five or six that they could have visited had they made the trip by plane. Their visas expire, and they have to leave after having seen nothing but vodka and caviar.

As the co-ordinating organization in these matters, our Committee maintains close contact with the Academy of Sciences of the U.S.S.R., the State Committee for Economic Relations with Foreign Countries, the Ministry of Foreign Trade, the All-Union Chamber of Commerce, and with many other organizations. All of them have within their ranks dozens of both GRU and KGB officers.

When I began my work in the Committee, I myself was not just surprised but simply astounded by the number of GRU and KGB officers working in the Committee. When one walks along the hall, one can see many saluting each other in the military manner. They have conspicuous difficulty getting away from their military habits and getting used to their civilian clothes.

Almost daily GRU officers are documented through our Committee, on their way abroad either as members of delegations or as tourists. It is very seldom that there is not at least one representative of the GRU Strategic Intelligence. If a delegation is small, let us say, two or three people, and it is difficult to insert a GRU officer into it, a co-optee is sent. If there is not one available, they will make one in one day. Summon a man to the General Staff, talk to him for a while, get his signature, and that is all. When a small delegation does not have among its members a GRU officer, there must be a KGB officer or a KGB co-optee in it. No delegation ever goes abroad without some form of KGB involvement. Not only is the KGB distrustful of the regular members of a delegation, but it does not even trust us GRU officers either. KGB officers travel with delegations even when it is hard to believe that there could be any intelligence officers in the delegation.

In October 1961, a Soviet delegation went to Paris to attend a conference of the International Oceanographic Commission. Among its members, by the decision of the Central Committee of the CPSU, were two officers of the GRU naval intelligence, Rear Admiral Chekurov and Captain Ryzhkov.

In November 1961, two senior GRU officers who worked with me in the Committee left for Cuba, Colonel Meshcheryakov and Lieutenant Colonel N. K. Khlebnikov. In

Cuba they will work as intelligence consultants in the Castro government, naturally against the U.S. and the Latin American countries. Khlebnikov was replaced in the Committee by Captain Boris Mikhaylovich Polikarpov.

Now a few words about misinformation. We have been given a special directive from the GRU leadership to spread, through our scientists, all sorts of provocative rumors and misinformation among foreign scientists and businessmen. This is done in the following way: Soviet scientists and engineers spread rumors among foreigners about various types of scientific work or construction work or about other major projects on which Soviet scientists are allegedly working at the present time, whereas in reality they are not even considering work on such projects. This makes the foreign scientists and their governments work seriously on expensive projects which are not of practical use, and they spend enormous sums of money on this. Sometimes it works the other way. The West builds or conducts costly scientific research work in some scientific or technical field while the Soviets just sit and wait and collect information on this work. Then, as soon as the West has basically finished the work on this project or problem, our scientists, having collected all the information, start working on the same project or problem, which costs them much less because all the preliminary scientific research work has been done by the West.

There are also many other ways this is done.

Back to my own specific role in all this. The GRU has assigned me to make a study of the members of British delegations visiting the Soviet Union. My job is to establish friendlier relations with these men, assess their intelligence possibilities, and establish the fact that they are of definite value to our intelligence service. Then I will write a detailed report on them to our *rezident* in London. After that, their processing will begin. Possibly the *rezident* will assign one of the intelligence officers, for example, either Shapovalov or Pavlov, to the case. I will then introduce the subjects to them, after which it will be up to the London *rezidentura* to work on their possible recruitment. It all depends on how they react. The basic material to be used in the recruitment operation is the collection of possible compromising information on these men, e.g., problems in their family life, gambling, personal finances, amorous adventures, the financial position of their companies.

My other task is to obtain as much scientific information as possible of some definite value for our industry. For example, when one British scientist visited us in Moscow, he gave me an unclassified brochure on how to get fresh water from sea water. Our specialists were very interested in this brochure. Using the methods by which we now get fresh water from sea water in the U.S.S.R., one cubic meter of water costs six rubles [old rubles]; using the method which was described in the brochure, it would cost ninety-seven kopecks. I received a commendation for obtaining this brochure. Thanks to visits to our country by foreign delegations, we obtain a vast quantity of such very valuable information on the basis of which new and improved methods are adopted by agriculture and industry in the U.S.S.R.

I often substitute for Andrianov, our GRU *rezident* in the Committee, who has twice gone on missions to Germany on Serov's orders; and then I formulate operational plans for our GRU officers and co-optees myself. I am permanently responsible for seven of our GRU officers assigned to the Committee.

Trips of Soviet delegations to foreign countries require careful preparation. The departure of each delegation requires a separate decree of the Central Committee CPSU. Take my second trip to London in July–August 1961. The decision of the Central Committee to send our delegation to London took place on July 1, and on July 4 the order was issued by the Chairman of the Committee to select and send forty-five Soviet specialists to the Soviet Industrial Exhibition in London. I was appointed leader of the delegation, inasmuch as I had already been in London once before, and at that time I had established some connections and made acquaintances with certain people.

I selected mostly people who already had their exit documents ready in the Central Committee CPSU. There was not enough time to provide new people with the necessary credentials. Among the forty members of the delegation were three employees of the Central Committee and two Central Committee analysts. At the same time, ten GRU military officers left for London in the guise of members of the delegation or tourists. Representing the interests of our Committee were three other GRU colonels besides myself: I. Ya. Petrov, A. P. Shchepotin, and V. F. Tebenko. Besides their special technical assignments, they were also carrying out several intelligence tasks: selecting dead drops in London, checking the existing ones, arranging locations for meetings with the agent network, etc. During our stay in London, we maintained constant contact with the GRU *rezident* in London, Lev Sergeyevich Tolokonnikov.

In order to demonstrate more clearly the way we work, I am enclosing several reports concerning my trip to London. For instance:

1. In traveling from London to Sheffield (Highway A-1), I observed for the second time in the southern outskirts of the city of Stamford a military airfield, on which were based planes of the British Air Force, and to the north of this same city a launch site for the anti-aircraft system. I had the opportunity to study more carefully the indicated objectives, their location, their co-ordinates, etc. I made additional sketches of the indicated objects, the description of which I have included as a separate reference. . . .

This is the sort of "scientific" reporting which our Committee favors.

Upon completion of my London duty, to satisfy the ego of my Chief, Gvishiani, A. Pavlov, the deputy *rezident* in London, wrote him a personal letter thanking him and wishing him further successes. It was, so to speak, a routine form letter to the civilian chief in Moscow from an "ordinary" counselor at the embassy to London. All the reports covering our trip were sent to Serov in the GRU and from him to the various GRU directorates and sections. The samples of my own reports indicate the kind of work in which I and other members of the delegation were engaged. I did not accomplish more because, in the first place, I did not want to. In any case, I would not have had the time, being the leader of the delegation.

Another of my tasks while in London was to make new acquaintances among the employees of the companies which our delegation visited, then report on them to the *rezident* in London and later in Moscow. If the London *rezident* decided that some of my new acquaintances were of interest to us, my job was to have them meet one of the members of our *rezidentura* prior to my departure for Moscow. Each GRU officer assigned to the delegation was obliged also to study the methods used by British counterintelligence against members of the delegation, e.g., what kind of provocative questions the British ask; what kind of anti-Soviet discussions they try to conduct.

Shortly before my departure for London all Soviet embassies and in particular all GRU and KGB *rezidenturas* abroad received a circular letter from the Central Committee CPSU. The letter enumerated 150 different targets or designations in the United States against which intelligence work should be directed—military, industrial, agricultural. Where it is impossible to obtain certain information directly in America, the letter directs the *rezidenturas* elsewhere to obtain this information through third countries.

A similar list was also given to the Canadian Desk, with thirty different targets for its intelligence work against Canada. These thirty targets include even such a marginal military secret as the manufacture of artificial fur. But this was important to us. Our specialists still do not know how to manufacture artificial fur with cloth backing. Such fur is manufactured in a very simple manner in Canada and in America, yet our scientific research institutes still have not been able to solve this problem. It is manufactured by two companies in the U.S. and one in Canada. One of them offered to sell us the machine. Of course, Moscow has no intention of buying it, but by studying its operations, they propose to learn the entire manufacturing process. Then, if possible, they will build this same machine in the U.S.S.R. at a much lower cost. The most important task of the delegation is to steal the secret formula of the glue by which the fur is glued on the cloth. We consider Canada to represent the synthesis of the high scientific-technical ideas of the Americans and the British. It is relatively difficult to steal secrets in the U.S. and Britain, but in Canada, in some cases, it is easier to get technical data. Also, it is much easier to get entry visas to Canada for various Soviet delegations. I cite this example to show the thoroughness of our Soviet technical intelligence operations.

When someone goes abroad, everybody wants him to buy some presents or just some things a person needs which are impossible to get in Moscow. But it is impossible to fulfill all the requests. Usually one makes up a long list of things to be purchased. Sometimes one cannot bring everything requested of him because of a shortage of foreign currency on hand or too much baggage. Nevertheless I always tried to satisfy everyone to the best of my ability.

Shortly before my departure for London as leader of a delegation, I was summoned by Serov. During the conversation which lasted a few minutes Serov informed me that his wife and his daughter were also flying to London as tourists. He asked me to look after them and render them any assistance they might need while in England. I told the general that I would do anything in my power to help his family while they were in London.

The next day at the airport Serov introduced me to his wife and his daughter and wished us a good trip. I was very surprised to see how Serov kissed his wife and his daughter good-by with genuine affection. Somehow I found it hard to believe that this cold, hard-boiled man with bloodstained hands could show such warmth toward those near to him.

When we arrived in London, nobody was there to meet us. Something apparently happened to the embassy automobile (although Serov had sent a telegram beforehand to the *rezident* in London). Finally the car arrived, and I took the Serovs to their hotel, promising to meet them the next day. During the next few days I showed them London. I took them shopping and escorted them to restaurants in the evening. They treated me very nicely, kept addressing me in the familiar form, and thanked me for everything.

Serov's daughter Svetlana is finishing the Mikoyan Aviation Institute in Moscow, where she is studying aircraft electrical instruments and equipment. She invited me to dance rock-'n'-roll in a London night club. One evening I hired a car and took them to several night clubs, including the Piccadilly. However, we did not do any dancing because we were afraid that we would attract too much attention. Both of them were extremely pleased by these outings in London. Serov's wife invited me to visit them at their country house near Moscow, saying that they had fresh strawberries there all year round and also had their own apiary. (Serov suffers from rheumatism, and he lets himself be stung by the bees, which is supposedly an old Russian treatment.) I also visited my new acquaintances several times at their hotel. I treated them to candy, fruit, and wine. They were very grateful. They would not have had the courage to go sight-seeing around London all by themselves. Had the English press known about their presence in London, there would have been much publicity.

While in London the Serovs had some trouble with money. I felt that they did not have enough pounds. Apparently they had spent most of their travel allowance shopping. I offered them my assistance and twice loaned them twenty to thirty pounds. At first Mrs. Serov refused to accept the money, but finally she agreed, saying that her husband would settle up with me upon my return to Moscow.

Mrs. Serov wanted to buy a swing for her grandchildren, but when she found out that both the price and the weight were high, she gave up the idea and asked me to get drawings of this swing so that her husband could have it made at one of the factories in Moscow. Knowing that they were to return by ship, I insisted that I would buy the swing for them, but Mrs. Serov asked me to buy something else for her husband; she suggested an electric razor.

I myself had no extra money left, especially pounds, because I had been issued only enough to cover my official expenses for my trip. It is interesting to note that all the presents bought by me for Serov and his family were purchased with money I had taken from our *rezident* in London—a handy use of the state treasury. Serov's family left London on board a Soviet ship. There were no incidents, and I was very happy.

After returning to Moscow I visited the Serovs several times. They live on Granovskiy Street, house no. 3, second entrance, apt. 71, and also have a fine country house near Moscow. They gave me a party including supper and drinks. I gave Serov the electric razor and several records by Leshchenko and Vertinskiy, two very popular Russian émigré singers of Russian gypsy songs and ballads. These are real rarities in the Soviet Union, almost impossible to find. Later, when Svetlana and I met alone, she told me that her father was very pleased and played the Leshchenko and Vertinskiy records almost every night.

Here are the survivals of capitalism in the minds of the Soviet people—razors and records from London, perfumes and eau de cologne from Paris. No, these traces will never be stamped out. After all, if they are so strong on the top level, what is there to say about the ordinary people?

Prior to my next regular trip abroad, I was called again by Serov to receive his instructions. He told me that he was very pleased with my work and wished me a successful trip. At the same time, he asked me to come to his apartment in the evening, as he put it, "to receive additional instructions from my wife." When I came to see them in the evening, Mrs. Serov gave me a long list of things to buy in Paris, and her husband asked me to buy him a lightweight tennis jacket. At the same time, they presented me with several jars of caviar and also offered me some good sausage for the trip. I accepted the caviar but politely refused the sausage.

Survivals of capitalism are in everybody's mind, especially love for good things. "We have everything in the Soviet Union, and everything we have is better than in the West," we keep saying every day. Yet all our best we bring from the West. Even underwear, which the wives of Serov and Churayev[3] asked me to buy for them abroad. One is asked to buy in London or Paris such things as socks, stockings, notebooks, eau de cologne, perfume, electric razors, dry-cell batteries, fountain pens, cognac, phonograph records, sweaters, shirts, neckties, etc., etc. During my last two trips alone I had lists with more than a hundred items which I was asked to purchase abroad.

There it is, our Soviet socialist society! "Everything is available, everything is better." Even such simple items as

---

[3] Viktor Mikhaylovich Churayev was the Chief Deputy Chairman of the Central Committee Bureau for the R.S.F.S.R., the largest of the fifteen Soviet Republics, and one of Khrushchev's right-hand men.

socks or neckties are hard to get. Everything has to be brought from abroad, for Central Committee members, marshals, and generals only. And what about night clubs and restaurants? If there were any worthy of the name in Moscow, I am certain that all the Central Committee members would patronize them, not to mention us ordinary officers.

On my second trip to London I bought many presents for Varentsov and his family. I bought two fountain pens, a wallet, several bottles of perfume, and some playing cards for General Smolikov, the Chief of the Personnel Directorate. He asked me especially to bring the cards because he is an ardent "Preferans" [Russian card game] player. I also brought back to Moscow perfume, face powder, lipstick, cigarettes, playing cards, and many other things for Gvishiani's wife. I brought some twelve-volt dry-cell batteries for Rudnev, the Chairman of the Committee. You see, here is a minister, Chairman of the State Committee for the Co-ordination of Scientific Research Work, and he asks people to bring some batteries from abroad! There are simply no batteries available in the U.S.S.R. I think that this alone is good proof of what we have, as against what we show foreigners.

During my trips to England and France during 1961 I was given the mission, just as other GRU officers were, of collecting information of a military and scientific nature. As I was in charge of the delegation, I did not participate in, as we call it, active operational work. I established contacts, made acquaintances, collected literature which would be of interest to the GRU, etc. I was well received in both France and England, and I met many interesting and prominent people in the scientific and business worlds.

I was very impressed with the completely free and easy attitude of these people. In Turkey, the only foreign country which I had visited before, I always felt that the population was not too kindly disposed toward Soviet people and that the Turkish police had me under surveillance. In France and England people talked to me freely, invited me to their homes, restaurants, and offices. I was astonished by this because in the Military Diplomatic Academy I was taught entirely different things about the French and British secret police. After spending some time in those two countries I saw how natural and unaffected the people behaved, as though there were no such thing as the secret police.

I did not find a single word in either the British or the French press about the arrival of our delegation, and all the people with whom I dealt were of the opinion that I was the same kind of businessman as they, sent abroad by my firm in the U.S.S.R. Are the British and the French really so naïve? Or is it that suspicions and denunciations, so widespread in our country, simply have no place in the life of England and France? I have not found the exact answer to this question, but this idea has become firmly implanted in my mind, and I cannot rid myself of it.

ADDITIONAL NOTES

Foreign Department of the Committee

The Chief is *Mikhail Fedorovich Kachalov,* a KGB officer, who served in Italy for a long time as deputy *rezident* of the KGB. His cover was Second Secretary of the Soviet Embassy in Rome.

The Deputy Chief is myself, Oleg Vladimirovich Penkovskiy, colonel in the GRU.

Following is a short list of other GRU and KGB workers known to me in our directorate:

Yuriy Borisovich Tikhomirov, senior specialist (Chief of Protocol), a KGB employee, specializing in American operations. He brags about the good contacts he established with American diplomats when he worked in Syria.

Ivan Petrovich Rybachenkov, senior specialist, a GRU employee and a military intelligence officer with great experience.

P. N. Ulyanenko, specialist, KGB captain, who spent approximately two years in London. A very high-strung person.

Georgiy Ivanovich Suvorin, specialist, Navy commander, employee of the GRU, is used at the present time for special assignments. He is often summoned by General Rogov.

Dmitriy Dmitriyevich Novoselov, specialist, KGB colonel. Levin uses him as an advisor.

Nikolay Ilich Kopytov, specialist, former major in the KGB, works together with Levin.

Vladimir Vasilyevich Krivoshchekov, senior specialist.

An intelligence officer, but I do not know exactly whether he works for the GRU or for the KGB.

Vladimir Nikolayevich Travkin, specialist, lieutenant colonel in the GRU. He worked for a short time at the UN in New York, but was recalled because of stupidity.

Aleksandr Mikhaylovich Bliznakov, specialist, GRU colonel. At one time worked in the Illegals Directorate under Admiral Bekrenev. He has been sent on temporary duty to India and to Japan.

Viktor Mikhaylovich Ryazantsev, specialist, KGB officer, in 1961 was sent to the U.S. to attend some conference.

Viktor Filippovich Golopolosov, specialist, employee of the KGB. Levin refers to him as "my boy."

Nadezhda Ivanovna Tsapp, specialist, is used by both the GRU and KGB as a co-optee.

Yuriy Yakovlevich Malik, specialist. I do not know whether or not he has anything to do with intelligence work, but his father, the former ambassador to Great Britain and Japan, at one time was Chief or Deputy Chief of the "Information Committee" under the Council of Ministers, U.S.S.R. That is what the Soviet intelligence service was called at the time when the GRU and the MGB intelligence were united into one single service called the Information Committee and headed at different times by Molotov and Vyshinskiy.

Igor Viktorovich Milovidov, specialist, KGB agent, travels abroad with Soviet delegations and watches Soviet citizens abroad. He approached me several times expressing the desire of working for the GRU, asking me to help him sever his ties with the KGB. When I mentioned the possibility of using Milovidov in GRU activities to Levin, he answered, "Leave him alone; we need him."

Vadim Vadimovich Farmakovskiy, specialist, GRU officer, lieutenant commander in the Navy, visited Italy and Sweden as a member of Soviet delegations, speaks English.

Valentin Dmitriyevich Khrabrov, specialist, GRU colonel, is a good friend of another GRU intelligence officer, Lappa. I believe he served in Paris as assistant military attaché.

Nazar Kalistratovich Lappa, specialist, GRU colonel, is responsible for receiving delegations from France, Italy, Belgium, and Holland.

Ilya Pavlovich Shvarts, senior reviewer, English language translator, KGB agent. He is avoided by the employees of the Committee because they know that he informs the KGB against everyone. His main job is to watch the Soviet employees of the Committee and see which of them have friendly contacts with foreigners. He made several trips abroad as an interpreter and KGB agent.

Nikolay Antonovich Berdennikov, KGB agent and senior specialist, works on the British Desk, which includes Canada and other English-speaking nations. He has made several trips to London and to the U.S. on KGB assignments as a member of various Soviet delegations. He knows English well and often goes to night clubs in Moscow with Levin.

Boris Vasilyevich Nikitin, senior specialist, GRU colonel, works on the Desk covering India, Pakistan, and Ceylon.

Aleksandr Yakovlevich Smurov, senior specialist, KGB employee, either a colonel or a lieutenant colonel, spent several years in Germany.

More names could be added to the list. Those already listed should be sufficient to give one an idea of the kind of espionage apparatus which exists under the cover of the State Committee for the Co-ordination of Scientific Research Work of the Council of Ministers U.S.S.R.

CHAPTER IV

The Khrushchev Cult

INTRODUCTION

ON May 6, 1961, Oleg Penkovskiy returned to Moscow with what was apparently a precise concept of his mission. He carefully stored his camera, film, and radio instructions in a secret drawer of his desk in the apartment which he and his family still occupied on Maksim Gorkiy Embankment. Then he began work in earnest. With free access to the Ministry of Defense and the GRU, as well as his own Committee, he photographed documents almost wholesale, most of them in the top-secret category. Some were technical papers or highly classified instructions and tactical manuals in use by the ground (tactical) missile force. Others were less technological, dealing with intelligence procedures, Soviet personalities or the goals and operations of the Committee.

On May 27 Wynne flew into Moscow, to resume some of his negotiations with the Soviets on behalf of the firms he represented. Colonel Penkovskiy met him at Sheremetyevo Airport and drove him back to the city. On the way he handed Wynne a packet of some twenty exposed films and other materials, which Wynne transmitted to a representative of British intelligence later in the day.

That evening Penkovskiy visited Wynne in his room at the Metropol Hotel. As he later admitted in their Soviet trial, Wynne gave Penkovskiy a package containing thirty fresh rolls of film and further instructions from the intelligence officers who had met him in London. It is hard to believe, from such goings-on, that Wynne was not himself an intelligence officer. He was not, however. It had simply happened that Penkovskiy chose him for his contact; and

115

when he reported this, British intelligence inevitably asked
him to keep up the connection and transmit certain packages, etc., to Penkovskiy. Wynne's position gave him a
facility for meeting Penkovskiy that could not easily be
duplicated—at least not without arousing Soviet suspicions.
(Even at the well-supervised Soviet trial, Penkovskiy insisted that Wynne never actually saw the information he
was passing.)

Far from suspecting anything strange in his behavior,
however, Penkovskiy's superiors at the GRU and the Committee were delighted by his British associations. People
like Greville Wynne were just the sort of contacts any
good Soviet intelligence officer in Penkovskiy's shoes might
be expected to make. They arranged to send him to London with another delegation of Soviet technical experts,
this time to attend the opening of the Soviet Industrial
Exhibition there.

The delegation arrived in London on July 15, 1961, but
Penkovskiy came alone three days later, since he was not
required to travel with the delegation. Fortuitously, no
one from the Soviet Embassy was on hand to meet him.
This oversight allowed him to telephone Wynne from the
airport, whereupon the Englishman drove out to meet him
—a pleasant encounter which was later related in painful
detail at the 1963 trial. Penkovskiy went along to Wynne's
house, shaved, bathed, and turned over another fat batch
of films and documents which he had brought with him.
Then Wynne dropped him off at the Kensington Close
Hotel, where he had a reservation—conveniently close to
the old mansions in Kensington Gardens which comprise
the working quarters of the Soviet Embassy.

Because most of his official work this time was concentrated in London, Penkovskiy was able to spend a great
deal more time than formerly with the four British and
American operatives who were waiting for him in one of
MI-6's "safe houses." He would spend most of the day
working at the Soviet Embassy or at the exhibition with
his delegates; but even this did not make too great demands on his time because the delegation was subdivided
by specialties. Each division had its own subleader. Penkovskiy handled only the over-all direction.

Evenings he reserved for the rendezvous with his new
friends: "Alexander," "Miles," "Grille," and "Oslav." They

went over the material he had previously given them in some detail, it having been checked by experts meanwhile. They made further assignments.

By this time, presumably, the first fruits of Colonel Penkovskiy's photography work with his new Minox had been received and evaluated in London and Washington. It was a tense summer in Europe that year. The Continent still reverberated from Khrushchev's threats over Berlin and the East Germany treaty. If anything, the Vienna meeting of Khrushchev and President Kennedy had only intensified the political electricity in the air. Against the background of a possible military showdown, therefore, in which Marshal Varentsov's missiles would play a heavy role, the personal reports and observations of his former aide had even greater value. That July, Penkovskiy's sessions with the intelligence officers lasted as long as ten hours at a stretch. To provide for the day when face-to-face communications might not be so easy, he was given further training in the use of a long-distance radio receiver.

Throughout this necessarily concentrated, grueling indoctrination course in Western intelligence procedures, Penkovskiy managed to preserve his amazing *sang-froid*. Only a few mortals are gifted with a natural talent for leading a double life and Oleg Penkovskiy was evidently one of them. Thanks to his diligent escort duty with General Serov's wife and daughter on his first London trip, he had accumulated quite a reputation among Moscow's upper crust as a man who knew his way around the West. This time he had a heavy shopping list with him. In his notebook, along with various orders and gift specifications, he had taken the trouble to draw the foot contours of various influential Soviet ladies and gentlemen, so he would make no mistake in purchasing the right shoes for them. (Shoes from abroad are a popular Soviet gift item, and ever since Khrushchev's famous Italian suit purchase, there had been much official leniency in the matter of foreign clothing articles.) The Colonel purchased as much as his official allowance would allow, more than enough to qualify him as a latter-day Grandfather Frost (the Russian Santa Claus) on the flight home. (It was fortunate that Soviet customs rarely touched his baggage.) With some of his purchases—a few shirts, a watch or two, and other oddments—Wynne helped him.

At the same time, Penkovskiy managed to keep up with his Soviet intelligence observations, which he forwarded in the normal way to GRU headquarters through Colonel Pavlov, the local deputy *rezident*. It can be assumed that his Western contacts gave him some "material" for forwarding to Moscow that was apparently valuable, if in fact relatively harmless. But such information was enough to continue his reputation as a hard-working "Chekist."

With what must have been a profound sense of irony, he also went on advancing his standing as a zealous Party man. One morning he quietly took a trip to Karl Marx's grave in Highgate Cemetery and discovered that it was in a bad state of neglect. Through Communist Party channels, he wrote a letter of protest direct to the First Secretary of the Central Committee in Moscow. Comrade Penkovskiy told Comrade Khrushchev that as a "loyal Marxist" he found such neglect appalling, a reflection upon Communism, the Soviet Union, and, specifically, the local Soviet Embassy officials whose job it was to take care of such things.

Moscow took swift action on receipt of the letter and Penkovskiy was commended for his "socialist vigilance." The London embassy was ordered to set things right immediately. Promptly the grave was cleaned up and decorated. Penkovskiy, although hardly popular in Soviet Embassy circles in London as a result of his letter, was treated with increased respect.

In two hasty visits to the open society, Penkovskiy had seen enough to confirm his admiration for the West and his wrath—the word is used advisedly—at the regime which kept his own people behind the walls and conventions of a garrison state. "Oh, my poor Russian people, my poor Russian people," he had exclaimed to Wynne, when looking through his first London department store in April. It was not the abundance which intrigued and amazed him so much as its obvious accessibility to people of all walks of life, in contrast to conditions back home.

He remained fascinated by London and enjoyed walking about the city, quietly observing its still stately manners. He dressed well, in conservative taste. Although a moderate drinker who generally contented himself with a few glasses of wine in the course of an evening, Penkovskiy was fond of socializing. In the midst of his other activities in London, he even managed to find time to take a few dancing lessons, in which he sampled the mysteries of the twist and the cha-cha.

He returned to Moscow on August 10, having already received commendations for his mission from his Soviet superiors. In an August letter to Gvishiani, at the Committee, Colonel Pavlov wrote his own endorsement of Penkovskiy's good work in England. The Western operatives were even more pleased. As his Soviet prosecutor later reported: "The foreign intelligence officers gave new assignments to Penkovskiy in which special emphasis was put on the collection of intelligence information on the Soviet armed forces, missile troops, troops assigned to the German Democratic Republic, and the preparation for the signing of a peace treaty with the G.D.R."

Penkovskiy had investigated the documentation necessary for applying for both British and American citizenship and received assurances that he would receive responsible employment and a decent position in Western society, whenever he was prepared to leave the Soviet Union forever. Two years later, Soviet investigators found in his apartment two photographs of Penkovskiy, taken in London, wearing the full uniform and regalia of a British and an American Army colonel.

All of this was clearly part of a deeply thought out transfer of allegiance, from a military man in whom the tradition of obedience and loyalty was ingrained. Penkovskiy was not merely interested in helping the West; he had to be part of the West himself. Moscow had never seemed to be so far away.

He went back there, however, and the depth of his disgust with the world he was going back to can be gathered from the next section of the Papers. It is clear to see, too, how this career soldier had developed a hatred for Khrushchev which was, originally, as much professional as it was ideological. Over the years, however, it had become something akin to obsession.

PENKOVSKIY'S TEXT

It is interesting to observe our prominent Soviet personages in the privacy of their own intimates. What a dif-

ference there is between them when they are on the
speaker's platform and when they are in their family
circles with a glass of vodka in their hands. They become
entirely different types. They are very much like the personalities which are portrayed by Gogol in *Dead Souls*
and *The Inspector General.* It is clear that such classic,
unfortunate Russian types have not become extinct with
the advent of the "Soviet Period." Indeed, I would say
that they are now more numerous and more obvious.

There are no more Communists such as our old Bol-
sheviks who used to operate in the underground [*pod-
pol'shchiki*], not to mention Marx or Lenin. Among my
friends, Party members of today, there is none that believes in Communism. They, like me, are looking for the
answer to the question: "Is our path a correct one? Where
are we going? What are we building? Why are we living
for someone else and for tomorrow rather than for ourselves and for today?"

Many months ago I had an interesting conversation
with one of my old friends, an instructor of a course on
"Foundations of Marxism-Leninism." We were discussing
that standard classic, the *New History of the Communist
Party of the Soviet Union.* "Poor *History of the CPSU;*
how many times it has been rewritten!" were my friend's
words.

I myself had studied the various editions of the *History
of the CPSU:* the Knorin edition, the Yem. Yaroslavskiy
edition, the edition of the CC, VKP (b) (Stalin's), and
now the CC CPSU (Khrushchev's) edition. Why are these
histories different? One reads them and wonders. According to one edition, Tukhachevskiy and Gamarnik were
enemies and foreign spies, yet another one treats them
as patriots and brilliant military leaders. In one edition
Stalin is called father of the workers of the entire world,
while in the other he is called a criminal, an enemy, and
a murderer. Yesterday nobody knew that Khrushchev was
at Stalingrad; today he is the Hero of Stalingrad. . . .

My friend explained this in a very simple manner: "Our
Party, as is well known, was founded by Lenin, who
carried on Karl Marx's cause. However, while Marx's
cause was carried on by Lenin, Lenin's cause was continued only by enemies and traitors. Let us classify our

leading Party members, as they have been celebrated in succeeding issues of the Party history:

Mercenary agent and imperialist hireling	Trotskiy
Traitor to the working class	Zinovyev
Rightist opportunist and double-dealer	Bukharin
Enemy of the people	Rykov
Saboteur and dissenter	Kamenev
Enemy of the workers	Pyatakov
Dissenter	Raskolnikov
Enemy and traitor	Yagoda
The enemy of Communists	Yezhov
Enemy of the Fatherland and spy	Tukhachevskiy
Generally speaking an enemy	Gamarnik
Imperialist agent and traitor	Beriya
Unmasked criminal	Stalin
Enemy of the Party	Molotov
Enemies in general	Malenkov, Kaganovich, Bulganin
Double-dealer	Shepilov
Khrushchev's enemy, etc., etc.	Zhukov

My friend stopped, and later added: "Only Khrushchev, the enemy of all our people, remains unmasked."

I did not know how to answer my friend. How clear and simple all this was. I myself used to think that our history was not a true history, but I never was able to put it in such a clear and witty form. And I think that it is clear to anyone now that to work for, and especially to serve, such a group of saboteurs is difficult and even impossible. This is the reason why I came to my final decision.

I am joining the ranks of those who are actively fighting against our rotten, two-faced regime, known by the name of Dictatorship of the Proletariat or Soviet Power [*Sovetskaya vlast*]. Yes, it is a dictatorship, not of the Proletariat, but of a small group of persons. It deceives my countrymen while they, being innocent, give their lives for this dictatorship, without knowing the entire truth. And they will probably never learn it, unless I or people like myself tell them the truth. I want to be with the common Russian people; I want to cry and laugh together with them; I want my old friends, ordinary human beings, to accept me back into their fold instead of avoiding me, because of my position. I want to be a soldier of my Russians, the common people. I am joining the ranks of a new army, the true people's army. I know that I am not alone; we are many. But we are still afraid of each other and we act only as individuals. The hour will come when we shall open our souls to each other, act together, serve the true people's representatives and ourselves instead of the group of saboteurs at the top.

Apparently we just cannot live without a dictator, without the personality cult. The big break came for Khrushchev in 1957, when he pushed back Bulganin, Molotov, Shepilov, Pervukhin, Malenkov, and others—the so-called anti-Party group. For three days before they were ousted by the Presidium and the Central Committee CPSU, Khrushchev was not in power. He had been voted the Minister of Agriculture. That was all. Khrushchev, however, dispatched his men all over the Soviet Union in order to call a Central Committee plenum in Moscow. Almost all Central Committee members, secretaries of *oblast* and *kray* committees, and also secretaries of the Union Republics came urgently by plane with the help of the KGB. Most of them were people previously appointed by Khrushchev, who were ready to support him. They did, successfully.

Now he has also created for himself a solid base in the Army: he elevated many to higher generals' ranks, promoted some of them to the rank of marshal. In 1961, three hundred colonels were made generals. They are the ones whose support he depends on now.

Khrushchev is not too clever, but he has vast energy. It is his energy that saved him during that period. When the necessary quorum was assembled for the plenum of the Central Committee CPSU which had been urgently called by Khrushchev, he announced the existence of the so-called anti-Party group. The majority of the Central Committee members supported Khrushchev. At that time Zhukov also was on Khrushchev's side. Zhukov hates Bulganin and Kaganovich, and at the plenum he said bluntly: "The Army is behind Khrushchev." And that was all! And so the anti-Party group was ousted. Khrushchev was victorious. Furtesva helped him a great deal; she worked day and night dispatching planes, and some say that she herself made some of the flights campaigning for support for Khrushchev. Everybody in Moscow calls her "Catherine the Third."

Anyhow, Khrushchev received the majority of votes and became czar, Chairman of the Council of Ministers and First Secretary of the Central Committee. And so again, a new cult of personality, a dictator.

However, there are still many people in the Central Committee who support Molotov, Bulganin (although the Army does not like him), Malenkov, Marshal Voroshilov, and others, as for instance Pervukhin, our ambassador to the German Democratic Republic.[1] Rumors have been seeping through that Khrushchev has frequent quarrels with Mikoyan.

I have seen Churayev many times, the R.S.F.S.R. Communist Party leader. Churayev says that there are many foreign policy questions on which Mikoyan disagrees with Khrushchev. When Varentsov asked Churayev one time why nothing had been heard about Mikoyan or his whereabouts recently, Churayev answered: "They are at each other's throats again." Incidentally, Mikoyan is against the hard policy on Berlin.

Thus there is smoldering opposition within the leadership, but it is not allowed to come out into the open for fear that Khrushchev may again announce the existence of some new anti-Party group.

There is also the possibility of a split in the top echelon, for instance, on the Berlin question. Many leaders realize that we are not ready for a major war; we have many bottlenecks in our economy as well as in our military problems. Steadfast, realistic people may say: "It is too early, we should not get ourselves involved in a war because small wars (we call them 'Khrushchev's adventures') may lead to a major war." Many generals bluntly say: "What in hell do we need this Berlin for? We have endured it for sixteen years; we can endure it a little more. One of these

[1] Mikhail Georgiyevich Pervukhin was a member of the anti-Party group and later Soviet ambassador to East Germany. He was replaced on November 30, 1962 and has not figured since in Soviet public life.

days Khrushchev will catch it good! They will hit him in his teeth so hard that he will lose everything!"

Of course, the opposite may happen. The restraining forces will be unable to keep this fool in check, and he will carry out his own policy. If the opposition wins, it will say that he is a sick old man, or that he himself asks to be released, the way he did with Malenkov. Or else he may simply be kicked out and they will tell him, "Go to your Kalinovka and stay there as chairman of the *kolkhoz* [collective farm]."[2] If this ever happens, the entire population will be very happy.

Khrushchev is not popular among the people. There are all kinds of anecdotes, jokes, and remarks about him. Everybody calls him an adventurer. Everybody criticizes him. Everyone laughs at him, especially at his slogan: "Let us catch up with and surpass America." The people are smart, and they immediately respond with a joke:

> In production of milk,
> We have overtaken America,
> But in meat we have failed,
> The bull's penis got broken.[3]

Or another one:

> Khrushchev had distributed a questionnaire
>   among the people with the question:
> "What are you going to do when we overtake
>   America?"
> One person answered: "I'll stay right there,
>   while you run farther if you wish."

Very clever. How long have we been overtaking America? We were overtaking America under Stalin; and now under Khrushchev we are still overtaking America. The fool. At least he could try to say something sensible. Of course, he personally has overtaken quite a bit: he has three

---

2 Kalinovka, a village in Kursk *oblast,* in the heart of European Russia, is Khrushchev's birthplace.

3 *My Ameriku dognali,*
   Po nadoyu moloka,
   A po myasu ne dognali,
   Khren slomalsya u byka.

country houses near Moscow, several in the Caucasus, in
the Crimea, near Kiev, and most likely in some other
places, too: first, a country house somewhere beyond the
university in Moscow; second, a country house along the
Rublevskoye Highway, beyond the settlement of Kuntsevo
(it is said that Stalin and Beriya's country houses were
located in that area; it would be very amusing if Khrushchev were living in Beriya's country house); third, a
country house along the Dmitrovskoye Highway. There
are large forests there and an atomic center nearby.

[EDITOR'S NOTE: After this disgression on Khrushchev
and his private reputation, Penkovskiy returns to his discussion of other Soviet regime leaders.]

Kozlov[4] is a devil and frequently attends the meetings
of the Supreme Military Council together with Khrushchev,
Mikoyan, and Suslov.[5] Kozlov is very much interested in
military matters. He sticks his nose into everything and
wants to know all the details.

Varentsov often attends the Supreme Military Council
meetings. He says that it sounds so ridiculous when the
others call Khrushchev Supreme Commander in Chief.
Even Kozlov and Suslov cannot help smiling. "It is a terrible mess all around," says Sergey Sergeyevich. "Stalin's
firm hand is missing."

He also regrets that Molotov and Malenkov are out.
But it is all the same to me. It is six of one or half a dozen
of the other. In private Varentsov criticizes Khrushchev,
but when he was given rank of Chief Marshal of Artillery
he made a toast, saying: "Let us drink to the health of our
dear Nikita Sergeyevich." Varentsov is my friend and I
like him, but why this pretense, why this hypocrisy?

Molotov's health is quite poor, and it is possible that he
will die soon. I have not seen him for more than a year.
I suspect that when he dies, it will not even be mentioned

---

[4] Frol Romanovich Kozlov was a member of the Presidium and
Secretary of the Central Committee CPSU. Before his stroke in 1963
he was a leading contender to succeed Khrushchev. On November
16, 1964, following the fall of Khrushchev, he was dropped from the
Presidium. He died on January 30, 1965.

[5] Mikhail Andreyevich Suslov is a member of the Presidium and
Secretary of the Central Committee CPSU and the chief Party ide-
ologist.

in the newspapers. One can expect anything from the scoundrel Khrushchev.

Kaganovich lives in Moscow, not far from Varentsov, on the Frunze Embankment. He often takes a walk in the evening. He looks rather well but has gained weight and looks older. He is not doing anything. His wife died recently, but this was not mentioned in the newspapers.

Shepilov is in Moscow and often walks along Gorkiy Street. He is clever. Once I met him near our Committee. He was in good spirits. In general, he is an interesting, smart person.

Malenkov is somewhere in Siberia. Once in a while he comes to Moscow.

Bulganin drinks, drinks from grief and disappointment.

Voroshilov used to drink a lot. Now he is quite an old man. Probably he will also die soon.

Pervukhin and Saburov[6] are nothing much, they are small fry, and nobody among the people remembers them at all. I have heard that Peruvkhin was rather smart, but that Saburov was nothing much, an upstart. Nobody seems to know why Stalin appointed him Chief of Gosplan.

Now Voznesenskiy was a true walking encyclopedia, he knew everything.

During one of my visits to Serov's apartment he told me an interesting incident about Khrushchev's personality cult. Serov said that when he was selecting materials for Khrushchev to use in his speeches on Stalin and his crimes, he tried to persuade Khrushchev not to attack Stalin too severely. Khrushchev would not even listen to him. And now, says Serov, all this has turned against Khrushchev himself. This was a serious error on Khrushchev's part.

A Party conference of the Frunze Rayon of the city of Moscow was held on September 9, 1960. Colonel Lazarev, head of a department in the Frunze Military Academy, made a speech at the conference as a delegate. He spoke out against the Khrushchev cult. Lazarev said: "Khrushchev did the right thing when he debunked Stalin's personality cult, but now he is creating the same cult for

6 Maksim Zakharovich Saburov, during the period of 1955–57, was the First Deputy Chairman of the Council of Ministers U.S.S.R., was connected with the anti-Party group and then disappeared from the scene.

himself." He was interrupted, and the chairman of the conference immediately submitted the question of Lazarev's speech to the conference for discussion. He called the speech apolitical and incorrect, and introduced a proposal to deprive Lazarev of his credentials as a conference delegate. The vote was taken immediately, and this department head of the academy was expelled from the Party conference. It must be assumed that for his bold speech against Khrushchev's cult he will also be expelled from the Party and from the Frunze Academy.

This is our Party democracy, our spirit of criticism and self-criticism.

If Khrushchev dies, the international situation may improve somewhat. Things may be quiet for one or two years, while the struggle for power is taking place in our country. What happens after that, heaven alone knows. Right now we do not have a single candidate who could be a good leader of the country. The most clever of them all is Mikoyan. He is a Leninist, but he will never be elected and will never win the struggle for power. Molotov is ill and probably will not join the struggle. Kozlov and Brezhnev both dislike Mikoyan. They have achieved their status only because of Khrushchev. If Khrushchev dies, both will be kicked out. Suslov is a possibility. I mentioned Suslov to Churayev, but his comment did not amount to much. He is afraid to foul the nest by any criticism. Among the leaders those who are opposed to Khrushchev keep their mouths shut because they are afraid of losing their positions.

In my considered opinion, as an officer of the General Staff, I do not believe Khrushchev is too anxious for war at the present time, but he is preparing earnestly; if the situation is ripe for war he will start it first in order to catch the probable enemy, i.e., the U.S.A. and the Western states, unawares. He would of course like to reach the level of producing missiles by the tens of thousands, launch them like a rainstorm against the West, and, as he calls it, "bury capitalism." In this respect even our marshals and generals consider him to be a provocateur, the one who incites war.

The Western powers must do something to stop him. Today he will not start a war. Today he is playing with missiles, but this is playing with fire, and one of these days he will start a real slaughter.

Today the Soviet Union is not ready for war. This is the precise truth. All this is agitation and propaganda— "on the one hand we stand for peace, and on the other hand we will cover you with missiles"—which some of the Western leaders take literally. This must *not* be taken seriously by the West. This is a policy of the moment, to gain time. On one hand we are for peace, on the other we frighten with missiles.

Look what happened during the Hungarian events and the Suez crisis. We in Moscow felt as if we were sitting on a powderkeg. Everyone in the General Staff was against the "Khrushchev adventure." It was better to lose Hungary, as they said, than to lose everything. But what did the West do? Nothing. It was asleep. This gave Khrushchev confidence, and after Hungary he began to scream: "I was right!" After the Hungarian incident he dismissed many generals who had spoken out against him. If the West had slapped Khrushchev down hard then, he would not be in power today and all of Eastern Europe could be free.

Kennedy must carry out a firm and consistent policy in regard to Khrushchev. There is nothing to fear. Khrushchev is not ready for war. He has to be slapped down again and again every time he gets ready to set off on one of his adventures.

Kennedy has just as much right to help the patriots of Cuba as we had when we "helped" the Hungarians.

This is not just my opinion. Everyone at the General Staff said this. It was said in Varentsov's home, even on the streetcars in Moscow. If the West does not maintain a firm policy, then Khrushchev's position will become stronger, he will think even more about his might and right, and in this case he might strike.

Everyone should know this. Once other countries begin to believe in his strength, Khrushchev will begin to dictate anything he wants. Khrushchev's government, and primarily he himself, thinks that if war is inevitable, we should strike first, create panic, and send our hail of missiles. This is calculated to produce a fast victory and stun the enemy. The Soviet Union is not capable of carrying on a long war. The internal situation is very bad, the standard of living is low, there is financial insecurity. There will be thousands of deserters on the very first day of the war. This is why Khrushchev prefers a lightning strike. It will stun the enemy, it will not worsen the situation internally, it will avoid mass desertion or surrender of troops, and it will allow him to retain the people's democracies in his camp.

This plan has been worked out in every detail and is on file in the General Staff. Staff exercises have been conducted in accordance with this plan. That is the Soviet position.

The people are very unhappy with Khrushchev's militant speeches. One can hear this everywhere. Now one can breathe a little easier than in Beriya's time, and one can hear and say a few things.

On the other hand, the world can be thankful to Khrushchev for his militant words. They forced Kennedy, Macmillan, and De Gaulle to double or triple their military budgets and defense preparedness. If Stalin were alive he would do all this quietly, but this fool Khrushchev is loud-mouthed. He himself forces the Western powers to strengthen their defense weapons and military potential.

The generals on the General Staff have no love for Khrushchev. They say that he is working to his own detriment. He blabs too much about Soviet military successes in order to frighten the West, but the West is not stupid, they are also getting ready. What else can they do?

Khrushchev will not consider the fact that our Army is not ready for a major war. Varentsov says that we have no confidence in our state of readiness, that we are taking a great risk. Certainly we are training our troops, keeping them in combat readiness every moment, but we are not certain that we are ready in all respects. The entire Central Committee CPSU, leading government officials, marshals, and generals spend all their time among the troops, checking, exhorting, making improvements, so as to be ready at a moment's notice.

Several hundred generals were present during maneuvers in the Odessa Military District; the entire General Staff was there. During the Berlin crisis the entire Central Committee visited factories and plants, especially those involved with defense production. The city of Moscow was empty. Everyone had gone out on Khrushchev's orders. Churayev also often has to leave on temporary duty to the provinces. All these representatives of the Central Committee visited factories and plants, appealing to the workers to work better and produce more. This happens not only during a crisis, it goes on all the time. It was especially noticeable during the Berlin crisis.

The General Staff works night and day formulating various plans of attack. Everything is marked on maps, including places where it is proposed to aim the first missiles. True, the marking is done in a secure manner; everything is directed against the "probable enemy." But this is simple deceit. It would be brazen and risky to name the enemy and the targets openly. Everyone knows, however, who the "probable enemy" is; it is America. (In our military and GRU literature we frequently refer to the U.S.A. as the "probable enemy," while in KGB and Central Committee CPSU circles I have heard the U.S.A. referred to as the "main enemy." This latter term is probably indicative of their true feelings.) I believe Varentsov and Churayev; it was they who claimed that Khrushchev said, "I will drop a hail of missiles on them."

Khrushchev does not want a world war because he knows he cannot win it; but he will keep on trying to instigate various local conflicts. But if he feels that he can win in a specific place, such as in Berlin, and thus in a way slap down the U.S., England, and to some extent France, he might order a general attack, hoping that the West and the NATO countries will get into a squabble and split. Recently even the General Staff has begun to agree with Khrushchev's concept of delivering a sudden lightning strike, as Hitler used to do. The General Staff believes that there are advantages in such an attack, particularly if a mass missile strike is used, and right now they are preparing strenuously for this. The General Staff considers that if it is impossible to strike at all the targets at once, it is at least possible to hit the United States and England first, cause a split in the NATO alliance, and then pick up the pieces without a general war.

The Western leaders should have a secret meeting, without Khrushchev, and quickly decide what to do. It is urgent that the leaders of all the Western states meet to work out a firm, common line. A summit meeting should not be called; Khrushchev would attend such a meeting with pleasure in order to increase his prestige and authority. He will again try to steer any summit conference in his direction, using his propaganda of peaceful coexistence and disarmament.

The West has already won a small victory in the Berlin matter. Khrushchev began to write notes and talk about new negotiations. But this is an old story. This shows that the Western leaders acted wisely. This is the only correct way. He should be treated the same way in the future. Of course, he will continue to make long speeches about peaceful coexistence and disarmament, he may even lower his voice at the conference in order to be believed. Actually he is holding a rock inside his fist and keeping his powder dry.

I always wonder: Why does the West trust Khrushchev? It is difficult to understand. We in the GRU sit around, talk, and laugh: What fools, they believed us again! Of course, the West must talk with Khrushchev, but it must maintain a firm policy. Do not retreat a single step from a firm policy, let Khrushchev know that the time of listening to his military psychosis has come to an end. Under no circumstances give any concessions to Khrushchev. He only gains time and by this prolongs his existence. If the West again makes even the smallest concession to Khrushchev, he will scream loudly about his power and will proclaim to the entire world: "See how powerful I am," etc.

It is said that Grotewohl, who is often very ill, has spoken out against the signing of the German treaty. Ulbricht, who enjoys no authority with the Germans, is fighting for the "obligatory" signing of the treaty. It is my personal opinion that Khrushchev is seriously considering signing a peace treaty with the German Democratic Republic, but just now he is looking for the best way to do it—so that at first glance it would appear to be acceptable to the West. Later Khrushchev would be the one to gain. Or else he would declare, at the end of the negotiations, that the West is to blame for everything.

Khrushchev has now become confused on the Berlin matter, particularly because he has realized that the West is firm there. He would like to pursue a hard policy and rattle his saber, but our country suffers from a great many shortages and difficulties which must be eliminated before the West is to be frightened further. Khrushchev will not scream so loudly if he feels that the West is holding a hard line in all directions.

When Khrushchev heard the categorical statements made about Berlin by Kennedy, Macmillan, De Gaulle, Adenauer, and Strauss, his reaction was the same as it was in 1961—he did not like it. He did not expect the Western powers to take such a firm stand and to undertake all possible measures in retaliation. The Soviet government and Khrushchev specifically expected the West to react in the following, unusual manner: ". . . let's wait a bit, in addition to everything else they have plenty of missiles, we really have no basis to start hostilities because of Germany. . . ." Khrushchev and his close associates expected everything to go according to plan, but it did not happen that way. This was well done by the Western states.

In 1961 the Soviet government was very unpleasantly surprised by the publication of Mr. Kennedy's statement regarding the three-billion-dollar increase in the military budget. This made a very strong impression. Good for him! That kicked them in the teeth! The Soviet High Command, moreover, is certain that the Western powers have still *other* secret funds (the Soviet Army has always had such funds) so they were sure that the budget was actually increased not by three but by six or nine billion dollars.

Our General Staff also knows that our nuclear weapons and plants are poorly hidden and camouflaged. The General Staff does not want a large-scale nuclear war, but it sometimes supports Khrushchev simply to please him, to curry his favor.

Our leaders proclaim loudly that our equipment is better, that we have more weapons in our arsenals, and that everything in the West is inferior. If this is indeed so, why do not the Western governments take urgent measures to improve their defense and increase their military forces? That is the elementary dialectic of survival. After all, they are responsible for the lives of their people! Every medium must be put to use—newspapers, radio, television; it must be demonstrated to the world where is truth and where is falsehood. It is Khrushchev, the Central Committee CPSU, and the Soviet government, together with the General

Staff, who are responsible for the continuation of the cold war.

There is no need to listen to Khrushchev any longer. It is enough. There is also nothing to be afraid of. His speeches are all the same, there is nothing new in any of them: "We are armed to the teeth, we have plenty of everything, life here is wonderful, I will punch the West in the nose so hard that it will fall apart. . . ." This is the essence of all his speeches.

The General Staff studies each of his speeches as part of its Party-political training. But one reads the beginning and the end and that is clear enough without having to read the whole thing. He is screaming about peace, and we in the GRU train hundreds of agents and saboteurs of all types and dispatch them daily to the west.

When I was in our embassy in London I heard many comments on Kennedy's speech. It was excellent. Everyone criticized Khrushchev, including the GRU and KGB *rezidents:* "There is no reason to be surprised. Kennedy's speech is the answer to Khrushchev's saber rattling."

In our embassy in London there was a very strong reaction to Mr. Kennedy's address and to the speech made by Nixon. Those were very good and wise words.

At the embassy, TASS intercepts and prints all communications which do not find their way into the Soviet press. This is done for all the ambassadors, ministers, and deputy ministers. In the GRU they are read by everyone down to and including the chief of a directorate. This is how they learn about everything that goes on in the world but does not get into their press.

At the embassy I saw a short comment on Mr. Kennedy's speech. The speech was called the militant speech of the President of the United States. That is what was said officially. The TASS reports, however, contain the entire speech, point by point: first, second, third. First, Kennedy's reference to the increase in the budget, next, the increase in the strength of the armed forces, in connection with the new Army draft, then the new specific categories of naval aviators, etc. If necessary, the increases must be even greater.

De Gaulle is a clever man, so is Adenauer. They brought a new element into politics. Why is this bald devil of ours allowed to do what he pleases? Why do the Western powers not call a conference and tell Khrushchev: "You scoundrel, you announced that you wanted to sign a separate peace treaty with Germany, but you have forgotten, we fought with you, fed you, gave you weapons, machinery, etc. If the Soviet Army did not have American Studebakers during the war, the entire artillery, of all calibers, would have been stuck in the mud of your impassable roads; and now you arbitrarily want to take the whole world and make it serve you"? The best way to handle Khrushchev is to throw him off balance—here, there, everywhere, by propaganda, and by actual deeds. Training is going on right now to prepare our troops somehow for combat readiness, to raise their combat spirit, train them better, and equip them better so that they will be ready for any emergency. At the present time there is no assurance that they are ready.

The essence of Khrushchev's policy is to frighten the whole world with his missiles. As soon as a problem arises, or a hot spot develops, Khrushchev immediately begins to talk about missiles.

Volodya Khoroshilov came home on leave. He is chief of the artillery staff of the tank army in Dresden under General Kupin. He was called back to duty, however, two weeks ahead of time. Before his departure we went to a restaurant for dinner and he told me: "As soon as the treaty with Germany is signed, an alert will be declared immediately, and the troops in East Germany will occupy all the control points and will take over their defense and support. Our troops will stand by on alert, but they will not occupy these routes immediately because this might be considered a provocation. We will simply say, 'Please, Americans, British, and French, go to Berlin, but you must request permission from East Germany.' If the Americans, British, and French do not want to confer with the Germans and try to use force, the Germans will open fire. Of course, the Germans do not have enough strength, and then our tanks will move directly into Berlin." I heard this from many officers, specifically from General Pozovnyy, and also from Fedorov and Varentsov. Varentsov, however, added, "We are taking a risk, a big risk."

In 1961, when Khrushchev decided to resolve the Berlin question, the General Staff, GRU, and KGB planned in advance not one but several provocations in order to feel out the Western powers and NATO. It was already planned to have one tank brigade standing by for an attack. If the Western powers knocked out this brigade, another one would be sent in, and then the second echelon would commence action. This echelon was brought to combat readiness on the border in the U.S.S.R. as well as in Czechoslovakia and Poland. That is the truth.

The NATO countries should give particular attention to antitank weapons. Why? Because East Germany has two tank armies in full readiness, this is in addition to the tank armies which are part of the second echelon located on the territories of the U.S.S.R., Czechoslovakia, and Poland.

Khrushchev personally attaches a great deal of importance to tank troops, especially in the fight for Berlin. These tank armies are equipped with guns and missiles which are mounted on the tanks, as well as with the usual machine guns and other automatic weapons.

So much importance is attached to tanks in connection with the Berlin crisis that controversies have already broken out in the General Staff regarding finances. They are afraid that too much money has been allotted for the tank troops and that there will not be enough for missiles, electronics, and other types of equipment.

CHAPTER V

Khrushchev's Army

INTRODUCTION

THE years 1960 to 1962 spelled crisis to a great number of professional Soviet officers. There was professional crisis, in the beginnings of an unprecedented military debate on the whole nature of the Soviet war machine. There was personal crisis, with the wholesale transfers of officers in the higher ranks and a gathering wave of forced retirements and replacements. There was political crisis, as the Soviet armed forces strained under the tight control of a Party politician whose flair for international military risk-taking was matched by the erratic nature of his domestic military decisions.

In January 1960, Nikita Khrushchev made his famous speech to the Supreme Soviet on the Soviet military posture. He reminded his audience, and his generals, that nuclear warfare in the missile age called for a new set of strategic plans and postulates. By Khrushchev's lights, the U.S.S.R. was strong enough to rely on its own nuclear might as a deterrent to any "imperialist aggression." "Firepower for manpower" ran the slogan. Given the new rules of nuclear warfare, Khrushchev went on, the Soviet Army no longer needed such heavy ground forces. The Premier and First Secretary accordingly proposed a reduction in strength amounting to one third of his military manpower.

What might be facetiously called Khrushchev's "more rumble for a ruble" policy was a direct parallel to similar attempts in the United States over the preceding fifteen years to cut mass military strength in favor of "more bang for a buck." The policy arose not only from Khrushchev's new look at Soviet strategy, but from his desperate efforts to stretch the resources of the Soviet Union, which were looking less and less inexhaustible, so he could pay for the expensive new missiles he kept brandishing, without skimping on the industrial expansion he kept promising. The announcement of this enforced demobilization particularly disturbed the Soviet generals, however, because it came at a time when the Army's very position in Soviet society, as well as its modern military concepts, was in a state of confusion.

Historically, a Soviet general's billet has never been noted for its job security, although the fringe benefits, in season, can be impressive. The collective mind of the Soviet General Staff—and there is one, with full consciousness of its own and the national tradition—has never forgotten the bloodbath of the late thirties, when Stalin virtually wiped out the higher echelons of the officer corps. Executions extended into the thousands, and there are few Soviet historians today who would defend any of them. The greatest strategist of the Soviet Union, Marshal Mikhail Tukhachevskiy, was shot in 1937 (along with his family) for allegedly plotting with the Germans. (Ironically it was Tukhachevskiy who kept warning Stalin about Hitler's military menace.) He was finally rehabilitated, by Khrushchev, and a two-volume edition of his works was published in Moscow in 1963.

The thought of Tukhachevskiy, Marshal Vasiliy Blyukher, and thousands less well known was not far from the average Soviet officer's mind after the regime's disgrace of Marshal Zhukov in 1957.[1] Under the umbrella of Zhukov's personal power, the post-Stalin Army had freed itself of Communist Party control to a degree previously unheard of. With Zhukov's removal, the Party bosses moved back into the Defense Ministry and their control apparatus had Khrushchev's name on it. By the spring of 1960 only two marshals were left on the active list who had *not* worked with Khrushchev in World War II, either at Stalingrad or on the Ukrainian front. Those two were Konev and Sokolovskiy; and Konev, at least, had temporarily bought favor with his two-page denunciation of

---

1 With Penkovskiy the memory of the old purges was particularly relevant. His uncle, the general, had been arrested in 1937 and spent two years in prison. He was lucky to have escaped alive.

Zhukov in *Pravda* three years before. They were both retired by the end of the year.

Khrushchev's drive to control the military was neither singular nor sinister, taken in its Soviet context. Every Soviet leader is put willy-nilly in the position of the juggler trying to balance three rusty balls in the air: the Army, the managerial leadership, and the Party—with the KGB, one might add, acting as referee. These are the time-honored components of the Soviet power structure. And, although the Soviet regime can increasingly be influenced by popular stirrings, the interplay of these three major forces remains the closest approximation of a democratic check-and-balance system which the Soviet society possesses. As long as a regime balances the three balls skillfully, plays them off against each other, and—above all—keeps them in the air, the regime is in good shape. If one of the balls drops out of sight, watch out. That is exactly what had been happening with the Army in the late fifties, and Khrushchev was out to restore the balance.

The two great domestic enemies of the professional soldier are politicians and budget cuts. When the budget cuts are accompanied by heavier political control, they are all the more painful. With the political control dominated by a mercurial amateur strategist who made decisions only fitfully but concentrated all power in his hands, the generals' resentment was bound to grow.

By the summer of 1961, with the Berlin pot boiling over and plans made for possible ground action in Europe, Khrushchev had frozen his 1960 demobilization project. As we see in the Papers, Penkovskiy thought they were a fraud anyway. But Khrushchev had meanwhile compounded the confusion among the generals by encouraging a semipublic debate on the new shape of the Soviet military machine. The debate was long overdue. It was essentially the same argument about deterrents and "first-strike" philosophies, mass retaliation versus the use of conventional armaments, which had raged in the U.S. years before. Because of the restrictions of the Stalin era, however, the Soviet strategists had not previously been allowed a forum to discuss the implications of their unprecedented new weapons.

The Soviet debate was something of a three-cornered battle. There were the "traditionalists" and the "modernists" within the Soviet General Staff. Then there was Khrushchev. A more headlong "modernist" than any of the generals, he was trying at the same time to keep the armed forces under the Party's thumb. In his recent book *Soviet Strategy at the Crossroads,*[2] Thomas W. Wolfe neatly summed up the problem:

". . . the debate . . . centered essentially on efforts of the political leadership, Khrushchev himself being deeply involved, to reorient Soviet military doctrine and forces in a direction considered more suitable for the needs of the nuclear-missile age. These efforts have met with varying degrees of resistance and dissent from some quarters of the military, perhaps with tacit backing among other elements of the Party-state bureaucracy whose interests were engaged in one way or another."

The outward sign of the great military debate was the 1962 publication of the journal *Military Strategy,* a collection of articles by Marshal Sokolovskiy and others, which also appeared a year later in a second edition with some meticulous revisions. This book, as Wolfe labels it, was "the most ambitious treatment of doctrine and strategy attempted in the Soviet Union in many years."

Although the Sokolovskiy articles wavered between the modernist and traditionalist approaches, they tended to favor the former. Sokolovskiy and his co-authors cover such topics as the dangers of escalating local wars, the use of nuclear power as a deterrent force, and the possible necessity of a nuclear first-strike theory, in case war threatened. Among American military commentators, these themes have long been familiar. But they were a novelty in the Soviet Union, where the regime likes to keep its military discussions intensely private.

Behind these published observations was a much more significant document, with a much more limited readership. The "Special Collection of Military Thought" was published in Moscow in 1960 as a result of Khrushchev's new look at military thinking. It was given a top-secret classification, its distribution limited to division commanders and above. Khrushchev had encouraged some of the younger generals to explore the possibilities of a blitzkrieg nuclear war, based on the premises that conventional warfare is hopelessly outmoded. The "Special Collection" was the result of their ponderings. (The Sokolovskiy papers and other segments of the military debate were directly inspired by the "Special Collection.")

The boldest of these thinkers, Lieutenant General A. I. Gastilovich, Deputy Commandant of the General Staff Academy, followed Khrushchev's lead in arguing that the Strategic Rocket Forces were now the main branch of the Soviet military. He advocated putting all the Soviet eggs in one big basket of missilery. "We will concede," he wrote, "that nuclear weapons and missiles alter the conditions of war, but having said 'a' we shrink from saying 'b.' After making our bow in the direction of missiles and introducing some minor revisions in the theory of the military art, we still maintain the old positions we held at the end of World War II. We strive without success to fit missile-nuclear weapons into the framework of the familiar needs of our military doctrine, only modernizing it slightly. We forget that this doctrine bases itself on the use of weapons not comparable with contemporary weapons."

The older marshals liked this not a bit. They pointed out to Khrushchev that the NATO countries were still expanding their armament (this was, of course, in 1960 and 1961.) Many of them were naturally conservative. An old artilleryman still likes to see battles in terms of howitzers, and old airmen are as dedicated to their obsolescent bombers as cavalrymen were to their horses. "Of course we must be interested in missiles," Varentsov used to say, "but we must not ignore conventional artillery, our old mother cannon."

Also, Khrushchev's obvious sponsorship of the modernist views in the "Special Collection" added a disturbing new dimension to their natural fears about new weaponry. As Penkovskiy notes in the Papers, some of the authors of the "Special Collection" went beyond the deterrent philosophy which Khrushchev publicly advocated. They pushed for a first-strike stance which was the next thing to preventive war. The older generals were not especially pro-American. But they were prudent men. And they were painfully aware that the Soviet armed forces were being moved to a cataclysmic first-strike mentality, when they lacked the weapons to carry it through.

Penkovskiy shared their qualms, as he shared their confidences. In 1961, when he himself first read the "Special Collection," it looked ominously as if the Soviet Union was being committed to a dangerous reflex principle of "strike first and ask questions after fallout." Now, as then, it remains a hair-raising prospect, completely out of line with the peaceful image which the Soviet public-relations machine continually propagates—and hopelessly compromising a nation whose people were then, as now, tired of war.

Penkovskiy was horrified when he reflected on these documents and their meaning. He was well aware of Khrushchev's capricious command qualities, which sometimes drove Varentsov and the other generals to despair. Now he had the added thought that the awful weapons Khrushchev was blustering with would be mobilized in a first-strike posture, leading ultimately to preventive war. Penkovskiy echoed the private opinions of Varentsov and other generals in holding that such "adventurism" would half-wittingly plunge the world into a war of thermonuclear extermination, a war which everybody would lose. Within the Soviet Army, Khrushchev's almost casual displays of brinkmanship were regarded as reckless to the point of folly. The First Secretary of the Party was not only committing the cardinal military sin of threatining a power he did not possess, but he was playing a gambler's game of diplomacy in an awesome new dimension of war.

As an intelligence officer with more than the average knowledge of the West's plans and people, Penkovskiy had long felt sure that aggression would not come on the Soviet Union from that quarter. He was less and less confident of his own leader's prudence on this score. And in 1961, we must remember, there was little sign that Khrushchev's reign could be overthrown three years later, or ever.

There is no doubt that this fear and confusion among his own officer friends helped form Colonel Penkovskiy's decision to work against his government. In the following passages, and elsewhere in the Papers, he constantly harps on the dictator's shabby treatment of a loyal officer class. As a military technician he had no objection to a modernization of forces. On the contrary, his own technological aptitudes fitted him remarkably well for the new nuclear-age Army. But Penkovskiy was bitterly critical of the brutal way in which career officers were thrown out of the service, with the scantiest of pensions and scanty prospects of finding another honorable, useful career outside the Army. This he blamed on Khrushchev, as did most of his friends. "His control of the Army is strong," Penkovskiy writes sadly in the Papers. "As a General Staff colonel, I hate to write this."

Penkovskiy's indignation expressed itself in a zealot's direct logic: if Khrushchev was betraying the Army, he would betray Khrushchev. This was no small part of his rationale for working with outside powers in order to bring down the regime he hated in his country. After all, Lenin had once invoked the Germans to war against the czar. Again, there emerges the Russian distinction between the *narod* and the *nachalstvo,* the people and the regime. If this distinction is hard for some Americans to comprehend, it is almost impossible for us to understand the kind of regime the Soviet people have always lived under— and the detached, relatively helpless feeling of a Soviet subject. In the U.S. the citizen thinks of the government as "we"; in Russia it has always been "they."

When the news of Penkovskiy's arrest and trial broke in the West, some newspaper articles suggested that he might have been part of a half-formed conspiracy against Khrushchev among high-ranking Soviet Army officers. The word "conspiracy" is overstatement. It is doubtful that Penkovskiy ever thought of recruiting any co-plotters in his lonely espionage activity. But there was a certain implicit silent conspiracy against the regime in the form of many like-minded protestors whose public silence was governed by their inability to communicate with one another. It is certain, as the Papers tell us, that Penkovskiy's hatred of the Khrushchev regime mirrored a large gathering resentment among the Soviet generals.

We know now that this resentment in the Army contributed heavily to Khrushchev's eventual ouster. As early as October 1961, Marshal Malinovskiy was at least implicitly criticizing Khrushchev's military policies. By the time the dam broke, in October 1964, Khrushchev's "more rumble for a ruble" policies had been put in the background. The huge conventional forces remained, with more than a little restored caution about the use of missiles and the advisability of a pre-emptive first strike.

By the early part of 1965, the generals had rushed into print with harsh words about Khrushchev's governance, as well as his military policies. "Bungling and superficial concepts," Marshal Zakharov, the new Soviet Chief of Staff, wrote in *Red Star*. It was dangerous to base a whole defense policy on the ICBM. "The Soviet Union," General Shtemenko wrote in February, "is prepared to face the fact that a war could last a long time." The first-strike philosophy, therefore, was not the only military answer. As another leading article in *Red Star* had it, in January 1965, the armed forces had been victimized by "bird-brained planning."

Their language was beginning to send like Penkovskiy's.

PENKOVSKIY'S TEXT

On Victory Day, May 9, 1961, Khrushchev promoted 372 marshals and generals to their next respective ranks. All those promoted to the rank of marshal and higher were announced in the newspapers, but those promoted to various grades of general were not. These latter promotions were classified as secret. Sixty generals were promoted to full general, lieutenant general, and major general. Over three hundred colonels were promoted to the rank of brigadier general. Sergey Sergeyevich Varentsov was promoted (at last) to the rank of Chief Marshal of Artillery. My relative Valentin Antonovich Penkovskiy was made a full general.

Among the GRU personnel, eleven men were given generals' ranks. Korenevskiy, Chief of the Information Directorate, is now a major general; his deputy, Kholoptsev, is also a major general; the other nine were promoted to brigadier general. Among those were: Chizhov, Deputy Chief of the 3rd Directorate; Mayorov, Secretary of the Party Committee of the Military Diplomatic Academy; Leontyev, who is now in Germany; V. I. Sudin (I believe

3. Ко дни победы /9 мая/ Председатель Совмина СССР - Хрущев присвоил
    372 первичных и последующих маршальских и генеральских званий.
    Маршальские звания были опубликованы в газетах. Генеральские - нет.
    Что присвоение новых званий засекречено.

he is going to Turkey soon), Patrikeyev, Vnukovskiy, and others.

This mass (and secret) promotion to generals' ranks explains much. This is how our "peacemaker" Khrushchev fights for peace, this is how he is disarming. His military "kitchen" is working at full speed.

There was another reason for the mass promotions—morale and discipline in the armed forces have fallen very low. They are too low for some cheap promotions to fix. It was not just the demobilization. It was Khrushchev's political intrigues.

On January 14, 1960 when Khrushchev made the announcement about demobilization, he actually had no thought of demobilizing either soldiers or officers. He simply carried out a self-styled purge, and saw to it that the first personnel dismissed were those who were either sick, old, or insufficiently trusted. But then many good officers followed, booted out for no clear reason. This was his self-styled purge of the armed forces of the Soviet Union.

The entire Army is in a state of turmoil; everyone in the Army recalls Stalin and says that under Stalin things were better, that is, Stalin never insulted the Army, but this scoundrel has dismissed good officers from the Army. And now this same scoundrel lifts his goblet high and drinks a toast, saying, "I love our Army." The officers say to themselves, "You scoundrel, right now you are drinking a toast to my health, and tomorrow I must die for you. If I do stay alive, then two years from now you will throw me out again."

When Khrushchev made a speech at the Military Academy graduation, he announced that we were slowing down demobilization and that the order had gone out to the military commissariats to recall demobilized officers, particularly the technical personnel. To this the officers answered—among themselves, of course: "Sure, now we are needed again because we have Berlin, Germany, Cuba. We may have to shed our blood again. When you dismissed us before, you did not even give us a decent pension, you just got rid of us because it was economically expedient. You gave 200 rubles to the officers and 300 rubles to generals —ten rubles, or one gold piece a day, that is your price for a general—and with this money I am supposed to live and support a family, etc.[1] You took away all our privileges after we had spent our entire life in the service."

The situation in the Army is bad, as bad as it is in the country. This old man Khrushchev wants to create marvels during his lifetime in order, perhaps, to get a golden bust or monument erected to himself while he is still alive. He is muddying the waters. He is the instigator, the inspirer, the creator. Everyone says that what he is doing is dirty and smacks of intrigue. If there were no Khrushchev, if he were to die or be killed, the situation in the country would undergo a very great change. He knows that he is old, but still he lies and lies and lies. He knows that his days are numbered, but he still acts like a maniac. Probably his age is making him senile. His thinking at the present time is all along in one direction to make all kinds of adventures. His control of the Army is strong, however. As a General Staff colonel, I hate to write this.

Here are some notes on our political direction. If I have time, I will discuss in detail the 1st Military Section in the Administrative Organs Department of the Central Committee CPSU, as well as the Chief Political Directorate of the Ministry of Defense with the status of a Central Committee's section. There is also a Supreme Military Council directly under the Presidium of the Central Committee CPSU, chaired by Khrushchev and in his absence by Kozlov or Mikoyan. There are always a few members of the Presidium of the Central Committee CPSU in attendance at the meetings of the Supreme Military Council. The Ministers of Defense and the commanders in chief of the service arms are automatically members of the council. Minister Malinovskiy is in this case just an ordinary member of this council.

Each council member had the right to state his views at meetings of the council on questions concerning his particular field of work. Each commander in chief speaks for his own arm of the service and presents his problems to the council members for their decision. In most cases Malinovskiy just sits there and says nothing. A very dull figure indeed! All the commanders in chief accept the orders of Khrushchev or of other members of the Presidi-

---

1 The rubles mentioned here are obviously new rubles, the inflated official value of which is approximately one dollar.

um because they consider them more authoritative than Minister Malinovskiy.

As a rule, the Supreme Military Council meets at definite intervals, but in cases of some extraordinary events its meetings may be called more frequently. The presence of all the commanders is not compulsory in cases in which the problems on the agenda concern certain specific arms of troops or specific types of weapons. None of the commanders in chief may have direct contact with any of the plants or factories doing defense work. All contacts and all instructions to civilian enterprises engaged in defense work and the production of weapons are effected through certain sections and directorates of the Central Committee CPSU and the Council of Ministers. From there directives are issued through the appropriate ministry to the specific plant or factory.

Each member of the Central Committee Presidium has under his control five or six ministries and state committees whose work he directs. And the ministers shake with fear before these members of the Central Committee Presidium.

Despite the fact that he is the President (Chairman of the Presidium of the Supreme Soviet of the U.S.S.R.), Brezhnev,[2] as a member of the Central Committee Presidium, is still responsible for many problems of defense and armament.

In case of disagreements between the Ministry of Defense and civilian ministries on problems of military deliveries or weapon production, breakdown of a plan, shortage of funds, etc., the Supreme Military Council and the Central Committee CPSU decide. Once during Khrushchev's absence Marshal Biryuzov raised the question of additional funds for missile tests in a council meeting. Suslov and Mikoyan, who were present at the meeting, failed to solve the problem. Varentsov said afterward: "They started beating around the bush and kept talking, but never reached a decision. If Stalin were alive, he would have given the word and the whole thing would have been resolved right then and there, but now it's a big mess, just like a *kolkhoz* meeting. There is no order."

---

[2] When Brezhnev became First Secretary of the CPSU in October 1964, he was replaced as President by Anastas Mikoyan.

The armed forces are also controlled by the Central Committee CPSU through the political organs. There is a Political Directorate in each Chief Directorate of the Ministry of Defense and in each military district. Below this level come political sections and Party organizations. All of them get direction from the central point, the Central Committee CPSU.

Political workers are the eyes and ears of the Army— or, at least, the Party's eyes and ears in the Army. I discussed this subject before. I myself was a political worker for a long time. But Zhukov was right in decreasing the political workers' importance. He understood the soldier's soul. He wanted to give the soldiers something besides political lectures and political information. Khrushchev was scared when Zhukov cut down the political aspect. He has now established a still greater political control. More hours have been allocated for political study and other kinds of propaganda—in order to distract the soldier from other thoughts. Nobody believes in Khrushchev's military policy. Of course, men go back and serve. One must feed his family. There is no other way in our country. But the Army's mood is bad. Khrushchev knows about this mood, and that is what he is so afraid of, afraid that if a major war starts, soldiers will start running. They will not fight for him. This is why he prefers all sorts of minor clashes at the present time

I remember that Varentsov once told me a very interesting story about two officers, a major and a lieutenant colonel, who were discharged from the Army and had no jobs. Both were engineers and they had been fine officers in the Soviet Army. They went to see Patriarch Aleksiy and told him they wanted to become priests. Patriarch Aleksiy, who has a direct line to the Kremlin, called Zhukov and told him: "Comrade Marshal, I have here with me two officers who want to become priests." Zhukov answered: "Send them to me, and thank you for letting me know about this." This happened a year before Zhukov's trip to Yugoslavia.

Zhukov saw the two officers personally. They told him the whole story, and Zhukov reinstated them in the Army. After that, Zhukov wrote a detailed report to the Central Committee and asked that the two officers not be arrested and that no drastic action be taken against them. For there might be other cases like this one and after all they were good officers. The officers stated that in a legal sense they had not done anything wrong because they knew that according to the Soviet law and the Constitution all clergymen in the Soviet Union are Communists and work either under the Central Committee CPSU or in the KGB. Why, then, could they not be priests? Besides, there is a special committee under the Council of Ministers of the U.S.S.R. which is responsible for all church affairs—a state institution. Everybody in Moscow was talking about this case.

During the time when Khrushchev denounced the personality cult and had the intra-Party struggle with the Molotov-Kaganovich-Malenkov group, Marshals Timoshenko, Rokossovskiy, and Konev had many points of disagreement with Khrushchev, while they often agreed with Molotov, Malenkov, and Kaganovich. In many cases Voroshilov, too, was in disagreement with Khrushchev, as was Pervukhin. But because all these leaders were quite popular and well known among the Soviet people, Khrushchev was afraid to have them arrested or take other strong measures against them. He just said: "Let them stay; the time will come when I can get rid of them."

Of course, he did get rid of Zhukov in the end. More on this. Georgiy Konstantinovich Zhukov is loved by all Soviet officers and soldiers as well as by the entire population. Our people call him "today's Suvorov" and "the military genius of our time."

At first Khrushchev bestowed on Zhukov the honors which he fully deserved. Zhukov was both Minister of Defense and a member of the Presidium of the Central Committee CPSU. Zhukov helped Khrushchev to consolidate full power in his hands at the time of the struggle against the anti-Party group. He supported Khrushchev. Later Khrushchev got scared of Zhukov. When Zhukov was still in power, Khrushchev began to reduce the supplementary pay for officers in order to save money for the production of armament. Zhukov opposed this and declared: "I do not want my officers to become beggars. If they become beggars, they will not fight; indeed, nobody will be able to recognize them as officers. An officer must be well fed and be able to provide more or less adequate support for his family." Zhukov hated Marshal Bulganin intensely. When Zhukov was Commander of the Sverdlovsk Military District, Bulganin telephoned him and said,

"This is Marshal Bulganin speaking." Zhukov answered, "I do not know any such marshal," and hung up.

Zhukov was for centralization of authority in the Army. He also reduced the time used for political indoctrination. As I said, he tried to lower the political workers to the second echelon. All these things, however, were not the main reason for Khrushchev's fear. A case in point: General Shtemenko, who at that time was Chief of the GRU, had organized a sabotage school near Moscow, where about two hundred inveterate cutthroats were being trained as saboteur agents and terrorists. Zhukov knew about this school, but he had not reported its existence to Khrushchev. At least this is what Khrushchev claimed. Actually I think this school had been in existence for years. Besides, Zhukov had once stated, "The Army will always follow me." All these things scared Khrushchev, and he decided to get rid of Zhukov. This question was decided secretly while Zhukov was in Yugoslavia.

When Zhukov returned from Yugoslavia, it was announced to him right at the airport that he had been removed from his post of Minister of Defense. After this, large meetings of Party activists were held in all cities, and Zhukov's "cult of personality" was discredited on Khrushchev's orders. A large meeting of the Moscow party *aktiv* was held which I myself attended. It was held in St. George's Hall of the Grand Kremlin Palace. It began with a speech by Khrushchev, who then left the hall. Next came a speech delivered by a minister, who also left the hall several times. Then came the regular propaganda speeches directed against Zhukov. Finally the minister returned once more and apologized for leaving the hall so many times but said that he had been called to the government.

In his speech at the meeting in the Kremlin, Khrushchev tried to prove that Zhukov was creating a new cult of personality, was displaying some Napoleonic ways, and was underestimating the role of the Party organs in the armed forces. As an example of Zhukov's cult of personality, Khrushchev cited the fact that there was a large picture of Zhukov on a white horse hanging on the wall at the Soviet Army Club. "What else can it be called but Zhukov's cult of personality?" But when Khrushchev had seen this picture before, he had always admired it, saying: "A fine picture! Zhukov is our hero and he has earned this honor!"

That is how this scoundrel Khrushchev operates. When he needed Zhukov, he called him a hero, but as soon as he felt that full power was in his own hands, he decided to get rid of this popular hero. Zhukov's cult of personality really scared him. But what about the cult of personality he has created for himself? There is not a word about it from him! Many people have already lost their heads for criticizing Khrushchev's cult of personality. So, here is truth for you, here are Lenin's standards of Party life! My poor Russian people!

Khrushchev criticized Zhukov also for his alleged attempt to fill government civilian posts with military personnel. Zhukov, ostensibly, had proposed that Serov be removed from the post of KGB Chairman, to be replaced by Marshal Konev. Khrushchev talked about this at the meeting of the *aktiv* of the Moscow Military District held on October 24 or 25. In the same speech Khrushchev accused Zhukov of creating the sabotage school, etc. Actually the school had existed long before Zhukov's time, and it exists now, and continues to train assassins for Khrushchev's purposes. This, of course, is all right! This is permissible! How I would like to see these cutthroats attack Khrushchev and the Presidium one fine day.

Soon after Zhukov's removal by a special decree of the Council of Ministers he was permitted to retire from service. He was given a pension of 5500 old rubles a month.[3]

Zhukov has a nice apartment, on Granovskiy Street, house no. 3, but he spends most of his time at his country house near Moscow, on the Rublevskoye Highway.

Later, in 1961, during the Berlin crisis Khrushchev proposed that Zhukov, Sokolovskiy, and Konev, to prove their loyalty to the Party and the country, return to active work with him. Sokolovskiy and Konev agreed, but Zhukov refused although he is still in good physical condition and could still do some work.

See what a scoundrel Khrushchev is! When Zhukov was needed, he gave him a fourth star of Hero of the Soviet Union. Then he dismissed him. Then for propaganda pur-

---

[3] This was not a large sum of money. A good pair of shoes, for instance, cost 400 rubles at that time.

poses he wanted to use Zhukov once more. Zhukov did the right thing by refusing.

The disagreement between Marshals Timoshenko, Konev, Rokossovskiy and others on one side and Khrushchev on the other began after Zhukov was removed from his duties. Another source of friction: Khrushchev had reduced their pay and discontinued payments of the additional money which they and other officers of the Soviet Army had been getting; he had also reduced generals' and officers' retirement pay. In addition, the marshals and generals mentioned above did not agree with Khrushchev's policy of cutting the Air Force, the ground forces, and other forces—including the Navy—in favor of missile armament.

In 1960 Sokolovskiy went to see Khrushchev and told him: "Just look at the military forces which are needed, and the money allocated for them. Under these conditions I cannot provide adequate defense for the country. Look how many enemy bases surround our country. I cannot maintain the strength of the troops at the level at which it should be especially in case of an enemy attack." Khrushchev answered him: "If that is what you think, then get out of here."

After that, Khrushchev recalled Zakharov from East Germany and appointed him Chief of the General Staff in place of Sokolovskiy. He also recalled Chuykov from Kiev, where he was Commander of the Kiev Military District; Grechko by that time was already in Moscow. Sokolovskiy, however, had prestige among the generals and within the Army as a whole. Khrushchev therefore had to play his game carefully, removing his adversaries one by one, until finally he had got what he wanted. He defeated the anti-Party group, then fired Zhukov, and also got rid of the unwanted marshals, moving those who disagreed with his policies to less important posts.

At the present time Khrushchev holds three offices: one at the Central Committee, one in the Kremlin (as Chairman of the Council of Ministers), and one at the Ministry of Defense.

Although it is amusing, Khrushchev is called "Supreme Commander in Chief." The Supreme Military Council chaired by him often acts as substitute for the Minister of Defense, making decisions concerning the least important matters. Often Khrushchev, bypassing the minister, issues directions to Vershinin, Moskalenko, Biryuzov, and others.

After Khrushchev's purge of the Army, many generals died from various illnesses, especially from heart attacks and nervous breakdowns. Those deaths that have been announced in the newspapers are just a few. Many took their own lives. A small number resigned themselves to their new status and tried to start a new life outside the Army. For example, one former general started growing strawberries, and his wife sold them at the market. The general was helped by a peasant from a *kolkhoz,* who was sick. So what happened? The general was accused of engaging in private enterprise activities and exploitation of another person's work; he was expelled from the Party and his pension was taken away. And all this after he had served more than thirty years in the Army and had participated in two wars. This is how Khrushchev cares for his people!

All officers, especially marshals and generals, were quite unhappy when Khrushchev cut their pay and took away many of the privileges which they had enjoyed under Stalin. The Chief of the General Staff is now paid a monthly salary of 2000 rubles; the commanders in chief of arms of troops, like Biryuzov, are paid 1800 rubles per month; Varentsov is paid 1200 rubles per month. This is the way Khrushchev is saving money for missiles. When cutting pay and other material advantages, Khrushchev said: "They have gotten fat! We cannot and must not raise such intelligentsia and capitalists." Generals' and officers' pensions were reduced by two to two and a half times. Because no other sources of income are available for these people in the Soviet Union, it is difficult even to make ends meet on this pension.

Many marshals were against this policy of Khrushchev's; but it is all carried out under the guise of reorganization of the armed forces, economy, etc. Marshals Konev, Sokolovskiy, and Timoshenko disagreed with Khrushchev and the dull-witted Malinovskiy on all questions dealing with the reorganization of the armed forces and especially on Khrushchev's policy in regard to the Army personnel. "The reductions among the middle-level Army officers will reduce them to a state of pitiful vegetation," they said.

At first the dismissed marshals and generals were not invited anywhere. Later Khrushchev began to send invitations to them to attend all sorts of receptions, banquets, conferences. Eventually some were invited to return to active service. Some of the marshals and generals submitted to Khrushchev and returned to the service. Others went to work for Khrushchev out of fear for their own fate. Besides, it must be remembered that all of them have families who have to be fed and clothed.

Discontent within the Army still continues, especially in connection with Khrushchev's reorganization of the armed forces and the reduction of pay. Here are some of the details.

As of January 1960, all previously established pensions for retired generals and officers of the Soviet Army were abolished. In the past, Soviet Army generals' and officers' retirement pay was 90 to 100 per cent of their regular pay when on active duty. Now the "ceiling" for colonels is 2000 rubles.[4] For generals it is 3000 rubles, and at that, only after twenty-five calendar years of active service in the Army. Those with less service than indicated above, according to the new Khrushchev decision, are paid: colonels from 1000 to 1400 rubles, and generals from 2000 to 2500 rubles per month. Because colonels and generals used to get 4500 to 7000 rubles per month while in active service, the difference is quite great. As a result, the mood among the retired is very bad. Everybody keeps his mouth shut. They know that any complaint will result in losing even this pension.

In the past the families of officers and generals who died or were killed in the war received a pension averaging 50 per cent of the salary of the deceased. As of January 1, 1960, even these pensions were cut by more than 50 per cent.

Khrushchev is carrying out a so-called "rejuvenation" of the Army. Large numbers of generals and officers who are not in the best of health or whose record has been marred in some way have been discharged after twenty years of service.

All the money made available as the result of Khrushchev's reorganization—the money saved in personnel,

---

4 Here Penkovskiy reverts to old rubles.

dismissals, reductions in pay and pensions—is used to train new cadres for the missile service and for the production of all types of missiles and *sputniks*. A new Engineering Missile Academy has been created. New technical schools of different specialties have been organized. And new military plants for the production of missiles and missile equipment are being built. They are spending many billions of rubles on the new equipment. An enormous amount of money is also spent on supporting the satellite countries and for other purposes. This is the economic reason for Khrushchev's reduction of the armed forces and its personnel. It was not merely a purge.

MANEUVERS IN OCTOBER

At the beginning of October 1961, the general strategic military exercises will commence. There have never been exercises like these in the history of the Soviet Army. All the staffs of military districts and groups will participate. All rear-area depots, etc., will also participate. That is, absolutely every Soviet military installation will take part in these games. The military establishments will support these maneuvers as if a real war had begun. The military staffs of all the people's democracies will also take part.

These exercises will take place over the entire territory of the Soviet Union and the territory of the people's democracies, with the main strike directed against Germany—on maps, of course. These maneuvers are called strategic because all troop arms of the Soviet Army will participate in them and because they are to be carried out in great depth. The exercises will last about one month.

What is the purpose of these exercises? To take a close look at everything as a whole, to see who is capable of what, who is able to carry out an order for an offensive, for an attack, for defense, etc.; to study staff training on all levels, take a look at the combat readiness of the troops, their co-operation and cohesion—and of course to give them some good training.

These will be almost actual combat exercises, with just one exception: there will be no actual enemy. Everyone understands, of course, that the "probable enemy" is the U.S. Recently included in this category are England,

France, West Germany, all the NATO countries, and, most recently, Japan.

If anything unfortunate occurs in Germany after the signing of the East German peace treaty (which will be signed immediately after the Twenty-second Party Congress), these exercises will have brought everything up to combat readiness and it will then be possible to deliver a strike. This is what Khrushchev is underwriting, under the guise of these maneuvers. He also insures that a peace treaty with East Germany will be signed—if, as Khrushchev says, the NATO countries will swallow this second pill. He considers that they swallowed their first pill on August 13, 1961, when Berlin was closed off and the building of the wall began.

I learned about the Berlin closing four days before the Soviet government actually closed it off.

Why is this done more or less in the open? Because under modern conditions and with modern intelligence it is very difficult to prepare for military operations secretly, or for war. Under the guise of military exercises, Khrushchev is getting everything up to combat readiness. It is even possible that during these military exercises actual hostilities will start.

All of Moscow is now swarming with military representatives of the countries of the people's democracies and various Soviet military commanders. The city is overflowing with the military. The General Staff works night and day. Some of these representatives from people's democracies wear their uniforms, but many wear civilian clothes.

Soviet troop maneuvers will be conducted jointly with the troops of the people's democracies. During maneuvers the divisions of the satellite countries are included in the T/O of the Soviet Army. This is necessary because we still do not trust them; they might turn their guns against the Soviets or run to the West.

The Twenty-second Congress of the CPSU, which opens on October 17, 1961, will be the aggressor-congress. At least that is what it should be called. The congress will be very polemic in tone, and strong propaganda speeches are being readied for it.

Decisive speeches against imperialism and colonialism have the following purposes: to untie our hands with the blessings of the congress from the Soviet Union, from the countries of the people's democracies, and from the Communist Parties of capitalist countries, support the decisions of the Twenty-second Party Congress. In other words, we support the policy of Khrushchev and his government. Then Khrushchev will act resolutely. That is to say: if, after the congress is over, he leads us into war by his policies, he will refer to the general support given these policies by the Soviet population, represented by the delegates at the congress, as well as by all the Communist countries and the world's Communist Parties. Many leaders of Communist Parties in capitalist countries are coming to the Twenty-second Party Congress—some of them illegally, in secret. In this manner, Khrushchev would like to win the support of all the Communist Parties in the world, as well as to learn in advance which way they will turn if his adventure is launched.

It must be noted here that a resolution of the Soviet government and the Central Committee CPSU was adopted not to admit a single foreign delegation into the Soviet Union during the month of October. They will make every effort during this period to have as few foreigners and foreign delegations in the Soviet Union as possible. Active preparations are already going on. The hotels are being cleared of foreigners and rooms readied for the visiting delegates and guests of the congress. Although many foreigners and foreign delegations continue to ask permission to visit the Soviet Union now, we are refusing them under various pretexts.

Our GKKNR specialists are also very busy right now because they are taking an active part in the work of the Twenty-second Party Congress.

All the Communist leaders who have been invited to the congress will remain to celebrate the October Revolution and to view the parade which will be held in Red Square on November 7.

Thorough preparations are already going on to set up a very strict counterintelligence system in Moscow and Moscow *oblast*.

To insure the success of the Twenty-second Party Congress, a great many KGB operational employees have been called back from the various *oblasts* and republics, including those employees in various educational institutions.

Immediately after the Twenty-second Party Congress,

Khrushchev wants to sign the peace treaty with East Germany. At the time of the signing he wants to have all of his armed forces ready to strike if the need arises. This is something which, by the way, he intends to be the first to do. If there is only a local skirmish, he will be ready to repel it, but if things reach a world scale, he feels that he must be absolutely ready to deliver the first strike.

At the present time a third army, the 8th Mechanized Army, is being sent into the territory of the German Democratic Republic. Before this there were only two. This was mentioned by Malinovskiy as he was leaving Varentsov's party before going to Lvov. He said that he must go and take a look at how our 8th Army was preparing to move to Germany. This army is being sent to Germany from the Transcarpathian Military District. It consists of three tank divisions and two motorized divisions. At the same time, six regiments of antiair defense of the V-75 type are being urgently sent to Germany; I do not know where these were previously stationed. The V-75 is a two-stage missile. These are individual regiments in the PVO [antiaircraft defense] system.

A decision has been made to defer the discharges from the Soviet Army of which Khrushchev spoke earlier. If these soldiers and officers are not discharged, troop strength will increase by 400,000. A decision has been made to put off demobilization until spring. This is Khrushchev's policy. If the Western states swallow the second pill, agree to a peace treaty with East Germany, and recognize it, then after this there may be a decision about demobilizing the Army. Not at present.

During the Twenty-second Party Congress, all military units have been instructed to be at combat readiness No. 1. Pozovnyy also told me that the PVO troops have been brought up to combat readiness and are ready to fire at any moment.

The Berlin problem is not on the agenda of the Twenty-second Party Congress. But during the sessions of congresses there are always various secret and so-called "official" meetings, to take advantage of the presence of all the members of the Central Committee even before the congress—to be announced subsequently to the members of the Central Committee CPSU. It may also happen that Khrushchev will be removed. Then there is the third possibility—that Khrushchev will overcome them all, carry through his policy, and run the risk of war.

CIVIL DEFENSE

On August 17, 1961, by a decree of the Central Committee CPSU and the Soviet government, a Civil Defense Command was created. Marshal Chuykov was appointed Chief of the Civil Defense of the Soviet Union, having been relieved of his duties of the Commander of Ground Forces.

A special regulation states that the Civil Defense Command will be directly subordinate to the Minister of Defense. This command was created for a "special period." It has the task of protecting the population from enemy strikes. This special period is set by the Party, the government, and the military command. The term refers to a time in which the Soviet authorities consider that hostilities may commence.

The regulations on Civil Defense list the duties of all the ministries, the vehicle industry, motor transport, railroads; what is expected of the Ministry of Defense, etc. Every government establishment and ministry in its own way takes care of defense and evacuation, procedures within its area of responsibility. These regulations indicate various underground structures, shelters for people, and equipment, etc. Although it is called the Civil Defense Command, Chuykov's title is not Commander but Chief of Civil Defense.

At the present time the post of the Commander of Ground Forces under the Ministry of Defense is vacant, because Chuykov left it. According to Varentsov, it has been suggested that the new commander will be Krylov. He is now Commander of the Moscow Military District. There are rumors that he has refused this new post. For the time being, the duties are being discharged by Zhadov. This man's name used to be Zhidov, but Stalin changed the "i" to an "a," and now he is Zhadov.[5]

The structure of the Civil Defense Command will be as

---

[5] Stalin considered the name "Zhidov" to have a "Jewish" sound to it, while Zhadov was more Russian. The word *zhid* in Russian means "Jew" and is derogatory, among generally anti-Semitic Soviet leaders.

follows: at the top will be the Civil Defense High Command, and in each military district will be subunits. The regulation states that the civil defense subunits must work in very close co-ordination with *oblast, kray, rayon,* and other local party and Soviet organs.[6]

CHEMICAL WARFARE

In preparing for atomic and hydrogen warfare, Khrushchev is also preparing for chemical warfare. There is a special 7th Directorate in the General Staff which is involved in working out methods of chemical and bacteriological warfare. The Chief Chemical Directorate of the Ministry of Defense is also concerned with the problems of chemical and bacteriological warfare. We also have the Voroshilov Military Academy of Chemical Defense, several military-chemical schools and scientific-research institutes and laboratories in the fields of chemistry and bacteriology.

Near Moscow there is a special proving ground for chemical defense. I know a new gas has been invented which is colorless, tasteless, and without odor. The gas is avowed to be very effective and highly toxic. The secret of the gas is not known to me. It has been named "American"; why this name was chosen, I can only guess.

Many places in the country have experimental centers for testing various chemical and bacteriological devices. One such base is in Kaluga. The commanding officer of this base is Nikolay Varentsov, the brother of Sergey Sergeyevich Varentsov.

Near the city of Kalinin, on a small island in the Volga, there is a special bacteriological storage place. Here they keep large containers with bacilli of plagues and other contagious diseases. The entire island is surrounded by barbed wire and is very securely guarded. But my readers must not be under any illusions. This is not the only place where there are such containers. Soviet artillery units all are regularly equipped with chemical-warfare shells. They are at the gun sites, and our artillery is routinely trained

---

[6] It is interesting to note that this new network of civil defense units, under Chuykov's command, was only recently announced officially. U.S. newspapers carried a news item about it on March 17, 1965.

in their use. And let there be no doubt: if hostilities should erupt, the Soviet Army would use chemical weapons against its opponents. The political decision has been made, and our strategic military planners have developed a doctrine which permits the commander in the field to decide whether to use chemical weapons, and when and where.

I recently read an article which wastes no time and minces no words on this subject. It opens with the statement that under modern conditions, highly toxic chemical agents are one of the most powerful means of destroying the enemy. Then the article describes the characteristics of chemical weapons and the principles of using them effectively in combat. There is no mention made of waiting until the enemy uses chemical weapons; there is no reference to the need for a high-level political decision for the use of such weapons. From start to finish the article makes it clear that this decision has been made, that chemical shells and missiles may be considered just ordinary weapons available to the military commander, to be used routinely by him when the situation calls for it. The article specifically states: "The commander of the army (front) makes the decision to use chemical weapons. . . ."

The authors add that one of the most important uses for chemical missiles will be the destruction of the enemy's nuclear-strike capability. Specific mention is made of the "Little John," "Honest John," "Lacrosse," "Corporal," "Redstone," and "Sergeant" units, the width and depth of their dispersed formations under tactical conditions, and their vulnerabilities to the chemical attack. Also American cruise missile and atomic artillery units. The article contains the usual precautions about the necessity of preventing damage to friendly troops, and discusses the operational situations in which chemical weapons could be used to greatest advantage. This is how it concludes:

"The purpose of this article is to present the main fundamental principles of using chemical missiles. Those principles should not, under any circumstances, be considered as firmly established, because they can be defined with greater precision *as practical experience is accumulated*."

Soviet officers generally consider Americans to be extremely lax in matters of training and discipline for defense against chemical attack. I have heard that American soldiers even boast of throwing away their gas masks and other protective equipment and claiming they have lost them. I can hardly believe this, but even if it is only partly true, it is a training deficiency which must be corrected immediately. Such crucial flaws in an enemy's defensive armor are not overlooked by Soviet planners.

THE NEW MILITARY DOCTRINE

In 1958 a seminar-discussion began in the General Staff on problems of military art and a future war. All high-ranking officers, from army commander up, representatives of all arms of troops, participated in these seminars. The seminars were of a secret nature, and the conversations and discussions that took place there must not be revealed to any outsiders. The basic questions discussed were those of a future war and the state of Soviet military art.

By 1959 all the top military brains of the General Staff agreed that Soviet military doctrine needed to be revised. Future strategy must be developed on the basis, first of all, of the availability of nuclear weapons and missiles.

Beginning in 1960, the magazine *Military Thought* started periodic publication of a top secret "Special Collection of Articles." It was devoted to a discussion of the problems of a future war and of the new Soviet military doctrine.

Among the authors of the collection are the Minister of Defense, his deputy, commanders of military districts, senior officers of the General Staff, chiefs of military academies, and the professors and teachers of the higher military educational institutions.

I have had my own interest in the "Special Collection." I have read it from cover to cover, making appropriate notes. I have jotted down some passages as particularly meaningful. The theme for the entire series was set by Lieutenant General Gastilovich in his article "The Theory of Military Art Needs Review" (Special Collection No. 1, 1960). Noting that wars formerly began on the borders of warring countries, where troops were concentrated, he says: "If war starts now, military actions will evolve in a different way because countries have available means of delivering weapons over thousands of kilometers. . . .

"About 100 nuclear charges, exploded in a brief period of time in a highly industrialized country with a territory of about 300–500 thousand square kilometers, will suffice to transform all of its industrial areas and administrative-political centers into a heap of ruins, and the territory into a lifeless desert contaminated with deadly radioactive substances."

This is their premise. Gastilovich concludes his long discussion of warfare under conditions of nuclear armament with an invitation to Soviet military leaders and theoreticians to contribute their thoughts in the form of articles to the "Special Collection." I hope the notes on the "Special Collection" will suffice to give my readers a clear picture of the military doctrine which is evolving in the Soviet Union. It would be more accurate to say this doctrine has already evolved.

One thing must be clearly understood. If someone were to hand to an American general, an English general, and a Soviet general the same set of objective facts and scientific data, with instructions that these facts and data must be accepted as unimpeachable, and an analysis made and conclusions drawn on the basis of them, it is possible that the American and the Englishman would reach similar conclusions—I don't know. But the Soviet general would arrive at conclusions which would be radically different from the other two. This is because, first of all, he begins from a completely different set of basic premises and preconceived ideas, namely, the Marxian concepts of the structure of society and the course of history. Second, the logical process in his mind is totally unlike that of his Western counterparts, because he uses Marxist dialectics, whereas they will use some form of deductive reasoning. Third, a different set of moral laws governs and restricts the behavior of the Soviet. Fourth, the Soviet general's aims will be radically different from those of the American and the Englishman. Here is an example—an article on nuclear/missile armament by Major General of the Engineering-Technical Service M. Goryainov. You will see how he uses American data, taken from open American sources, on the characteristics and effects of nuclear weapons, and you will see that the conclusions he reaches are quite different from those which were reached by the Americans who used the same facts.

Goryainov complains that nuclear weapons are not yet being evaluated properly. He thinks the necessary reshaping of tactical and operational doctrines to take best advantage of this new warfare is proceeding too slowly and somewhat in the wrong direction. To quote him:

"Specifically, the reason for this is that the new weaponry is for the most part considered as a way of increasing the firepower of the Army to a considerable degree; therefore from the organizational viewpoint, there is basically nothing new here. There has appeared a new technical means of combat—a new arm of troops has been created, as happened with aircraft, tanks, and even earlier, with artillery. The old arms of troops are modernized as much as possible and 'assimilate' nuclear charges and missiles. Armies continue to consist of the usual arms of troops (modernized, of course)—plus missile troops.

"In other words, the process of assimilating the new weapons which is occurring now can be characterized in the following way: based on the experience of the past and considering the achievements of the present, armies are adapting nuclear/missile weapons to the established views on the preparation for and conduct of war.

"This is a logical process—sanctified by past experience —of an empirical approach to the solution of problems which have not been greatly explored. Such an approach, the only one which is possible and normal for the military science of capitalist countries, is completely out of the question for the armies of the socialist countries, whose military science is built on Marxist-Leninist teachings on war. It is obvious that we must go faster and further both in the theory of using nuclear/missile weapons and in their production."

Having set the proper political tone, he assumes a very serious, studious air of objectivity—what a fraud—to explain why he is forced to use American data in his study: *He can't get access to similar data on our own Soviet weapons!*

What is at the heart of Goryainov's views? The fact that maximum radioactive fallout is now to be considered a military advantage. After citing pages of facts and figures from American sources, he says clearly in his text: *". . . radioactive contamination of terrain by megaton bombs can be a principal factor of combat."*

At another point in his text he says, "In our view, it

should be absolutely clear from the above that *nuclear bombs of great yield are above all a means of radiological contamination of vast areas* with all the resulting consequences."

There is the difference between Western logic and Marxist dialectics! The Americans are always trying to reduce fallout, and on the basis of their own data General Goryainov concludes that fallout should be maximized! With this in mind, he goes on to say:

"The chemical composition of the ground and soils of the blast areas can also be very influential in increasing the effectiveness of the blast products. Such elements as sodium, iron, silicon, and others can increase substantially the radioactive mass of particles which are blown up into the air. An exact knowledge of local meteorological conditions in possible strike areas acquires enormous significance in the proper use of powerful bombs. One should study these conditions well in advance. . . ."

In this statement we can see the germ of a requirement for the GRU. Soon some of my colleagues, perhaps assistant military attachés in Washington, London, or Paris, will be out buying unclassified geologic studies and maps of the areas of the major population and industrial centers, so that Goryainov and his analysts can calculate the precise size and type of weapon, and the exact height of burst to create optimum radioactive fallout in each target area. Goryainov goes on to extol the military virtues of large bombs (in the megaton range) over small bombs. This is because the large bomb can contaminate with radioactive fallout a much larger area. He analyzes the number of weapons required to defeat the United States (he figures it would take about 120 bombs of twenty-megaton yield, properly placed) and moves on to study the question, "Is victory for one side possible in the age of nuclear weapons?"

It is, he says. Probably not under conditions of a prolonged nuclear/missile war, but to quote the most significant statement in his paper:

"Victory by one side depends on readiness and ability to finish the war in the shortest possible time."

The implications of this statement are clear.

It is important for Westerners to know and understand the new Soviet military doctrine; it is equally important to know and understand the *Soviet concept of Western military doctrine.* The Soviet concept of Western doctrine could be and, in my opinion, is vastly different from Westerners' concept of their own doctrine. For the official Soviet concept of the U.S. and British military doctrines must fit the Marxist concepts of the nature of capitalism and the course of history. If objective facts (for instance, intelligence reports) do not seem compatible with the Marxist concepts, it is the function of dialectics to warp and bend them until they are; Goryainov gives a politically correct analysis of the Western position:

"How are these new conditions reflected in the interests and the ideology of the warring classes?

"First of all, it must be kept in mind that no normal man can be interested in the destruction of mankind. This is seen differently, however, from the viewpoint of the ruling classes, which are disappearing from the historical scene.

"History has shown more than once that a dying class, a dying social order, produces theories and dogmas of human destruction characterized by such phrases as, *'après moi le déluge'* and 'better dead than Red.' For reactionary forces, who are doomed to perish because of historical hopelessness, a long war (like any other war) is not ruled out, particularly because preparation for such a war is economically advantageous for certain monopolistic circles.

"Preparation for an extended war is immensely more costly than for a short war and thus the profits of capitalists immensely higher.

"Therefore, because of economic reasons and partly because of the aspirations of groups connected with military production which are out to preserve the commanding position they hold in the economy of a country like the U.S.A., the theory of an extended war is circulated very widely. This theory ties in well with the necessity of keeping colonial and economically underdeveloped countries under the threat of war and even to thrust wars upon them.

"The interests of the progressive forces of the world dictate a different approach. The material prerequisites for the victory of the socialist system over the capitalist system by using peaceful means have already been created.

Therefore the progressive forces are keenly interested in avoiding war. But if war becomes inevitable, the new world, of course, must strive to keep war losses to a minimum and it should, therefore, do everything possible to keep the war short and, in any case, to put an end to the decisive phase of the war prior to substantial atmospheric contamination over large areas!"

In striving for political correctness, from the Marxist point of view, an author is frequently led into contradictions. For instance, Goryainov says that the capitalist countries favored blitzkrieg because they were afraid that arming the masses and conducting wars would lead to revolution. On the very next page he says that capitalists favor long wars because they lead to greater profits. Now, I fear for the health of any Soviet citizen who dares to say that arming the masses in capitalist countries would *not* lead to revolution, and also for any Soviet who might say capitalists prefer shorter wars and smaller profits. Probably no one has pointed out this contradiction to Goryainov, because it is safer to avoid such prickly questions.

I am sorry that I cannot copy here the entire "Special Collection." I have sent it to my intelligence contacts. I will, however, give my views on it, for in my opinion the trend in it is unmistakable, as is the nature of the final doctrine which will emerge from this discussion.

First, let me say that virtually all the authors recognize the importance of the first thermonuclear strike.

In the first place, to be the first one to deliver a nuclear strike is important not only as far as the initial stage of the war is concerned, but also because it concerns the entire course and the outcome of the war.

Secondly, strategic nuclear missiles, which will play a tremendous part in the initial stage of the war, will also make it possible to achieve the necessary strategic goals of the war within the shortest possible time.

All military men understand perfectly that the final decision "to attack" rests with the political leadership, in this case with the Presidium of the Central Committee CPSU and with Khrushchev personally. Participating in the discussion, the Soviet generals naturally try to do everything in their power to prove their abilities to Khrushchev and earn his praise.

This new military doctrine must become, or perhaps has already become, a sort of guide for the Soviet state in preparing its armed forces for a war, and it sets forth in detail where and how future military actions should start.

A future war will begin with a sudden nuclear strike against the enemy. There will be no declaration of war. Quite to the contrary, an effort will be made to avoid a declaration of war. When circumstances are favorable for delivering the first nuclear strike, the Soviet Union will deliver this strike under the pretense of defending itself from an aggressor. In this way it will seize the initiative.

All operational-strategic plans of a future war are being developed in this direction. This does not mean that the plans exclude so-called local wars; on the contrary, Khrushchev is for local wars as a prelude to a future "big" war, for which intensive preparations are being made.

Knowing the meaning of Khrushchev's slogans on "peaceful coexistence" and "the struggle for peace," Soviet military leaders are making intensive preparations for a future war, although many of them are against any kind of war—actually they are for peace. They are working out war plans as professional soldiers, carrying their Party cards in their pockets. These cards compel them to carry out implicitly the directives of the Presidium of the Central Committee CPSU and those of Khrushchev personally. After all, they occupy their high posts only thanks to the Party card, which, as we say, "gives them food and drink."

Despite the fact that all authors of the "Special Collection" agree with the importance of the initial sudden strike, some of them realistically suggest that the following term be included in the doctrine: "Try to achieve victory with a short war (by a lightning strike) but be prepared for a prolonged war."

The Soviet Union does not wish to wage a long war. The Soviet Union will not be able to achieve victory in a long war because the country's economy and the people's morale will not endure prolonged ordeals. Gastilovich's article says: "One cannot replace strategic art by urgent demands on the moral fiber of the people, and neither can one plan strategy on the basis of fear of calculated risk and the sacrifices connected with it."

As a General Staff officer, as a true fighter for peace, and as a soldier of a new army fighting for freedom and democracy, I have made my own conclusions about the new Soviet military doctrine. I do not wish, however, for my countrymen here in the U.S.S.R. as well as the people of the West and of the entire world to think that these are my own personal conclusions alone. I have tried to substantiate all I said above about the new Soviet military doctrine and Soviet plans for a sudden attack with facts and documents which I saw due to my official position. I am certain that I and many others like me have provided sufficient military information to the Western intelligence services to confirm my words fully.

Khrushchev's peculiar variety of "peaceful coexistence" has advanced so far that Khrushchev could decide for the period of 1962–63 ". . . basically to complete the production of the necessary number of strategic missiles with nuclear warheads so that by adding them to the weapons of mass destruction which are already available one may be capable of directing these weapons against *all* the NATO countries and their bases." (Such missiles are already directed against England, Italy, and the U.S.A.; ballistic weapons have been made combat-ready. A large number of launching mounts against West Germany are in the Carpathian Mountains.)

Once and for all, preference has been given to Moskalenko's missile troops. His staff and control will *not* be combined with Varentsov's. The infantry and tanks will not be given so much attention and money as was done previously, in 1960. The number of Moskalenko's troops will be increased quickly, and a very large portion of the budget will be given to them. In the near future new units will be deployed under Moskalenko's command. It is considered that the large number of tanks and other infantry weapons which are at hand are sufficient for the present, and it is necessary to make a mass shift in the country's material and technical potential toward weapons for Moskalenko's troops. This does not mean that the production of missile and other weapons for an infantry army will cease completely, but the scale will be reduced.

Although at the present time Khrushchev prefers to wage small wars and to avoid a world war, Khrushchev and the members of the Presidium of the Central Committee CPSU have adopted the new military doctrine of the sudden strike employing atomic and hydrogen bombs for their strict guidance. The entire economy of the country is directed toward this end. An urgent reorganization of all the armed forces of the U.S.S.R. is being conducted. It should be taken into account here that the Anglo-American forces, as well as NATO as a whole, are capable of a strong counterblow, in connection with which the antiair defense troops are being quickly reorganized and strengthened. That is why the Chief Headquarters for Civilian Defense was created.

Having failed to resolve the Berlin and other international crises according to his own taste and desire by shouts, threats, etc., Khrushchev continues to struggle to gain time. He uses this time to continue further the mad nuclear and missile armament race.

People of the world, be vigilant!

CHAPTER VI

Espionage Notes

INTRODUCTION

IN the days before the revolution quiet old ladies used to sell flowers *(tsvety)* along the broad center strip of Tsvetnoy Boulevard. Some still do. The boulevard, a pleasant, tree-lined double thoroughfare between Trubnaya Square and Samotechnaya Square, lies in the heart of Moscow, not far from the old "Birds Market" which Chekhov lovingly recalls in the essay "On Trubnaya Square."

Late in the afternoon, one bright September day in 1961, three pleasant English children were playing by a sandbox along the boulevard, while their mother sat watching them on a bench nearby. A well-dressed Russian civilian stopped for a moment near the children, evidently in the course of a leisurely walk. He smiled, talked to them for a moment or two, and offered one child a box of candy which he had pulled out of his pocket. The child accepted the candy and the smiling stranger walked on. Then the child brought the candy box over to the mother, as children often do.

It was in this moment that Oleg Penkovskiy transmitted a highly important package of exposed film concealed in the package of Drazhe candy drops, to Mrs. Janet Anne Chisholm, the wife of an attaché in the British Embassy in Moscow.

Penkovskiy had met Mrs. Chisholm during his second trip to London and he had been drilled in this procedure by his Western intelligence contacts. A month before, Greville Wynne had arrived again in Moscow to attend the French industrial fair. Penkovskiy as usual had visited

171

him at his hotel. In Wynne's room at the Metropol, Penkovskiy had turned over film and several packets of information, as well as a broken Minox camera (he had dropped it during one of his nocturnal photography sessions). Wynne gave him a replacement camera, as well as the little box of Drazhe lozenges to use in the contact with Mrs. Chisholm, along with detailed instructions for meeting the children. The box was just big enough for four rolls of film.

The meeting with Mrs. Chisholm was the first contact Penkovskiy made with a person other than Wynne. In a city where foreigners are as closely watched as they are in Moscow, the novelty of "the meeting" was understandable, to say nothing of their caution in arranging it. Wynne, however, Penkovskiy could meet without fear of suspicion, virtually as often as he wished. Not only was Penkovskiy Wynne's official contact on the Committee, but Wynne represented a promising prospect for the GRU, which was anxious to recruit a British businessman for use as an agent. As far as his military intelligence superiors were concerned, Penkovskiy was "developing" him. When Penkovskiy saw Wynne in August, he told him that he was about to take a trip to Paris himself with another Soviet trade delegation for the purpose of attending the Soviet industrial fair there.

When Penkovskiy arrived at Le Bourget Airport, near Paris, on September 20, 1961, Wynne met him and drove him to his hotel. Not knowing the exact day of his arrival, Wynne had gone to the airport for two weeks, watching every Moscow flight. From the standpoint of Western intelligence, his vigil was well spent. Penkovskiy brought with him at least fifteen rolls of exposed film: photographs of documents, secret processes, missile design, highly classified military memoranda, and other pieces of scientific and technical information which his Soviet accusers later nicely lumped together under the heading "espionage material."

Three days after Penkovskiy's arrival, Wynne drove him to one of the Seine bridges, where he was met, a few minutes later, by one of the Anglo-American intelligence officers. The four members of the Anglo-American intelligence team evidently saw a great deal of Penkovskiy during the next month, when he was not conferring at the Soviet Embassy or visiting the Soviet exhibition in Paris, which had been the pretext for this trip.

Penkovskiy worked hard with his intelligence contacts during this third visit to the West. He not only discussed his information at some length, but he laid the groundwork for a system of contacts in Moscow by which he could later transmit information and receive instructions with a minimal amount of risk. Here, ironically, the terse language of his Soviet trial provides a concise account of a most successful intelligence mission:

"While in Paris, Penkovskiy repeatedly met representatives of the British and American intelligence services at secret apartments. At these meetings he reported about the official assignment which he had been given for his stay in France, discussed a number of workers at the Soviet Embassy in Paris in whom the intelligence officers were interested, identified those persons for them in photographs, gave them brief histories of these persons, and on a floor plan of the Soviet Embassy showed them the places where those persons worked. In addition, he recognized and identified for them, on the basis of photographs, several other Soviet citizens who were of interest to the intelligence services, he gave important information, underwent instruction in espionage work, and received this assignment: to continue to photograph secret materials; select in Moscow and describe in detail eight to ten dead drops for impersonal contact with the intelligence services; establish new friendships among officers and workers of the State Committee for the Co-ordination of Scientific Research Work; study the possibility of obtaining espionage information from them; and collect information concerning new Soviet military equipment by making use of his acquaintance with members of the rocket forces. In addition, in Paris, Penkovskiy continued to study espionage radio equipment which the foreign intelligence officers promised to send him in Moscow through Wynne or Janet Anne Chisholm.

"During one of the meetings Janet Anne Chisholm was present and specific details were worked out for maintaining contact between her and Penkovskiy in Moscow. At the next meeting in Paris, Penkovskiy was introduced to a highly placed person in American intelligence. . . .

"Having received from the foreign intelligence services

in Paris thirty rolls.of film and new treated paper for the preparation of secret reports, Penkovskiy returned to Moscow on October 16, 1961. . . ."

What the Soviet indictment naturally did *not* include was the fact that most of the "Soviet citizens" Penkovskiy discussed were themselves members of either the GRU or KGB. It is clear that Penkovskiy gave precise details of the large Soviet intelligence and subversive network operating out of the Paris embassy. In intelligence terms, he "blew" a major segment of the Soviet spy network.

In this Paris visit Penkovskiy behaved with his customary energy. He continued to handle a multitude of varied tasks and interests conjointly—performing all with Faustian zest. (This is probably one reason why his Soviet superiors took so long to credit the suspicion that he might be playing a double game.) We can only conclude that the Colonel took more than a little pleasure in playing his perilous double game. In Paris as in London he was an avid tourist. The paintings in the Louvre and the nightclub extravaganzas at the Lido he absorbed with apparently equal interest. The experience of the West was still new, still strangely free.

In his own memoirs, published in London in September 1964,[1] Wynne recalled some of his companion's impressions. By now they had become good friends:

"He used to attend the Embassy or the exhibition during the day; go to some official dinners at the Embassy; but whenever he got away I was always waiting for him in a car at a prearranged rendezvous and in Paris you can easily lose yourself. So we had quite a lot of amusement there, doing the usual tourist things, and he seemed to enjoy it very much. But he said he preferred England.

"Later, when we were in Paris, we went to cabarets at the Lido and Moulin Rouge. It was the first time he had ever seen such spectacular shows, with the chorus girls in line: they don't have that in Moscow. 'Why can't the Russians have this, too?' he said. 'It is a lively and happy art, and not so serious as the ballet.' "

Yet Oleg Penkovskiy was hardly the Russian version of the stereotyped "How you going to keep 'em down on the farm" Parisian tourist. When he had time to himself

[1] Copyright London *Sunday Telegraph*. Reprinted with permission.

in Paris, as in London, he would simply walk the streets, observing people and looking in shop windows. The differences between this open society and his own were borne in upon him in the smallest ways, e.g., rather vain about his looks and growing bald, he even reveled in the large available store of Western European hair tonics.

He was surer than ever that the course he had chosen was the correct one. The only remaining question in his mind was: should he escape now? He knew the risks he took by returning to Moscow. And the intelligence officers with whom he was in contact were, by Wynne's later testimony, perfectly willing to have him remain in the West. The information he had already given was so great that they were concerned about his future personal security and were thus extremely careful not to jeopardize his security in Moscow.

For days Oleg Penkovskiy debated with himself as he walked the streets of Paris. He had family considerations at home—a pregnant wife, a mother, and a daughter. Could he cut them off from his life forever? To leave his own familiar society, much as he hated the regime, meant a considerable wrench.

On the other hand, he was captivated by the bright new world in the West. There were the lights, the stores—and, it might be added, the girls. For Penkovskiy, who could not be accused of puritanism, had managed to make a few pleasant acquaintanceships in the course of this trip. Everything in his immediate surroundings argued that he stay.

He almost did. His plane back to Moscow had been delayed by fog and the omen did not escape him. He hesitated, literally, at the customs barrier, but at the last second he turned, said good-by to Wynne, and marched back into a world from which he had emigrated in spirit. He had a job to do in Moscow. He had said this many times to Wynne as he argued aloud the pros and cons of his departure. He felt himself a "soldier" of his new allegiance. He said as much in the Papers, shortly after his return to Moscow: "I feel that for another year or two I must continue in the **General Staff of the U.S.S.R., in order to reveal all the villainous plans and plottings of our common enemy, i.e., I consider, as your soldier, that my place** during these troubled times is on the *front line*. I must remain on this front line in order to be your eyes and ears, and my opportunities for this are great. God grant only that my modest efforts be useful in the fight for our high ideals for mankind." To have stayed in Paris seemed too easy, when there remained a force in Moscow which he wished to stop.

PENKOVSKIY'S TEXT

While the events of my recent trips to Europe are fresh in my mind, I shall put down some notes on the work of Soviet intelligence in foreign countries and its direction by the KGB and by the GRU. Some of this pertains directly to the work of Communists and Communist Parties in the West. More and more, as I see this work, I realize the overriding power of the KGB.

There was a period at the end of Stalin's reign when the Central Committee CPSU issued an order restricting the active use of Communists in intelligence work. At that time, contact with some of the GRU Communist agents was ended. There had been several exposés of Communist agents, and the prestige and authority of the Communist Parties in the West was somewhat undermined.

Experience later showed that it was much more difficult to work without the help of the Communists. So Khrushchev and the Central Committee put out a directive to the KGB and GRU to activate recruitment of Communist Party members for intelligence work. In 1956 and 1957 we again began to recruit Communists in the West. We would use them as spotters and agents, and, through them, spread misinformation and propaganda. Contact was re-established with former agents, and in general Communists in the West proved of invaluable help. Because the Communist Parties in the West are able to exist openly, they have every opportunity to organize conspiratorial activities in their respective countries in support of Soviet intelligence work. Many of the leaders of these Communist Parties move in the highest circles of their governments, and many are ministers or members of parliaments. For example, after the Khrushchev and Kennedy conference in Vienna, a secret letter was sent out by the Central Committee CPSU directly to certain leaders of the Communist Parties of the West (France, England, Italy, and others). The Soviet ambassador in Rome personally read this letter to Togliatti.

Pavlov, Shapovalov, and Milovidov also said that a directive had been received from the Central Committee and the GRU to employ all agents and friendly contacts with England in order to collect information. The ambassador had a conference with the GRU and KGB *rezidents* and gave them instructions from the Center. Shortly after this all the officers in the embassy took off in various directions all over England to gather the needed information. The entire force of operational, strategic, and political intelligence services was mobilized for this.

I cannot understand at all why the Communists are permitted to operate so freely in England and France. Why are they not shown who is boss? Where are the counter-intelligence services of the Western countries? What are they doing? Everything is being stolen right from under their noses, and they are doing nothing to fight the Communists. The Communist Parties of West Germany and the U.S.A. have been declared illegal; why are not similar measures taken in England, France, Italy, and other countries? These are all "fifth columns" which support our work.

Ananyev, our officer in Paris, told me that the GRU and KGB have very close working relations with Communists, especially those who work in the government, Army, and NATO. Ananyev and Prokhorov had both told me that it was very easy to carry on Illegal operations in France, especially in Paris. Prokhorov also remarked that in comparing the working conditions in France with, for instance, those in Turkey, France does not present any particular difficulties in our dealings with agents, especially if they are French Communists.

It is true that if we approach an ordinary Frenchman and he learns that he is speaking with Russians, he will immediately run and report the contact to the police. But French Communists, generally speaking, readily agree to work for us, asking only directions on how and what to do. They act as spotters and obtain military information. According to Prokhorov, we could not work so well in France without Communist help. He actually made the statement that we bought France easily and for a cheap price. A great many Communists in France have direct contact with Khrushchev. They can cause much trouble for the Western governments.

The GRU has levied a requirement on all *rezidenturas*, especially those in France, to obtain information on the new models of NATO weapons. They are to obtain this information by any means available to us—for cash, through agents, through confidential sources, by stealing when there is the need and opportunity to steal, by simply picking up information in those instances when vigilance and security measures were weak. They are to use all possible contacts, including all the representatives of the countries of the people's democracies, acquaintances, and Communists.

Other assignments made by the GRU were to obtain a model of the NATO American rifle, equipped with a NATO cartridge; to obtain samples of some kind of new, improved American and British gas masks. Soviet intelligence is very interested in charcoal, which absorbs poisonous substances in these gas masks. Also they want to get information on the anticorrosive coatings used for submarines and ships. There were many other requirements regarding the collection of information of various sorts, including approximately twenty to twenty-five items directly concerned with electronics, especially electronic technology as used by missile troops of the American and British Armies. We were also directed to obtain information about certain kinds of small American missiles launched from aircraft, which create various forms of interference in the air and disrupt radar scanning. All operational intelligence officers were assigned the task of visiting chemical enterprises in France, America, and England in order to learn the process and ingredients of solid fuel for missiles. Information was desired on heat-resisting steel; there seemed to be some reason to believe that the U.S.A. had done some very good work in this field. The GRU considers that the French have an excellent solid fuel for missiles and have made great progress in this direction.

Here is a copy of my own orders to Paris. This shows how we subordinate everything to the intelligence task.

Approved. *Top Secret*

Major General *Single Copy*
A. Rogov

September 1961.

MISSION

for Colonel O. V. Penkovskiy, departing for a short official trip to France from 13 September through 8 October 1961.

Through the channels of the State Committee for the Co-ordination of Scientific Research Work of the Council of Ministers of the USSR you are sent to France as leader of a group of Soviet scientific research representatives in order to get acquainted with some French enterprises and to maintain contacts with business circles while the Soviet Industrial Exhibition is being held in Paris.

During your stay in France, you must fulfill the following intelligence tasks:

1. In case of interest by officials of the local *rezidentura*, together with them you will seek opportunities to transfer your acquaintances to the local case officers. It would be desirable for you to recruit two or three people from among French scientific research specialists.

2. You will give a description of the measures taken by counterintelligence organs against Soviet representatives.

3. In traveling about the country in order to visit French enterprises, pay attention to any military objectives you may notice (missile launch sites, airports, troop locations, etc.). As far as possible, try to photograph these objectives and also determine their coordinates.

4. Acquire information on equipment produced by firms for military purposes.

After your arrival in Paris, establish contact with the *rezident,* to whom you must report the task assigned to you. In case of need, he may assign additional tasks.

In fulfilling this assignment, act in strict accord with your official position.

After you have finished your work in France, report to the *rezident* about its results, and after your return from the trip, submit a report on fulfilling your assignment.

Lieutenant Colonel of Engineers

N. Khlebnikov

12 September 1961

I have studied the assignment and will fulfill it.

Colonel

O. Penkovskiy

12 September 1961

I told the *rezident* in Paris that I would be traveling through France and could select suitable sites for dead drops. The *rezident* replied that they had all the dead-drop sites needed. He told me not to waste my time on this.

Ananyev has said that in Paris one can travel 600 kilometers and have surveillance all the way. It is, however, an ostentatious type of surveillance which the French employ. It can be eluded when you leave your apartment or the embassy. Everyone loves Paris very much, there are many famous places to see and visit, and many convenient places for intelligence work because there are all kinds of alleys, courtyards, gateways—it is easy to lose surveillance. The *rezident* also said that it was very easy to arrange agent meetings in France, to transmit and receive materials, etc. He even indicated that dead drops were seldom used because it was simple to arrange direct meetings with agents. These are not set up very frequently, however, only when necessary.

I have mentioned Soviet operations in the U.S. There Soviet Intelligence officers, in order to evade FBI surveillance, sometimes stay in the assembly overnight, sleeping on desks, then get up early in the morning to leave the embassy unnoticed. In this way they manage sometimes to avoid surveillance.

In London there are three GRU officers working under the cover of the Soviet Trade Delegation.

Shapovalov loves England. He says, "It is pleasant to live and work in Mother England."

While I was in London I asked about Gagarin's visit to England.[1] Gagarin does not speak English but he had some excellent translators. Everyone assigned to him was selected from our "neighbors," the KGB. Shapovalov told me that it was uncomfortable to see so many KGB types surrounding Gagarin. While he was in London he lived in house no. 13, on the second floor (Kensington Palace Gardens). People by the hundreds stood in the streets in order to see him, and one British girl waited eighteen hours to catch a glimpse of him. When Gagarin was told about this, he said, "What a fool! It would have been better if she had shared my bed for a couple of hours." Here is the new historical personality for you.

During my stay in London, by chance I met a chauffeur from our embassy; the number of his car was 603. This chauffeur was the one who taught me back in Moscow how to set up a concealment device for carrying classified documents in an automobile. He gave me lessons on Gritsevets Street, the motor pool for GRU operational cars. He is also extremely clever in making all kinds of operational modifications in cars. For instance, one trick he told me about was the installation of a switch which would enable the driver to turn off the inside dome light and the outside rear brake lights. Thus when one of our people is picking up an agent at night the brake lights do not come on when he stops and the dome light does not come on when he opens the door to let the agent get in the car. Thus even if the local counterintelligence service is following at a discreet distance, quite possibly they will not even be aware that he has stopped and picked up someone. Here is a typical embassy chauffeur for you!

[EDITOR'S NOTE: Here Penkovskiy digresses, with more fragmentary notes on Soviet intelligence operations elsewhere.]

When I was in Turkey, we never hired any local specialists or technicians to do work in the embassy. Even the charwomen were sent from Moscow. In Moscow, however, the foreign embassies have a great many Soviets working

[1] The successful Cosmonaut Yuriy Gagarin arrived in London on July 11, 1961.

for them. Each and every one of these Soviets is either
an agent or has been co-opted by the KGB, as was my
aunt, for instance.

The KGB sets up audio-surveillance devices in all the
embassies in Moscow. Hundreds of Soviet intelligence
technicians sit and listen day and night.

Our GRU officers, in Moscow as well as abroad, have
the right to invite foreigners to a restaurant, to their apartment or to receptions and affairs at Soviet embassies, provided that the foreigner is of some interest, from the intelligence viewpoint, or is already being developed and
prepared for recruitment. We have no right to carry on any
other type of friendship with foreigners; they are all our
enemies. For instance, during 1954 and 1955 Shikov was
working with a secretary of the Egyptian Embassy who
was passing information to him about codes. For contact
with the Egyptian, Shikov had a special telephone line
installed, and a separate telephone instrument was set up
on his safe. Shikov and the Egyptian conversed in French
and met either in a restaurant or in a safe-house.

There are Soviet agents also among the Scandinavian
diplomats. Some of these are quite valuable. I learned this
from several officers who worked with Slavin in Sweden.

After the conviction of Soviet agents in London (one
of whom was given a forty-two-year sentence)[2] the *rezidentura* received a special letter from the GRU, which
issued the warning to maintain greater security in their
work. The mood in the *rezidentura* was bad; everyone
was depressed. They were afraid that the arrest and trial
would tend to keep many Britishers from making contact
with the GRU.

My good friend Vasiliy Vasilyevich Petrochenko was
an Illegal for a long time in Austria, Switzerland, and
France. He was graduated from two academies, the Zhu-
kovskiy Air Force Academy and the Military Diplomatic
Academy. He was almost caught in France and was recalled to Moscow. They wanted to send him as *rezident*
to London instead of Pavlov, but they were afraid that the
British would not give him a visa. Petrochenko speaks
French, German, and English. After his return from

---

[2] George Blake was sentenced to a total of forty-two years in
prison in May 1961 for spying for the Soviets.

2. М е л е х И.Я. - советский разведчик. Имеет воинское звание -
подполковник. Отлично знает английский язык. В свое время окончил
военный институт иностранных языков и после очень долгое время был
преподавателем английского языка в военно-дипломатической академии,
которая готовит офицеров стратегической разведки. Получив некоторую
специальную подготовку Мелех был послан под"крышу"ООН для выполнения
разведывательных заданий.
Отсюда сами судите чего стоит цена советских правительственных заяв-
лений и протестов?

Советская стратегическая разведка имеет на территории США ТРИ своих
резидентуры: одну в Вашингтоне - под прикрытием военных аппаратов
/куда входят и отдельные секретари советского посольства,торговые
представители и другие работники/, и две резидентуры-в Нью-Йорке:
одну под прикрытием ООН и одну нелегальную резидентуру, имеющую прямую
самостоятельную связь с Москвой.
В Вашингтоне в составе резидентуры много советских оперативных работни-
ков и незначительное количество агентов, в основном "старых", завербо-
ванных уже очень давно.
В Нью-Йорке резидентуры мощнее. Есть новые агенты, из числа которых
отпачкавали и нелегальную резидентуру.
Во всех резидентурах советские оперативные работники занимаются /при-
чем активно/ поисками подходящих людей /часто по наводкам/, их разра-
боткой. Засылаются агенты и из третьих стран, которые легализуются и
и переходят на связь этим резидентурам. Среди агентов много иностранцев
живущих и работавших в США.
Советские оперативные работники занимаются большой информационной рабо-
той по США и др.странам - вероятным "противникам".

France, he worked in the school for Illegals. I made a copy of his GRU identification card, and a copy of his work book which clearly shows when he was an Illegal in France.

Sudin (*Sudakov* is his alias), a brigadier general, was in charge of the Illegals in Turkey. He organized an Illegal *rezidentura* consisting of Iranians, Afghans, Bulgarians, and one Swede. He was the First Secretary of the Soviet Embassy in Turkey. He knows many jokes, speaks Turkish and a little English and French. His wife's name is Yekaterina, and they have three children.

Ivan Yakovlevich Melekh is a Soviet intelligence officer. He has the military rank of lieutenant colonel. He knows English very well. At one time he graduated from the Military Institute of Foreign Languages, and for a long time after this he was an instructor of English at the Military Diplomatic Academy, which trains officers for the GRU. After receiving some special training, Melekh was sent under the cover of the United Nations Secretariat in New

York in 1955 to carry out his intelligence missions. This should help us to judge the value of Soviet protests and declarations at the UN.[3]

INTELLIGENCE WORK IN THE U.S.A.

The Soviet strategic intelligence service has three *rezidenturas* on the territory of the United States. One is in Washington, D.C.—under the cover of various military apparatuses (which include individual Soviet Embassy secretaries, commercial representatives, and other employees). There are two *rezidenturas* in New York, one under the cover of the UN. The other, the Illegal *rezidentura*, has direct, independent contact with Moscow. The Washington *rezidentura* has a great many Soviet operations officers and an insignificant number of agents; these are basically "old-timers" who were recruited a long time ago. The New York *rezidenturas* are of greater strength. They have new agents from whose ranks they built up the Illegal *rezidentura*.

In all the *rezidenturas* the Soviet operations officers are actively engaged in locating suitable prospects (often through spotters) and in their development as potential agents. Sometimes agents are sent in from a third country. Once properly documented, these will be transferred to the local *rezidenturas*. Among the agents are many foreigners who reside and work in the United States. Soviet operations officers are active in collecting large amounts of information on the U.S. and other countries, but mostly on the U.S., "the principal enemy."

After the Powers affair (after May 5, 1960, approximately) Khrushchev issued an order to all units of the intelligence services, especially those in the U.S., to cease their active work temporarily—in order to take no chance of putting into the hands of the enemy any evidence pointing to Soviet espionage against the U.S. and other countries. In November 1960 this order was rescinded. Intelligence activities began again in full swing.

In addition, at the beginning of 1961 a resolution was adopted about training all agents in one-way communica-

---

[3] On October 27, 1960 he was arrested by the Federal Bureau of Investigation on charges of espionage. In April 1961 the U.S. government dropped its charges on the condition that Melekh leave the U.S. before April 17.

tions. This was done in the event of a worsening agent or political situation in a certain country, and also by way of creating more secure working conditions for Soviet intelligence officers. The agents began to be taught coding, receipt of cables from headquarters, and the use of dead drops. Accordingly, the agents receive the needed technical equipment and guidance for maintaining impersonal, one-way contact, i.e., from top to bottom. This last precaution is being carried out also because in the summer of 1960 there were several incidents of Soviet establishments and embassies being visited by agents attempting to re-establish contact with their Soviet superiors. (These superiors had had to suspend agent meetings abruptly immediately after the Powers affair.)

While I was in London I talked with one of the *rezidentura* members, my old friend Shapovalov. When he was preparing to go to England, we were afraid that the British would not grant him a visa, and we were very surprised when they did. He sought my advice in regard to some difficulties he had encountered in his agent work.

This is the way our *rezidenturas* work. Every day something happens. One person gets his fingers burned, the other just washes his hands and laughs at the first person's misfortune. This joy in another's misfortune is not just a personal thing. The GRU and the KGB rejoice over each other's failures. When the GRU *rezident* in London found out that the "neighbors" had had two agents arrested, he gleefully rubbed his hands and said, "That is just fine, thank heaven that everything is all right with me."

The KGB has more representatives everywhere, especially in the U.S. and England. Both the GRU and the KGB try to be the first to send information to the Central Committee in order to receive praise. Neither of the intelligence services shares any information with the other in the *rezidenturas,* although sometimes we hold conferences together and even exchange agents. For instance, Colonel Pavel Dmitriyevich Yerzin, the former KGB *rezident* in Turkey, never gave me any intelligence information, not even of a military nature. He was always in a hurry to deliver all his information to Moscow, trying to show how actively he was working. The morning after he had sent it off, he would boast to me about the information which he had given the Central Committee. He was in Ankara for approximately one year. He had some sort of unpleasantness with Serov at that time, even though he had recruited some Western diplomat and paid him 5000 Turkish liras on the spot. He borrowed this money from my operational fund and returned it a few days later when he received the money from Moscow. Yerzin's deputy, Vavilov, was a good friend of mine and I advanced him this money on his signature.

After Yerzin returned from Turkey, he had quite a bit of trouble with Serov. Yerzin had bought an automobile in Syria and subsequently exchanged it in Odessa for a Volga. This is so that he would not attract too much attention with a car of foreign make. When we met in Moscow, he gave me a ride in his new car, and during our conversation he used some very "choice" words to describe Serov. He said that Serov did not want to listen to anything that he, Yerzin, had to say.

For some time Yerzin worked as a KGB representative with the State Committee for Cultural Relations with Foreign Countries, at the time when Georgiy Zhukov[4] was Chairman of the Committee. (Often his name is written as Yuriy Zhukov—not to be confused with the marshal.) Yerzin had a complete operational staff on this Committee, and there were, and still are, some GRU officers there. There was one colonel from the tank troops (I have forgotten his name) who had been in Afghanistan twice at an earlier date.

Yerzin was recently promoted to the rank of brigadier general and was appointed as prorector of the Patrice Lumumba Friendship University. The entire faculty of that university is made up of KGB employees, even the people in charge of the dormitories. Only a few professors work there as co-optees. Yerzin told me that he wore two hats there, as the Chief of a KGB section and the other as the prorector. The university is located in a building which formerly housed the Voroshilov Military Academy

---

[4] For a time, Zhukov served as a Soviet correspondent in Paris. He was also co-opted for espionage activities by the KGB. He was extremely successful in his espionage activities in Paris, and after his recall from Paris he was used extensively by Khrushchev for contacts with foreign Communist Parties and other prominent foreigners.

under the General Staff. The basic task of the Friendship University is to prepare a fifth column for the African countries. Many of the students have already been recruited and are now working for Soviet intelligence service. They are studying Marxism and Leninism, being prepared politically to become the future leaders of African countries. As a first step, after their return from Moscow, they are directed to organize strikes, demonstrations, overthrow governments, etc. In the university they are well fed, clothed, and given money. They live better than the average Soviet student; almost everything is paid for.

To understand our "neighbors" fully, one must recall something of their background—and Khrushchev's association with them. Terrible things were done to our people under Stalin and Beriya. We all knew this even without Khrushchev's denunciation of the personality cult. Khrushchev did not justify himself by this; he only threw more dirt upon himself. He was right there together with Stalin and Beriya. Many people even say that there was more order under Stalin, that this fool has ruined everything, in both industry and agriculture. He liquidated the machine-tractor stations, not using his stupid head. Now he wants to organize them again, but he fears the people will laugh.

I have my own accounts to settle with the KGB. My great-uncle (my grandfather's brother) spent several years in prison before the war—because his brother had been a judge in Stavropol before the revolution! His brother died in 1919. I was afraid to maintain contact with this great-uncle, thinking that it might reflect upon my career. This although he is a general. Even now we do not maintain close relations. When Malinovskiy was at Varentsov's birthday party and Varentsov introduced me to the minister, Malinovskiy asked me: "Are you a relative of General Penkovskiy?" I replied: "Only very distantly." When Varentsov told Malinovskiy that I was from Serov's outfit [GRU], he answered, "Oh, that is very good, very good."

I know from Varentsov that Malinovskiy does not particularly care for Serov, but he can do nothing about it. They removed Serov from his position as Chairman of the KGB in 1958 and sent him to us in the GRU. He is Deputy Chief of the General Staff and at the same time

Chief of the GRU. Everyone in the GRU is unhappy with this appointment. Serov should have been shot together with Beriya and not given the rank of general. But this was impossible. One hand washes the other.

I am an officer of the General Staff, I work with generals and marshals. They all say: "Why do we need this Serov? If they shot Beriya, they should hang Serov." We do not say this openly, but sometimes we get together, drink, and talk about it. The old Russian proverb is correct that says: "The sober man thinks what the drunkard says."

There are various rumors about how Beriya was shot. I heard from Varentsov and Churayev that he was shot in the basement of the Moscow Military District Headquarters building. General Kozlov shot him in the presence of other generals. During this operation all the Moscow Military District buildings were surrounded by tanks and armored cars; all the troops had been brought to combat readiness. There was some apprehension that Beriya's MVD cohorts would try to seize the headquarters and free him. After the execution, Beriya's corpse was soaked with gasoline and burned there in the cellar.

In the basement of the MVD (now the KGB) building there is a prison and also many "investigation" rooms with special equipment. These are the rooms where innocent Russian people—prominent people, intelligent people, patriots—were subjected to inhuman tortures. There was a special room with special pipes leading into it, through which rats could be let into the room. Persons who did not confess and who did not say what the investigator wished to hear from them were led into this room. Someone said to them over a microphone: "Well, now will you confess, you scoundrel?" If a man did not confess, they would first release one hungry rat, which began to run around the person, biting him. If he still did not confess, they would release more rats, which would all throw themselves upon the victim.

Through the microphone interrogators shouted: "Now, will you confess, you dog?" It was terrible. People went out of their minds. And they confessed. Then the guards would release a stream of cold water with terrible force, to wash out the rats. The innocent man had confessed, the investigator was satisfied, the death sentence was signed, the victim was written off.

Khrushchev lies when he says that he knew nothing of this. He worked together with Beriya, and Serov was Beriya's deputy. It may be true that Khrushchev no longer has rats, but technology has indeed moved ahead and now it may be possible to get a confession without rats.

Of course, lately this terror has slackened. Khrushchev has eased it. He has released those who were held illegally in jail and rehabilitated those who were shot. And their families—their families who were banished God knows where, they have now received rooms and little pensions for those who have perished. "Excuse us," they were told, "a little mistake."

There are thousands of families in this situation. There were thousands of acknowledgments like that. Thousands! "Their enemies did that for enmity's sake. We apologize. Here is an order allocating a room to you; here is a pension of two or three hundred rubles. Excuse us that a small error was committed."

Before, Stalin and Khrushchev shot and poisoned people like rats, those who confessed and those who did not. Now Khrushchev without Stalin shoots people for speculation and petty thievery. And they shout: "We are strengthening socialist legality!"

The Russian people are fools. They are good, fine people, but they are fools. They allow themselves to be tied up with ease. They cannot organize themselves. But if they could only establish conditions in which the KGB could not shoot them from behind, then these people could cry out that they had been deceived too long and suffered too much. That is why Lenin sprang forward with such a surge in 1917—the czar had taken so many wrong attitudes to the people's grievances.

Khrushchev wishes to justify himself and the organs of the KGB, he wishes to gain the love of the Russian people by announcing some amnesty and rehabilitation for those innocent people who had been executed and eaten up by rats. But the people at least see through this artifice. The people say: "You have thought of that too late. One cannot resurrect the dead. Who needs your rehabilitation, when the people long ago rotted away?"

When Khrushchev accompanied Sukarno to Leningrad, the Leningrad workers (known of old as the Petersburg

proletariat) shouted during the meeting: "Long live Sukarno, away with Khrushchev!" Churayev told me that
Khrushchev was struck dumb. He did not know what to
say. The Leningrad people are good fellows. Churayev
said frankly: "The devil only knows what is going on.
Stalin hated the Leningrad party organization, but nonetheless the Leningrad people prefer Stalin and Molotov,
anyone but Khrushchev."

If it were not for the KGB and Serov, Khrushchev
could never have become the Supreme Commander in
Chief. And Khrushchev handled even Serov in typical
fashion. After he had replaced many of the leading KGB
personnel with his own party cadres from the Central
Committee and the Ukraine and was sure that he was
securely in power, he removed Serov. He gave him the
rank of full general and sent him to us at the GRU. In
place of Serov he put his toady Shelepin, the former First
Secretary of the Komsomol Central Committee.

KGB employees are everywhere, literally everywhere.
I saw fewer of them even under Stalin than now. They
control our whole Army and especially the GRU. Here
with us in the Committee they comprise more than 50 per
cent of the key staff. During preparations for the Twenty-
first Party Congress thousands of KGB employees were
summoned from the provinces to help. Guards were
everywhere, documents were checked, and the streets of
Moscow were patrolled at night.

We all were very happy when they jeered Serov and
threw him out of England.[5] But the English did not know
that during Khrushchev and Bulganin's trip to England,
Serov was aboard the ship where they stayed the whole
time. He directed their security.

These KGB scoundrels even forced my aunt to be an
informer. She worked for them the whole time while she
was a cleaning woman and housemaid in the Afghan and
Italian embassies in Moscow. My poor aunt often came
to my mother, crying and complaining about the degrading
and dishonest things she had to do. She eavesdropped,
stole documents, cleaned out waste baskets, wrote reports

[5] In 1956 Serov visited England to make security arrangements for
Khrushchev's visit. The press raised such a hue and cry about "the
butcher" that he was not a part of the official party when Khrushchev finally arrived.

on diplomats, helped with provocations against them, etc. Many times she complained to me, but this was still before I began working for the GRU, and I could give her no advice, just sympathy. After she was discharged because of age, she was forbidden not only to receive presents which the foreigners gave her on holidays, but even to be seen close to their embassies. If this were to happen now, I could give her much useful advice. Now I myself am a senior officer in strategic intelligence. I could teach her how to talk to KGB employees.

When Khrushchev arrived on his ship in New York for the session of the UN General Assembly in 1960, one sailor fled the ship. This put Khrushchev on the spot, as he could not control the questions put to him by the foreign press. But what did Khrushchev say to the foreign journalists? One of my friends, a GRU general who at that time was with Khrushchev's ship in New York, told me that Khrushchev promised to give the sailor financial aid if he needed it. But this was only in public. In private Khrushchev bluntly commented that the U.S.S.R. now had "one scoundrel less." Here is real propaganda. But the Klochko case did not put Khrushchev in such a spot, and his reaction to it shows clearly who is the real scoundrel.

When our scientist Klochko, who went to Canada through our Committee, refused to return to the Soviet Union, the whole Central Committee was alarmed.[6] For two weeks the KGB looked for one of Klochko's friends or acquaintances to send to Canada, to meet him and persuade him to return. After Khrushchev had received the report, he said: "That is enough. Take all measures to find and bring him back. If it is impossible to bring him back, destroy the wretch. Let this be a lesson to others." Here is Khrushchev for you, a fine peasant. Who said that he was no criminal or murderer?

When one goes to the Central Committee CPSU, one does not know whom one will meet, a Central Committee man or one of the KGB. They are in almost all sections

[6] Mikhail Antonovich Klochko asked for political asylum from the Canadian government on August 16, 1961. He is the author of a book, recently published, on his experiences as a Soviet scientist in Communist China.

and directorates there. They enjoy greater confidence. Under Stalin they worked only on Dzerzhinskiy Square, but now they work also in the offices of the Central Committee CPSU, the Council of Ministers, in ministries, and in all state institutions.

Khrushchev himself directly supervises the work of the KGB. In this matter he trusts no one else; he controls the KGB organs as First Secretary of the Central Committee CPSU and not as the Chairman of the Council of Ministers. It is said that Shelepin spends more time in Khrushchev's office than in his own office on Dzerzhinskiy Square. Khrushchev and the Presidium of the Central Committee CPSU regularly receive reports from the KGB on the activities of our intelligence services and the moods of the people. Also we make and regularly send GRU reports to Khrushchev and the Central Committee.

The Central Committee has a so-called Administrative Organs Department. Its Chief is Nikolay Romanovich Mironov. He is a former high officer of the KGB. This section has nothing at all to do with administrative matters. It directs the work of the KGB, the Ministries of Internal Affairs of the Union Republics, the courts, the procurator's office, and us, the GRU. This Mironov is czar and god over us. Everything goes to him, and from him to Khrushchev and other members of the Presidium of the Central Committee CPSU.

The newspapers write that he is the Chief of the Administrative Section of the Central Committee CPSU, but they never write what this section does. It is a secret. From whom? From their own people. All of the people in Mironov's section are KGB, MVD, and GRU personnel; only a few are from the court and procurator's office of the U.S.S.R.

Mironov is a member of the Central Committee CPSU and a deputy to the Supreme Soviet of the U.S.S.R. Our General Serov stands at attention before him, indeed before any employee of his section. All appointments and replacements in the GRU and KGB go through Mironov.

OVERSEAS SPYING AND THE KGB

The Exit Commission of the Central Committee CPSU had close relations with us in the GRU—I encountered this section before my trip to Turkey. The head of the commission is Aleksandr Semenovich Panyushkin, former Soviet ambassador to China and to the U.S.A. Panyushkin also is an intelligence officer and a KGB employee. Panyushkin's commission is concerned with selecting and placing personnel abroad. It selects and confirms all ambassadors, counselors, trade representatives, military attachés, *rezidents*, etc., that is, everyone connected with work abroad.

If a dispute arises between the GRU and the KGB over a question of cover, or over the allocation of positions in embassies and representative agencies abroad, then the sections under Mironov and Panyushkin act as an arbitration commission. The KGB always wins out. They enjoy greater trust than we and they always get more. To put it briefly, we suffer much from the KGB directly in the GRU, where they have their Special Section, and in the Central Committee, where both Panyushkin's and Mironov's sections are made up almost entirely of KGB workers. Panyushkin's commission is never even mentioned in the newspapers. One can see how secret it is. And from whom is this hidden? Again, the answer is—from their own people.

At one time Panyushkin was Chief of the First Chief Directorate of the KGB (at that time called the MVD), which was responsible for foreign intelligence. This First Chief Directorate of the KGB now is called the Intelligence Directorate. We frequently correspond with it, but we do not use the word "intelligence." We just write: to the Chief of the First Chief Directorate of the KGB under the Council of Ministers of the U.S.S.R.

All intelligence *rezidents* of the GRU as well as of the KGB are approved by the Central Committee CPSU. All of them are summoned to the Central Committee before their departure overseas. Periodically, approximately once a year, all *rezidents* are summoned to Moscow to the Central Committee CPSU for the briefing [*instruktazh*], where they report on their intelligence activities and receive instructions for their future work. One of the secretaries of the Central Committee CPSU, and sometimes even Khrushchev himself, conducts such conferences of *rezidents*. Suslov directed the work of one such conference.

In Turkey our military attaché was Brigadier General Kazakevich, who simultaneously was the secretary of the embassy Party organization (overseas we call Party organizations "trade unions"). When he was called to Moscow, Suslov conducted his briefing. On Ambassador Ryzhev's suggestion Kazakevich pointed out to Suslov that in Ryzhev's and his opinion our government was pursuing an incorrect policy in regard to the new Turkish government (the Turkish people were poor, the lira had dropped, Americans did not provide enough help, etc.). He held that a large loan should be given to the Turks, so as in this way to win them over from the Americans. Suslov answered: "What kind of experiments are you proposing, to spend millions of rubles! And what assurance do you have that the Turks will turn to us? They will probably accept the loan, eat it up, and again fall into the American fold."

As a result of this proposal, Kazakevich was accused of political short-sightedness. He was removed from both his position as military attaché and as secretary of the Party organization. This is the way we are treated by the Central Committee. One makes a proposal and then waits to see what happens to him. For this reason we all keep our mouths shut, ambassadors included, and wait until the Central Committee tells us what to do.

To process people traveling abroad for long as well as short trips, there is a Special Commission on Trips Abroad under the Central Committee CPSU. It consists entirely of KGB members.

Any person, even a tourist, going overseas comes for a conference to the Central Committee CPSU. He thinks he is talking to a member of the Central Committee, but in reality he is talking to a KGB officer. The majority of the instructors of this commission are KGB colonels and lieutenant colonels, but they all wear civilian clothes. A person is called by the commission only after a full clearance has been completed on him by the KGB. At the commission the departing person fills out a special form and acquaints himself with the instructions—which include the rules for his conduct abroad. He also signs a secrecy agreement and a Party and Soviet government loyalty pledge.

The form includes the following questions to be answered:

1. Last name, first name, and patronymic.
2. Was the last name, first name, or the patronymic ever changed? If so, where and when?
3. Year, month, and date of birth.
4. Nationality.
5. Party status.
6. Education.
7. Country of travel.
8. By whom and in what capacity is the person being sent abroad?
9. Family status (indicate full names of wife and children).
10. Members of the family accompanying subject.
11. Had subject ever been abroad before? In what capacity and where?
12. Had subject any relatives abroad?
13. Home address and telephone number.
14. Date. Signature.

When I was leaving, this scoundrel Daluda from the KGB poked through my file for two hours. What was he looking for? I have been a Party member since 1940. He questioned me about *all* my relatives, living and *dead*, about my family life, whether I quarrel with my wife, about drinking, whether I want to go abroad, etc. He even asked me some questions on international problems. This was done to me, an officer of the General Staff and of the GRU! I was graduated from two academies, and here he was talking to me as if I were a first grader.

How many forms and autobiographies must be filled out before a trip abroad is processed! And all of them in four and sometimes in five copies! One even has to bring with him a residence registration certificate when it is perfectly clear to everyone where one lives, because no one can live in Moscow without registering. I submitted eighteen photographs! What are they going to do with them, marinate them? This is such a tremendous job! My wife and I worked on it for two days, and still we could not finish it all.

The instructions also state that when you are traveling

by train the conductor should seat you with your own sex. The instructions further state: do not drink, do not talk too much, and do not say anything you are not supposed to say, report all incidents to the ambassador or the consul or some other embassy representative who is responsible for these matters. Do not carry any secret materials or letters with you, do not make any notes, but if you have made some, keep them on yourself at all times, do not leave them in your hotel room, etc.

I remember that early in 1961 we sent a delegation to the Federal Republic of Germany. An engineer from Leningrad went with this delegation. He was co-opted by the GRU and making notes in his notebook. He put this notebook in his raincoat and forgot the raincoat in a car when he left. A search was conducted. The raincoat was found, but no notebook. He became so upset that when his comrades went to do some shopping he hanged himself in his hotel room. He used the cord of an electric iron which he had attached to the light fixture in the ceiling. They had taken this portable iron with them to save money on pressing. He used the cord of this iron.

His body was sent to Leningrad by plane. Later, at the place where he had worked, it was announced that he had not been normal and that he had suffered from constant headaches. This is how things are done in our country.

I have already mentioned the scientist Klochko, who defected in Canada. Our Committee for the Co-ordination of Scientific Research Work did not suffer because of his defection, although we felt very uncomfortable, because all the Committee had done was to obtain his passport for him. (Because it is designated as a Co-ordinating Committee, all requests for passports go through it.) For example, if the Academy of Sciences processes its individuals for a delegation, they do all the basic work and all the Committee does is to submit the formal request for a passport to the Consular Section of the Ministry for Foreign Affairs. There was a tremendous upheaval in the Academy of Sciences, however, and a number of people were discharged. It was later discovered that at one time Klochko was up for dismissal from the Party, allegedly for having a personal argument with someone in which he was accused of calumny. This action had been dropped as unsubstantiated.

I became involved in the Klochko case when Lieutenant General Rogov called me, Serov being in Poland at the time, and asked me to get whatever files the Committee had on this man. As I noted before, Khrushchev and the CPSU Central Committee issued an order to have Klochko assassinated. The Academy of Sciences submitted all its files on him to the KGB, which took whatever action was necessary. I was sent to the Personnel Section of the Committee where I told them that GRU headquarters was interested in knowing what the Committee had on this man, because it had processed his passport application forms.

There was a tremendous upheaval, because he was the author of some seventy works, a member of the Communist Party since 1930, the holder of a Stalin Prize. He was fifty-nine years of age and he had knowledge of some three hundred special chemical formulas in his head. When the balance of the delegation returned they were questioned by Andrianov and myself. They told us all the details of how Klochko sneaked out of his hotel. Later we heard what was said at the conference when he announced that he would not go back. The counselor of the embassy was there and one of the members of the delegation (a KGB man) was also present. Therefore although it was uncomfortable for our Committee, the real upheaval and blame was on the Academy of Sciences. Klochko had worked seventeen or eighteen years at the Academy of Sciences and was the director of a laboratory. One of the workers in the Central Committee involved with the exit permits was dismissed. Three more received reprimands in Party proceedings for short-sightedness and for letting a man of that age "who does not have a long tail" (i.e., insufficient hostages left behind in the U.S.S.R.—Klochko has no family) go abroad.

Apparently both the embassy counselor and the KGB *rezident* had tried to talk Klochko into returning, but they failed. The first day Klochko hid in the cellar of a Canadian police station. Before the first meeting Klochko declared to embassy representatives that he would not talk to them until they brought his suitcase with his belongings from the hotel. This was done. Then the embassy counselor declared: "Comrade Klochko, the way the case stands now, we are examining your deed simply as an error and delusion on your part, but in two hours it will become a crime against the state." Klochko replied: "I am sick and tired of this propaganda, and if you continue to try to persuade me, I shall simply not talk with you any more." All his life, Klochko told them, he had been persecuted and bullied. He had decided to defect a long time ago but never had the opportunity. Only by leaving the Soviet Union could he do anything good and useful—and that was his only good in life. He said: "I have decided to continue my scientific work here in the West and will endeavor to develop those ideas I have in my head. And you can just go to hell!"

The order on doing away with Klochko is still in force. Measures ought to be taken for his security, or he ought to be warned about it. There were also other similar cases —one man was assassinated in Iran and another one in Turkey. So here is your peace-loving Khrushchev! Who believes that Khrushchev has abolished terror? I do not, and nobody else does in the U.S.S.R.

ADDITIONAL NOTES

Fedor Fedorovich Solomatin was graduated from the Frunze Academy and also the Military Diplomatic Academy in 1950. He is a KGB employee and was in the U.S. Formerly Solomatin worked on the British Desk in Moscow. His wife Katya bought several dozen fur coats and then sold them in Moscow. Katya also worked in the KGB. She was fired for speculation. Now through connections she is trying to get a job in the GRU. It goes without saying that it would be a good candidacy; we have many petty tradesmen of our own.

Anatoliy Mikhaylovich Tudin, chief of the Inturist group in France, is a KGB employee.

Deterkin is a former KGB employee. He finished the KGB school or institute which is near the Belorussian

Station in Moscow. Now Deterkin works for us in the GRU.

In the last graduating class of the Military Diplomatic Academy, 30 to 40 per cent of the graduates were taken by the KGB. This was done by decision of the Central Committee CPSU.

CHAPTER VII

The Great Ones

INTRODUCTION

IT is customary to say that the spy lives in "a netherworld of shadows," or words to that effect. Nothing could be further from the truth. Netherworld it may be; but the world of the spy, the intelligence agent, or whatever term we use, is far from shadowy or vague. On the contrary, it is furnished with incidents, images, and interior decoration of the most precise nature. A meeting scheduled for 1900 hours is useless, or at best dangerous, if it occurs at 1911. If a black briefcase is to be picked up, a brown one must be ignored. If three rings of a telephone are set as a prearranged signal, a phone that rings twice is nothing more, nor less, than an object of suspicion. The whole success of an undercover operation hangs on its exploitation of the commonplace act, word, or gesture to conceal a most uncommon transaction.

As a professional intelligence officer himself, Penkovskiy needed to be told little about this aspect of his craft. In his earliest conversations with British and American intelligence, he took pains to specify exact locations and exact dimensions. In Paris that autumn he had painstakingly researched every detail of the methods by which he would transmit his information. He knew better than most the degree of surveillance exercised on the streets of Moscow. He knew the consequences of a careless act and the importance given by Soviet counterintelligence to the slightest occurrence or meeting that seemed out of the ordinary. Accordingly, he delivered his information to the West in three ways: 1. by chance encounters which could take place without exciting suspicion, yet were regulated in a most precise manner by the participants; 2. by meetings at the homes or offices of British or Americans whom he would be normally expected to visit; and 3. by the safe but often circuitous device of the dead drop, the inconspicuous hiding place where a packet can be left for a later pickup. Each contact, however, was prearranged to work in a clear, specific manner.

On October 21, just two weeks after his return from Paris, Penkovskiy had his first meeting with one of his contacts. At 9 P.M. he was walking along the Sadovnicheskaya Embankment near the Balchug Hotel, smoking a cigarette and holding in his hand a package wrapped in white paper. A man walked up to him, wearing an overcoat, unbuttoned, and also smoking a cigarette. "Mr. Alex," he said in English, "I am from your two friends who send you a big, big welcome." The volume changed hands and another hoard of documents and observations on Soviet military preparations was on its way westward.

"Alex," for such was his code name, coolly kept on with his work of collecting and transmitting information, without skimping on his normal daily rounds. More than ever, he kept up contacts with his friends in the Army. He showed himself at his favorite restaurants and cafés, the Baku on Neglinnaya Street, the Peking on Bolshaya Sadovaya, or the restaurant at the Gorkiy Park of Culture and Rest, but no more than was expected of him. Because of his work on the Committee, he was expected to do a good bit of entertaining. He exuded confidence. In mid-November he took his wife off for a month-long vacation. First they went to the quiet spa at Kislovodsk in the Caucasus, where most of the Soviet ministries have rather large rest houses. Then they traveled south, to the Black Sea beach resort of Sochi to round out a lavish Soviet-style vacation. They returned to Moscow on December 18.

In December and January, Penkovskiy resumed meetings with his Western contacts, this time—according to the Moscow trial—with Mrs. Chisholm, the same lady to whom he had passed the candy on Tsvetnoy Boulevard. But he quickly alerted himself to possible surveillance. On January 5, after he had passed some more film to Mrs. Chisholm in an elaborately casual encounter, he noticed a less than casual third party hovering in the background. A small car, violating traffic regulations, had entered the small lane, then swung around, while its two occupants surveyed the scene, before moving off in the direction of Arbat Square.

On January 12, the date of the next meeting, nothing happened. But the week following, the same car appeared again, a small brown sedan with the license plate SHA 61-45, driven by a man in a black overcoat—enough to warn anybody off. Penkovskiy wrote a letter to a pre-arranged address in London, advising that no further meetings with Mrs. Chisholm be attempted.

From that time on, Penkovskiy relied on the two remaining methods of communication. He either handed over material in the houses of Westerners, to which he was invited in the course of his duties, or relied on the relative anonymity of dead drops. Over the course of the next six months his intelligence contacts supplied him with some more ingenious methods of transmitting his film, including a can of Harpic disinfectant, with a removable bottom, in which film could be inserted. (The Harpic jar was to be found in the bathroom of a British attaché's house, where Penkovskiy would occasionally be invited for receptions. The occasion to use it never arose, however.) But he was able to pass on his packages at the few social occasions to which he might be invited, without causing undue suspicion. He was sometimes invited to formal parties or, on occasion, to informal British or American parties like the special Moscow showing of Shelagh Delaney's film *A Taste of Honey*.

The dead drops were, of course, the safest way to communicate. But they had their own peculiar suspenses and horrors. An agent must take the gamble that whatever he puts in a dead drop will not be disturbed and that neither he nor the receiver of the item will look suspicious in the transaction. In some ways, an agent working through dead drops finds himself playing a grown-up game of blind man's buff.

Through the spring of 1962 Penkovskiy's existence was bounded by a collection of these inconspicuous hiding places. Drop no. 1 was located in the doorway of No. 5/6 Pushkin Street. To the right of the doorway, as one entered, stood a radiator painted dark green and fastened with special hooks. Between the radiator and the wall was a gap about three inches wide. The message to be sent was placed in a matchbox wrapped in light blue paper, bound with cellophane tape and wire, and hung on a certain hook behind the radiator.

When Penkovskiy had something to leave there, he was to make a black mark on post no. 35 on the Kutuzov Prospect. He would then put the materials in the drop, and make two telephone calls to nos. G 3-26-87 and G 3-26-94, each with a set number of rings. When the person answered he would hang up. But the "interested parties" would then know to expect something.

Most of the caches where Penkovskiy deposited his notes and films were to be used only once, to minimize the danger of detection. There were selected places of mutual convenience, but always with the thought that they should be normally accessible to foreigners in Moscow. One of them which he selected himself was in the Vagankovskoye Cemetery, near the grave of the celebrated Soviet poet Sergey Yesenin,[1] another in a house entrance on Gogol Boulevard, where there was also a public telephone. In his trial Penkovskiy described a third location: ". . . I chose one place on Brusovskiy Lane, in the vicinity of a church which was in use, a corner house—I do not remember the number, but it was the first entrance from the corner, where I had seen a whole system of radiator pipes, a convenient place for putting magnetic containers. . . ."

Later in the trial the prosecution read from a document purporting to be from Western intelligence, which was found by Soviet investigators in the hidden drawer of Penkovskiy's desk. Although it is hard to vouch for its authenticity, the instructions have the ring of truth about them and they suggest the regularity with which Penkovskiy transferred his information.

". . . B. Caches. They will be the basic method for sending reports and materials by you. For the effectiveness of this method, we need a description of the caches which you have promised. You will have to find others in the future also. In choosing caches, keep in mind they should be in places normally accessible to foreigners. We consider that it would be best if we co-ordinate in advance the day and the hour when you will place the prearranged

---

[1] Sergey Aleksandrovich Yesenin was born in 1895. He committed suicide in the Angleterre Hotel in Leningrad on December 26, 1925, after a checkered career as an international man of letters.

cache, so that we can immediately remove it without waiting for a signal. We propose the following basic plan:

1) You will fill a cache no oftener than once a month.

2) Each cache can be used only once (we will consider a cache used once we have checked for material, even if you did not place anything there).

3) You will inform us in advance of the dates and times when you will place caches and which they will be, during the next three months. . . . We will confirm by radio when a cache is emptied. . . ."

If there were to be any changes in his assignment, or sudden travel orders, Penkovskiy was to inform Western intelligence through use of some prearranged postcard messages. (The postcards, already written out, were supplied him.) For example, one postcard addressed to a Miss R. Cook in London said: "I am having a very interesting time and enjoying myself. There are so many interesting things here that it is difficult to decide even where to begin. I'll see you soon." Signed "John." (This was presented as evidence at his Soviet trial.)

This meant that Penkovskiy was scheduled to leave the U.S.S.R. within the next two weeks.

As the Soviet record of Penkovskiy's activities grimly continued: "Subsequently the espionage meetings between Anne Chisholm and Penkovskiy were carried out at official diplomatic receptions, to which he was invited because of the nature of his work.

"On March 28, 1962, at a reception given by an employee at the British Embassy in Moscow, Penkovskiy transmitted to Anne Chisholm a written report and six rolls of film on which he had photographed secret materials.

"On March 31, 1962, at a reception in the British Embassy in Moscow which was held in honor of the Queen's birthday, Penkovskiy received from Anne Chisholm a letter of instruction from the intelligence headquarters. . . ."

While thus continuing what historians of espionage will probably record as one of the great information leaks of modern times, Penkovskiy managed to keep up his normal life in Moscow, now become an elaborate cover: a constant and rather intimate association with the highest Soviet military circles. Since his arrest the Soviet regime has been nervous about revealing how high Penkovskiy's contacts actually reached. For a whole year the Soviet press attempted to play down his influence, as witness the characterization from *Izvestiya,* on May 10, 1963: ". . . a rank-and-file official whose contacts and acquaintances did not go beyond a limited circle of restaurant habitués, drunkards, and philanderers. . . ."

How true this characterization was may be gauged from the Papers themselves, a record of which the regime was, of course, ignorant.

PENKOVSKIY'S TEXT

At the beginning of my notes I promised to tell the entire world about our important personages, members of the Central Committee CPSU, marshals, generals, etc.— about the cream of Soviet society, as our people say. Many of these highly placed figures are my good friends or acquaintances. With most of them I enjoy considerable respect.

At first I thought that perhaps it would be better not to mention some of them at all, but after thinking it over I decided to tell everything I know about all of them. I myself am part of this society, and I have told everything about myself.

I shall begin with the one who is closest to me, *Sergey Sergeyevich Varentsov.* I have already mentioned him in my notes and I will again, but now, if time permits, I shall try to set down everything I know about him and his family without concealing anything.

Sergey Sergeyevich was born on September 15, 1901. His rank is that of a Chief Marshal of Artillery; his official post is Commander of Missile Troops and Artillery under the Commander in Chief of the Ground Forces, Ministry of Defense, U.S.S.R. Simultaneously he is a member of the Supreme Military Council of the U.S.S.R., whose Chairman is "Supreme Commander" Khrushchev. That title sounds most ridiculous. When talking about Khrushchev as Supreme Commander, Chuykov once said that Khrushchev was better fit to lead a herd of swine than to chair the Supreme Council.

Varentsov has been serving in the Army since 1919 or 1920. He comes from a peasant family. He is a real

Russian *muzhik:* He did not even finish a secondary school but he has attended several different artillery courses. Prior to the war he was a junior artillery commander. During the war he proved himself a capable artillery officer and advanced rapidly, until he reached the post of artillery commander of a front.

He became a Party member much later, I believe, at the beginning of the war, 1940 or 1941. After the war he was artillery commander of a military district and then was transferred to Moscow. Because his post of Commander of Missile Troops and Artillery is such a responsible one, Varentsov was elected a candidate member of the Central Committee CPSU.

There were those who were against promoting him to the rank of Chief Marshal of Artillery, including Malinovskiy and other officers of the General Staff. Khrushchev personally reprimanded Malinovskiy because he did not include Varentsov on the promotion list. Khrushchev has known Varentsov personally since the time Varentsov commanded the artillery of the 1st Ukrainian Front under Vatutin. Varentsov would also like to be promoted to a higher post but he lacks formal education—many call him a *muzhik* behind his back. He has many enemies, although it must be said that Marshal Konev always supports him.

Varentsov once ran into very serious trouble with Malinovskiy. Working very hard and delving into everything, Varentsov was very concerned about shortcomings in the missile units. When he realized how many deficiencies there were, Varentsov wrote a personal letter to Khrushchev complaining about poor management in missile production, lack of funds, and other trouble of the missile artillery. To see Khrushchev personally was impossible, so Varentsov sent a top-secret letter to him. But it so happened that at that moment Khrushchev was not in Moscow, and the letter was given to Suslov. Having read the letter, Suslov called up Malinovskiy and told him: "Varentsov, your Commander of Missile Forces, sent us a letter complaining about serious shortcomings in the missile artillery, and it seems to me that he is right. Investigate this and take the necessary measures." Later Khrushchev found out about the letter, but by that time it had already been forwarded to Malinovskiy's headquarters. Malinovskiy had a very serious talk with Varentsov: "What are you doing?" asked Malinovskiy. "You write denunciations of me to the Central Committee behind my back. Why did you not come to me directly with your problems and proposals?" The Commander in Chief of Ground Forces, Chuykov, was also upset when he found out about Varentsov's letter.

Varentsov is very strict with his own officers and generals and always teaches them by personal example. In short, Varentsov sticks his nose into every little detail and in that way tries to achieve improvements.

It was only by personal hard work and persistence that Varentsov achieved the rank of Chief Marshal of Artillery. Many plain, ordinary persons often come to seek help from Varentsov as a deputy of the Supreme Soviet. He works a great deal, and writes all kinds of letters to various government offices asking help for people. He gets very angry and upset when his requests remain unfulfilled or unanswered, due to bureaucracy.

At the present time Varentsov must be considered one of the best artillerymen. Voronov, who for a long time was the only Chief Marshal of Artillery, is more intelligent than Varentsov, but now he is ill and old. As far as his military career is concerned, he is through.

In addition to his apartment in Moscow, Varentsov has a country house outside Moscow, not far from the town of Babushkin. In the same area, not far away, there is a large base of the Chief Artillery Directorate. Soldiers from this base often go to Varentsov's house to do some work: dig around the trees, take away the trash, etc.

Varentsov's old mother and two sisters live near the city of Dmitrov, not far from Moscow, in the direction of our atomic center at Dubna. I often go there with Varentsov to take groceries to them or just for a visit. There is a nice little garden there where it is pleasant to rest. They need help and Varentsov gives them 500 [old] rubles a month.

Varentsov's daughter Natasha, who was born in 1946, lives with her father and mother in Moscow. Varentsov's brother, Nikolay Sergeyevich Varentsov, a colonel in the engineers, is a very nice fellow. He, his brother, and I fought together in the 1st Ukrainian Front during the war. Nikolay is married to his brother's former *"PPZh"* [literally *polevaya pokhodnaya zhena*, a campaign wife —a woman with whom one could live while at the front]. One day during the war when Sergey Sergeyevich and his *PPZh* were together at the front, his wife arrived at the front and caught them by surprise. When she found some items of female attire in Sergey Sergeyevich's dugout, she gave her husband hell. At this point Sergey Sergeyevich's brother Nikolay came to the rescue, saying that he had been in the dugout with his girl friend. Soon after this, Nikolay married his brother's *PPZh*, although by that time she was pregnant by Sergey Sergeyevich. So, of the three children they now have, the father of one daughter is not Nikolay but Sergey Sergeyevich Varentsov. They arranged the whole thing in a friendly family way.

Varentsov's daughter Yelena is married to Artillery Captain Leonid Goncharov. They live in Leningrad. He is attending the Leningrad Artillery Academy. Prior to that he served in East Germany, then Sergey Sergeyevich helped him to get a transfer to Leningrad and enter the academy. They come to Moscow quite often and stay at Varentsov's country house. Sergey Sergeyevich helps them; he gives them 1000 [old] rubles each month. They have two children, Sasha and Seryezha. Yelena is very capricious and spoiled; her father spoiled her. The Varentsovs have two maids and a gardener. Besides this, several soldiers come to the house, as they say, to help with the housework. Varentsov has a car with a chauffeur, an Army sergeant. All this is paid for by the government— except the gardener, whom Sergey Sergeyevich pays out of his own pocket.

Varentsov is getting old. He drinks only in moderation. Before my trip to London he asked me to bring back from England some pills against sexual impotence. At least the desire is still there and that is good.

Preparations for the celebration of Varentsov's sixtieth birthday in 1961 took some time. His family, relatives, friends—everybody wanted to contribute. Everyone had a present for him. Although Varentsov's birthday is September 15, the celebration was to take place Saturday, September 16.

On the morning of September 15, I met Varentsov at the station in Moscow. He had gone to Leningrad to be elected delegate to the Twenty-second Party Congress. I was the first one to congratulate him on his sixtieth birthday and give him my presents: a razor, a cigarette case, and a cigarette lighter made like a missile with his name inscribed on it. I had purchased all these presents during my trip to London. Then I gave him the package which contained a bottle of French cognac with the vintage year 1901 appearing on its label. His sixtieth birthday and sixty-year-old cognac! (Actually, I had to buy a fifty-year-old cognac and affix a 1901 label to it.) Sergey Sergeyevich was quite touched, and we kissed each other. Two of Varentsov's assistants also met him at the station. They offered their congratulations, and Varentsov shook hands with them warmly.

The party was held at Varentsov's country home. Many guests were invited, including Marshal Malinovskiy. My whole family, including even my mother, was invited long in advance. Yekaterina Karpovna, Varentsov's wife, asked me to be master of ceremonies [tamadan].

On September 15, as soon as he returned from Leningrad, Varentsov went to his headquarters and found the entire directorate assembled and waiting for him. A speech of congratulations was read, and a decree of the Presidium of the Supreme Soviet was read awarding Varentsov the Order of Lenin. The old man was quite touched by all this, and he almost cried.

Some actors, singers, and musicians were also invited to the birthday party.

On the evening of September 16 the guests began to arrive: Marshal Malinovskiy with his wife; Churayev, Khrushchev's right-hand man in the Central Committee Bureau for the R.S.F.S.R.; Lieutenant Ryabchikov; Major General Semenov; and many others. All the military were in civilian clothes with the exception of Malinovskiy, who came wearing his uniform. Some of those invited could not come because they were busy, many of them out of town on business trips. The most important guests, of course, were Malinovskiy and Churayev. Both arrived in Chaykas.[1]

Malinovskiy presented Varentsov with a large (three-liter) bottle of champagne, Churayev gave him a large

1 This is a luxury Soviet automobile used by high officials.

carved wooden eagle, someone even gave Sergey Sergeyevich a black dog. The best and the most original presents were those from me and my family. They were the things I had bought in London. Varentsov openly admitted it by declaring loudly: "My boy has really outdone himself this time!" And my presents went from one guest to another. Everyone asked where and how I had managed to get such beautiful things. Mrs. Varentsov and my wife quietly explained to the guests about my latest trip to London. The answer was always the same. "Oh, well, that of course explains it."

While the table was being arranged, everybody went for a short walk in the garden. Many of those who were not known to Malinovskiy introduced themselves to him, the military giving him their respective ranks, and the civilians the names of the offices in which they worked. I presented myself as "Colonel Penkovskiy," to which Varentsov added: "A Serov man." Malinovskiy shook my hand and asked me if I was related to Lieutenant General Penkovskiy who served together with him in the Far East. I answered, "Yes, like a second cousin twice removed."

When everything was ready, Yekaterina Karpovna invited us to the table. When everybody was seated and it had become quiet, as the master of ceremonies I opened the bottle of cognac, announcing that this cognac was sixty years old and had been purchased especially to mark the "sixtieth birthday of our dear Sergey Sergeyevich." When people heard about this cognac, again their eyes popped, and again they asked the same question: "Where did you get it?" And when told, they again had the same reaction: "Well, that explains it," while somebody jokingly said: "I hope we will not be accused of admiring the West because we are drinking French cognac brought from London."

After I had poured cognac into everybody's glasses (I half-filled everybody's glasses except those of Malinovskiy, Varentsov, and Churayev, whose glasses I filled to the top), everybody turned toward Malinovskiy, who was ready to propose a toast. He said a few congratulatory words, everybody clinked glasses with Sergey Sergeyevich, and some of those closer to him kissed him. After the noise had subsided, Malinovskiy began to praise the cognac; he called it an incomparable drink, with a real bouquet. The second toast was a reply from Varentsov, who thanked all those who had come.

Then I got up. In my congratulatory speech I put the emphasis on the Order of Lenin, which had been awarded to Sergey Sergeyevich (somehow everybody seemed to have forgotten about this fact and it had not been mentioned by anyone). This statement of mine was followed by a loud round of applause.

The cognac lasted only three rounds at half a liqueur glass for each person. Malinovskiy relished each sip, and one could see that he liked cognac and was a connoisseur of its taste. When the cognac was gone, Malinovskiy asked me to open the bottle of champagne he had brought. While opening the champagne bottle, I did a little apple-polishing by saying: "And now champagne presented by our dearest guest Comrade Marshal of the Soviet Union Malinovskiy." Everybody applauded and drank bottoms up. Sometime during all this, Varentsov took the empty cognac bottle and said to me: "Oleg, I am going to save this bottle as a most cherished relic; after all, it has the year 1901 on its label."

A short toast was proposed by Churayev, and from then on, the guests kept having drinks informally for Varentsov's wife, for Malinovskiy's wife, and for others present at the party. Mrs. Varentsov and one of the maids served hors d'oeuvres to the guests and attended the table.

The first name and the patronymic of our Minister of Defense Marshal Malinovskiy is Rodion Yakovlevich. My mother's patronymic is the same as his: Yakovlevna.

At some point while the party was in full swing, my mother approached Malinovskiy and out of a clear sky asked him: "Forgive me, an old woman, Comrade Minister, my dear Rodion Yakovlevich, tell me please, will there be a war? This question worries all of us so much!" Marshal Malinovskiy answered her in these words: "It is hard to tell, Taisiya Yakovlevna, but I would rather not discuss it now because I think almost all of the time about whether there will be a war or not. But generally speaking, the situation is difficult. Our enemies refuse to yield. It is true that they swallowed one pill;[2] the whole thing

2 The erection of the Berlin wall and closing of the border between East and West Germanies.

was handled very skillfully by us. As for the future, I can tell you only one thing: we are totally prepared for any eventuality. We keep our powder dry." Not only my mother but everybody present was listening with interest while Malinovskiy answered my mother's question. I was so afraid that my mother might blurt out something foolish, but everything went fine without any hitches.

Soon after this, Malinovskiy departed, saying that the next morning at ten he was flying to Lvov. He was going there to attend a Party conference at which he was to be elected a delegate to the Twenty-second Party Congress. In addition, as he said, he had to see how the preparations for the coming large-scale maneuvers were progressing.

After Malinovskiy had left, the real drinking began. People drank Armenian cognac, *starka* [a special type of aged vodka, stronger and more expensive than the regular kind], and just plain vodka. Churayev drank mainly *starka* and vodka. He soon got drunk and began to say all kinds of foolish things; he even embarrassed Varentsov several times.

While Malinovskiy was still at the party I went out to the street several times to see if everything was in order, and was surprised to find security men stationed around the country house. Until then I never knew that besides his aides and various orderlies Malinovskiy also had a special security force.

Churayev approached me several times during the party asking me to buy him some Chanel No. 5, Arpège, and other perfumes for his wife if I went on another temporary duty trip abroad. Other guests asked me to buy them razors, batteries, and some of the generals wanted attaché cases. At first I wrote these things down, but later I simply said I would try to get them.

Later Churayev began to brag about having 20,000 roses and other flowers at his country house, as well as having various small structures, etc., there. I thought to myself: "What a louse, he has 20,000 roses while ordinary people are starving." It was especially unpleasant for me to listen to his boasting about his wealth and fine life because he told us at this very party about the unrest among the people in a small town between the towns of Mineral'nyye Vody and Groznyy in the northern Caucasus, where things had gotten so bad that several militiamen had been killed.

A similar incident had occurred in the city of Aleksandrov near Moscow, where the local population had attacked some militiamen and members of the MVD. He also told about the city of Murom, where during a strike the militia had fired on the crowds; several people were killed and many were wounded.

When Varentsov tried to stop Churayev, the latter would not listen to him. Churayev went on to tell us about a larger hunger riot that had taken place in Ivanovo, where approximately four hundred people attacked the militia. According to him this was a real hunger riot. The people demanded that they be supplied the same food as people in Moscow and asked, "Why is it that they have almost everything in Moscow while we here have nothing? In Moscow and Leningrad one can fill his stomach somehow, while here we and our families are starving." The militia began to drive the crowd away from the *oblast* Party committee and the *oblast* executive committee. Then the crowd attacked the militia, and the shooting began. The militiamen aimed at the ground near the feet of the crowd in order to scare the people and make them disperse. There was a great scramble, and many were arrested.

The *oblast* Party committee secretary came out on a balcony and tried to quiet the crowd. The people booed him and would not listen to him. The militia then once more opened fire on the crowd but were unable to disperse it. At this point troops were called out in support of the militia. They did not fire and just pushed the people with their own bodies and rifles, and finally drove the crowd away. The food situation in the country remains extremely serious. There is much dissatisfaction. Street holdups, burglaries, and murders are frequent. Furthermore there have been more instances of people attacking the militia. Those who attack the militia are not hooligans; they are ordinary citizens who want to vent their anger on somebody representing the government.

Finally, when Churayev started telling how the Central Committee employees wrangle with each other, how much drinking and gambling takes place among them, how they chase after women, Sergey Sergeyevich took him by the arm and led him outside to get some fresh air.

After listening to all these stories many people felt

depressed, and in order to somehow enliven the spirits of the guests I proposed another toast, filled everybody's glasses with vodka. After everyone had drunk, conversation ceased, and everybody began to listen to the singing and the anecdotes told by the actors.

So, there is Churayev, an "authoritative" representative of the Central Committee: 20,000 roses, a Chayka limousine, two maids, a personal chauffeur, an apartment in Moscow, his own country house in the outskirts of Moscow, a gambler, a drunkard, and a blabber. But he is on the Central Committee. It is impossible to touch him because he is next to Khrushchev! And one would not be surprised if this man soon became one of the secretaries of the Central Committee and one of our leaders and his pictures would be carried during the parades on Red Square.

But to me he is just scum, a drunkard and a bloodsucker. Just think, 20,000 roses. The scoundrel! And all this while people in Voronezh have to stand in line for horsemeat! Just see what is the result of all this. Although Sergey Sergeyevich is my friend, his table almost collapsed with food, salmon, fish in aspic, sprat, cheese, ten different kinds of sausage, over fifty bottles of vodka and cognac, champagne, cakes, pastry, ice cream, and so on. And yet people are hungry! I cannot remain indifferent to this. I myself have a fairly comfortable life; my pay is about ten times that of an ordinary laborer, but what can I do alone? I simply do not know how to help my people. I, too, could move higher along the bureaucratic ladder, but I just cannot, I do not want to do it, it is against my personal convictions. I do not wish to become part of our elite.

Perhaps this attitude of mine has already been detected by others. I do not care, I am even glad if this is true. After all, one has to stop and think; today the people are venting their anger on the militia, but tomorrow who knows, they may start doing this to those who are dressed well, who are fed well, to such persons as Churayev, perhaps to me, because I, too, wear civilian clothes. I do not think the people will turn against the Army; they know that the Army consists of their sons, the same peasants and workers as they themselves are. But against the well-dressed, well-fed, fat-bellied leaders—yes, one fine day something may start, especially against the Party members.

Malinovskiy is a member of the Central Committee CPSU, and a deputy of the Supreme Soviet. During the war he was commander of one of the fronts, but he did not distinguish himself in any particular way. He is the most colorless of all the marshals, of limited mental capacity, and has not contributed anything new or come up with any original ideas in the military field. In short, he is one of those men whose principle is: "Don't bother me, and I will not bother you." These are probably the very reasons why Khrushchev chose him for the post of Minister of Defense.

Malinovskiy is a yes man. He does not have the firmness that Zhukov has. Khrushchev feels safer and happier with Malinovskiy. There is never any opposition from Malinovskiy. But things are not so well organized under him as they were under Zhukov. The General Staff does not respect him either. Malinovskiy is taciturn by nature. At the meetings of the Supreme Military Council he usually keeps silent and waits for Khrushchev to speak, and then, like a record, he repeats: "I agree. Yes, Sir, it will be done." There are never any objections nor any opposition to Khrushchev's ideas. He always agrees with Khrushchev.

Malinovskiy has very few friends. His closest friend is Lieutenant General of Artillery Fomin. They served together somewhere in the past, I believe, in the Far East or in China. There have already been rumors about Malinovskiy's being replaced, yet, on the other hand, frequent changes in that post are considered unwise. Just the same, the rumors about his replacement are quite persistent. Who his replacement will be is hard to say. The well-known marshals have gotten old. It may possibly be Biryuzov, or Grechko, and Chuykov has also been prominently mentioned as his successor.

[EDITOR'S NOTE: The following passages tend to be fragmentary, as Penkovskiy provides brief biographical notes about various highly placed acquaintances in the Soviet Army.]

General Antonov. Under Stalin he was Chief of the General Staff and also Commander of the Transcaucasian Military District. Now he is Chief of the 10th Directorate of the General Staff, which concerns itself with the satellite countries.

Marshal Moskalenko, Commander in Chief of all Missile Troops. At one time he was Commander of the Moscow Military District. He is about as dull as Malinovskiy, but he has some kind of pull with Khrushchev. He suffers from stomach ulcers. He has to apply hot-water bottles to his abdomen even at work. When he was promoted to marshal, Varentsov was indignant and said, "Can you imagine, they made this stupid ox a marshal."

There has been a rumor that if Marshal Grechko became Minister of Defense, Moskalenko would be made his deputy and Commander of the Warsaw Pact Forces.

Moskalenko's headquarters is located not far from the Golitsyno Station near Moscow, on the territory of the small town where the School for Advanced Military Political Studies used to be located. The headquarters are hidden in a large forest next to the village of Perkhushovo along the Mozhaysk Highway. There is a large lake there and a very nice recreation area, but there is only limited access to it. Swimming and fishing are prohibited. The entire area is fenced in.

Nearby are Marshal Budennyy's cottage and the writers' settlement. The country house which formerly belonged to Fadeyev, the writer who committed suicide, is also located there. Other writers including the old lady Marietta Shaginyan also live in the same area. Although the writers are not particularly pleased with the neighbors, there is nothing they can do; there is no other place for them.

It is not so important to be the commander of a certain category of troops as it is to belong in the category of deputy minister. That means a better car, better food supply, more esteem, larger allowance for domestic help, a better country house, i.e., definite and highly advantageous privileges. This is the position Moskalenko[3] occupies: he is at the same time Commander in Chief of the Missile Troops and Deputy Minister of Defense.

[3] Moskalenko has now been put out to pasture. He is in the Inspectorate of the Ministry of Defense.

Marshal of the Soviet Union Ivan Kh. Bagramyan, Deputy Minister of Defense, Chief of the Chief Directorate for Rear Area Administration, a rear-area pen-pusher. He is considered a rather intelligent marshal but is getting too old; he is about sixty-five. He holds the title of Hero of the Soviet Union and is a member of the Central Committee CPSU. I do not know exactly when he joined the Party, but I heard people say that he was criticized for being a late-comer, and was asked why he joined the Party so late. Most likely he joined the Party during the war in 1941 or 1942. He has two offices: one at the Ministry of Defense and the other at Building No. 2 on Red Square.

Lieutenant General Beloborodov used to be the Commander of the Voronezh Military District. At the present time he is Chief of the Chief Directorate of Personnel of the Ministry of Defense. The Chief Directorate of Personnel is one of the largest in the Ministry of Defense.[4]

Brigadier General Ivan Vladimirovich Kupin, my good friend through Varentsov. He is Varentsov's protégé and a distant relative of his; Varentsov's daughter Yelena is married to Kupin's nephew. Kupin is the Commander of Artillery and Missile Troops of the Moscow Military District. Prior to this post, Kupin served in the German Democratic Republic as Commander of Artillery of the 1st Tank Army. He was in a lot of trouble due to his amorous escapades. While in Germany he lived with his cipher clerk, Zaytseva. After Kupin's departure from Germany she hanged herself because Kupin had left her pregnant. During the investigation a photograph of Kupin had been found among her belongings. Kupin confessed that he had lived with Zaytseva while concealing this fact from his wife; he admitted that he promised Zaytseva to marry her. When he arrived in Moscow, General Krylov, Commander of the Moscow Military District, refused to see him, but, because the decision concerning Kupin's assignment had already been approved by the Central Committee CPSU, the case was hushed up. Varentsov persuaded Krylov to forget the whole thing.

This is the way it goes in our country. As long as the Central Committee approves, as long as one has connec-

---

[4] At present he is the Commander of the Moscow Military District.

tions, one can get away with anything, even crimes; but if a similar incident happens to an ordinary officer without any connections, he is punished immediately—either his rank is reduced or he is discharged from the Army entirely.

Marshal of the Soviet Union Vasiliy Ivanovich Chuykov, the hero of Stalingrad, Commander in Chief of the Ground Forces, recently appointed Chief of the U.S.S.R. Civil Defense.

Varentsov says that Chuykov is a boor and scum. Once during maneuvers Varentsov got the best of Chuykov. When Chuykov tried to hurry Varentsov in obtaining the co-ordinates, Varentsov answered him in a singsong manner: "Comrade Marshal of the Soviet Union, one does not fry co-ordinates like pancakes."

General Krylov, former chief of Chuykov's staff in Stalingrad, now Commander of the Troops of the Moscow Military District. He was offered the post of Commander of the Ground Forces but turned it down. I am certain that he will go far and will be appointed to a higher post.[5] I knew him well through mutual friends. Krylov's son, a lieutenant colonel, is serving in the 1st Tank Army in East Germany.

Marshal of the Soviet Union Filipp Ivanovich Golikov, head of the Chief Political Directorate of the Soviet Army, one of Khrushchev's protégés. He supported Khrushchev when Marshal Zhukov was removed. He is a member of the Central Committee and deputy of the Supreme Soviet. He is completely bald.[6]

Vice Admiral Platonov, Commander of Submarines in the Soviet Navy.

Brigadier General Arkhangelskiy, former Deputy Chief of the Lenin Military Political Academy. Last September, Arkhangelskiy was summoned by the Chief of the Academy, Lieutenant General Zheltov, who told him: "We have decided to retire you." Arkhangelskiy was stunned by the unexpected news and began to cry: "This is a tragedy. . . . What will I tell Nina, my children . . . ? That their husband and father, a general in good health, is being dis-

[5] Krylov is now a marshal, a Deputy Minister of Defense, and the Commander in Chief of the Strategic Missile Troops.

[6] Since 1962 he has been one of the main advisors in the Ministry of Defense.

missed because he did not do his work well? That I am lazy, stupid? Or that I am a criminal, or something else?"

Arkhangelskiy used to be a division commander. His wife is a doctor, and they have three children. After his dismissal Arkhangelskiy used all his connections in an effort to remain in the service but without any results. Lieutenant General Beloborodov, head of the Chief Directorate of Personnel, told him: "There is nothing I can do for you. I have not dozens but hundreds of generals who have to be dismissed. The old ones go, and new ones take their place. You know yourself that a new broom sweeps clean. It was not my decision. It came from above." After this discussion Arkhangelskiy suffered a heart attack, was taken to a hospital, and soon died.

I participated in his funeral as one of the honor guards. Permission was not given to have him buried at the Novodevichye Cemetery, so after much difficulty a plot was obtained by his family at the German Cemetery and he was buried there. After his death it was discovered that Arkhangelskiy had written a letter to Malinovskiy in which he complained like a child. The letter was never answered.

My father-in-law Major General Gapanovich was not buried at the Novodevichye Cemetery either; no approval was given. Apparently he also had not quite reached the political stature necessary for being so "honored," as some others have been.

After being dismissed, many generals could not find a place for themselves in civilian life, they turned to drinking and became regular alcoholics, as for example *Lieutenant General Biryukov*. Biryukov was well known during World War II and was respected by Stalin himself. After Stalin's death he quarreled with Zheltov, who was then the head of the Chief Political Directorate of the Soviet Army, and the latter did everything he could to have Biryukov dismissed. Biryukov was a good friend of Krupchinskiy's. They drank, played chess, and chased after women together. Biryukov is married to a Jewish woman. Now one can see him often either drunk or in the company of some woman.

Lieutenant General Georgiy Spiridonovich Kariofilli, Varentsov's Chief of Staff. On his sixtieth birthday he did not get the Order of Lenin but only a gold watch. This was probably because he had a fight with General Zhadov,

Chief of Staff for the Commander in Chief of the Ground Forces.

Krupchinskiy, head of the School for Nurses and a friend of General Smolikov's. They drink together and indulge in sexual orgies with girls attending the school. Krupchinskiy also provides girls for other generals of the General Staff.

Mamsurov, Serov's deputy; he almost died from a heart attack he suffered during the New Year's celebration from dancing too much.

Lieutenant Colonel Mikoyan, the son of Mikoyan, Khrushchev's First Deputy; at one time he was commander of a small airbase in Kubinka.

Lieutenant General Perevertkin, was Deputy Chairman of the KGB; he was killed during maneuvers. He had offices in both the General Staff and the KGB.

Marshal of the Soviet Union Klimentiy Yefremovich Voroshilov, well known to everybody. At one time the President-Chairman of the Presidium of the Supreme Soviet of the U.S.S.R. He was the first one to be given the rank of Marshal of the Soviet Union. Now retired because of old age. He participated in the anti-Party group against Khrushchev.

Marshal of the Soviet Union Semen Mikhaylovich Budennyy. Retired, but he has his own office and a staff of several officers. I believe he is writing his memoirs. His office is located in the Antipyevskiy Lane, but he lives at his country house near Moscow. He receives the full pay of a marshal, 1200 new rubles a month.

Marshal of the Soviet Union Meretskov, chief of some kind of special group of senior military advisors under the Minister of Defense. This group consists of a small number of marshals and generals.

Marshal of the Soviet Union Rokossovskiy, one of the cleverest marshals next to Zhukov. At the present time he is in retirement because of ill health, but he belongs to the same special group of advisors under the Minister of Defense.

Marshals Konev, Vasilevskiy, Sokolovskiy, and *Timoshenko* are all in retirement because of "ill health." Actually all of them are perfectly healthy. They were forced to retire "on their own" or were requested to retire. Why? None of them agrees with the new Khrushchev military doctrine, putting the main emphasis on missiles in all branches of the Soviet armed forces. Many of them are listed as counselors or consultants to the Minister of Defense, and they have their own offices at the Ministry. *General Tyulenev* also belongs to this group of advisors. At one time he was the Commander of the Moscow Military District.

One can see Rokossovskiy, Konev, and Sokolovskiy quite frequently, the others very seldom.

Lieutenant General Zhdanov, Head of the Chief Artillery Directorate. He wants to become a marshal very much but so far has not been promoted. In the past this post was occupied by Marshal of Artillery Yakovlev, who was put in jail by Stalin for having done a poor job of organizing the country's antiaircraft defenses; as a result they proved inadequate. Zhdanov is very sick, and recently he suffered a heart attack. Zhdanov and Varentsov do not like each other. When Zhdanov was taken ill, Varentsov said that the only thing left to him was to retire.

Commodore Vasilyev, retired, one of my old acquaintances. He refused to go to Red Square to watch a parade. He said, "That is another parade demonstrating military power. I am for peace."

Marshal of Artillery Yakovlev, at the present time Biryuzov's deputy in the Antiaircraft Defense of the country. When Yakovlev was put in jail during Stalin's rule, his wife went crazy, and his son was discharged from the Army.

Lieutenant General of Artillery Volkotrubenko, former deputy of Yakovlev, at the present time he is chief of the artillery school in Voronezh. He was in jail with Yakovlev.

Chief Marshal of Artillery Nedelin, former Commander in Chief of the Strategic Missile Forces of the country and Deputy Minister of Defense for New Weapons, one of the smartest artillery marshals. He was killed in October 1960, during the testing of a new long-range missile, although the official government announcement made in behalf of the Central Committee CPSU and the Council of Ministers stated that he was killed in an airplane crash. This, of course, was just a big lie.

Marshal of the Soviet Union Grechko, Commander of the Warsaw Pact Forces and First Deputy of the Minister of Defense. It is said that he is in some way related to

Khrushchev, and there are already rumors that he will be the next Minister of Defense. He is the youngest of all the marshals. Biryuzov considers him a narrow-minded person.

Brigadier General Andrey Romanovich Pozovnyy, Chief of Political Directorate of the Antiaircraft Defense Troops. He used to be Varentsov's deputy at the First Ukrainian Front. They are close friends.

Pozovnyy is married and has two children. When his son was entering the Artillery Academy I got the examination questions for him in advance. This is a normal thing with us: people gain admittance to schools of higher education with the help of influential friends, by using pull or pressure or money.

General Pozovnyy says that he has been very nervous lately and that the doctors found that he is suffering from nervous exhaustion. I brought him some pills against sexual impotence from abroad.

Pozovnyy also refused to attend the parade on Red Square. He called it a pure provocation and called Khrushchev all kinds of dirty names.

I have absolutely no intention of defaming the marshals and generals mentioned above. Many of them are fine old soldiers and Russian patriots. I did not wish to go into their biographic data or to describe all their exploits and heroic deeds. I mentioned only those whom I know and I have said about them only what I know about them personally. I intentionally omitted the subject of moral degradation and drunkenness among the top military personnel—because there are already too many dirty stories on this subject. I know one thing for sure, though: all our generals have mistresses and some have two or more. Family fights and divorces are a usual occurrence, and nobody tries to keep them secret. Every month at our Party meetings in the GRU we examine three or four cases of so-called immoral behavior and lack of discipline among our officers. The Party committee and the Chief Political Directorate of the GRU examine the cases involving generals and colonels, while those cases involving marshals are examined by the Central Committee CPSU. The Central Committee naturally discusses such matters behind closed doors, in order to conceal from the general public and the rank-and-file officers the dirt in which our high-command personnel is involved. Besides, marshals are not punished so severely as others. In most cases they are just given a warning. The explanation for this given by the Central Committee is the same simple answer once given by Stalin: "A marshal and his services are more valuable than a female sex organ."

The Central Committee employees themselves are not exactly saints when it comes to morality. Drunkenness and sexual relations with office secretaries and other women are a usual thing among the Central Committee employees as well as in all Soviet ministries and departments. Khrushchev and Furtseva have set the example. Moral decay penetrates all levels of Party and government leadership.

Khrushchev's son-in-law Adzhubey got himself so deeply involved with some actress that it almost led to a divorce. He was given a warning by Khrushchev himself to be more careful in his adventures. Adzhubey is the chief editor of the newspaper *Izvestiya,* and every day he writes articles about Communist morality. Yet look at his own behavior. All the other journalists hate him. Even Satyukov, the editor of *Pravda,* has slid down to second place after *Izvestiya.* Adzhubey received a Lenin Prize for his so-called work about Khrushchev's trip to the United States. This "work" was compiled and written by the Central Committee. All Adzhubey did was put his signature to it as its editor.

It helps to be Khrushchev's son-in-law. There is an old Russian proverb: "It is better to have 100 friends than 100 rubles." There is a new variant to this: "It is better to be married like Adzhubey than to have 100 rubles."

Here are some other examples of our "Communist morality." Podtserob, who at one time was the Soviet ambassador in Turkey, was living with his stenographer, Shura Andrianova. The entire embassy knew about this. I do not know how this affair ended, but I remember that everybody called this Shura, Podtserob's bed companion.

Our naval attaché in Turkey was living with one of the embassy typists whose husband was also in Turkey at the same time. When we lived in Turkey, my own wife was boldly approached by one of my brother officers, who wanted to sleep with her.

[EDITOR'S NOTE: Another case of repetition. Penkovskiy had discussed this before.]

In our own Committee in Moscow, Yevgeniy Ilich Levin, KGB worker and Gvishiani's deputy, is a drunkard and dissolute man. The stories he tells about the cheap dives he frequents are hardly consonant with what the Party tells us about "socialist morality." After his nightly drunken escapades and amorous adventures, Levin invariably sleeps until noon. Almost every morning Gvishiani looks for him: "Where is my deputy?" Someone says: "He has not arrived yet. Probably he is at his other office (that is, KGB)." Gvishiani is afraid of Levin. He knows very well that Levin is at home sleeping off his rough night, but he will do nothing.

The relatives of the highly placed do very well in our Socialist society. Almost all of the marshals' sons have finished the Military Diplomatic Academy. All of them would like to be sent abroad to work, but the government will not let them. There is a special decree of the Central Committee CPSU forbidding the sons of marshals to go abroad. Many of them tried, but to no avail.

Marshal Sokolovskiy's son was given a twenty-five-year prison term. He belonged to a large group of sons of marshals and ministers—some of our so-called "Golden Youth"—who had organized drunken orgies at their country houses outside Moscow. At one of these orgies, a girl who had just come to Moscow from Leningrad was raped by the gang. She happened to be the niece of some minister. After she was raped the girl was placed in a car and taken somewhere behind the Belorussian Railroad Station, where they dumped her. Because the whole gang was drunk, the driver of the car was driving very poorly. A militiaman noticed this and blocked the car. One of the boys in the car grabbed a pistol and fired a blank shot. The car was stopped. This happened under Stalin, and he said, "I respect Sokolovskiy very much, but there will be a trial just the same." And so a trial was held, and Sokolovskiy's son was given a twenty-five-year prison term. He stayed in jail only three years, however, and then he "became ill," allegedly suffering from an ulcer or something of that sort. He was released.

Marshal Konev's son, Geliy Ivanovich Konev, is a woman-chaser and a drunkard. He is also a member of that same group of sons of marshals and other high officials. He is a motorcycle enthusiast, and he loves to play the horses.

I studied with Geliy at the Military Diplomatic Academy. During that time Geliy had an accident while riding his motorcycle. He hit a man who later died. Papa, however, took care of everything, and Geliy was not jailed. He was graduated from the academy in 1953, and is now working in the Information Directorate of the GRU, on the American Desk. He knows English well.

Konev's present wife is not Geliy's mother. After the war was over, Marshal Konev left his wife and two children, his son Geliy and daughter Irina, and married the directress of a mess hall of the 1st Ukrainian Front, where he then commanded.

Colonel Pavlov, a good friend of mine, is married to Voroshilov's daughter. Pavlov is the GRU deputy *rezident* in London.

Rogov's son (Rogov is Serov's deputy) also works in the GRU. They did not want to allow him to attend the Military Diplomatic Academy because during the war he had worked with British and American flyers.

Gorkin, Chairman of the Supreme Court, has taken good care of his two sons-in-law. One of them, Colonel Konstantinov, a GRU employee, was the Air attaché in Great Britain; he is married to Gorkin's elder daughter, Irina. Serov wanted to dismiss Konstantinov from the GRU but was unable to because of Gorkin's intervention. Konstantinov likes to drink and loves women, especially the fat ones.

Gorkin's other son-in-law is Lieutenant Commander Ivanov, a GRU employee.[7] He and I studied together at the Military Diplomatic Academy. At present he is the assistant naval attaché in Great Britain. His wife is one of

---

[7] This is the same Ivanov who was connected with the Profumo scandal in England.

Gorkin's daughters. He loves going to night clubs in London.

As one can well see, all the sons and relatives of our Soviet leaders and high-level personnel are well taken care of. I have told only about those who are in the Central Committee, the Council of Ministers, the KGB, and various other ministries. The sons, daughters, sons-in-law, etc., of all our important Party and government officials finish higher educational institutions and have good jobs even though some of them are quite stupid. All roads are open for them. They are the first ones who get promoted to higher ranks and better jobs. Everything is done by pull, through friends and family connections. The newspapers scream that a struggle must be waged against such practices. But what happens? They punish some factory director for giving a job to his niece, and he is criticized for it in the newspapers. But we must look higher and see what is going on at the top level. That is where all the big crimes are committed. It is they who set the example for the others to follow.

CHAPTER VIII

Atomic Weapons and Missiles

INTRODUCTION

PENKOVSKIY celebrated the Fourth of July 1962 by attending a reception at the American Embassy in Moscow. There he apparently made contact with the U.S. intelligence officer to whom he later turned over a detailed plan of new Soviet missile construction. Two days before, Greville Wynne had arrived in Moscow. Penkovskiy met him at the airport in a borrowed car and drove him to the Ukraina Hotel. He was nervous. Wynne later observed that he had never seen Penkovskiy so agitated. "I am under observation," he said.

Wynne passed some materials to Penkovskiy and a letter from the West, which visibly improved his spirits. Western intelligence officers had apparently arranged a passport for Penkovskiy to use, under another name, within the Soviet Union, in case the surveillance on him intensified to the danger point. Penkovskiy was now actively considering methods of escape. At one point, in his European visit, the possibility of his leaving Moscow and making a rendezvous with a submarine in the Baltic had been at least scouted. He had been thinking of this, how feasible it was, and whether it would be possible—by some means or other—to get his family out as well.

Through this period Penkovskiy continued to get out his information at an almost frantic pace. Although he was well aware of the dangers involved, he was equally well aware of the need to get his information to the West. Soviet military preparations which were to culminate in the Cuban missile crisis had already begun. So he was caught in the age-old vise of the spy who has been all too

229

successful. A less bold character would have sharply curtailed his activities, but this was not Penkovskiy's way.
Yet while he continued to send out ever-increasing amounts
of information, he worried about his predicament. He had
never wholly faced up to the idea of the danger to his
family. Now he did. And now that he had a skillfully
forged domestic passport to use for an escape, he pondered
over the best way to bring the family out with him.

He knew that the KGB was at least somewhere on his
trail. As early as January he had written:

"Supposedly the 'neighbors' have information that my
father did not die and is located abroad. This information
appeared at the end of 1961. An immediate search of the
place where my father was buried did not produce anything—the grave was not found. Also, no document concerning the death of my father was found. My command
does not give this special attention and believes that my
father is deceased."

By early spring the degree of interest in his investigation
had obviously grown strong enough to block any of his
pending travel plans. For months he had counted on making a trip to the U.S. in April with a Soviet mobile book
exhibition. This had not worked out. With some agitation
he wrote in the Papers:

"If all is well, I will take off for the U.S. on April 19.
But at present things go badly. They are continually searching for my father's burial place. They cannot find it—and
therefore they are conjecturing that my father is alive.
And therefore in the future it would not be suitable to
send me on overseas assignments. My command considers
these fears meaningless and they defend me from all these
conjectures of the 'neighbors'—everything must be decided
soon."

He was relieved by the messages which Wynne brought
from the outside. But he had grown progressively more
nervous about his contacts with Wynne himself. Greville
Wynne had taken a terrible risk in returning to Moscow
at all, and he knew it. But in his own agitation Penkovskiy
worried whether Wynne had kept up the high degree of
caution necessary at this point in their relations. Wynne
was a very circumspect man. Penkovskiy's fear was probably the result of his own jumpiness.

On July 5 he had a last meeting with Wynne at the

Peking Restaurant, where it was obvious that they both were under heavy surveillance. Trying to sort out the events of this day in his mind he wrote down this account in the Papers:

"Up to his recent trip to Moscow everything went normally, there were no questions, and the embassy was given approval for his visa. The first days of his work passed normally, but a day before his departure Levin told me that his people [KGB] were interested in the aims of Wynne's visit. I told him that besides the Committee, Wynne must visit the Trade Council or the Ministry of Foreign Trade about the question of organizing the mobile exhibition. Levin said that he knew all this, but that for some reason they have become interested in Wynne. I learned all this in the afternoon—after I had given Wynne the second batch of material. I had made a date with him for 2100 hours that same day for a farewell supper. I was working officially with Wynne, and the organs [KGB] had been informed of this—in such cases the 'neighbors' are not supposed to surveil us. On approaching the Peking I noticed surveillance of Wynne. I decided to go away without approaching him. Then I became afraid that he might have some return material for me before his departure from Moscow. I decided to enter the restaurant and to have dinner with Wynne in plain sight of everyone. Entering the vestibule I saw that Wynne was 'surrounded' (and that surveillance was either a demonstrative or an inept one). Having read that there were no free tables, I decided to leave, knowing that Wynne would follow me. I only wanted to find out if he had material for me and then to part with him until morning, having told him that I would see him off. Having gone 100–150 meters I entered a large through courtyard with a garden, Wynne followed me, and the two of us immediately saw the two detectives following us. Exchanging a few words, we separated.

"I was very indignant about this insolence, and on the following day, after seeing Wynne off, I reported officially to my superiors that KGB workers had prevented me from dining with a foreigner whom we respect, have known for a long time, with whom we have relations of mutual trust, with whom I have been working for a long time, etc. I said that our guest felt uncomfortable when he saw

that he was being tendered such 'attention.' My superiors
agreed with me that this was a disgrace, and Levin [the
KGB representative] was equally indignant about the surveillance. Levin said that the Committee and I as its
representative granted the necessary courtesies to Wynne
and that 'we' [KGB] do not have any claims on him. . . ."

Wynne's own report of the meeting, as given in his
memoirs, bears repeating:

"I happened to get to this restaurant a little earlier than
I should and I walked up and down the pavement. I saw
some characters standing around, but they didn't pay too
much attention, for the moment. But then, after about ten
minutes, Penkovskiy came along with his briefcase on his
arm. I crossed the road and went up to him, but instead
of greeting me, he just put his hand to his nose, lowered
his head, and went straight into the doorway.

"I followed him into the hotel, where there were people coming and going. He went up to the entrance door,
and looked into the restaurant, walked about and as he
was passing me he said something that sounded like,
'Follow *behind* me.' I gathered there was something wrong
and I took the hint.

"Penkovskiy went out into the street and walked for a
few hundred yards to where there was a gap in the buildings leading to a tenement area of wooden houses. He
went in there. As I was coming by he spoke to me,
'Grev, quick!' I went into the alleyway and he said, 'You
must go away now, quick. I might see you at the airport tomorrow, but you are being followed. Go.' And he
went the other way.

"As I came out of the alley I saw two men standing
there. And of course later in Lubianka I saw photographs.
They had had cameras. . . ."

Wynne had already booked passage to London on a
flight which left Moscow the next afternoon. He decided
to check out of his hotel as quickly as possible and go to
the airport, before the KGB might make its own decision
to apprehend him. (Despite the widely vaunted omni-
science of Soviet security forces, they do not move without something of the same consultations, approvals, and
countersignatures which are necessary in any bureaucracy.)
He reached Sheremyeteyevo Airport at five thirty the next
morning.

At the airport, Wynne at first made no move to change his ticket. He merely sat down on an outer bench in the waiting room, to see if Penkovskiy would come. Wisely, he set out to make himself as inconspicuous as possible.

Forty-five minutes later, after two taxis had rolled up to the airport entrance, Wynne saw a private car come up to the outer gates of the airport, then park outside. Penkovskiy quickly got out of the car and walked into the terminal. He first walked past Wynne—as was his custom —to check any possible surveillance. Then he turned and sat beside him. He told Wynne he must leave immediately.

Using his authority with customs officials and the airport staff, Penkovskiy personally changed Wynne's tickets, rushed him through customs, and booked him on the first available flight to the West, an S.A.S. flight to Copenhagen leaving about 9 A.M. Although Penkovskiy succeeded in overawing the airport guards, it was obvious that for the long term this precipitate action killed whatever chances remained to him of neutralizing the regime's suspicion, or at least explaining away his connection with Wynne. It was an act of self-sacrifice and Wynne never forgot it.

For the next two months, instead of lying low, Penkovskiy redoubled his intelligence activity. Perhaps he knew that the game was up. But it was more likely that he was driven by the importance of what he had to communicate. In the following passages of the Papers he underlines again and again his concern about Khrushchev's nuclear preparations.

PENKOVSKIY'S TEXT

The responsibility for all nuclear equipment and its safekeeping rests with the Chief Artillery Directorate (CAD) of the Ministry of Defense. This directorate is also responsible for the production of nuclear equipment. In accordance with the decision of the Central Committee and the Supreme Military Council, CAD supplies the necessary nuclear weapons to the military districts, military groups abroad (as for example, in Germany), separate armies, and all other units which, according to the General Staff's plans, must be armed with nuclear weapons.

Of course, the CAD is also responsible for supplying nuclear weapons to all the missile troops.

The KGB is responsible for the security of all nuclear plants, scientific research institutes, laboratories, and the installations where the nuclear bombs and missiles are stored. KGB troops escort nuclear equipment while it is being transported. For this purpose the KGB has special vehicles, railroad cars, aircraft, etc.

The U.S.S.R. conducts scientific research work on the uses of nuclear energy for peaceful and strictly scientific purposes. But this represents a very small portion of our activities in nuclear energy. Only a few projects, such as the icebreaker *Lenin* and several atomic reactors, are devoted to peaceful purposes. All the others are military.

Many of our nuclear explosions (tests) have been conducted in the central part of the U.S.S.R., mostly in Kazakhstan. Some of the smaller tests were not noticed at all and were not recorded by the Western states. The large nuclear explosions are reported by TASS and the Soviet press, but nothing is ever said about the smaller ones. At the General Staff we sometimes know of tests being conducted on a certain type of nuclear weapon, and we wait to see what TASS will say about this. If TASS keeps silent, then we keep silent, too.

Testing of various new types of nuclear weapons is conducted daily. Nuclear test explosions take place more often than reported by TASS or the Soviet press. All this talk about the Soviet Union advocating the prohibition of nuclear tests is nothing but lies. Khrushchev will fire anyone who mentions complete suspension of nuclear tests. He is not ready for it. He will sign an agreement prohibiting nuclear tests only after he becomes convinced that the U.S.S.R. is ahead of the U.S. in the use of nuclear energy for military purposes. The negotiations can last another ten years without any results.

When our first atom bomb was detonated, the entire event was recorded on movie film, from the preparations to the explosion. This film is classified Secret, and it was never shown publicly. I saw it when I was studying at the Military Diplomatic Academy, where it was shown to us as intelligence officers. At the beginning the film showed the transportation of the bomb by a truck with heavy rubber tires. Officers and soldiers are guarding the vehicle.

The film showed the airport and the airplane—it was hard to tell its type—and the transfer of the atom bomb from the truck to the airplane. Then there were pictures of a forest, birds singing, etc.—and a spot on the ground, indicated by a circle, where the bomb was to be dropped. Within a radius of two kilometers or more around this spot were placed all sorts of vehicles, tanks, ordinary and reinforced concrete buildings. Animals—cows, horses, sheep, dogs, and others—were tied to trees or the structures, or simply put to graze in designated areas. This sort of arrangement was made around the target in several echelons, beginning at a distance of two kilometers from the target.

The bomb was dropped from the aircraft at a great altitude by a radio signal sent from the ground. The pilot had no control over the release of the bomb. The bomb fell not far from the prescribed target.

For a long time after the explosion various studies were conducted as to its effect on vegetation, animals, structures, vehicles, etc. These studies lasted several months. A number of prominent scientists, doctors, engineers, and various other specialists participated, using the latest scientific methods.

As a rule, neither Khrushchev nor Malinovskiy is present at atomic tests, but there are always some representatives of the Central Committee CPSU, the government, and the Ministry of Defense in attendance.

Khrushchev did attend twice, however, during practice firing of missiles. This took place at Kapustin Yar[1] and also somewhere else in the South. Often it happens that the missiles do not leave their launching pad. This occurred once during practice firings in the presence of Khrushchev himself. As always happens in cases like this, there was a big uproar, followed by an investigation, etc.

Foreign observers, including those from the satellite countries, are not allowed at the nuclear bomb and weapon tests. When practice firing of missiles is conducted, observers from countries of the people's democracies are sometimes allowed—with the exception of China.

There is a shortage of atomic raw materials needed for

[1] Kapustin Yar is a town about seventy-five miles to the east of Volgograd, formerly Stalingrad.

the atom bombs and missiles with nuclear warheads. This problem is being dealt with by the Chief Directorate for Atomic Energy under the Council of Ministers of the U.S.S.R. They control the consumption of raw materials. Almost all the ore containing uranium comes to the Soviet Union from Czechoslovakia. Recently some uranium ore deposits have been found in China, but they are very insignificant. Soviet monazite sands and ore deposits are not particularly rich either in elements necessary for atomic energy.

In view of this shortage of atomic raw materials, it is small wonder that our government is so interested in establishing Soviet control in the Congo. The largest uranium ore deposits are in the Congo. When Lumumba was temporarily in power the Soviets sent twenty-three planeloads of officers (including generals) there via Egypt and Sudan. The aircraft were of the IL-14 and IL-18 types; heavier types could not land on the Sudanese airfield, and other countries would not give permission for the Soviet aircraft to land for refueling.

A good friend of mine, GRU Major Aleksey Guryev, was the first one to fly to the Congo with the Soviet generals. The primary task of this mission was to establish Soviet control over the uranium ore in the Congo.

Major General Semenov, Varentsov's second deputy, spends almost all of his time in Central Asia where the nuclear tests are conducted. One of Moskalenko's deputies always goes with Semenov, too. Lieutenant General Pyrskiy, another of Varentsov's deputies, could not be present at his chief's birthday party because he was attending atom-bomb tests on the island of Novaya Zemlya. There is a large nuclear base on Novaya Zemlya, as well as a missile base equipped with R-12 and R-14 missiles. Malinovskiy told this to Churayev at Varentsov's party.

Other nuclear bases and storage areas are located in Norilsk, on the island of Franz Josef Land, and not far from Vorkuta. These are all in the North. In the South there are bases in Krasnovodsk, Kirovabad, and on Artem Island. Varentsov, Kariofilli, and Buzinov sometimes travel to these bases.

On September 8, 1961, there was a regular experimental

atomic explosion of a sixteen-megaton bomb. This was the first test explosion of a bomb of such force in the Soviet Union. An R-12 missile was used in this test. The missile was launched from Kapustin Yar. Varentsov was present when the missile was launched.

Later, when a fifty-megaton bomb was tested, to everybody's surprise the explosion's actual force equaled that of eighty megatons. Such great force was not expected. It was believed that some unforeseen chemical changes in the charge must have taken place after it was prepared. It is now thought that such a bomb with a calculated force of 100 megatons may actually produce an explosion equaling that of 150 or 160 megatons.

5. При испытании бомбы мощностью в 50-мегатонн, совершенно неожиданно получился разрыв равный по силе разрыву бомбы в 80-мегатонн. Такой силы разрыва не ожидали. Полагают, что произошли какие то химические изменения в заряде, после его изготовления. Полагают также, что подобные бомбы мощностью в 100-мегатонн, могут быть выше расчетной и дать разрыв, равный разрыву бомбы в 150-160-мегатонн.

More on uranium ore deposits: Uranium is mined in the area of the city of Pyatigorsk in the Caucasus. The mines are located in the mountains and are named as follows: "Byk"—where the rock contains high percentage of uranium; "Beshtau," "Verblyud," and "Zolotoy Kurgan." Twelve kilometers from Pyatigorsk is the new town of Lermontov, where the workers engaged in the mining and processing of the uranium ore live. A uranium ore concentration plant is located on the outskirts of Lermontov. Uranium is mined in the area of the city of Nalchik, near the small town of Kendzha. Uranium ore deposits have also been found in the area of the city of Elista.

Why did Khrushchev unexpectedly begin to conduct new nuclear tests?[2] All nuclear tests have had and some still have two phases. The first phase deals with the explosive force in TNT equivalents. In these tests the bombs were dropped from aircraft or from special masts. The second phase tests nuclear payloads lifted by missiles.

[2] The Soviets resumed nuclear testing on September 1, 1961. They continued the practice until the nuclear test-ban treaty of 1963 with the U.S. Subsequent Soviet tests have been underground, apparently, to suit the terms of the test-ban treaty.

The present tests are almost exclusively of the second-phase type. Almost all of them are conducted with missiles. First, the missiles are fired for distance and accuracy without a nuclear charge. Next, the same types of missiles are launched at the same targets, with nuclear warheads. Thus, for example, the R-12 missile, now being mass produced, has a range of 2500 kilometers. The R-14 missile is only in the development stage and is being readied for mass production. The range of the R-14 missile with a nuclear warhead is 4500 kilometers. The range of the R-14 missile with conventional warhead is much greater.

According to Buzinov, the cost of the missiles is very high. For example, the R-11 missile with a conventional demolition warhead costs 800,000 rubles; the same missile with a nuclear warhead will cost from five to ten times as much, depending on the particular TNT equivalent of the warhead. That is where the people's money goes. That is the reason why a laborer is paid sixty to eighty rubles a month.

Why is Khrushchev pushing his nuclear tests? Why is he unwilling to sign the agreement forbidding nuclear weapons' tests? Because most of our missiles have not even passed the necessary tests, let alone reached the mass-production stage. There have been many instances of missiles and satellites exploding in the air or disappearing completely. But Khrushchev persistently does everything possible to improve missile weapons. He wants to seize the initiative and to show the West that he is ahead in the field of missile production, as regards quality as well as quantity. Khrushchev and our scientists are still quite far from being able to prove such a superiority; but they are working hard to improve all types of missile weapons.

Khrushchev often boasts about the Soviet missiles or spreads all kinds of propaganda about them. Often a new-model missile is still only in the testing stage—in fact, the tests may have proved unsuccessful—but there he is, already screaming to the entire world about his "achievements" in new types of Soviet weapons. The idea of Khrushchev and the Presidium of the Central Committee is to demonstrate somehow Soviet supremacy in the nuclear field by any possible means: by launching new *sputniks,* by nuclear explosions, etc. In short, Khrushchev often brags about things we do not yet have. Varentsov, when commenting on Khrushchev's behavior, often says: "We are only thinking about those things, we are only planning. Even if we have actually achieved some successes here and there, we still have a long way to go before we actually achieve the things about which Khrushchev keeps talking and boasting." Varentsov has always stressed the fact that we do not have enough qualified personnel, that their training is inadequate, that the quality of production is poor, and the quantity is inadequate.

Sometimes this pushing of Khrushchev's for premature achievement has disastrous results. The sudden death of Marshal Nedelin, chief of our missile forces, was a case in point.

Хрущев требует от своих специалистов создания двигателя для ракеты на атомном сырье, т.е. на атомном горючем. Лабораторные работы по этому вопросу были завершены и к 43 годовщине Октября хотели сделать "подарок" - ракету, движимую атомной энергией. При испытании этого нового двигателя и присутствовал НЕДЕЛИН, многие специалисты по реактивной технике, представители правительственных комитетов.
После подачи команды "старт" - ракета не сошла с пускового стола. Прошло 15-20 минут. НЕДЕЛИН вышел из убежища; за ним последовали другие. В это время произошел взрыв атомного вещества, используемого с другими компонентами. Погибло до 300 человек. Несколько человек чудом спаслось. Они получили тяжелые травмы. Некоторые из них уже умерли. В Москву привезли не тело НЕДЕЛИНА и других погибших, а землю в урнах.

Khrushchev had been demanding that his specialists create a missile engine powered by nuclear energy. The laboratory work concerning such an engine had even been completed prior to the forty-third anniversary of the October Revolution in 1960, and the people involved wanted to give Khrushchev a "present" on this anniversary—a missile powered by nuclear energy. Present during the tests on this new engine were Marshal Nedelin, many specialists on nuclear equipment, and representatives of several government committees. When the countdown was completed, the missile failed to leave the launching pad. After fifteen to twenty minutes had passed, Nedelin came out of the shelter, followed by the others. Suddenly there was an explosion caused by the mixture of the nuclear substance and other components. Over three hundred people were killed.

A few people miraculously survived, but all of them were in deep shock. Some of them died soon afterward. What was brought to Moscow were not Nedelin's and other victims' remains, but urns filled with dirt. Yet we all had read in the "truthful" official government statement printed in the newspapers *Pravda* and *Izvestiya* only that Nedelin died, ". . . in the line of duty—in an air accident," and we also read about how these bodies were cremated, as well as other details about the funeral. The rest of the victims were buried quietly, without any fanfare. A period of mourning was announced in cities where some of the scientists who perished had lived or gone to school. I know that a long mourning period was announced in the city of Dnepropetrovsk.

This, incidentally, is not the first time that a missile accident took place. There had been others before this, but the government keeps silent about them. It would be appropriate at this point to tell of another terrible accident that happened to a helicopter about which Khrushchev at one time bragged to President Eisenhower.

In May 1961, near Odessa, practice firing of combat missiles was being conducted with representatives from the satellite countries attending. On May 17 a group of Soviet generals including General Kolpakchi, Chief of Combat Training of the General Staff; General Perevertkin, Deputy Chairman of KGB; General Goffe, Varentsov's deputy; General Morozov, Chief of the Operations Directorate of the Odessa Military District; and others were flying to the proving grounds near the city of Nikolayev in a helicopter belonging to Lieutenant General Babadzhanyan, Commander of the Odessa Military District. While they were already over the proving grounds, one of the large rotor blades broke loose, and the helicopter crashed into the ground. Everybody including the crew was killed. All bodies were mangled terribly, and the relatives were not even allowed to see them. Soviet newspaper accounts of this tragedy merely said that they died in an air accident. After the cremation the urns were placed on display at the Central Theater of the Soviet Army. The funeral was attended by hundreds of generals and officers, including Varentsov, who was very much upset by the death of his deputy. There were also other accidents involving this same type of helicopter.

Here is a striking example of effrontery and deceit! After that, how can one trust the statement of the central Party organ and the government, which always claim that they say nothing but the truth? Let the entire world know that Marshal Nedelin perished in a nuclear explosion, and that there had been such an accident!

The Dzerzhinskiy Artillery Academy (now the Missile Academy) has a total of 2500 students. From 450 to 600 officers are graduated from this academy every year. But there is only one Missile Academy, and even after their graduation from it the officers will have to have several years of special training in order to become qualified and valuable missile specialists, capable of controlling modern equipment. A missile is not a cannon on two wheels which can be turned in any direction. Khrushchev is blabbing that we are ready, we have everything. This is just so much idle talk. He himself probably does not see the whole picture. He talks about the Soviet Union's capability to send missiles to every corner of the world, but he has not done anything about it because he knows that we are actually not ready. Of course, we can send our missiles in different directions as far as the United States, or Cuba, etc. But as far as launching a planned missile attack to destroy definite targets is concerned, we are not yet capable of doing it. We simply do not have missiles that are accurate enough.

According to the information acquired from Varentsov and others, many of our big missiles are still on the drawing boards, in the prototype stage, or are still undergoing tests. There are altogether not more than a few dozen of these, instead of the "shower" of missiles with which Khrushchev has been threatening the West.[3] The launching of the first *sputnik* required the combined efforts of all Soviet scientists and technical personnel with the entire technological capacity of the country at their disposal.

Several *sputniks* were launched into the stratosphere and never heard from again. They took the lives of several specially trained astronauts.

---

[3] Here Penkovskiy is referring to the ICBM, not the IRBM, which was in production at that time.

Khrushchev's boasting is also meant to impress the Soviet people and to show them that we are strong. Of course, there have been some fine achievements in the development and improvement of tactical and operational short-range missiles. It is still too early, however, to speak of strategic missiles as perfected. Accidents and all sorts of troubles are daily occurrences. In this connection, there is much talk about shortcomings in the field of electronics.

There have been many cases during the test launchings of missiles when they have hit inhabited areas, railroad tracks, etc., instead of the designated targets, after deviating several hundred kilometers from their prescribed course.

The vigilance of the Western powers, however, must not be weakened by the shortcomings mentioned above. If at the present time the Soviet ballistic missiles are still far from being perfect, in two or three years—perhaps even sooner—Khrushchev will have achieved his goal; this is something for everyone to keep in mind.

Right now we have a certain number of missiles with nuclear warheads capable of reaching the United States or South America; but these are single missiles, not in mass production, and they are far from perfect. Every possible measure is taken to improve the missiles and their production. Money is saved everywhere and allocated to the building of "kindergartens," the slang expression we use for missile production. Scientific and technical personnel are being mobilized.

Many different towns have been built for the scientists and the technical and engineering personnel. Not only have scientists and engineers been awarded decorations and medals, but some have been awarded the title of Hero of Socialist Labor three or four times. They have received the Lenin Prize and other prizes. The work of these people is not publicized and their pictures do not appear in the newspapers. Sometimes they may be seen at some important conferences or at Party congresses which they are invited to attend. From this it may be deduced that they are secretly given awards, Lenin Prizes, titles of Hero of Socialist Labor, etc.; this is not made public.

Thus, for example, Vladimir Nikolayevich Chelomey, a missile designer, is the foremost specialist on missiles. He has two laboratories in Moscow. Khrushchev's son works in one of them. Chelomey is a civilian engineer. He developed the "cruise" missile which has been adopted as armament on submarines. It is also used by the ground troops.

The cruise missile will have several different combat designations. A very sensitive altimeter and a special range finder have been developed for this missile, which will enable it to fly around various heights and mountains when launched to the height of 200 to 300 meters above the horizon. Soviet specialists claim that when launched to this height (200 to 300 meters) and with its high speed of flight, this missile will be extremely difficult, if not impossible, to destroy in the air along its trajectory. Tests conducted with regard to these features proved completely successful. In its flight around obstacles over 300 meters in height, the missile's maneuvering will be automatic, i.e., all changes in its flight will be controlled by instruments on board the missile.

For example: Suppose the missile is launched to the height of 250 meters above the horizon. Thirty seconds later it must fly over a mountain 1000 meters high. At twenty-five seconds after the start the missile instruments record the approaching mountain and the missile begins its gradual ascent remaining at 250 meters from the mountain slopes, i.e., when the missile flies over the highest point of the mountain, it will be 1250 meters above the horizon. After flying over the mountain it will come down 1000 meters, etc.

When Khrushchev announced at the beginning of 1960 that the Soviet Union possessed a completely new and terrifying type of ballistic missile, he actually had in mind the order he issued to invent or prepare a new type of propellant based on nuclear energy. Some of the work in this direction has proved quite successful, but it is still far from what Khrushchev had in mind. There is a big lag in electronics. There were many accidents during tests. In this respect my sympathies are with the Americans. If they have an accident, it is all in the papers; everyone knows about it. But in our country everything is kept secret.

There were several unsuccessful launchings of *sputniks* with men killed prior to Gagarin's flight. Either the missile would explode on the launching pad, or it would go up and never return.

When Gagarin made his flight, it was said officially that there was not a single camera in his *sputnik*. This was nothing but a big lie. There was a whole system of cameras with different lenses for taking pictures and for intersection. The photographic equipment was turned on and off during the flight by the astronaut. But Khrushchev tells everybody that nothing was photographed. Photographic equipment has been installed on all *sputniks,* but this has been denied in order to prevent the Americans from launching espionage *sputniks* or, as we call them, "spies in the sky."

Our people in the General Staff felt very uncomfortable when they learned that the Americans had launched a satellite which would fly over the territory of the U.S.S.R. They denounced this as a spy satellite. They believe that this satellite can make photographs, which frightens them. Immediately an order was issued to all major Soviet military targets to improve their camouflage.

All Soviet missiles made at the present time are of the two-stage type. In the past we had some three-stage missiles, but then it was decided that the two-stage missiles were easier to control.

General Grigoryev, commander of a brigade of strategic missiles under Marshal Moskalenko (his brigade is stationed in the Far North), told Pozovnyy that his depot, which contained nuclear warheads, was flooded by water. Therefore it was necessary to move the warheads to another location. Malinovskiy has two launching pads. The launching capacity of each pad is one missile a day.

Colonel Fedorov is commander of a ground-forces missile brigade in East Germany.

Brigadier General Vinogradov is also the commander of a missile brigade in East Germany.

There is a large, well-equipped airfield in the area or city of Zhitomir, where long-range heavy bombers capable of carrying atom and hydrogen bombs are based. Training flights by bombers with these bombs are made regularly from this airfield. Serving at this airfield is General Pozovnyy's nephew, a lieutenant, who recently visited Moscow and told Pozovnyy that he frequently makes flights in the

westerly direction all the way to the border of the U.S.S.R., with atom bombs in his bomb bay.

2. В районе гор. Житомир имеется большой, хорошо оборудованный аэродром, на котором базируются тяжелые бомбардировщики дальнего действия /ДД/, могущие нести атомные или водородные бомбы. С этого аэродрома производятся регулярные полеты /тренировочные/ бомбардировщиков с указанными бомбами. На этом аэродроме служит племянник генерала Позовного А.Р. /лейтенант/, который был недавно в Москве и рассказал Позовному, что он часто летает в западном и юго-западном направлениях до границы СССР, имея наборту атомные бомбы.

Recently in Moscow I saw Colonel Igor Andreyevich Gryzlov, Deputy Chief of the Missile Artillery Supply Directorate of the Soviet Army (the Directorate's Chief, Colonel Gorelikov, has been recommended for promotion to a general), who was on a ten-day visit. Gryzlov is a close friend of mine, and when I was studying at the Dzerzhinskiy Academy, he was Deputy Chief of the 4th Faculty of the Academy.

Colonel Gryzlov told me that the 34th Artillery Division is included in the composition of the Soviet forces stationed in East Germany.

Colonel Nikiforov, Varentsov's former Chief of the Personnel Section, had arrived in Germany and assumed command of a missile brigade (same type of brigade as the one commanded by Colonel Fedorov.)

Besides the missile-firing ground at Kapustin Yar, two new firing grounds have been equipped and put in operation, one at Shklo Yar in Lvov *oblast*, and one in the area of Nikolayev in Odessa *oblast*. The command-staff exercises of the Warsaw Pact Command personnel held last April in Moscow at the General Staff were followed in May by practical exercises with troops and with field firing of missiles. They were attended by representatives of those satellite countries which have received missile equipment.

Missiles were fired from two firing ranges. The Yauer firing range's missile impact area is in Poland, and that of the Nikolayov firing range in Rumania (the impact bases are located in some marshy areas).

So, we fire at Rumanian cornfields, or as we say, at Rumanian *"mamalyzhniki."* [*Mamalyga* is a Rumanian national dish which is made from corn.]

At the end of 1961 a firm directive was issued to equip the satellite countries with missile weapons. This was by a special decision of the Central Committee CPSU. In this regard Marshal Varentsov made the following comment: "They say we must give our brother Slavs missile weapons. So we give them missiles now, and later they will stick a knife in our back."

Marshal Varentsov flew to Poland, to Hungary, and to other countries of the people's democracies, including North Korea and China. This was approximately at the beginning of 1961. To this day Varentsov still receives presents from the Chinese—real Chinese tea which he loves to drink.

The first country to receive missiles from the U.S.S.R. was East Germany, in 1960.

There have been many cases in which the construction of small factories, apartment houses, or office buildings was suspended in order to divert funds to the defense industry and give assistance to the satellite countries.

In my opinion as a General Staff officer, it will take a year or a year and a half for us to be able to equip all our satellite countries with missiles. In order to stop this armament of Khrushchev's and his attempts to launch an attack, the Western countries must triple both their efforts at unity and then increase in armaments. Only then will Khrushchev realize that he is dealing with a strong adversary.

I wish to repeat that I know the exact location in some areas of the launch sites for missile troops where nuclear warheads have been set up: Novaya Zemlya is the number-one center; Norilsk; farther, in the area of Franz Josef Island; in the Vorkuta area. This is all in the North. Now the South: in the areas of Krasnovodsk and Kirovabad; these are directed against Iran, Pakistan, and Turkey.

Here is an interesting note. A Japanese by the name of Sato was on a visit in the U.S.S.R. He wanted us to show him the island of Artema near the city of Baku because he was interested in the problems of drilling underwater oil wells. We sent a special inquiry to the General Staff. The answer, which was classified Secret, stated that no foreigners were allowed on the island; a missile base and an antiaircraft defense base were located there.

The *sputnik*-launching base is located near Orenburg (formerly Chkalov). Gagarin was launched from there.

Missile bases directed against England are located north of Leningrad, in Karelia.

There are missile plants in the Urals and in Gorkiy. Also, there are so-called "powder candies" [*porokhovyye konfety*] in the Ukraine. Everybody calls missiles "modern weapons," i.e., when someone does not want to discuss secrets, he refers to missiles as "modern weapons."

The warheads for atomic shells are manufactured in the city of Klintsy.

One very important airbase is located near Zhitomir. There is also a large airbase near Lvov. By order of Khrushchev, the personnel of this airbase have been trained in handling and carrying atomic bombs. The aircraft can fly across Rumania and Bulgaria.

I have heard already some talk about a woman astronaut being readied for a flight into the stratosphere in a *sputnik* for propaganda purposes. All the higher commanders think that such a flight will have a strong propaganda effect. The launching is planned for the beginning of 1963.[4]

A huge artillery base is located in Mozhaysk.[5] A certain Captain Yevgeniy Mikhaylovich Sklyarov works there. He was not allowed to go abroad because he has no parents. In the Soviet Union persons who have no parents or close relatives are not allowed to go abroad because it is feared that they will leave and never return.

China has not been given a single nuclear missile, nor any other kind of nuclear weapons. The Chinese have been given conventional missiles just as the other countries of the people's democracies, and it is possible that they will be given nuclear missiles if it becomes necessary. But so far they have not received any. The Chinese themselves can manufacture conventional missiles, using our blueprints.

A kind of headquarters has been built underground in the Urals to be used in case of war by the Central Committee CPSU, the Ministry of Defense, and all the other vitally important government agencies. Also in the Urals

---

4 Valentina Vladimirovna Tereshkova was launched into orbit on June 16, 1963.

5 Town about sixty-five miles west of Moscow.

are many aviation plants and hangars, hidden deep underground.

A new type of aircraft with a delta wing has been designed and is undergoing extensive tests. The ceiling of this aircraft is higher than thirty kilometers.

A few more words about artillery and missiles. There are two higher educational institutes in the U.S.S.R. which train personnel for conventional and missile artillery; this is not counting the schools and separate courses which provide training in narrow fields.

The academies are: The Dzerzhinskiy Military Engineering Artillery Academy in Moscow and The Leningrad Artillery Academy in Leningrad; it is a command school rather than an engineering school.

For a long time there was a Foreign Department in the Moscow Academy in which officers of the satellite countries of Eastern Europe as well as Korea and China were trained. But after two Germans, one Pole, and one or two Hungarians were arrested for spreading anti-Soviet propaganda and having contact with foreign embassies in Moscow, this department was moved to the city of Voronezh. Each department also has its chief, deputy chief, and a full-time secretary of the Party bureau. Then there are the senior instructors, instructors, teaching assistants, and laboratory technicians.

Periodically, higher academic courses are organized by the academy to teach the latest missile techniques and other problems of artillery art. I finished one of these special courses in 1959. When I was there, there were eighty students attending this course—twenty of them upon finishing the course were assigned to the ballistic missile troops.

In 1959 the Military Academy for Antiaircraft Defense was organized in the city of Kalinin, in close conjunction with the Dzerzhinskiy Academy. It is now training artillery missile personnel for antiaircraft defense.

Besides this academy, on Khrushchev's orders, a special scientific research institute has been organized to work on the problems of control and communications in the field of electronics, etc. One experimental missile battalion has been attached to this institute. The entire work of this institute is directed toward the development of means of antimissile defense, or antimissile missiles. Varentsov, Pozovnyy, and Buzinov told me, "Thank goodness, Khrushchev is finally turning from loud words to deeds."

I must say frankly that on the basis of what I heard from Varentsov and others, we have no existing means to fight enemy missiles. Work is being conducted, however, in that direction with a considerable rate of speed.

Noting such shortcomings and gaps in the missile artillery, Varentsov and the other artillery men often express their views approximately in this manner: "Our approach to things is always one-sided. We were carried away by missiles. Of course we must be interested in missiles, but we must not ignore conventional artillery, our 'old mother cannon.' We have ignored conventional artillery, which still exists in all our regiments and divisions, and therefore, because of these missiles, we are suffering shortages in the old classical artillery. And in general, because of these missiles, we are also short of other types of armament."

CHAPTER IX

Trouble in Moscow and Abroad

INTRODUCTION

AFTER Wynne had left Moscow, Penkovskiy prepared for trouble. His Committee and the GRU still maintained confidence in him—or said they did. As he noted in the Papers, representations were being made to the KGB to obtain clearance for another trip abroad with a delegation. "Only God knows what their answer will be," he wrote. But he knew himself that a second denial of his travel request could well mean that he was under suspicion, and for something far more serious than the matter of his father's allegiance to the White Army.

In the event, he decided to await the decision of "the neighbors" and plan his course of action accordingly. It was possible that he might simply be removed from the Committee and further contact with foreigners. The exposure of his father's identity, if pressed by enough people, would be enough to warrant such treatment. If this happened he planned to appeal to Varentsov and Serov, if necessary, in an effort at least to stay in the Army. He might have to leave Moscow. If so, he would try to remain somewhere in European Russia, preferably in Leningrad. (He said at his trial that his Anglo-American advisors had suggested Leningrad as the best alternative.)

In the midst of this uncertainty Penkovskiy kept up with his dangerous photography work and attempted to pass on the information he was accumulating. On September 5 he brought some film to an American Embassy reception, but he could find no safe opportunity for transmitting it. The next day he tried to make contact with one of his British sources. That effort, too, proved abortive.

251

On October 22, according to Soviet sources, Oleg Penkovskiy was arrested by the KGB. On November 2, Greville Wynne was kidnapped by the KGB in Budapest, where he had gone with more plans for a mobile trade exhibition in Eastern Europe. He was taken to Moscow. He next saw Penkovskiy through a peephole in Lubianka Prison.

The inevitable question occurs: what betrayed them? It was probably not shrewd, farseeing detective work either on the part of the KGB or the GRU. That is where real life so often departs from the spy stories of fiction. According to the canons of espionage literature, there must have been a lynx-eyed KGB colonel somewhere who had been patiently accumulating a mosaic of fact and hypothesis in the "Penkovskiy case," each element of which was innocent in itself but damning as part of a totality. The Soviet authorities, in fact, finally produced this master sleuth, one Lieutenant Colonel A. V. Gvozdilin, although he was not unveiled until two years after the trial. (See Epilogue.)

Yet the real-life KGB, with or without Colonel Gvozdilin, took twenty-three years to find out that Penkovskiy's father was a White officer, a fact which does not suggest the presence of any Soviet Arsène Lupins or even Sam Spades buried in its Table of Organization. There is no evidence available that the KGB acted with any greater speed or shrewdness in determining that the GRU colonel was betraying the Soviet regime.

Penkovskiy had detected signs of surveillance early in 1962, but such KGB activity was hardly a rarity in the life of the most trusted Soviet official. Although his chance meetings with Mrs. Chisholm look suspicious in hindsight, actually none of Penkovskiy's associations with foreigners —not even the circumstances of his casual meetings— had been out of line with his normal duties on the Committee and in GRU. Only by the summer were the signs of surveillance multiplying. Even then, Greville Wynne himself felt that, at worst, the KGB thought he and Penkovskiy might have been engaged in some black-market trading.

A cautious man would have run to cover at the first signs of continuing surveillance. In July, for example, Penkovskiy could have sent off a message to London that he was breaking off communication, eased off his Western contacts for some months, and—above all—destroyed the incriminating home-espionage kit in the hidden compartment of his desk drawer.

Penkovskiy was a cautious man by training, but not by nature. Every human has his own "hubris," as the Greek dramatists used to tell us, and Oleg Penkovskiy was no exception to the rule. In some lines of work pride goeth before a fall and rises again; the victim of hubris can recover and go on to great heights, if humbler and wiser for having had his overconfidence shaken. But a spy can make only one mistake. He receives no second chance.

The same private personal assurance which made Penkovskiy so successful was undoubtedly what brought him down. Ivan Berzin, who had commanded the GRU in 1934, once made the classic comment about his craft: "In our work boldness, daring, risk, and great audacity must be combined with great prudence. Dialectics!" Penkovskiy never lost his audacity or his sense of risk. He chose to sacrifice his prudence.

When in January 1962 he suspected that he had been observed during at least one rendezvous with one of his contacts, he quickly called off further meetings at that time and resorted to the use of the dead drop. But he continued to pass on documents and write down his observations. His friends and superiors at the Committee continued to trust him. He continued to feel secure in the GRU offices on the Arbat. He knew that the danger, if it came, would come from the KGB, which had presumably been tinkering with his dossier since the discovery of his father's allegiance to the White Army. As the Papers indicate, he was aware of the danger.

It is easy to explain, by hindsight, how the KGB could have worked up its case against Penkovskiy. KGB agents abroad as well as in Moscow were trained to report any Soviet official's contacts with foreigners, as a matter of routine. By the spring of 1962 Penkovskiy's frequent meetings with Wynne and other foreigners must have occasioned many individual routine notations in his KGB file. Although they could be explained by virtue of his position, the number of observations were probably enough to cause the faintest kind of question mark.

The mass of gifts and presents which Penkovskiy brought

back from the West must also have aroused the suspicions of the KGB in Moscow—even if most of them were destined for his superiors or co-workers. The presents were obviously worth more than Penkovskiy, given his earnings and expense allowances, could have spent for them. This might add up to another question mark on his record— not enough evidence of any trouble, but enough to deepen suspicion a little, even if only suspicion of black-market dealings.

There is another important factor. Through the spring and summer of 1962, as tension with the West increased, the KGB was tightening its surveillance of all foreigners. Thus even the casual contacts which Penkovskiy had made in Moscow with British and American attachés were now noted with more care than they might have been—since the foreigners were under closer watch.

Penkovskiy continued to feel free in meeting Wynne because he knew Wynne was not himself an intelligence officer but a businessman who was exactly what his calling card stated. The KGB, however, obviously regarded Wynne as a suspicious character, if only for his repeated trips to Moscow—and despite the fact that the GRU looked on the Englishman as a possible recruit.

Penkovskiy kept up his visits to libraries in the Ministry of Defense, where he read classified literature on many areas obviously not in his immediate purview. Given the volume of information that he transmitted, it is reasonable to assume that someone must have seen him and, again, made some small notation.

Penkovskiy constantly relied on his well-placed connections with people like Marshal Varentsov and General Serov to divert suspicion. But to the KGB mind these connections could arouse suspicion, as well as respect.

At the first hint of suspicion, the KGB is apt to make its own secret search of a suspect's apartment. Someone must inevitably have taken a close look at his desk. Once the secret drawer was found, the jig was up. But when this happened, no one here knows.

We do know that Penkovskiy's meeting with Wynne in July was recorded and photographed. Wynne notes this in his own recollections of his trial: "They would produce a tape recorder and there would be Penkovskiy's voice, and mine. That was sufficient to tell me they had been listening to conversations. . . . In the conversation I could be heard saying, 'I wish you well, Alex,' and, 'I have a letter for you from them,' and Penkovskiy's voice—'Yes, in the letter they say very good things. . . .' "

Either Wynne's room happened to be bugged, as the rooms of so many foreigners in Moscow are, and the transcript led to Penkovskiy's search—or Penkovskiy's apartment was searched, which led to the KGB's watch on Wynne's room. In any event, someone in the KGB finally put two and two together.

We still do not know when this moment of truth came to the KGB. It was probably not in July. We assume that Penkovskiy was still sending out information to the West late in August, at the time of the last notations in the Papers. And it is highly doubtful, given the tensions of the Cuban missile effort, then abuilding, that someone of Penkovskiy's station would be allowed to continue sending out information, even for the purpose of tracking his contacts. He was too big a fish for any counterintelligence agency to dangle on a line.

More probably, given the normal mill of Soviet bureaucracy—imagine the job of recording and processing thousands of taped conversations by foreigners each day—it took weeks before the evidence against Penkovskiy and Wynne was put together and brought to the proper authorities.

What follows was evidently the last entry in the Penkovskiy Papers.

PENKOVSKIY'S TEXT

The ordinary Soviet man in the street has learned to speak out a little. We are not so afraid as before. Even in restaurants one can hear Khrushchev criticized: "Why is he bothering about Berlin again? Why do we need Germany? We have already fought twice against the Germans in this century—do we have to lay down our lives there again? So many have died before. . . . We live in semistarvation, there are shortages everywhere. What will we gain by fighting for Berlin? We have lived without the treaty for sixteen years and nothing happened, why change things now? To hell with Germany."

The intelligentsia is of the same opinion.

Similar sentiments are expressed about Cuba: "Well, what about Cuba? It is thousands of kilometers away from us. We never heard anything about Cuba before, and now we have to feed Castro while we are short of clothing and bread."

Everyone knows that Khrushchev is playing the demagogue when he states that we shall catch up with America in the production of meat, milk, etc. In Moscow one can see long lines, and in the provinces there is neither meat nor milk. People are butchering rabbits and horses.

Varentsov says the same thing, that the people's morale is very bad. They do not believe Khrushchev, they do not believe the government, and they are just as hungry now as they were before. The people are very unhappy about his militant speeches. They say that Khrushchev is forcing Kennedy, Macmillan, and De Gaulle to arm themselves. Then what will we do? People say that if Stalin were here, he would at least keep quiet. Khrushchev is criticized for his garrulity, his stupid bluntness, for the way he himself indiscreetly blurts out state secrets.

At the present time even Moscow and Leningrad are feeling the shortage of vodka. The only vodka sold on the market comes from old reserve stock, since alcohol is presently being hoarded by the government for use in the missile program. For the present, people drink cognac and wine. Whenever any vodka from the old reserve stock appears for sale, there are long waiting lines in the stores, and people come to blows in order to get a bottle.

Why is Khrushchev constantly threatening everyone with nuclear war? It is because he fears dissatisfaction among the people. He thinks that by mentioning nuclear war every day, he will hold the people in fear and obedience.

By nature I am not a religious man. I do not go to church, but I remember that when I was a boy my mother used to take me there. I know that I was baptized—my mother told me. She is very religious and attends church every Sunday and on religious holidays. She knows that I am a member of the Party and an intelligence officer. In our family we have worked things out as follows: Mother does not talk to me about church and religion, and I do not talk to her about my beliefs. She is very old now, and I never attempted to discuss these matters with her, as I did with soldiers and officers in the days when I was the chief of the political section for the Komsomol and conducted antireligious propaganda. But here is something interesting: I remembered God during the war and often in thought crossed myself and prayed. This is something within me which cannot be explained.

Since I moved to the Maksim Gorkiy Embankment, I pray silently every day. Across the street from my apartment is a pretty little church, and, in my heart, I go there and pray. I say again that in this I am not alone. Most officers have the same sentiments in this respect as I.

Recently the number of ordinary people attending church services has grown considerably, and, what is more interesting, even the young people are now having marriages performed in church. There are even instances of church marriages among officers, something which was almost impossible before the war.

In order to turn the young people away from church marriage ceremonies, the Komsomol, at Khrushchev's direction, has organized a campaign to promote so-called "Komsomol weddings." Although to some extent this acts as a deterrent to religious practices, nevertheless young people, even if only a small percentage, today have their marriages performed by the church. Baptism of children, even those of important Party officials, can be described as a widespread phenomenon. Antireligious propaganda has been intensified during recent years, but the population continues to attend church. Khrushchev rants and raves, but can do nothing.

There are even jokes circulating about "religious freedom" in the U.S.S.R. For example: during the Vienna conference Kennedy and Khrushchev were discussing the question of freedom, specifically freedom of religion.

KENNEDY: Mr. Khrushchev, you are talking nonsense, you do not practice religious freedom; you do not even allow people to go to Church.

KHRUSHCHEV: Not only do I forbid them to go to

church, I am conducting antireligious propaganda. . . . There is only one problem—the people still
persist in attending church.

KENNEDY: May I give you some advice?

KHRUSHCHEV: Yes, please do; after all, you are a Cath-
olic yourself.

KENNEDY: Take all the icons out of the churches and
replace them with your portraits. No one will go into
the churches after that.

That was a typical Soviet joke in the year 1961.

In this connection a few words should be said about the
building of the Palace of the Soviets. The area selected
for the site was occupied before the revolution and in the
1920s by the Cathedral of Christ the Saviour. On the
orders of the Central Committee of the All-Russian Communist Party (Bolshevik), this cathedral was dynamited
and razed, to make room for the Palace of Soviets. This
was before World War II. Construction was halted because of the war, and after the war it was discovered that
all the cellars of this palace were flooded. The ground
was too soft for the construction of a multistoried building. The people, however, have their own explanation for
this: because the Cathedral of Christ the Saviour was destroyed, no palace could stand in its place. The place belongs to God, they say.

A large swimming pool has now been built there. However, during the summer months many people drown there,
and the people persist in their explanation along the same
lines: nothing can be built on the site of the Cathedral of
Christ the Saviour because this belongs to God. Subsequently the government spread a provocative rumor in
Moscow that the Baptists had specially trained a few
good swimmers who would dive, grab swimmers by their
feet, and pull them down so that they would drown! This
talk is all over Moscow now.

To support their falsehoods about the Baptists, a special anti-Baptist film was produced on orders from the
Central Committee CPSU. I went to see this movie myself, but I do not remember its name now. Everyone
ridicules the story, but because it is a well-produced film,
people still go to see it.

ANTI-SEMITISM

We have almost no Jews in the GRU. They have all been thrown out. Anti-Semitism is in full bloom. The Jews were just weeded out of the intelligence services under Stalin, and now no Jews are taken in. We had quite a few Jewish generals, a good sprinkling of colonels and other officers. Their purge began under Stalin and finally ended in 1954 or 1955. There has not been a single Jewish student in the Military Diplomatic Academy for many years. In the GRU there is to my knowledge only one Jew, Major Rabinovich. He is retained because he knows Urdu, Hindi and other languages. He even translated the Koran.

There are a few Jewish engineers working for our Committee. They are excellent specialists and very intelligent people. In conversations, however, we refer to them as Armenians or Georgians. Some of the Jewish population, specifically those engaged in trade, live quite well, but in general their situation is not to be envied. None of them is in any type of supervisory work, and none is employed by the KGB.

Here is one of the jokes on the subject, currently circulating: A Jew is called into the KGB Headquarters, and the investigator is interrogating him:

Q. Why are you concealing the fact that you have a brother residing abroad?

A. I have no brother living abroad, and I have never concealed such a thing.

Q. Have you forgotten, you scoundrel, that your brother lives abroad? Why are you concealing the fact that he is in Israel?

A. I am concealing nothing. My brother is living in the homeland, not abroad; I am the one who is living abroad.

So much for jokes. They can tell much about the grimness of our situation.

[EDITOR'S NOTE: After these observations on religion and popular morale, Penkovskiy switches back to his principle themes of international relations and the war danger.]

More on Berlin. There is talk in higher military circles, especially among Kupin's group and others stationed in East Germany, that in case of a Berlin crisis or a war we would have to kill both West and East Germans. Everything is ready to fight against not only West Germany but East Germany as well, because the Germans have anti-Soviet sentiments. In this connection various bases of operations and military points are being readied to be used not only against West Berlin and West Germany, but also against the East Germans.

In September 1961 a directive went out, ordering families of military personnel to be evacuated from East Germany.

Fedorov specifically told me that the military, in spite of their great strength, are afraid that the Germans will set up barricades, trap them, and make it impossible for them to get back to their bases. The Soviets stationed in East Germany are afraid that during the very first night of hostilities the Germans will begin to massacre all the Soviet military personnel in East Germany.

Last year Fedorov made a special report on the existing situation in East Germany to his commanding officer in that area. The latter in turn sent a special political report to the Central Committee CPSU regarding our relations with the population of East Germany.

Varentsov and Fedorov are good friends. Varentsov visited East Germany twice for a so-called inspection of artillery units. During both of the trips he spent all his time with Fedorov.

Kupin's headquarters is in Dresden. The Army Headquarters is located in Dresden, and Kupin is the Commander of the Army Artillery.

Fedorov used to say to me: "Oleg, let us make a jump with our brigades and mechanized regiments and make a riot in Germany. We shall kill all the Germans, one after another because the average German in East Germany hates us." Here are his exact words: "The leadership of East Germany does not treat us too badly because we feed them, give them money, clothes, shoes, etc., but the ordinary East Germans hate us. If it comes to war, they will stone us, shoot us, start fires, commit all kinds of sabotage, etc."

Pozovnyy has also been very critical of Khrushchev for his reckless policies. He used to say that Khrushchev had a big, loud mouth but that we were not yet ready to make a big noise. He came right out and said that the Western states could slap us down so hard that the people's blood will flow. There is no doubt about this.

All this has also been corroborated by Major General Korenevskiy, the GRU information chief, by Zasorin, and by others who work with me in GRU. Korenevskiy has good connections in the Central Committee CPSU and is called there occasionally to give reports.

I repeat again—Khrushchev will someday sign a peace treaty with East Germany after he has brought everything up to combat readiness. Khrushchev has already prepared nine armies for operations in East Germany, and now he is preparing a tenth army. There are only two armies in Germany itself, but the rest are standing by on the German border and can be brought in very quickly.

Khrushchev decided to kill not two but three birds with one stone. First, to have everything in combat readiness in order to frighten other countries. If the West adopts a hard line and shows Khrushchev who is boss, he will certainly feel it. Otherwise there will be trouble. Although many in the command echelon do not agree with Khrushchev's policies, the Army is still under Khrushchev. If the command is given, the Army will fight.

Fedorov told me that many acts of sabotage were committed by German civilians who were sometimes permitted to do odd jobs at the Soviet military installations in Germany. They drill holes in equipment, break automobile parts, let out the fuel. There was an instance when they drilled a hole in a missile, and the fuel leaked out. There were three instances of sabotage in his brigade. Similar instances were discovered in other units of the Soviet army stationed in East Germany.

Kupin says there are insufficient defense facilities in case of war, particularly as regards defense against radioactive substances. Although we tell our people working in defense plants that everything is under control and that there is no danger of contamination, they are still afraid. Many become ill after working for six months or a year.

Even our nuclear-powered icebreaker *Lenin* is a floating deathtrap because of its badly designed valves which allow radioactive leakage.

Whenever possible, our soldiers try to escape to West Berlin or West Germany. Surveillance, however, has been increased to such a point that it is almost impossible to escape. Fear is another controlling factor. The soldier is told that if he is captured he will be shot immediately. Even the East German police have been instructed to capture our soldiers. No German girl is allowed to enter an area where a Soviet military unit is stationed. Soldiers and officers are dissatisfied with service in East Germany because they stay in the barracks day and night and cannot leave. They hear nothing but propaganda. Khoroshilov and Kupin told me that the officers stationed in Germany no longer receive a supplement in German marks. Our regular soldier gets eight to ten marks per month, not even enough to buy cigarettes.

Fedorov, Kupin, and Varentsov all agree that our combat readiness in Germany is at a low level. Every month various commissions from the Central Committee CPSU and from the General Staff are sent to East Gemany to check on the combat readiness of troops and lend assistance. Fedorov is sick and tired of his duty in East Germany and is constantly hoping that Varentsov will transfer him back home.

The West must be ready. They must be prepared to retaliate with antitank forces, etc. The troops must be trained as well as possible. The Soviet plan to create a conflict in Berlin is simply a bid to win without a fight, but to be ready for a fight if it comes. It is planned to use tanks to close all the roads and thus cut off all routes to East Germany and to Berlin.

The first echelon will consist of East German troops, the second of Soviet troops. As a whole, the plan provides for combined operations by Soviet and German troops. If the first echelon is defeated, the second echelon advances, etc. Khrushchev hopes that before events have reached the phase of the second echelon, the West will start negotiations in which East Germany will also participate. This will result in recognition of East Germany.

The Soviet and German troops will participate jointly in this operation because the Germans cannot be trusted to act independently. In the first place, the East German Army is poorly equipped and insufficiently prepared because we are afraid to supply them with everything. The Germans have no love for us, and there is always a chance that in the future they may turn against us, as it happened with the Hungarians.

The entire East German Army is only at 80 per cent of full strength. We are afraid. One of my friends among the Soviet troops in Germany told me that the Germans, especially the civilians, are very dissatisfied with us. He also said that East German officers cannot be relied upon either. About 50 per cent of the soldiers are against us.

KHRUSHCHEV AND CHINA

Judging by what I know and what is known in the Committee and in the GRU, our relations with China are getting worse day by day.

It is not only a matter of ideological differences, but of differences on all matters of, so to speak, a practical nature. We are even conducting intensive intelligence operations against China. We have almost stopped calling China the Chinese People's Republic.

It is interesting to follow the way this name has been changed by us. At first there was the Great China, then the Chinese People's Republic (C.P.R.), and now simply China. And it would not surprise me one bit if we soon started calling them what we called them under the czars: "Salty-Eared Chinks" or "Chinks with a Queue." Right after the revolution of 1917 we used to tease the Chinese by saying: "Do you need some salt, Khodya?" And the Chinese would answer: "And do you need your Soviet power?"

The fact that we are conducting intelligence operations against China is a deep secret. But we have orders from the Central Committee CPSU to conduct active intelligence work against the C.P.R. with the purpose of obtaining objective information on the internal situation in the country and about the immediate plans of its present leadership.

Almost all intelligence operations against China are

conducted by our "neighbors," the KGB, who are responsible for all intelligence work directed against the countries of the so-called socialist camp. Khrushchev wants to know who among "our friends" are his true friends. Naturally he was distressed when Marshal Peng Te-huai was dismissed as Chinese Minister of Defense in 1959. He is especially interested in the opinions and activities of the younger cadres among the leading officials of the Chinese Communist Party. Khrushchev and some of the other Soviet leaders think that Chairman Mao is too old and that this, as well as his poor health, makes it quite obvious that soon the time will come when they will have to deal not with him but with representatives of the new, younger generation. Khrushchev hopes that the younger leaders will renounce Mao's mistaken Trotskyite policy of world revolution and the inevitability of another war, and instead respect the first socialist state in the world, the Soviet Union. They should be more concerned with the problem of how to provide more rice and trousers for their peasant hordes.

The differences with our "Chinese brothers" brought us to the brink of severing diplomatic relations with them. After Khrushchev exposed Stalin's cult and his crimes, the Chinese took the position that Khrushchev had made an irreparable mistake. They held he not only had delivered a crushing blow to the cause of building Communism in the U.S.S.R., but had even betrayed the interests of the world Communist movement. When representatives of labor and Communist parties gathered in Moscow in a special conference to celebrate the forty-third anniversary of the October Revolution in 1960, the Chinese delegation brought up this matter for discussion. A heated argument developed between Khrushchev and Liu Shao-chi. Khrushchev lost his temper and in a fit of anger almost shouted at Liu Shao-chi: "If you need Stalin that badly, you can have him, cadaver, coffin, and all!" Ninety per cent of the conference time was spent on the Soviet-Chinese differences, e.g., the subjects of peaceful coexistence, the inevitability of war, the correctness of the U.S.S.R. foreign policy.

The efforts of all the participants of this assemblage were directed basically at preventing a break between the Soviet and Chinese Communist Parties. To a certain degree they were successful. The Chinese refused to yield on some points, but by means of compromises and proposals a general "understanding" on several questions was achieved by the conference.

Despite the fact that the only differences mentioned in the declarations of the conference were those on questions of tactics and strategy, actually the differences on all questions were so great that there is almost no hope that they can ever be reconciled.

Later, apart from the conference declaration, the Central Committee CPSU issued a special letter for the information of CPSU members in the U.S.S.R. only.

Since the conference the split has become even wider. The Chinese "comrades" (we still call them that) are not only publicly denouncing the Soviet leadership and challenging it. They are also propagandizing the correctness of their views among other Communist and fraternal parties and are seeking active support from them against the CPSU leadership and Khrushchev personally.

Of course, this is something new for the leadership of our Party. Under Stalin our Soviet leaders were accustomed to keeping other Communist Parties under their strict control, making them dance to the tune of their choosing. Thus, when the Hungarian revolution and the events in Poland took place in 1956, our leaders were confused; in the first few days no one knew what to do and what measures to take. Some proposed crushing the revolution (in the Soviet Union it was called a "counterrevolution") by all possible means, others were against using drastic measures for fear that it would further complicate the situation and make the revolution spread into other countries. This was still the time when the Chinese comrades were giving us advice, telling the Soviet leaders what to do and how to do it. Later, Khrushchev of course felt too ashamed to thank the Chinese for their advice. This, naturally, made them angry.

It is interesting to note that Khrushchev is trying everything, including deceit, and, if one may call them that, all sorts of speculative machinations, hoping that the Chinese will finally capitulate because they cannot get along without Soviet economic, technical, and other assistance which they need to make the big leap, as we say, "from the wooden plow to the blast furnace." And therefore there is much talk in the Central Committee CPSU about whether Khrushchev is right. It is known to me that we have curtailed, and in many cases completely stopped, our help to China because we reached the conclusion that the Chinese could not be bought—therefore it was useless to waste our gold and our machinery on them.

Another very important question is: Who is the better Marxist-Leninist, Khrushchev or Mao Tse-tung? After Stalin's death Mao decided that he was much better trained in the matter of a correct understanding and practical application of Marxist-Leninist teachings than Khrushchev and the other leaders of the CPSU; and that because he had been a professional revolutionary all his life he was better prepared to be head of the world Communist movement. He looks upon the present Soviet leadership, and especially upon Khrushchev, as smalltime politicians who found themselves at the helm of the CPSU by accident, without possessing any particular talents for it. Without any real revolutionary background, he feels they cannot remain at the head of a world revolutionary movement.

I personally have little to do with China, but I have many friends in the GRU and here on the Committee who are concerned with Chinese problems. One of my friends who lives next door works as an engineer in the Ministry of Light Industry. He spent eighteen months in China, and he told me that there were no friendly feelings between us and the Chinese. The majority of our representatives in China live isolated from the Chinese, and their relations with the Chinese are strained. Our engineers and technicians do not get any moral satisfaction working with the Chinese because the latter are not sufficiently educated and trained and do not know the basic principles of respect. On the other hand the Chinese, without realizing this, act with suspicion and at every opportunity try to insult our specialists or simply ignore their advice.

In conversations with the Soviets the Chinese Communists always try to show off by quoting from Marx and Engels, thus upsetting the Soviet people even more. I have also heard that the Chinese, on their part, consider our people uncultured and insufficiently civilized. The higher the position of the Chinese leader, the more noticeable this becomes, and the Chinese actually try to stress their superiority.

Varentsov visited China several times and, it seems to me, found a common language with them. [As already noted,] whenever some group of Chinese comes to the U.S.S.R., they always bring Varentsov two or three boxes of real Chinese tea.

The fact that China does not possess any nuclear weapons keeps it from breaking its relations with the U.S.S.R. Research work is being conducted there in the field of atomic energy, and we have given them much help, but I doubt very seriously that we would ever give them nuclear weapons. Varentsov is of the same opinion. Of course, if something very serious takes place and Khrushchev feels that the Chinese need help, then we will simply send our own troops with nuclear weapons and will give them the necessary help. I think it will be three or four years before China has its own nuclear weapons.

Judging by the way our relations with China have been developing, our leaders must be quite apprehensive about the time when China will have its own nuclear weapons. As I have already said, our relations with China are getting worse every day. Still, as Party members, we are told that nothing serious will come from it and that our relations with China will eventually improve.

I wish only to warn the Western states that despite the serious differences that exist between the U.S.S.R. and China at the present time, these differences could disappear if a serious situation develops in the world. The argument and the differences between Khrushchev and Mao Tse-sung are basically concerned with the problem: which is the best and quickest method of burying capitalism. This must not be forgotten.

Khrushchev would like to combine his provocations in Berlin with the Iranian problem. He already has a plan worked out: If any complications develop in Berlin or Cuba, Khrushchev will send his troops into Iran. The Soviet troops' entry into Iran would not be a single isolated act, but would coincide with the start of military operations in other directions. In fact, many of our GRU officers now stationed abroad have been instructed to tell their Western contacts that the Cuban problem would be solved in Iran.

It is not considered expedient to take the troops into

Iran at the present time because this would create even greater tension, and possibly even war. Soviet troops are being prepared for such an entry, however. It is conjectured that this may take place in October.

In connection with this problem, the GRU *rezident* in Iran, Panteleymonov, was summoned to Moscow to receive some instructions. Other *rezidents* from countries in the Middle and Near East were also summoned to Moscow for a conference.

There are maps in the General Staff on which the missile bases of the Western states are indicated, including three American missile bases in Iran. Buzinov and Zasorin told me about this. So did Varentsov.

While I am on the subject of neutral countries I should mention Egypt. Khrushchev is very unhappy because Nasser is oppressing the Communists there; the Communist Party of Egypt has been banned. Khrushchev once said frankly that Nasser was Tito No. 2. Nasser's nationalism, his policy of independence, and his insignificant support of the Soviet Union worry Khrushchev considerably. The Soviet Union, however, has no intentions in the near future of straining its relations with Egypt further— this might have an adverse effect on its relations with other Arab states. In addition, as everybody knows, the Soviet Union is building a large dam in Egypt. It would be rather awkward to abandon this construction now and spoil relations with Egypt. It is better to maintain the status quo with Egypt than to have nothing.

Khrushchev has tried since the Suez crisis to exploit Nasser's nationalism. So far he has not got anywhere. At the present time Khrushchev prefers to have Nasser's position grow weaker and weaker, and he is even disposed to having Nasser removed and replaced by someone else. The friendship which exists today with Egypt is not to Khrushchev's taste at all.

When the American troops disembarked in Lebanon in July 1958, Marshal Rokossovskiy was appointed the Commander of the Transcaucasian Military District. At that time Varentsov was also in the Transcaucasian Military District, although he was not officially stationed there. This was done not because the Soviet Union was ready to go to war, but simply to show the world: "See what an important military leader has been appointed! Take care, we are ready to fight!" It is true that Khrushchev ordered everything brought to combat readiness, but actually he did not intend to send his troops into Lebanon.

Some notes on our international aircraft incidents:

The RB-47 Incident: The U.S. aircraft RB-47 shot down on Khrushchev's order [on July 1, 1960] was not flying over Soviet territory; it was flying over neutral waters. Pinpointed by radar, it was shot down by Khrushchev's personal order. When the true facts were reported to Khrushchev, he said: "Well done, boys, keep them from even flying close."

Such is our way of observing international law. Yet Khrushchev was afraid to admit what had actually happened. Lies and deceit are all around us. There is no truth anywhere. I know for a fact that our military leaders had a note prepared with apologies for the incident, but Khrushchev said: "No, let them know that we are strong."

When it became known about the Berlin tunnel and the monitoring of Soviet telephone conversations by Western intelligence,[1] there was great commotion in Moscow, especially among the GRU and KGB people. An investigation was conducted by the KGB, and many Soviet military and civilian personnel in East Germany were punished. We heard lectures on this subject at the Military Diplomatic Academy in which we were told that many important secrets and much valuable information had fallen into enemy hands. This incident is considered a very serious failure on the part of the Soviet counterintelligence.

At a dinner at Varentsov's house, Churayev, while discussing intelligence work with me, bragged to me that he, too, knew a few things about intelligence. "An American industrialist, after having a few drinks, offered Nikita Sergeyevich his services as an informant. This industrialist supposedly has a friend who occupies an important position in high U.S. circles."

The U-2 Incident: Prior to the Powers flight, other U-2 flights had been made in the Kiev-Kharkov direction, but Khrushchev kept his mouth shut because at that time there

---

1 In April 1956, Soviet military authorities in East Germany admitted that U.S. intelligence agents had tunneled into East Berlin to set up and operate an elaborate system for wiretapping telephone lines.

were no missiles that could be effective at the altitudes at which the U-2 aircraft were flying.

When Powers was shot down over Sverdlovsk, it was not a direct hit but rather the shock wave that did it. The aircraft simply fell apart from it. During his descent Powers lost consciousness several times. He was unconscious when they picked him up from the ground; therefore he was helpless to do anything and did not put up any resistance. This incident happened on May 1, when I was duty officer at the GRU. I was the first one to report it to the GRU officials. Powers was brought to Moscow by plane after he had been shot down, and the KGB at the moment did not have an English interpreter. I was supposed to talk to him because I was the only one around who had some understanding of English—I had already reported the incident to some generals. If they had not found a KGB interpreter at the last minute, I would have been the first one to interview Powers.

Ultimately they called up to say that I was not needed and the KGB Chief, this young fellow Shelepin, who used to run the Komsomol (he replaced Serov at the KGB), wanted to make the report to Khrushchev personally. So he got an interpreter and picked Powers up. But the military had knocked Powers down and Powers was considered to be a military man. He should have been turned over to the General Staff. Nonetheless the KGB seized him, took him to Dzerzhinskiy Square, and made their own report. He was being treated medically because he was still in shock.

Marshal Biryuzov was reprimanded because he had not correctly estimated the probable direction of the U-2 flights —he misgauged the importance of the targets. They wanted to fire when the aircraft from Turkey flew over Kiev, but there was nothing to fire with and the aircraft escaped. Powers would have escaped if he had flown one or one and a half kilometers to the right of his flight path.

On the fifth of May, after Powers was knocked down, Khrushchev ordered a suspension of agent operations to avoid the risk of being caught by a Western provocation or of possibly furnishing material for Western counter-propaganda [a fact Penkovskiy reported previously]. There were many protests about dropping scheduled meetings and other contacts, but it had to be done. The *rezident* in

Pakistan decided on his own to pick up material from a dead drop which was already loaded in order to avoid possible compromise to the agent. For this he was severely reprimanded by his superiors at the GRU, even though he did the right thing. Thus, Khrushchev ordered cessation of agent contacts during the period when he was going to capitalize on the Powers incident—despite the damage it did to the agent nets.

Khrushchev followed Powers' investigation and trial with great interest. He personally conducted the propaganda activity connected with the case. He was the first who began to shout about the direct hit, although actually there had been no such thing. Khrushchev wanted to brag about his missiles.

Khrushchev lied when he said that Powers was shot down by the first missile fired. Actually, fourteen missiles were fired at his plane. It was the shock wave produced by the bursts that caused his plane to disintegrate. The examination of Powers' plane produced no evidence of a direct hit; nor were there any missile fragments found in it. One of the fourteen missiles fired at Powers' plane shot down a Soviet MIG-19 which went up to pursue Powers. Its pilot, a junior lieutenant, perished.

Things are going very well on the Arbat and in the Committee. In these organizations I am treated in the best manner. Serov, Smolikov, Gvishiani, and other friends very much want to send me on another temporary duty mission abroad: either to Australia or Japan or the U.S.A. with the mobile book exhibition or to France with Rudnev and Gvishiani. They will try to talk the KGB and the Central Committee into granting the necessary temporary duty orders. If the KGB clears me of suspicion, they will sanction my travel.

I have already grown used to the fact that I note periodically some degree of surveillance and control over my movements. The "neighbors" continue to study me. There is some reason for this KGB activity. I confuse and lose myself in guesses and suppositions. I am very far from exaggerating the dangers. Still, I am an optimist and I try to evaluate the situation objectively.

I am not disappointed in my life or my work. The most important thing is that I remain full of strength and desire to continue this work. To tell the truth about this system—it is the goal of my life. And if I succeed in contributing my little bricks to this great cause, there can be no greater satisfaction.

August 25, 1962

Epilogue: The Trial

On May 7, 1963, in Moscow in the Court Session Hall of the Supreme Court of the U.S.S.R., there began an open trial in the criminal case of the agent of the British and American intelligence services and citizen of the U.S.S.R., O. V. Penkovskiy, and the subject of Britain and spy go-between, Greville Wynne.

> —Information release, Military Collegium of the Soviet Supreme Court

THE trial of Colonel Penkovskiy and Mr. Wynne lasted all of four days, and one of these days was occupied by a closed session. The verdict of "guilty" was never in doubt. Both defense attorneys devoted themselves, principally, to arguing for a slight mitigation of the sentences; for most of the trial their arguments and attitude varied little from that of Lieutenant General A. G. Gornyy, the chief military prosecutor. Both defendants confessed their guilt, although Wynne displayed some obvious reservations. As he intended, he left little doubt about the extent of his coaching and coercion. When a telling point was made by the prosecution, or a damaging admission by Penkovskiy, the two-hundred-odd "representatives of the workers of Moscow" who had attended the trial cheered and jeered, per instructions.

Yet the trial emerges as far from the document the KGB had hoped for. Penkovskiy and Wynne were no road-show Rubashovs, already preconditioned to play whatever parts were assigned them in a display trial like those of the thirties. They were the knowing, unrepentant victors in a long battle of wits with Soviet counterintelligence; and even under their captors' thumbs they could

273

not be squeezed too far. Anxious to preserve the newly avowed Soviet respect for judicial form, the prosecutors did their best to avoid the avenger stereotype of Andrey Vyshinskiy at the prewar purge trials. At times they were hesitant, and by their hesitance betrayed the uneasiness about repression which has characterized recent Soviet leaderships. This experience in court was no Stalinist invasion of the Baltic States, so to speak. But it did recall the backing and filling before the Khrushchev reconquest of Hungary.

The very fact that a trial had to be held must have been embarrassing. Other Soviet officers had been arrested for espionage against their government and shot out of hand. In December 1962, just a month after Penkovskiy's arrest, an infantry officer known in the Soviet press as Lieutenant Colonel P. was shot for treason, as a spy of the American intelligence service. While the comments lavished on him ("egocentric and secretive . . . lacked common, everyday courage . . . an obviously weak individual") prefigured the "moral" case later made against Penkovskiy, there was no thought of a public trial. Penkovskiy, however, *had* to have a public trial. Not only had eight British and U.S. diplomats been declared *personae non gratae* for their connections with him. Not only was a foreign national, Wynne, directly implicated. But Penkovskiy himself was too big a fish to dismiss with the minimal angler's report reserved for most such offenses. The wave of transfers and demotions in the Soviet intelligence service and the Army was too large to avoid explaining. And Penkovskiy's associates in the Army were too highly placed to avoid the most public sort of warning. Deep down, the trial of Colonel Penkovskiy may have represented the Communist Party's warning to the military that seditious thoughts about the regime's leadership could meet with only one unfortunate end.

For six months the prosecution worked out the details of these four swift days in court. Thanks to his subsequent exchange in 1964, Greville Wynne returned from the Lubianka to give the outside world an uncensored version of this preparation—a subject's view of how Soviet intelligence stages its juridical proceedings.

Wynne had been flown to Moscow in a Soviet aircraft on November 3, less than twenty-four hours after his abduction in Budapest by Soviet and Hungarian security men. He had gone to Budapest in the first place with deep reservations, for it was clear after his last meeting with Penkovskiy that July that they were both under heavy surveillance. But he felt that to renege on his scheduled trip to Eastern European countries would kill whatever slim hope remained to Penkovskiy to pass off their meetings in Moscow as routine business conversations. Wynne was apprehended about two weeks after he arrived in Hungary.

From the day of his arrival in the Lubianka, Wynne was subjected to interrogation, some of it not very gentle, by a KGB general and his assistants. He was shown some of the evidence against Penkovskiy and himself, which included photographs of their meetings and what was apparently a taped transcript of their last conversation in Wynne's room at the Ukraina Hotel. Ultimately his jailors arranged a meeting with Penkovskiy, a joint interrogation designed as prelude to an arranged public trial.

As Wynne described his experience, he had first hoped that the only charge would be that of bribing Penkovskiy with presents—much was made of the packages he had brought with him from the West. But the KGB general and his colleagues soon made it clear that Wynne, like Penkovskiy, was to be charged with espionage. He was allowed to make the distinction that he had no direct knowledge either of the intelligence information or the instructions which he had passed to the Soviet colonel. The prosecution was content to describe him as the dupe of British intelligence. He was a man "forced by threats to do this dirty work," the Soviet defense attorney stated.

At their meeting inside the Lubianka, Penkovskiy begged Wynne to co-operate in a public trial. Unless there was one, he said, "I am sure I will be shot." But if he co-operated, he said, "they have promised me my life."

It was certain that the KGB had also promised some degree of protection for Penkovskiy's family if he and Wynne faithfully played the roles assigned to them. Wynne agreed to co-operate with the KGB, within limits. After six helpless months in a solitary cell of the Lubianka, there was little option left to him. But his limits were important ones. It took great courage for anyone to observe them—most especially for Greville Wynne, who was not an intelligence officer himself, but a patriotic

British businessman who simply had carried through an operation in which circumstances had put him, because he was aware of its importance.

In the pretrial interrogations Penkovskiy, who had obviously had a rough time of it, made no attempt to disguise his motives and his actions. He told the KGB interrogators that he had acted not primarily to help the West, but in the best interests of his own people, the Russian people. This was hardly a defense which the Soviet court would permit to be repeated. (It is of interest that the final statements of both defendants were made in closed session.)

The two defense attorneys assigned to Wynne and Penkovskiy went through the motions of talking to their "clients," but only after the KGB interrogation had finished. (Wynne's attorney, who spent most of his time in court agreeing with the prosecution, later presented him with a capitalist-sized bill.)

Soviet publicists in fact went to great lengths to dramatize the work of their "vigilant Chekists" in the Penkovskiy investigation. As late as 1965, in a little paperback book called *The Front-line in the Secret War*,[1] one Lieutenant Colonel Aleksandr Vasilyevich Gvozdilin, who was apparently Penkovskiy's chief interrogator, was publicized in the best spy-story tradition. "On this overcast November evening," the story begins "in one of the windows of a building standing in Dzerzhinskiy Square in Moscow, a light glowed for longer than usual. . . . Aleksandr V. tilted back in his chair, closed his weary eyes and before him as if in a kaleidoscope there passed most of what he had discovered and heard in recent times. . . ."

The authors of *The Front-line* continued their dramatization. "Only under the pressure of irrefutable evidence presented by the investigator did [Penkovskiy] finally confess that he was a spy. . . . He still hedged for a long time and spoke confusedly of the concrete facts of his treachery and espionage. . . . However the keen mind and patience of Aleksandr V., his clear logic and his skill in conducting an investigation had their effect. . . ."

In the Soviet authors' version, Lieutenant Colonel

[1] Published as Front Taynoy Voyny by S. I. Tsybov and H. F. Chistyakov. Military Publishing House, Defense Ministry, Moscow.

Gvozdilin established that Penkovskiy—"long since discharged from the Army"—had ferreted out his military secrets only from "the irresponsible chatter of a number of servicemen with whom this enemy met and caroused." About Penkovskiy's motives they were silent. Although the question was asked "When and how had he gone astray?" neither Aleksandr V. nor, as we shall see, the prosecution at the trial was ever able to establish a satisfactory answer.

When the trial was finally staged, both defendants had been rehearsed thoroughly, even to the point of visiting the courtroom in advance. The trial went on in the flat, prosy manner of most such proceedings. The military court, presided over by Lieutenant General V. V. Borisolglebskiy, called four witnesses, two of them acquaintances of Penkovskiy's, and produced nine experts to certify the equipment found in Penkovskiy's apartment, the security nature of the information which he gave, etc. In an orderly process of question and answer the whole story of Penkovskiy's espionage against the Soviet Union was repeated and summarized, from the first confrontation with the British and American intelligence officers in London. General Gornyy summarized it at the outset: ". . . the accused Penkovskiy is an opportunist, a careerist, and a morally decayed person who took the road of treason and betrayal of his country and was employed by imperialist intelligence services. By the end of 1960 he attempted to get in touch with the American intelligence service, further exploiting the undeserved trust placed in him and his position as deputy head of the Foreign Department of the State Committee for the Co-ordination of Scientific Research Work—having, through the nature of his work, the opportunity to meet foreigners visiting the Soviet Union as members of the various scientific and cultural delegations. . . ."

In the humdrum legalese of the court's question and answer, packets of intelligence material were again passed and received, dead drops were utilized, and contacts were made; radio frequencies were identified and coding sets discussed.

Occasionally Penkovskiy and Wynne disagreed on matters of fact, but not seriously. Penkovskiy, to his credit,

did insist that Wynne had no knowledge of the contents
of the packets. But the first few hours of testimony were
enough to reveal that Penkovskiy had successfully transmitted information of considerable if undisclosed value to
the West. Representatives of foreign news organizations
were invited to the trial. They reported no evidence either
that the defendants had been drugged, or that any undue
coercion was used to elicit their answers.

Nonetheless the KGB took few chances on any un-
timely disclosures. Greville Wynne tartly notes in his
memoirs that the Moscow police department blocked off
traffic on some streets near the Supreme Court building,
rerouting it so that it ran directly under the courtroom
windows. Western representatives at the trial confirmed
that they had difficulty hearing the testimony.

Since Wynne threatened to deviate from the prepared
script, the microphone was turned off whenever he spoke.
This made almost all of his replies unintelligible. Once he
managed to make a noticeable departure, when he said:
"Well, it is no secret to people in my country and people
in other countries that there are microphones planted in
diplomats' apartments in Moscow." (This was rendered
in the Soviet transcript of the trial as "I must also say—I
have been told that in apartments occupied by diplomats
in Moscow there are very often microphones for listening
in.") At this, the presiding officer of the court immediately changed the subject. Wynne was later threatened by
KGB interrogators with severe consequences if he made
another such gaffe again.

With the facts of the case, the prosecution might have
rested. Had General Gornyy been content with stating that
espionage had been done and had he then demanded the
punishment for espionage under Soviet law, he might have
shown the world an irreproachable example of standard
judicial procedure. The evidence against Penkovskiy and,
to a lesser extent, Wynne admitted of little dispute. There
was the secret drawer in the Colonel's desk at home, the
rolls of exposed film with the most compromising sort of
military information, the instructions from Western intelligence officers, the Continental typewriter, no. 213956,
which experts testified had been used to write the intelligence reports found in Penkovskiy's apartment.

The catalogue of material confiscated, as read off at the

Soviet trial, would in itself offer ample grounds for an espionage conviction:

"During the search at Penkovskiy's apartment, in addition to the already mentioned records with the telephone numbers of the foreign intelligence officers, six message postcards with instructions for them, the report, and the exposed rolls of film, the following articles were discovered in a secret hiding place installed in his desk, and were attached to the file as tangible evidence: a forged passport, six cipher pads, three Minox cameras and a description of them, two sheets of specially treated paper for writing secret text, a memorandum with an indication of the frequencies on which Penkovskiy received instructional radio transmissions from the foreign intelligence services, the draft of a report from Penkovskiy to the intelligence headquarters, the article which Penkovskiy had received from the foreign intelligence services and which he intended to publish in the Soviet Union, fifteen unexposed rolls of film for the Minox camera, and various instruction manuals provided by the foreign intelligence services: on taking photographs with the Minox camera, on the encipherment and decipherment of radio communications, on the procedure for receiving radio transmissions from the intelligence headquarters, and on the selection and use of secret drops.

"In addition, during the search at Penkovskiy's apartment, the following were also confiscated and attached to the file as tangible evidence: the Soniya [Sony] radio receiver which he had received from the foreign intelligence services and which he used to receive enciphered radio messages from the intelligence headquarters, and the typewriter on which Penkovskiy typed his reports."

Nor was there much doubt about the fact that British and American officers had kept up constant contact with Penkovskiy in his intelligence mission for them. Under questioning at his trial Penkovskiy described his contacts in great detail. The summation of General Gornyy, toward the trial's close, makes an instructive piece of reading material; and in the following concrete illustrations, at least, there is little reason to doubt its accuracy:

"While he was in Paris Penkovskiy was told of a secret American hiding place in the entrance to the building at 5/6 Pushkin Street in Moscow and the rules were explained for using it: before depositing espionage materials in the hiding place Penkovskiy was to make a black mark on the no. 35 lamppost on Kutuzov Prospect then, after depositing the materials, was twice to call the telephone numbers G 3-26-87 and G 3-26-94, and having heard an answer, to hang up the receiver. This would mean that the intelligence officers could come to the pickup. One of the calls should be answered 'Jones' and the other 'Davison.' Later Penkovskiy was told that instead of 'Jones,' the answer would be 'Montgomery.'

"Penkovskiy was to use the same telephone numbers also in case he found himself in difficulties. Then he was to make a black cross on no. 35 lamppost and then, having called the numbers mentioned, was to blow three times into the mouthpiece.

"Penkovskiy wrote all this down on a piece of paper which was taken from him when he was arrested and offered as material evidence [Vol. 8, point 110].

"As the telephone book declares and as you, members of the court, know, the telephone G 3-26-94 is located in the apartment of the assistant Army-Air attaché of the U.S., Aleksis Davison, and the telephone G 3-26-87 in the apartment where the Second Secretary of the American Embassy William Jones lived until February 1962.

"They will tell you that the fact that Penkovskiy had telephone numbers of diplomatic representatives in his possession is no evidence at all that he had traitorous relations with such persons since Penkovskiy's official duties required him to maintain contact with foreigners, to attend diplomatic receptions, and that, in general, to know such telephone numbers is not so difficult.

"The investigation foresaw the possibility of such statements and, not simply taking Penkovskiy's explanations at face value, made an objective check on them.

"As you already know, for this purpose a check was carried out in accordance with Art 183 of the Criminal Procedure Code RSFSR on November 2, 1962. Observations were made of the visits of intelligence officers to the hiding place which had been shown to Penkovskiy. You also know that thirty minutes after the telephone calls the assistant Army-Air attaché of the U.S., Davison, was examining lamppost no. 35 on Kutuzov Prospect, and some time later on the same day Richard Jacobs, an official of the U.S. Embassy, came to the hiding place where he was apprehended.

"Penkovskiy's statements together with the materials taken from him and the results of the experiment constitute convincing evidence incriminating Penkovskiy himself and the American diplomatic personnel Davison and Jacobs. The nature of their activities is truthfully revealed and cannot be evaded.

"Moreover, in accordance with the principles of Soviet law of evidence we have grounds for believing Penkovskiy's statement that, in addition to the telephone numbers mentioned, he was given the number K 4-89-73 for calling intelligence officers to the pickup place by calling any Monday at 21:10 hours twice with an interval of one minute and hanging up after blowing three times into the mouthpiece. This telephone is located in the apartment occupied to June 1962 by the former British assistant naval attaché in the U.S.S.R., John Barley, and from July 1962 to March 1963, by the embassy official of the same country, Ivor Russell.

"Upon returning from Paris Penkovskiy, it was learned, on October 17, 1961 called the number G 3-13-58 and after blowing three times replaced the receiver, which signified his safe return to Moscow. This telephone is located in the apartment in which the British Embassy official Felicita Stuart lived in October 1961.

"Carrying out the instructions of his 'bosses,' Penkovskiy selected places for spare pickups in various sections of Moscow and for such very prosaic purposes planned to use the grave of the poet Sergey Yesenin in the Vagankovskiy Cemetery.

"In July 1961 Wynne came to Moscow with assignments from British intelligence. He was received at the British Embassy and handed over to Penkovskiy further instructions, warning postcards, 3000 rubles in cash, and an article prepared by intelligence officers which Penkovskiy wished to have published in the Soviet press for the purpose of publicizing his name.

"Penkovskiy studied the photographs shown to him by Wynne of persons with whom he was to maintain espionage contacts; these included the attaché of the U.S. Embassy in the U.S.S.R., Rodney Carlson, and also the wife of the second secretary of the British Embassy in Moscow,

Gervaise Cowell—Pamela Cowell. Penkovskiy was to identify Carlson by his necktie pin encrusted with red stones.

"Penkovskiy was to transmit spy material to Pamela Cowell by depositing it in a container in a jar of Harpic powder.

"You will remember, comrades of the court, the story of this jar of Harpic. Wynne first studied it with Chisholm and there was a silent scene: Chisholm opened the jar, took the material out, and showed the container while Wynne watched carefully. Then, in the Ukraina Hotel the roles were reversed: Wynne displayed the material and Penkovskiy observed.

"During this meeting in Moscow with Wynne Penkovskiy transmitted to him various espionage materials.

"The warning postcards received from Wynne were ordinary Soviet picture postcards with views of Moscow, with English texts and addresses. Penkovskiy was to mail these postcards in order to give notice of changes in his activities.

"For example, in case he changed his place of work, he was to send a card with a view from the Kotelnicheskiy Embankment addressed to Mrs. N. Nixon, Berks, England, with the message 'I am having a pleasant time and have even found that I like vodka. Moscow actually looks this way and you should see the size of the streets. I will give you all the details on my return. With love, Dick.'

"Penkovskiy succeeded in sending only one postcard; the others were taken from his hiding place and lie before you. During this time he was not spending his time enjoyably and was not delighted but was looking around him in all directions in a cowardly fashion and sweating from fear. He felt that the noose was closing on him and that the end was near.

"On July 4, 1962 at a reception at the American Embassy on the American national holiday, Independence Day, Penkovskiy became acquainted with Carlson and in August, at a reception at Khorbeli, handed over to Carlson seven exposed photographic plates with secret material and a report on one of the Soviet missiles. At this meeting Penkovskiy received from Carlson a package with a fictitious Soviet passport in case he had to go underground and a letter of instructions in which the foreign intelligence agents demanded information on the state of the defenses of the capital of our Fatherland and on the troops in the Moscow Military District."

All of this secret maneuvering would have made a real-life James Bond proud (although the intricate communications details might have taxed Bond's attention span). The prosecutor's indignation at Western attachés' "unceremoniously violating the norms of international law" is, to say the least, ironic, considering how Soviet diplomats have trampled on international law throughout the world as a matter of standard operating procedure. Nonetheless the expulsion of Western attachés after Penkovskiy's arrest was to be expected and, from the official Soviet point of view, the prosecutor's fulminating against the Western intelligence services was amply justified:

"A leading role in this belongs to the Central Intelligence Agency of the U.S.—the support of the most adventurist circles in the U.S. Like a giant octopus it extends its tentacles into all corners of the earth, supports a tremendous number of spies and secret informants, continually organizes plots and murders, provocations and diversions. Modern techniques are put to the service of espionage: from the miniature Minox cameras which you see before you up to space satellites, 'spies in the sky.'

"The British Intelligence Service, which has been in existence for about three hundred years, is no less insidious and astute in its methods but it attempts to remain more in the background. The activities of these major espionage centers against the U.S.S.R. are connected and closely coordinated, as can be clearly seen in the present case, but this, however, does not reduce the contradictions between them or their struggles against each other."

But a straight verdict of "guilty" was not what the Soviet prosecutors sought. The Soviet system is still too brittle to permit what to the Western mind seem commonplaces of the judicial system, like an accused defending and explaining his motives, with a defense attorney actively seeking a verdict of "not guilty." A Western traitor like Klaus Fuchs or Julius Rosenberg could give voice to whatever protest against his system he wished to make. Even a professional Soviet agent, like Rudolf Abel, could avail himself of a skilled American defense counsel, sworn to defend Abel to the best of his ability, whose legal expertise could make things quite difficult for the U.S. government prosecutor. But an Oleg Penkovskiy had to "confess." Because the Soviet system cannot admit any open controversy or disagreement within its ruling Party, Penkovskiy's trial would be useful only if he admitted utter guilt in Marxist theological terms. He could not be allowed to be simply a lawbreaker. He had to join the demonology of "wreckers, diversionists, assassins, and spies," to use Andrey Vyshinsky's old 1938 term, for, obviously, only a serious moral character defect could lead a Soviet citizen to betray his regime.

The trial of Oleg Penkovskiy, in short, was held not to establish guilt, but to establish a motive and publicize it. We must understand that the Soviet managers of the trial were not remotely conscious of any immorality, not to say illegality in this rigging process.[2] In a system whose ideological underpinnings have been steadily weakening, the trial of a Penkovskiy was something of a last rally.

All other considerations, therefore, were sacrificed to the cause of proving Penkovskiy's Communist immorality and holding him up to the world as a horrendous example. And it was precisely there that the staging broke down.

To begin with, the Soviet prosecutors could not properly identify their man. His real identification cards could not be used as elementary evidence. To have given Penkovskiy's real service, title, and function would have been tantamount to unmasking his Committee, an important and on its face respectable Soviet organization, as little more than an intelligence machine. So Colonel Penkovskiy had to be classed merely as a "colonel in the reserve." There was never a mention in the trial that Penkovskiy's primary position was that of an intelligence officer in the Soviet General Staff and that he had been occupied since 1949 exclusively with intelligence missions. The GRU "experts" who testified at the trial were described simply as officers belonging to the Ministry of Defense.

Similarly the Soviet court was very cautious about Pen-

2 In the words of the popular textbook *Communist Morality* (Molodaya Gvardiya Publishing House, Moscow, 1963): "Devotion to Communism—behavior appropriate to the needs of the construction of Communist society—is the moral behavior of people. We judge the moral image of a man from the point of view whether his actions are in accordance with the needs for the construction of Communism."

kovskiy's associations. As he tells us in the Papers, he moved constantly in senior military circles of the Soviet Army. His friends were generals and colonels, of his own rank and outlook. According to the trial, however, Penkovskiy operated in an ephemeral Moscow demimonde of cabarets and high-priced restaurants. Witness *Izvestiya's* comment on May 10, 1963, summing up the trial testimony: "A rank-and-file officer whose contacts and acquaintances did not go beyond a limited circle of restaurant habitués, drunkards, and philanderers." The only two witnesses summoned who allegedly knew Penkovskiy were I. P. Rudovskiy and V. Ya. Finkelshteyn. Finkelshteyn was identified as "the director of a shop for applied art" and Rudovskiy merely as a translator and the owner of a car.[3]

The prosecutor did his best to characterize Penkovskiy as a sort of overage hipster, in the Soviet sense, who concentrated most of his energies on having a good time. In his own well-rehearsed statement, throwing himself on the mercy of the court, Penkovskiy himself admitted to "the meanest qualities, the moral decay caused by almost constant daily use of alcoholic beverages and dissatisfaction with my position in the Committee. . . . I lost the road, stumbled at the edge of an abyss, and fell. Vanity, vainglory, dissatisfaction with my work, and the love of an easy life led me to the criminal path. . . . Morally base qualities and complete corruption—I admit to all this. . . ."

Both Finkelshteyn and Rudovskiy were questioned almost exclusively about Penkovskiy's alleged dissipation and womanizing. Hence this typical exchange:

Prosecutor: "Witness Rudovskiy, tell us please, were there any evening or other meetings when the slippers of his beloved were used as goblets?"

Witness Rudovskiy: "One time on the birthday of a friend Penkovskiy, his lady, and I were at the Poplavok restaurant in the Park of Culture. I had no woman with me and did not drink from the slipper. I don't know if it

---

[3] It is significant, too, that both of these "friends" questioned bore Jewish names. This little touch of the anti-Semitism for which the Soviet regime is famous could still be counted on to strike a popular note with Russian newspaper readers. There was more than a little hint in this positioning of "close friends" that Penkovskiy was Jewish himself.

was to show his love for the girl or because it was Western practice, but Penkovskiy poured wine into the slipper and drank it."

It was all very bizarre and very suspect. The accusations of his drinking champagne from a slipper suggested that Penkovskiy's KGB interrogators were at least men of imagination. But it hardly sounded like the accused's behavior.

Despite such official efforts to paint Penkovskiy's life as a latter day "Rake's Progress," the witnesses themselves, inadvertently, did much to substantiate Penkovskiy's contrary description of himself in the Papers. And the picture they give of him is consistent with everything we know of his character. As Finkelshteyn remarked, "Penkovskiy was always tense, always hurrying, always agitated, very vain; he always wanted to express his own opinion and reacted strongly to those who did not agree with him. He was punctilious in small things, very obstinate; he loved to pose, there was much of the histrionic about him."

There is this passage, also from Finkelshteyn: "We usually met with Penkovskiy on his initiative, always somewhere in the city. He usually telephoned and named the place of meeting—either in the Moscow Restaurant or somewhere else. As a rule, Penkovskiy proposed having a glass of champagne, sitting in a cafe or dining. If we had dinner, then Penkovskiy always attempted to pay the check. It was decided that we should pay according to the so-called German principle—that is, each for himself, but very often Penkovskiy impulsively threw money on the table and paid for all, explaining that he earned more money than the rest of us and that it meant nothing to him to spend ten to twenty rubles."

The prosecution was anxious, also, to portray Penkovskiy as strictly a lowbrow. As Finkelshteyn again noted under questioning: "Penkovskiy was not attracted to the theater. It would seem that a person with a higher education would have some interest in theatrical matters, movies, various events, art, literature, etc. but Penkovskiy, to my knowledge, was not so interested. In my opinion, he did not read books or if he did, it was only best-sellers, although he bought books. I also like books very much and often buy them. Penkovskiy's interests were mainly concentrated on his work about which I, to speak honestly, know very little. I explained everything by the extreme pressures of his work."

This kind of reticence about his work and the tendency to concentrate on small talk were less the characteristics of a rake than those of a good intelligence officer. And the lack of intellectual interest in the theater was not necessarily a black mark against a professional military man whose hobbies were tinkering and inventing. It says something for the insularity of KGB interrogators that testimony which they obviously selected as particularly damaging to Penkovskiy redounds somewhat to his credit when viewed outside a Soviet courtroom.

The second basic problem the Soviet court had with Penkovskiy was to identify the kind of information he had revealed to the West. Prosecutor Gornyy made the point that the information Penkovskiy gave was "90 per cent economic," as befitting a reserve colonel who had long been working in the civilian sector. Yet here the prosecution kept tripping itself up. Almost every mention of Penkovskiy's information in the Soviet trial involved something of a military nature: "information concerning one type of Soviet rocket," "information on the Moscow Military District," information on "a state and military secret," "two military journals." . . . Such citations occur continually.

Once again the prosecution faced a dilemma. While General Gornyy wanted to emphasize the serious nature of Penkovskiy's crime, he did not want to explain either the extent of what Penkovskiy had *really* told the West or the fact that this apparently ineffectual reservist had had access to such a store of top-secret military information. Inevitably, propaganda yielded to security. The real story of the information delivered and the charges made was told in closed session.

Even after the trial was over, Chief Prosecutor Gornyy felt it necessary to give the following statement to *Izvestiya:*

"After the trial certain Soviet citizens had the impression that Penkovskiy had given away to the enemy almost all our secrets connected with military equipment and the defense capacity of the Soviet Union. Such claims are without foundation. Penkovskiy in his position was far removed from information connected with the armament of our troops and their deployment and with the employment of new types of weapons. He passed on to foreign intelligence services information on some technical reports of Soviet specialists who had gone abroad and some scattered data of a military nature that he had pumped out of loose-tongued friends and had taken from classified publications. He also passed on various materials of an internal political nature."

The prosecution fell into its worst pitfall with the attempt to establish Penkovskiy's motive. With Wynne, there was no problem. He was an Englishman and thus could be expected to have furthered his own country's interests, although as a courageous man he did not go nearly so far in his "recantation" as the Soviet prosecution wished. But it was more than sufficient for the Soviets to slander Wynne as a weak "middleman," a foreigner suborned by his own intelligence service to "work in a dirty business."

Penkovskiy's problem the Soviet prosecutors were never able to solve. On the one hand they had to concede a promising record as an exceedingly competent soldier, a vigilant Party man, and a clever worker. The worst that could be said of him was that he was a careerist. They struck a note of perplexity throughout that someone who had advanced so far in their system could so thoroughly betray it.

Witness the comment of Prosecutor A. G. Gornyy: "From outward appearances, Penkovskiy looked like quite a good worker. He rose rapidly up the ladder in his career, but by dint of the development of his base inclinations, he became more and more preoccupied not with the interests of state and society but with his personal career and well-being. . . ."

Or, as A. V. Apraksin, the state-appointed attorney for the "defense," summarized things: "Over a short period of time he spanned an important career—from a student artillery officer to colonel and commander of a tank-destroyer regiment.

"He received many awards for his battle service. The ease and brilliance of manner with which he carried out his military service particularly strikes me. . . .

"The war over, Penkovskiy went back to his desk to resume his studies. Thanks to his capabilities, to his love of work, and to his stubbornness—all this cannot be taken away from him—he managed to graduate from two higher educational institutions in the postwar period. Then, out of the Army, he found his place in life and had considerable success in his civilian profession. The job he last held, with the State Committee for the Co-ordination of Scientific Research Work, was a high position, a position which carried sufficient authority. . . ."

Penkovskiy's past credentials were thus certified: a war hero, a brilliant officer (and even more brilliant if one included his real record in the GRU), and a responsible Soviet official. Then suddenly came The Fall in 1960. Despite all the prosecutors' attempts to trace the beginning of careerism, it was as they depicted it, a fall as abrupt as original sin and about as rationally explainable. An extraordinary gap yawned between the able, hard-working, trusted Soviet official and the cringing specimen of "moral depravity" whom General Gornyy presented, in a summation labeled on the Soviet trial transcript as "Penkovskiy's path from careerism and moral degradation to treachery."

The result was inevitable. "Penkovskiy is dead," General Gornyy told *Izvestiya,* and the world, a few 'days later, "The sentence was carried out on May 16, in the second half of the day. . . . When it was announced to him that the Supreme Soviet of the U.S.S.R. had denied his petition for mercy and he was to be executed, there was not a trace of the poseur's manner which he had maintained in court. He met death like a despicable coward. . . ."

Having so said, General Gornyy returned to the editing of the trial transcript, of which 100,000 copies were printed, for use as information and object lesson, within the Soviet Union.

In the unlikely event that the trial had taken place in a Western court and in the even less likely eventuality that a Western court had been so desperately interested in developing the defendant's motives, the prosecution would undoubtedly have drawn from Penkovskiy something of the same explanation which he fortunately sent out in the Papers. There would have been the protests against the Soviet system, the anger at Khrushchev, the fear of a nuclear war, the fascination with the freedoms of the West, the gathering contempt for Communism, along with the arrogance, the ambition, the fancied slights, the rest-lessness, the snobbery of one man's exceedingly complicated character. But no such explanation could be permitted by a regime which still must rely for its *raison d'être* on a political theory of temporal infallibility. Penkovskiy was of course required to forswear his original statement to his interrogators about his hostility to the regime. In its place he substituted, according to orders, a careful statement that he had never the slightest political disagreement with the Soviet system.

Some explanation for his behavior had to be constructed, however. Here are Comrades Gornyy (for the prosecution) and Apraksin (for the defense) busy with hammer and saw:

Gornyy:

"In reviewing the present case, this question inevitably arises: how can it be that a man like Penkovskiy, who was born, was brought up, and received his education during the years of Soviet power, within our society, could so completely lose the moral qualities of a Soviet man, lose his shame, conscience, and elementary feelings of duty, and end up by committing such serious crimes?

"A partial answer to that question was provided by Penkovskiy himself when he pointed out, in his testimony in court, that it was the base qualities which have brought him to the prisoner's dock: envy, vanity, the love of an easy life, his affairs with many women, his moral decay, brought about in part by his use of liquor. All of these blotches undermined him; he became a degenerate, and then a traitor. . . .

"The exceptional careerism, egoism, and ambition of Penkovskiy manifested themselves long ago. He sought constantly to mingle with people of authority and influence, to please and to fawn upon them, and to glory in his closeness to them.

"He lived it up at the restaurants, drank wine from the slippers of his mistresses, having learned such habits from night clubs in London and Paris which Wynne took him to in the process of acquainting him with the 'charms' of Western culture.

"He was mercenary and, although he was well paid by the state, was fully provided for, and had savings in the bank, his 'appetite' grew excessively. He was particularly partial to trips abroad. Strictly speaking, his dissatisfaction with his job and his bitterness were born out of the fact that he was not offered a job abroad.

"Of course, such degenerates and renegades as Penkovskiy, who evoke a feeling of indignation and loathing in all Soviet people, are a passing phenomenon in our society. But this example shows clearly what danger is hidden in the vestiges of the past, vestiges resurrected by an ideology which is inimical to us, and what they might develop into if we do not take notice of them in time and decisively uproot them."

Apraksin:

"What indeed was it that led Penkovskiy into the camp of agents of the British and American intelligence services?

"A difference in views as to the path to be followed in the development of our society? The existence of some sort of private political postulates? A difference or lack of agreement with the policy of the building of a Communist society being conducted by our Party and our government? Or hatred for the people, whose son he happens to be?

"No, I do not think that it was any of these. Crimes for political motives have not been committed in our country for a long time now. When this question was put to him, to Penkovskiy, during the preliminary examination as well as in the courtroom, he replied: 'I had no political conflicts whatsoever with Soviet authority.' (Vol. 3, file 25)

". . . such motives for the crimes committed by Penkovskiy did not exist and could not exist, because there were no grounds or basis for such conclusions in the life of Penkovskiy.

"Thus, to say and to think that Penkovskiy became a criminal out of some sort of political motives, well, neither you nor I, nor the representative of the state prosecutor, have any basis for it.

". . . Penkovskiy himself was dazzled by his career. He began to take stock of himself again. He wanted more than he actually had, and he learned to be respectful and obliging to those upon whom his career depended, upon whom his promotions depended. His head was turned by success.

"It is sad, but he did place great hope in souvenirs, trinkets, bracelets, French cognac, as well as telephone calls from abroad, more than he did on conscientious work for and selfless service to his Motherland. He got used to this and made use of it.

His views on life changed, his comrades changed, and his social interests changed.

"There was, it is true, someone else who saw that something bad had come of Penkovskiy. It was his wife, who, upon being queried at the preliminary investigation, testified that:

" 'Over the past year, in general, he became nervous and suspicious. By his very nature, Penkovskiy was vain, touchy, and inclined toward adventures. These negative features in his character had been developing over the course of his entire life. These were promoted by the praise of his achievements which he received from his relatives, comrades, and friends. He and his job went along at rather an easy pace. He had never suffered any great hardships in his life.' (Vol. 4, files 152–158)

"The entire conscious life and the activities of Penkovskiy, to the day of his fall, forces us to realize that, for our society, he is a man who is not lost but who has wandered, that he is not an enemy of our society, a society which raised him. He is a Philistine who is far along into his own delusions, a man who by dint of his activities has come to the logical end for all Philistines—to crime."

To any Western reader of this book, an obvious superficial explanation of Penkovskiy's Philistine "crime" against the Soviet Union was the fact that his father was a White officer. Whether from an extraordinarily green memory or from resentment at the Soviet social and political prejudice shown against White Army family connections, he would have a basic motive there. "Here was a man whose own father was a White Guardist, the blackest of reactionaries. From the beginning he plotted secretly in his father's memory to destroy the revolution, to sabotage the work of his comrades. . . ." We can almost hear any spirited Soviet prosecutor heating up his violin on this theme. But one problem intervenes. Any allusion to Penkovskiy's ancestry would throw an even more embarrassing question back at the prosecution: Why had the KGB and GRU Chekists allowed a man with *this* damaging a background to rise to *this* level of prominence in Soviet society? Why had they never found out? What was wrong with the system?

From the KGB's point of view, therefore, this solution was impossible. The only "out" possible for the prosecution was to portray Penkovskiy as a man hopelessly corrupted by greed and debauchery. Yet their own evidence at the trial produced nothing more than the sum of 3000 rubles which was given to him by Wynne, of which he paid back more than two thirds, plus promises of a steady income in the event he managed to reach the West. If this represented greed, the definition was an extremely scholastic one.

As for debauchery, the only evidence to be introduced was a few meetings with an unidentified lady named Galya, in company with Mssrs. Finkelshteyn and Rudovskiy. At one of these meetings, apparently, Penkovskiy had attempted to drink out of Galya's slipper. The existence of the slipper—and of Galya—remains open to question.

The real underlying motivation of Penkovskiy, of course, was the one thing which the Soviets could never admit. He was making a protest against the regime on behalf of the people. It mattered little to Penkovskiy that the Russian people did not particularly solicit his services. He neither possessed nor sought accomplices. But many Russians before him had made a lonely personal violent gesture of protest. He declared war on his society and he used whatever weapons were at hand. He was in a tradition.

It would be idle to conclude that Penkovskiy was a reasonable, stable citizen. He was a zealot. He was an angry, driven man. He was vain and overconfident, surely, in thinking he could carry on his secret work indefinitely. He was hardly mindful of the great danger in which he had placed his family, although he loved them and ultimately made his confession to save them.

Is Penkovskiy alive today? No one knows. Perhaps, somewhere. Greville Wynne thinks so, as his articles reveal, basing his belief on the Soviets' continuing interrogation of Wynne himself *after* the trial. We know that Prosecutor Gornyy went to the trouble of insisting that sentence had been carried out, on May 16, in a press conference a week after the trial.

By some intelligence standards, the KGB would have been wise to keep him alive, so they could have a constant check on what he really told the "American and British intelligence agents" memorialized in the Moscow trial.

Needing information, the Soviet authorities would be unlikely to eliminate their best source. But if he is alive, he must be paying a dread penalty. Then again, pressure must have been strong to have him executed and seal his lips forever—especially by those whose secrets he must have known.

Was Penkovskiy completely committed to the West? From the intensity of what he wrote and the extent of what he did, there is no doubt. For, it must be repeated, no man before or since has succeeded in such a daring and sweeping intelligence operation, with such powerful consequences in its train.

It is probable that Penkovskiy represented a current trend of thinking within the ranks of Soviet Army officers and officials, albeit to an extreme degree. As Wynne had said, "He was like the top part of an iceberg." Certainly the Penkovskiy Papers bear out this discontent. There is no doubt that the Khrushchev version of personality cultism was highly unpopular within the Soviet Union, and played a major role in bringing Khrushchev down, two years later. There is no doubt that pressures were then and are now mounting in this closed society, pressures for greater personal freedom, greater creature comforts, greater personal initiative. As the Papers well demonstrate, the motives of people working toward a freer society within the U.S.S.R are not unmixed ones; but the important thing is that they exist. What Penkovskiy wrote in 1961 is five times truer in 1965.

Oleg Penkovskiy's initial overtures toward the West were made from disgust at his own Soviet system. His visits there turned this into a more positive sentiment. He was almost awe-struck at the experience of the Open Society. He wanted his own people to have this society at home. He wanted to share in it himself, whether the Russian people could or not.

If he was a flawed hero, he was a hero nonetheless. His struggle was one of heroic proportions, as was his achievement. If he served by this struggle to blunt the forces of aggression and reaction within his own country, he will have served well.

In any case, by any standard, Oleg Penkovskiy was a most uncommon man.

APPENDIX I

Organizational Chart of the State Committee for Co-ordination of Scientific Research Work

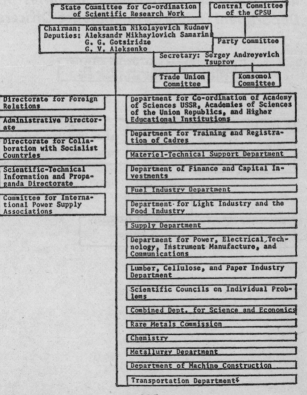

Council of Ministers of the USSR

State Committee for Co-ordination of Scientific Research Work

Central Committee of the CPSU

Chairman: Konstantin Nikolayevich Rudnev
Deputies: Aleksandr Mikhaylovich Samarin
G. G. Gotsiridze
G. V. Aleksenko

Party Committee

Secretary: Sergey Andreyevich Tsuprov

Trade Union Committee

Komsomol Committee

Directorate for Foreign Relations

Administrative Directorate

Directorate for Collaboration with Socialist Countries

Scientific-Technical Information and Propaganda Directorate

Committee for International Power Supply Associations

Department for Co-ordination of Academy of Sciences USSR, Academies of Sciences of the Union Republics, and Higher Educational Institutions

Department for Training and Registration of Cadres

Materiel-Technical Support Department

Department of Finance and Capital Investments

Fuel Industry Department

Department for Light Industry and the Food Industry

Supply Department

Department for Power, Electrical, Technology, Instrument Manufacture, and Communications

Lumber, Cellulose, and Paper Industry Department

Scientific Councils on Individual Problems

Combined Dept. for Science and Economics

Rare Metals Commission

Chemistry

Metallurgy Department

Department of Machine Construction

Transportation Department

APPENDIX II

The Directorate for Foreign Relations (to Which Penkovskiy Belonged) of the State Committee for Co-ordination of Scientific Research Work (Penkovskiy Identifies the Department Heads as Intelligence Officers)

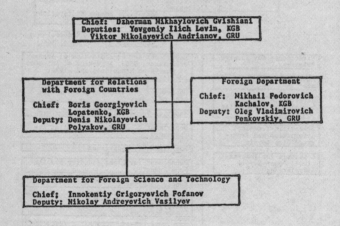

Chief: Dzherman Mikhaylovich Gvishiani
Deputies: Yevgeniy Ilich Levin, KGB
Viktor Nikolayevich Andrianov, GRU

Department for Relations with Foreign Countries

Chief: Boris Georgiyevich Lopatenko, KGB
Deputy: Denis Nikolayevich Polyakov, GRU

Foreign Department

Chief: Mikhail Fedorovich Kachalov, KGB
Deputy: Oleg Vladimirovich Penkovskiy, GRU

Department for Foreign Science and Technology

Chief: Innokentiy Grigoryevich Fofanov
Deputy: Nikolay Andreyevich Vasilyev

APPENDIX III

Pravda *Editorial and* Izvestiya *Interview Concerning Penkovskiy's Trial and Execution*

LET'S INCREASE
OUR REVOLUTIONARY VIGILANCE!

Editorial, *Pravda,* May 17, 1963

The entire Soviet nation, with a great degree of approval, met the just sentence of the Military Collegium of the Supreme Court of the U.S.S.R. in the criminal case of the traitor to his Motherland and agent of the British and American intelligence services, Penkovskiy, and the spy go-between, Wynne. The sentence of the court is the highest measure of punishment—execution for Penkovskiy and eight years of imprisonment for Wynne.

During this entire period there has been a steady flood of letters to the editorial office of *Pravda* and other agencies of the press and to radio stations in which Soviet citizens of the most varied professions and ages have expressed their feelings of profound satisfaction with the manner in which the glorious Soviet Chekists have decisively suppressed the foul work of the British and American intelligence services. From the pages of these letters one can loudly hear the voice of laborers, workers in agriculture, and Soviet intellectuals angrily holding up to shame the reactionary circles of the capitalist countries which are carrying on subversive activity against the Soviet Union.

In their letters the Soviet citizens recall the words expressed by Comrade N. S. Khrushchev at the Twentieth Congress of the Communist Party of the Soviet Union, to the effect that subversive activity against the Soviet Union is being openly supported and paraded by reactionary circles in a number of capitalist countries. "Therefore," N. S. Khrushchev said, "we must do everything possible to increase revolutionary vigilance in the Soviet people. . . ."

From the first days of its existence, the Soviet state has been the object of continuous hostile acts on the part of international imperialism. During the years of the civil and Great Patriotic wars, enemies attempted to destroy the world's first socialist state by force of arms. They were defeated by the Soviet people. They also failed disgracefully in their computations that our nation would prove to be unable to provide for the development of our economy, technology, and science, and would be forced to return to the path of capitalism. During all these years the imperialists, in addition to open political, economic, and military warfare, carried out a "secret war" against our Motherland, resorting to espionage, diversion, and other types of subversive activity. In a number of imperialist states, subversive and intelligence activity has been raised to the level of state policy. But all these criminal plans and actions of the reactionary forces were doomed to failure.

In our time, when the ratio of power on the world scene has changed radically in favor of socialism, open military acts against countries in the socialist camp inevitably end in the destruction of those undertaking them. However, international imperialism has still not renounced its vile plans against the socialist state, and continues to organize various intrigues against socialism. The trial of Anglo-American spies which ended several days ago is only one of the acts of this "secret war."

The imperialist states are attempting, at any price and by any means, to gain information about the outstanding achievements of the Soviet Union in the field of economy, science, and technology, and about the armed forces of our country. At the trial it was irrefutably proved that, by unceremoniously trampling the norms of international law, they also use the diplomatic service of those powers for purposes of espionage. A private decision of the Military Collegium of the Supreme Court of the U.S.S.R. contains the names of seven British and five American diplomats, accredited to the U.S.S.R., who, by abusing their official status, engaged in activities hostile to our country. Certain foreign businessmen, tourists, and members of various foreign delegations are also drawn into the dirty work of espionage.

Does that mean that Soviet citizens, as Western propaganda states, are inclined to see an enemy in every foreigner? Is it really necessary to say that such statements are completely without foundation and are stupid, or that they are malicious slander against Soviet citizens?

The peace-loving Soviet nation, educated by the Communist Party in the spirit of proletarian internationalism, has always come out, and will continue to come out, for the strengthening of friendly relations with other nations, for the complete development of international contacts, and for the broad exchange of cultural values. The whole world knows the hospitality with which we greet everyone arriving in our country with a pure heart and an open one. Let everyone know that Soviet citizens do not put an equal sign between vigilance and suspiciousness: they are far from presupposing that all their guests have bad intentions. But let everyone also remember that the striking sword of the Soviet agencies of State Security inevitably falls on any snake that tries to crawl into the beautiful building of Communism which was erected by our people.

Any intrigues of foreign intelligence services are doomed to failure, since they do not have and cannot have any social support in the Soviet society. The moral and political unity of our people, the high degree of patriotism of Soviet citizens, constitutes the most reliable of the walls standing in the way of the scouts of the capitalist world. That is why the intelligence services of the imperialist powers persistently search out individuals affected by the wormholes of idealistic unreliability and moral turpitude, adventurers, careerists, and persons with self-interests, who, under definite conditions, might yield to recruitment and take the criminal path of treason against one's Motherland.

In our socialist society, degenerates like Penkovskiy are doomed to universal contempt and annihilation. Two hundred and twenty million Soviet patriots have unanimously expressed their anger against the traitor. The raising of the vigilance of the Soviet people against the intrigues of the imperialist powers constitutes the answer that Soviet citizens give the subversive actions of the British and American intelligence services, which have been unmasked before the entire world at the trial which was held in Moscow. One should not forget that any connivance with respect to the survivals of the past or to their bearers, any leniency toward vices, and any gullibility manifested by individual persons are inadmissible; they lead to the loss of political vigilance.

In addition to espionage, enemies of our Motherland, enemies of peace and socialism, have been resorting more and more persistently in recent times to methods of ideological subversion. Attempting to undermine the might of the Soviet system, they are searching for any and all holes through which they can exert their pernicious influence upon individual unstable characters. Therefore any lessening of the struggle against bourgeois ideology, which serves as a means of keeping alive the survivals of capitalism, can create conditions in which it is most convenient for the petty soul-hunters sent by the imperialist intelligence services to operate. And the more actively the Soviet citizens fight the influence of bourgeois ideology, and the dog-eat-dog morality of the capitalist world, the greater their political vigilance and their ability to recognize an enemy, in whatever guise he appears—the more reliably we will be able to close up all the chinks through which enemy agents might penetrate.

In the name of the Motherland, in the name of the people, and in the interests of peace on earth, the Soviet court has punished the criminals in full measure for the crimes that they committed. The far-reaching plans of the ruling circles of the imperialist powers to penetrate into the state secrets of the Soviet Union have failed. The high vigilance of Soviet citizens who remember well the instructions of V. I. Lenin that, having undertaken peaceful construction, it is necessary to be constantly on alert, and to cherish as the apple of one's eye the defense capacity of our Motherland, constitutes the most reliable guarantee that no one will ever be able to prevent us from achieving our great goal. Let us always be on the alert, let us increase our revolutionary vigilance!—that is today's motto of the Soviet people, the builders of Communism.

THE OLD FOX'S TAIL

Interview Given to Correspondents of Izvestiya *by Chief Military Prosecutor General Lieutenant of Justice A. G. Gornyy.*

The trial of the spy Penkovskiy and his accomplice Wynne attracted the attention of the world. The world's newspapers were filled with comments. In many of these papers the progress of the trial was treated objectively, and the fairness of the sentence given was acknowledged. But there were also those press organs which carried articles containing quite a bit of malicious fabrication.

The Soviet people have unanimously approved the sentence passed on the spies. In their letters to the editors, readers hold up to shame the organizers of this subversive activity—the American and English imperialists. Readers have also asked the editors to answer several questions connected with the spy case.

To fulfill the request the editors of *Izvestiya* turned to Chief Military Prosecutor General Lieutenant of Justice A. G. Gornyy, who was the state prosecutor at the Penkovskiy trial. Following are Gornyy's answers to the questions of our correspondents V. Goltsev and V. Kassis.

Correspondents: "The editors of *Izvestiya* have received a number of letters in which readers have wanted to know how great is the damage to our defense capacity as a result of Penkovskiy's activities."

A. Gornyy: "After the trial several Soviet citizens had the impression than Penkovskiy had given away to the enemy almost all our secrets connected with military equipment and the defense capacity of the Soviet state. Such claims are without foundation. Penkovskiy in his position was far removed from information connected with the armament of our troops and their deployment and with the employment of new types of weapons. He passed to foreign intelligence services information on some technical reports of Soviet specialists who had gone abroad and some scattered data of a military nature that he had pumped out of loose-tongued friends and had taken from classified publications. He also passed on various material of an internal political nature.

"It should be noted that in the initial period of his spy activity Penkovskiy was closely watched and checked by the foreign agents so they afterward could give him assignments to collect material that particularly interested them. But by the beginning of 1962 Penkovskiy was put under conditions that made liaison with foreign intelligence services difficult. This is shown by the fact that a large amount of secret material he had collected was discovered in his possession when he was arrested. These materials later served as material evidence at the trial. Penkovskiy was not able to pass material at will. He was hindered by the vigilance of the Soviet people and our Chekists [KGB agents].

"After becoming a spy, Penkovskiy passed to the American and English intelligence services certain important information, part of which was connected with a state secret of the U.S.S.R. He committed a most serious crime against the Motherland, for which he was sentenced to death. However, it can be asserted with full responsibility that the materials he passed could not cause any serious harm to the defense capability of the Soviet Union."

Correspondents: "Readers in their letters have been asking: what got Penkovskiy started on the path of treason and espionage?"

A. Gornyy: "The material of the court examination convincingly shows that Penkovskiy became a hireling of foreign intelligence services as a result of his amorality, careerism, and egoism. A poseur and careerist, Penkovskiy sought personal glory and personal mercenary successes. Embittered at everyone and everything because he was discharged from the regular Soviet Army and was not given a permanent job overseas, Penkovskiy sold himself to foreign intelligence services."

Correspondents: "Several readers want to know why Penkovskiy was not arrested immediately after his activities became known to State Security organs."

A. Gornyy: "I already said that after the State Security organs noticed the suspicious contacts of Penkovskiy with foreigners he was placed under difficult conditions. Despite his persistency in trying to get overseas he was not given such an opportunity. There were also set up obstacles to his collecting information and meeting with untrustworthy persons. However, there was still not enough evidence to arrest him. In addition, all of his criminal contacts with foreigners, in our country and abroad, had not been found out. I have in mind the diplomatic employees of the Moscow embassies of the U.S.A. and Great Britain. It was necessary not only to collect irrefutable proof of Penkovskiy's spy activity but to establish his criminal contacts and to collect irrefutable proof that foreign intelligence agencies and diplomats were engaged in subversive activities. The spy was surrounded like a bear in his den. As a result the State Security organs were able to collect important evidence that not only convicted Penkovskiy and Wynne as spies, but also exposed the subversive work against the Soviet state of a large group of American and British diplomats."

Correspondents: "Our readers are interested in knowing whether the persons closely associated with Penkovskiy and who knew of his amoral and suspicious conduct will be punished in any way."

A. Gornyy: "Penkovskiy was associated with many people both officially and in his private life. Some of them turned out to be gullible and loose-tongued. Others used to drink with Penkovskiy and contributed to his degeneration. However, the majority of the Soviet people he associated with were honest and loyal to our Motherland. They were very helpful to the security organs in convicting Penkovskiy as a spy. It was their warnings that formed the basis of the active work of our Chekists in exposing Penkovskiy and Wynne. By the way, I should mention that the group of Soviet citizens who helped to expose the spies was officially thanked and awarded with valuable gifts by the Committee of State Security under the Council of Ministers of the U.S.S.R.

"As concerns the friends and drinking companions of Penkovskiy, they, as was established at the preliminary investigation and in the court examination, did not know about his spy activity and therefore cannot be held criminally responsible. But their conduct deserves the sternest public condemnation. I should say that they have all been subjected to strict administrative and Party punishment. For example, former Chief Marshal of Artillery S. Varentsov has been demoted in rank and position because he gave credence to Penkovskiy's 'complaints' that he was allegedly illegally discharged from the regular Soviet

Army. S. Varentsov succeeded in having a negative efficiency report re-examined and was instrumental in getting Penkovskiy a job in the State Committee for Coordination of Scientific Research of the U.S.S.R.

"Penkovskiy's close acquaintances, General Major A. Pozovnyy, Colonel V. Buzinov, and former employees of the State Committee for Co-ordination of Scientific Research, U.S.S.R., V. Petrochenko, all of whom shared official information with Penkovskiy in violation of existing regulations, received strict disciplinary punishment.

"His drinking companions V. Finkelshteyn and I. Rudovskiy were also condemned by all the personnel at their places of work.

"I would hope that all these people will reform, learn their lessons, and get on the right track."

Correspondents: "In the Western bourgeois press various 'doubts' have cropped up about the sincerity of Penkovskiy and Wynne's confessions in court. What can you say on this point?"

A. Gornyy: "I must say that the respectable bourgeois press organs and telegraphic agencies that were represented at the trial were compelled to admit the irrefutability of the evidence presented by the prosecution against the spies in the dock. For example, in reference to the trial the American papers *The New York Times* and New York *Herald Tribune* wrote that no one even doubts that the defendants are guilty. The correspondent for the Swedish newspaper *Svenska Dagblaget* reported from London during the trial that 'judging from unofficial English commentaries one cannot help seeing that the Wynne trial has put the English government and security service in a difficult position, because nothing has been presented to counter Wynne's confession to espionage.'

"Similar statements were contained in other newspapers. But as always, there were attempts to sow distrust of Soviet justice. Malicious and fantastic fabrications are favorite methods of the cheap bourgeois press. The Turkish newspaper *Eni Istanbul* claimed that a 'brainwashing operation' was performed on Wynne while in prison. I think that such fabrication can only provoke laughter even from readers who have no objective information.

"The fact that Wynne and Penkovskiy confessed to such serious crimes is explained simply by the irrefutability of the evidence so laboriously gathered during the preliminary investigation and presented at the trial. The prosecution had available and presented to the court ample proof of the defendants' guilt. This proof was completely objective and not dependent on the testimony or confessions of the defendants. Wynne and Penkovskiy understood this perfectly. Even during the preliminary investigation they became convinced that they had been exposed and caught red-handed. For this reason the spies decided to confess their guilt and to repent in some measure.

"Incontrovertible, objective proof of their guilt is represented in the spy equipment seized from Penkovskiy and Wynne upon their arrest: Minox miniature cameras, cipher books, diaries, instructions from spy headquarters, radio receivers, numerous written documents, and the experiments carried out during investigation. Under such conditions Penkovskiy and Wynne had no choice but to admit their guilt and confess to the crimes."

Correspondents: "There are rumors that link Penkovskiy and the family of the late Chief Marshal of Artillery M. I. Nedelin."

A. Gornyy: "These rumors are nonsense. Penkovskiy had no connection at all with the family of Marshal M. I. Nedelin. He was married to the daughter of General G., a former political worker who died several years ago. General G. did not serve in the missile troops, so Penkovskiy would not have been able to get any information on our missiles through family channels. It was established by the preliminary and court examinations that Penkovskiy's wife and relatives did not know of his criminal activity. They were deeply shocked and indignant when they found out his true face. Penkovskiy managed to give foreign agents fragmentary information concerning old-model missiles that he had obtained during his Army service."

Correspondents: "What can you tell us about the activities of imperialist intelligence operations against the U.S.S.R. on the basis of spy cases heard in recent years by the Military Board of the Supreme Court of the U.S.S.R.?"

A. Gornyy: "Espionage and subversive activities against the U.S.S.R. have been raised to the level of state policy in a number of imperialist states. The leading role in espionage against the U.S.S.R. is played by the Central Intelligence Agency of the U.S.A. The best and most modern equipment has been made available for espionage —from Minox miniature cameras to space satellites, the so-called 'spies in the sky.'

"The trial of Penkovskiy and Wynne gave a pinch to the old fox's tail—that is, the British Secret Intelligence Service. It has been in existence for around three hundred years and continues to use more and more deceptive and refined methods. In so doing it tries to remain in the background, but not very successfully, as is clearly shown by the Penkovskiy-Wynne trial.

"It is becoming ever more difficult for the imperialist intelligence services to conduct their subversive activities in the U.S.S.R. and the other socialist countries. In our country there is no social base for recruiting agents for foreign agencies. Therefore the English and American agencies rely on professional spies who are trained in special schools and then sent by various means to our country. But they all end up facing Soviet justice.

"Trampling standards of international law, American and English intelligence agencies utilize as spies members of various delegations, scientists, businessmen, cultural figures, students, and tourists who visit our country. This is shown particularly by the unmasking of tourist spies such as Kaminsky and Makinen, Sonntag and Naumann, the Werner couple, Yakher Lou and Reydon, and others.

"It was also proved at the trial of Penkovskiy and Wynne that seven English and five American diplomats were involved in spy activity. All of them have been shamefully expelled from the Soviet Union—one during investigation, the others after the trial. These facts allow us to conclude that the imperialist intelligence services do not hesitate to turn the diplomatic missions in the U.S.S.R. into espionage centers. Is it necessary to say that such dirty actions by the English and American intelligence services cause great harm to the cause of increasing trust among peoples and states and hinder the development of scientific and cultural co-operation and international trade?

"At the same time, as was revealed by the Penkovskiy trial, the intelligence services of the bourgeois states strive to find even among Soviet citizens individual renegades who might work for them and betray the interests of the

Motherland and the people. Such people are usually morally degenerate, unprincipled careerists, and egoists who are
willing to sell out to the enemy for pieces of silver. But
these renegades do not take root in our Soviet life, which
is why they inevitably and quickly fail. They are quickly
exposed by the organs of State Security with the active help
of the workers."

Correspondents: "Some persons in the West doubt that
Penkovskiy's sentence was carried out. What can you say
regarding this?"

A. Gornyy: "Striving to discredit the Penkovskiy trial,
which nailed the intelligence services of the U.S.A. and
England to the pillory, the cheap Western newspapers are
resorting to monstrous lies and fabrications. The reactionary English paper *Sunday Telegraph* wrote on May 19,
after Penkovskiy's sentence had already been executed, the
following: 'Western officials in Moscow think that Oleg
Penkovskiy's death sentence is a complete fake.' As one
diplomat put it, Penkovskiy's execution 'amounted to having his passport destroyed and then being issued another
one.'

"This report is a shameless newspaper lie. Penkovskiy
is dead. The sentence was executed in the second half of
the day of May 19. The evening before Penkovskiy was
allowed a meeting with his mother. During the night he
wrote several letters. When it was announced to him that
the Presidium of the Supreme Soviet of the U.S.S.R. had
denied his petition for mercy and that he was to be executed, there was not a trace of the poseur's manner that
he had maintained in court. He met death like a despicable
coward."

Correspondents: "What lesson should our people learn
from the Penkovskiy case?"

A. Gornyy: "This case is a reminder to all Soviet people that it is necessary to maintain revolutionary vigilance
and be firm against gullibility, loose talk, and carelessness,
which can help foreign spies to carry out their dirty work.
I think that the evidence produced at the trial also convincingly shows the need to intensify the fight against nar-
row-mindedness, Philistinism, lack of principle, and vestiges
of the past that eat away the conscience of certain morally
unstable people. From Philistinism to moral degeneration
is just one step, and moral degeneration and lack of prin-

ciple can lead a person into the nets of imperialist intelligence services.

"In connection with the Penkovskiy case there has been started in the West a noisy campaign about alleged spy mania in our country. This is of course a propaganda trick. The Soviet people are not disposed to see a spy in every foreigner. They hospitably open their doors to all who come to our country with good intentions. We are against spy mania and unnecessary suspiciousness, which only bring nervousness and actually harms the struggle against the real enemies of our socialist state. But we are for revolutionary vigilance, which must be the standard of conduct for every Soviet man."

From *Izvestiya*, May 29, 1963.

APPENDIX IV

The Prikhodko Lecture

INTRODUCTION

I have mentioned that some of Penkovskiy's Papers read like lectures. Like many Russians he had a strongly didactic cast of mind. But along with his own injunctions and observations he did send out a few lectures which were formally delivered in a classroom—probably many times. They were part of a series given in 1960 and 1961 to the students of the Military Diplomatic Academy, the GRU higher training school from which Penkovskiy himself was graduated in 1953. Penkovskiy mentions several lectures dealing with agent work in Western Europeon countries, as well as various aspects of the intelligence trade. One of them, however, is particularly interesting. Its title is "Characteristics of Agent Communications and of Agent Handling in the U.S.A."

The "American" lecture was delivered by Lieutenant Colonel Ivan Ye. Prikhodko, presumably of the GRU's Anglo-American Affairs Directorate, a veteran intelligence officer who had been, ostensibly, a working member of the Soviet Delegation to the United Nations in New York, between 1952 and 1955. Behind this scholarly title the lecture itself is something of a hair-raiser. Although the language is dry and rather technical at times, it should be read assiduously, for it is nothing less than a professional operating manual for Soviet spies in the United States.

To get Prikhodko's lecture out of the GRU's security files was an extraordinary coup. Never before have the operating methods of a modern intelligence service been laid bare with such embarrassing clarity. Rarely, also, has a single document so heavily underlined the limitations of the Soviet mind, in any of its attempts to make an objective appraisal of another country and another culture.

We assume that Penkovskiy sent copies of this lecture and any other material of a similar nature to his Anglo-American intelligence contacts. But Penkovskiy's motive in sending the Prikhodko lecture along with the Papers was a wider one than the mere dissemination of intelligence information. As his few words of introduction state, he wanted to warn "the American people" of the espionage effort which was being directed against them. Penkovskiy, in all his writings, displayed an almost obsessive fear that the British and the American publics were disastrously unaware of the real extent of Soviet intelligence work. By sending the lecture he hoped to convince them. In this, as in all the Papers, Penkovskiy had a case to state. He was a zealot who wanted to be heard, if not appreciated. He was after a wider audience than the sophisticated experts of the Anglo-American "intelligence community."

In the lecture quoted, Colonel Prikhodko was trying to be objective. Essentially his comments are intended as a handy little secret agent's Baedeker, with strong overtones of Emily Post, a technical and social set of do's and don't's for the man with a Soviet secret mission. For one thing, the Colonel advises, a good Soviet intelligence officer must get to know the New York subway system (". . . the subway system there is quite complicated and should be studied carefully before planning to use it for operational purposes"). Motels are excellent places for meetings with agents, because of their separate entrances. Rental cars are an excellent means of conveyance. The intelligence officer must develop the habit of walking a lot to accustom counterintelligence surveillances to his peripatetic journeys to contact points. Public telephones are a fine means of communication ("The telephone is an integral part of the American way of life"). But officers should be on their guard against counterintelligence wire tapping.

Prikhodko cautions officers living in the U.S. to make the acquaintance of a laundry and a good dry cleaner's: Americans "try always to have a clean suit, well pressed with a good crease in the trousers. . . . It is customary to change white shirts and socks daily."

He was impressed by both bars and brand names. For example: "Americans like to spend a great deal of time in bars. . . . In order not to attract undue attention the intelligence officer must know how to order sufficiently well; for example, to ask, 'Give me a glass of beer.' It also is necessary to name the brand of beer ('Schlitz,' 'Rheingold,' etc.)."

As for the movies, he observes that "Americans are not content with only a single feature film. Therefore, movie-theater proprietors show two films one after the other." Prikhodko finds nearly empty movie theaters excellent for agent rendezvous purposes, while drugstores are just fine for making fast phone calls.

Classified ads, Prikhodko suggests, are a great way to keep in touch with one's agent network in the U.S. and easy to insert. (Because of their dependence on advertising profits, he advises, American newspapers accept ads "very readily.") A good Soviet intelligence operative will avoid meeting agents near banks, jewelry shops, the United Nations building in New York, or the vicinity of the Soviet Embassy in Washington. And he is cautioned not to schedule meetings on Staten Island—accessible at that time only by ferry or by bridge from New Jersey.

Flawed GRU linguists in New York need not worry about their foreign accents showing ("since a large segment of the city's population speaks with an accent"). But they must study up on their sports. A golf course, Colonel Prikhodko advises, is an excellent place for an agent meeting, but would-be golfers must get their practice in Moscow before going abroad. The Colonel cautions: "To hold successful meetings at golf courses . . . a basic requirement is to know the game and how to play it. Therefore students should learn this game while still at the academy."

Officers on duty in the U.S. must check carefully the restaurants where they are to have their meetings. (If they follow Prikhodko's advice, however, they may not be overly popular—he anachronistically suggests that a 10-per-cent tip is adequate.) Typewriters should be used wherever possible, handwritten notes avoided. Parks are excellent locations for leaving communications for agents, although they have their disadvantages. "One must bear in mind," Prikhodko writes, "that a number of American parks (for example, Central Park in New York) have many squirrels which can destroy the dead drop[1] (especially in hollow trees) and carry off our material." Officers in the U.S. must remember the conversion to daylight-saving time when they arrange their rendezvous and they should avoid being caught at department-store sales. ("In their efforts to advertise the sale, the proprietors invite news photographers to the opening of the sale. To avoid being caught by the photographer's lens, our intelligence officers and members of their families should not visit the store during the beginning of the sale.")

The American reader should not be deceived by the unintentional humor into thinking of the GRU officer's life in the United States as a jolly round of mischievous squirrels, department-store shopping expeditions, and bracing walks to the agent rendezvous at the sixteenth hole. The bulk of Prikhodko's lecture consists of warnings to secure communications, to avoid any unnecessary agent contacts, to report all meetings immediately after they occur. Speed is of the essence. The methods of dodging surveillance are almost endlessly elaborate, involving hours of dull, apparently unnecessary travel. Through the entire lecture runs a certain professional and personal horror of getting caught.

There is no doubt that American counterintelligence makes life difficult for even the most accomplished GRU visitor. To the GRU and the KGB, the FBI is more than a set of initials; it is a shrewd, relentless, and omnipresent enemy. That the number of Soviet agents apprehended in the U.S. has steadily risen attests to the Justice Department's steadily growing efficiency in this area.

The Federal Bureau of Investigation, as Prikhodko says over and over again, runs "a severe counterintelligence regime." On almost every page of his lecture he refers to "constant surveillance." He warns of listening devices which the FBI can install in automobiles, allowing them to track an agent down and/or listen to his conversation. He notes that even the U.S. Customs Service uses the latest achievements in technology to detect smuggled material. "Not long ago," he adds, "the chief of the Federal Bureau of

---

1 A dead drop (called *taynik* in Russian) is the technical term used for a hiding place where an agent can leave a packet for an officer to pick up later, at a set time, without the two parties meeting.

Investigation, Edgar Hoover, proposed the use of X rays to screen baggage transported in aircraft." Thanks largely to the FBI, working conditions for Soviet officers in the United States are what Prikhodko understandably calls "complex."

A great deal of planning in the Soviet intelligence network involves the business of communications. Besides the use of normal radio channels Prikhodko even suggests the possibility "of a radio station on an earth satellite" to speed up Soviet agent communications with the Center in Moscow. Much of the communications planning centers on wartime conditions. "In time of war," Prikhodko warns, "the maintainance of direct communications between the Center and the *rezidenturas* will be considerably more difficult." Among other things he warns officers to locate themselves and their agents, whenever possible, in areas away from big population centers and hence liable to Soviet attack. He adds: ". . . one of the most important tasks of the *rezidentura* under official cover during peacetime is to train agents and prepare agent nets . . . for operation during wartime."

The most revealing and distressing part of this lecture, however, is its curiously uneven picture of the American character. Note some of his typical observations. "An American's circle of interests is often rather small." "Many Americans do not read books. Their main interest in newspapers lies in advertisements, sports news, and cartoons."

"Generally speaking bourgeois society demoralizes people." "The absolute power of money in the U.S.A. arouses one desire in many people—to make more money." "Wall Street does everything possible to keep Americans from devoting their free time to meditation and deliberation. Movies, cheap concerts, boxing, parks, horse races, baseball, football, restaurants—all these are used to divert the masses from the realities around them."

Yet at the same time "most Americans are energetic, enterprising, and open people, having a great sense of humor." Also, "They can be described as having business acumen and as being resourceful, courageous, and industrious."

Over and over again he warns the visiting Soviet intelligence officer to develop a sense of humor, "something which is valued highly by American agents." The urbane

GRU man should be able to tell jokes appropriately "despite the fact that very important problems are being discussed at a meeting." The lecturer warns that American intelligence agents, despite their love of jokes, are apt to be hard to handle. ("Americans do not like discipline and are always demonstrating their independence.")

Above all, the intelligence officer must not knock things American. Prikhodko notes that "an unfortunate statement, for example, about some popular U. S. President (George Washington, Abraham Lincoln, Thomas Jefferson) might offend the agent."

Thus, "The intelligence officer who knows the national traits of Americans should be able to establish rapport quickly with the agent and positively influence him." Officers are advised to play on the American's desire for financial gain by upping the ante when more work needs to be done. ("Americans like money. Money is their favorite topic of conversation.")

On the other hand Prikhodko concedes that "Americans are distinguished by their efficiency and their resourcefulness," and "that the technical knowledge of the average American is rather high." Finally: "Americans, to a larger degree than representatives of many other peoples, have a natural love of freedom and independence."

Seen through American eyes, the cautious analyses of Colonel Prikhodko are sometimes hilariously incongruous —De Tocqueville as translated by Charles Addams and Milton Berle. The overriding impression is one of confusion. The Americans, as the GRU sees them, are an independent, resourceful, fun-loving people hopelessly undermined by the "demoralization" of bourgeois society, yet doing their best "to save money for a rainy day" because of their desperate greed for material things. The lecture reminds us that to a great extent even the best-informed Soviet officials can be victims of their own propaganda. Prikhodko's observations, a dialectical interpretation of GRU experience in the field, are a mixture of operational shrewdness and country-cousin gullibility, the work of men whose own indoctrination and upbringing has left them a little like Plato's bound prisoners in the cave, who saw the world only in terms of the fire-lit images cast on the opposite wall.

For all its humorous sidelights, the estimate of the

American character is a bit frightening. Consider that men like Prikhodko are the same people who prepare the position papers predicting American reactions to Soviet initiatives and some very frightening reflections come to mind. Are the Americans always "swayed by money" and "indifferent" to anything not connected with business? If the Presidium of the Central Committee in Moscow thinks we are, it may one day make some irretrievable miscalculations.

In its own curious way this document constitutes a powerful argument for a greater, not a lesser degree of international exchange. No country wants to be deluged with GRU and KGB representatives, yet we could do worse than introduce as many of these Soviet gentry as possible to the real facts of American thought processes and living conditions. Perhaps the GRU training at the Military Diplomatic Academy, by tacit arrangement, might be supplemented by a tour of U.S. college campuses, Iowa small towns, Chicago conventions, etc. There the serious Soviet Army Staff officers might be encouraged to look more closely at a society which they now see through their own red-shaded glass, rather darkly.

PENKOVSKIY'S TEXT

We spy everywhere. Sometimes it is the neighbors, sometimes it is our own *residents* who take the lead. But there is no country on earth where we do not have our intelligence officers recruiting, arranging meetings, doing everything possible to establish permanent networks of Illegals. Whether the country is friendly or not is not important. We spy on neutrals as much as we spy on the NATO countries. The officers who teach in the Military Diplomatic Academy have acquainted themselves with the most intimate aspects of other countries, so we can use this knowledge. Our experts in Italy, for example, give our officers detailed information about where to plant agents and how to organize contacts in Rome.

Rome is a good place for intelligence operations. So our officers say. There are many foreigners there and the Romans themselves get along well with foreigners, seeing in them a source of income. Therefore we can operate inconspicuously. The Italians are excessively talkative. That helps us, too, even though the police are alert and often conduct surprise document checks, which can be embarrassing. There is a large Communist Party in Italy. Instructors at the academy advise our officers that "our Italian friends"[1] can be of great service in operations.

Operations in a large country like Italy might be expected, yet we work even in a small peaceful country like Denmark. Our "brave" Chekists are even working in little Denmark. Officers are given detailed information about such things as automobile travel between Copenhagen and various towns in Jutland. They are advised about the best times to make trips to remote areas, as well as the extent of counterintelligence surveillance possible. Everything is detailed for them. There is a special lecture on Italy and Denmark given at the Military Diplomatic Academy.

Some of these lectures I had heard myself and later seen in written form. With the GRU's instructions on the U.S.A. I am particularly familiar.

When the question of my trip to the U.S.A. as chief of a delegation was under discussion, my supervisor, Colonel Rogov, sent me for a briefing to our GRU 3rd Directorate, which is responsible for Anglo-American affairs. There I was instructed on the agent/operational situation in the U.S.A. I was given the lecture to read, "Characteristics of Agent Communications and of Agent Handling in the U.S.A." by Lieutenant Colonel I. Ye. Prikhodko. Prikhodko is quite a young officer of the GRU. From 1952 to 1955 he was in New York City as an intelligence officer under United Nations cover. This short lecture is one of the better training lectures for our intelligence officers operating in the U.S. It reveals all the hypocrisy of our "peaceful coexistence." I have never visited the U.S. and it is very hard for me to judge what is true and what is false in Prikhodko's lecture. But even the ordinary American, untutored in intelligence, will understand what we conceal under the wing of the United Nations. Because this lecture was given to me only for a few hours and I have no time to make comments on it, I made a photocopy of it and include it together with my papers. And I will be more than glad if one day this lecture

_____
[1] This of course refers to the Italian Communist Party.

reaches the shores of the U.S. It is part of my warning to the American people.

Lieutenant Colonel I. Ye. Prikhodko

CHARACTERISTICS OF AGENT COMMUNICATIONS
AND OF AGENT HANDLING IN THE U.S.A.

Training Manual[2]

1961

In this training circular we shall examine only those questions of operating conditions in the U.S.A. and those facets of American counterintelligence tactics which affect our own agent communication and handling.

The great distance which separates the U.S.A. from the Soviet Union complicates the organization and support of direct agent communication between the Center and our intelligence units in the U.S.A. This forces our intelligence to employ duplicate communications along many lines. There is a wide use of the most modern radio equipment with a large operating radius, and, in case of need, we resort to radio relay stations. Radio communication is of vital importance to *rezidenturas* operating on the territory of the U.S.A. At the same time, the extensive economic relations which the U.S.A. has with other countries of the world facilitates the support of direct communications between the intelligence units located on the territory of the U.S.A. and the Center and by postal and telegraph communications.

The factor of time has always played an important role in agent operations. Under modern conditions, when our potential enemy is preparing for a war with widespread use of nuclear missiles weapons and intends to launch a

---

[2] EDITOR'S NOTE: Certain portions of this lecture have been deleted because of excessive repetitions and technical discussion of scant interest to the general reader.

surprise attack on the U.S.S.R. and other countries of the socialist camp, this factor has become even more important.

Therefore it is necessary to work out in advance, during peacetime, a reliable system of communications techniques which an agent can use to inform the Center instantly about enemy measures directed toward unleashing a sudden war.

To transmit these messages one must use the most modern and most highly developed electronic technology, which should be improved on continually.

If the imperialists unleash a war, the U.S.A. will be the target of a crushing retaliatory strike causing damage to all the most important political and economic centers of that country. Soviet intelligence should thus adopt timely measures to guarantee the security of its intelligence net. To achieve this it is necessary to disperse operating *rezidenturas* and to move valuable single agents some distance outside the limits of large cities. As for agent nets engaged in collecting intelligence on atomic and missile bases, they should preferably consist of individual sources equipped with radio having direct communication with the Center.

We must mention that, to a significant extent, success in performing intelligence tasks in the U.S.A. depends on agent handling. Therefore we must devote serious attention to this subject.

I. CHARACTERISTICS OF AGENT COMMUNICATIONS

The characteristics of agent communications basically amount to the use of specific methods in organization and utilization. These depend on the characteristics of operating conditions.

The way of life, customs, temper, demeanor, and personality traits of Americans have specific significance. Most of Americans are energetic, enterprising, and open people, having a great sense of humor. They can be described as having business acumen and as being resourceful, courageous, and industrious.

The over-all situation and the absolute power of money in the U.S.A. arouses just one desire in many people—to make more money. In describing a person Americans often use the expression, "He knows how to make money," which means that such a person has a lot of money. The other side of the question, specifically, where the money comes from or how it is "made," is not, as a rule, of interest to anybody. It can be said that Americans encourage any method of getting rich.

American bourgeois propaganda tries in every way to convince the population that anyone can make money if he is sufficiently resourceful.

Such a one-sided upbringing engenders in some of the people an indifference to everything unconnected with business, profits, and gain. An American's circle of interests is often rather small. Many Americans do not read books. Their main interest lies in advertisements, sports news, and cartoons; on the front pages they only glance at the large sensational headlines.

Generally speaking, bourgeois society demoralizes people.

Every American family tries to save money for a "rainy day"; therefore a certain amount is set aside from each pay check.

Wall Street does everything possible to keep Americans from devoting their free time to meditation and deliberation. Movies, cheap concerts, boxing, parks, horse races, baseball, football, restaurants—all these are used to divert the masses from the realities around them.

In general, an American's wants consist of having his own automobile, a comfortable apartment, and a good time. Most Americans, both men and women, smoke.

Americans are very concerned about clothes and outward appearances. They try always to have a clean suit, well pressed with a good crease in the trousers, a clean shirt, and shoes well polished. They send their suits regularly to the cleaner and their shirts to the laundry, both of which are everywhere in the U.S.A. It is customary to change white shirts and socks daily.

Clothing styles in the country change every year. Just as one can determine accurately from specific features the year and make of an automobile, so can one determine from outward appearances the class level of any American.

Despite the frequent change of styles, several general characteristic features of American dress can still be noted: narrow and short trousers, short sleeves, white shirt with a starched collar (on important occasions), and always with a necktie. In clothing, light colors predominate. Americans like loose-fitting shoes, as a rule one or two sizes larger than necessary.

In his free time, when not at work, and especially during the summer, the Americans wear sports clothes: light trousers, short-sleeved shirts, no necktie. Sunglasses are in common use. Outside the office an American's behavior is free and relaxed. Many Americans like to keep their hands in their pockets and chew gum.

Agent communications and agent handling involves first and last working with people, as a rule from the bourgeois world. For this work to be successful, it is necessary to know these people well, their characteristics and their personality traits, and the political and economic circumstances which condition their behavior.

An intelligence officer who does not know the characteristics of the American way of life or who neglects those aspects cannot be a full-fledged agent handler. Thus, for example, an intelligence officer who has an outward slovenly appearance will not command respect from an agent. If an agent does not have sufficient dedication to our intelligence service, the result of this and similar errors on the part of an intelligence officer may leave the agent with the impression that he is working with an inadequate and unreliable organization.

In the organization and utilization of agent communications knowledge of the local area and local conditions is of the utmost importance. Not only the country as a whole, but even every city, has its own individual features which influence agent communications. They may complicate them or, on the contrary, facilitate their successful accomplishment.

New York, for example, is distinguished by its large size and by the great number of its parks, museums, athletic grounds, movie houses, libraries, and other public buildings. People of the most different nationalities comprise a large segment of the population. The city public transportation system, especially the subways, is extensive, and there are a great many buses and taxis.

In New York it is easy to establish a cover story for going downtown either during the day or at night, because New York has many public places. Skillful use of transportation facilities makes it possible to make a good check for the detection of surveillance. Finally, an intelligence officer who speaks with an accent in New York is quite acceptable since a large segment of the city's population speaks with an accent.

There are many large cities in the U.S.A. including such giants as New York, Chicago, San Francisco, etc. The large cities in the U.S.A. offer favorable conditions to organize agent communications and to establish a cover story for them.

On the other hand the organization and utilization of agent communications in Washington are full of difficulties because of the city's small size, its limited number of public places, no subways, and an inadequate public transportation system, especially in the suburbs.

As we know, there are essentially two types of agent communications: personal and impersonal.

Because they do not involve personal contact between case officer and agent, impersonal communications afford the greatest degree of secrecy to the activities of operational agents and they greatly complicate the work of counterintelligence in the identification and exploitation of our intelligence officers.

In the U.S.A., a country with a highly developed counterintelligence effort, the basic type of agent communications is impersonal communications, the importance of which is constantly growing. The task of operational agents consists of using impersonal communications creatively and perfecting their manner of organization.

However, one must remember that proper agent handling and the development of the greatest effectiveness in working with agents require periodic personal meetings with them.

1. *Personal Communications*

Only by personal contact between intelligence officer and agent is it possible to study the agent better, to discover his real feelings, to check on and control his work, and finally—and this is of utmost importance—to instruct the agent, to train him in new methods and in professional intelligence skills, to develop him, and to exert an influence on him through personal example.

The basic types of direct communications are the meeting, the recognition meeting,[3] and communications through a cut-out or transmission points.

Meetings

A meeting betwen intelligence officer and agent is one of the most vulnerable means of communications. Therefore, in organizing a meeting, an intelligence officer must anticipate everything in order to guarantee security.

In organizing a meeting, the closest attention must be paid to such questions as the meeting time, the meeting place, the meeting agenda, the meeting cover story, and the measures to ensure security.

Meetings should be varied as to time of day, days of the week, and dates of the month. For example, meetings should not be held on the fifth day of each month, on Wednesday of every week, or consistently at 8 P.M., because such consistency in the activities of an intelligence officer makes the work of counterintelligence easier. In fact, in order to compromise an operation it would be sufficient for counterintelligence to intensify its surveillance on our intelligence officer for only one day of the month (for example, the fifth of the month), for one day of the week (for example, on Wednesday), and even for only a certain time—until 8 P.M.

Neither, however, should there be an unlimited juggling of times. In choosing a time for a meeting, one must take into consideration the agent's working conditions, his hours of work, his family situation, and the meeting place and area. Consideration should be given to the fact that the agent must have a plausible explanation for his absence from work or his departure from home.

Most Americans spend their days off and holidays with their families or with relatives and friends. Besides this, an agent has family holidays—birthdays of members of the family. An intelligence officer must consider these circumstances, hear the agent's views, and not schedule a meeting on days which are holidays for the agent and for members of his family.

---

3 A "recognition meeting" is an intelligence contact at which a Soviet intelligence officer and an agent meet first for the purpose of mutual recognition, on the basis of prearranged place, time, and identifying marks.

Most meetings are held in the evening. As a rule, the agent does not work in the evening and does not have to ask permission of his boss to leave. In addition, evenings provide the greatest security. It is not recommended, however, to hold meetings in a park, because, unlike Europeans, Americans visit parks only during the day. At the approach of darkness nobody uses the parks. At that time of the day only criminal elements and persons who are mentally ill can be found in the parks. In the press one can find special warnings concerning the danger in going to parks in the evening. It is not unusual for the newspapers to publish detailed accounts of rapes and murders which were committed in the parks during the night.

One may also hold meetings in the middle of the day and during lunch (Americans have their lunch from 1 to 2 P.M.). If it is within his pattern of activities, the agent may leave his office during the day. If such is the case, one can meet him at any time of the day.

Finally, meetings can be held in the morning, before work, because the majority of office workers start work at 9 A.M. and some even at 10 A.M.

We know that at certain periods, which may last from one to several months, counterintelligence concentrates its main efforts on working days during the working hours of Soviet installations, while during preholiday days and holidays, as well as during the morning hours, only preventive measures are in force. Our intelligence officers must always take into consideration all aspects of the counterintelligence agents' *modus operandi* and conduct their clandestine activities during those days and hours when counterintelligence is least active. The selection of times and dates must always be selected with the agent.

As a rule, meetings should be as short as possible; therefore very careful preparations are necessary. In organizing communications from a third country, or from the Center to the U.S.A., and especially in organizing radio communications, one should consider the American practice of changing the time during the summer to be one hour ahead of standard time. Clocks are moved ahead one hour (so-called summer or daylight time, "daylight-saving time") starting at 2 A.M. on the last Sunday in April and ending at 2 A.M. on the last Sunday in September, when clocks are moved back one hour throughout the U.S.A., with the exception of Indiana and Nebraska where daylight time is in effect all year.

In choosing a meeting site, it is necessary of course to consider the characteristics of the country as a whole and, above all, the characteristics of the area. As a whole, conditions in the cities of New York and Washington, for example, are favorable for the organization of agent communications. However, not all areas of such cities are suitable for this. For example, of New York's five sections, which are called "boroughs," Richmond is less suitable than the other areas for organizing agent communications. The reason for this is its isolation from the main city. One can reach the island only by ferry (ferry crossings for Richmond are made from Manhattan and from Brooklyn) or by the bridge connecting Richmond with Bayonne and Jersey City.

New York's other four sections—Manhattan, Bronx, Brooklyn, and Queens—are widely used by our intelligence officers for the organization of agent communications.

However, differences exist not only among the five sections of New York, but also among different sections of the city within the very same area. For example, let us take Manhattan, which is the business area of the city. Negro Harlem is unsuitable for the organization of agent communications in Manhattan. It is located north of Central Park, and the Chinese quarter, located downtown, is also difficult for agents. Extreme squalor distinguishes the Chinese quarter. A properly dressed person will stand out sharply there. As for Negro Harlem, white people cross it only by automobile. A white person is unsafe there, because the Negroes regard every white person who comes there as a curiosity-seeker who came to view them much as people go to the zoo to view the animals in cages.

We do not recommend that meetings be held in the area between Forty-second and Thirty-fourth Streets. This is the busiest part of midtown and therefore has the widest coverage by the police and by counterintelligence.

Likewise, it is inadvisable to hold meetings in the vicinity of the UN Building (along the shore of the East River, between Forty-second and Forty-eighth Streets), near buildings of the permanent representations of various countries to the UN and, above all, the delegations to the UN of representations of socialist countries (the representation of the U.S.S.R. to the United Nations is located at 680 Park Avenue), nor in the vicinity of large banks, jewelry stores, etc.

In Washington, meetings should not be held in the central part of the city, where Congressional buildings, the White House, departmental buildings and other governmental offices, large banks, stores, and restaurants are located. Neither should they be held on the main streets of the city, or in areas where foreign embassies and, especially, the embassies of the U.S.S.R. and other countries of the socialist camp are located. Meetings should also not be held in areas near military objectives or in the Negro district.

Generally, an operation can be compromised through the improper selection of a meeting site. For example, an intelligence officer, who did not know the city well, once selected a meeting place with an agent on a street corner in the evening. A large bank stood on this corner. The intelligence officer arrived for the meeting exactly at the appointed time. The agent was late. The intelligence officer was there for less than two minutes when a policeman approached, asked him what he was doing there, and requested him to move along. The intelligence officer had to leave quickly. In addition, two plainclothesmen followed him until he entered a subway station. The meeting was not held.

In another instance, the site selected for a recognition meeting was a bus stop served by only one bus. Our intelligence officer who was supposed to meet an agent at an appointed time arrived at the meeting site. To guarantee the security of the meeting, another intelligence officer countersurveilled the meeting from a bench in a square near the meeting site. Because the agent did not appear for the meeting that day, both intelligence officers went home. This was repeated two more times. On the third day the agent himself approached our intelligence officer, not the one waiting for him at the bus stop, but the one sitting on the bench in the square, and made contact with him. It was later learned that the agent passed the meeting place each time, sat on a bench in the square, and watched the intelligence officers. He had decided not to come to the bus stop, as he considered it unnatural to wait there because he had no plausible cover story. Only on the third day was the agent convinced that the man sitting in the square was a Soviet intelligence officer. He then approached him, because he considered the square a more appropriate meeting site.

The best boroughs for holding meetings are the Bronx, Brooklyn, and Queens, as well as various parts of Manhattan (the area near Columbia University, the area adjoining Riverside Park, the area east of Lexington Avenue, and others).

As we know, we must select a meeting site that is secure and convenient for holding the meeting. It must also be such that an appearance there can be explained plausibly and convincingly by a cover story. Among such places are crowded streets, parks, sports fields, sports clubs, restaurants, motels, beaches, etc.

Most streets in American cities, including Washington and New York, are quite regular and well planned, and intersect at right angles.

In New York many streets have ordinal numbers as names. In Manhattan, for example, only the far downtown district has word names for streets. North of Houston Street begins the numbered streets: First, Second, etc., through 207th. Fifth Avenue divides Manhattan into two parts: west (in the direction of the Hudson River) and east (in the direction of the East River). Addresses therefore are indicated as follows: 302 W. Fifty-sixth St., N.Y. This means: house (more often, the entrance) no. 302, the western part of Fifty-sixth St., N.Y. One should also give an address this way when speaking. Manhattan avenues run north–south, and many of them are numbered. Streets cross from east to west. In general, the city is well planned, and a person can learn his way around with relative ease. Queens and the Bronx have a good many quiet streets which are good places to meet.

In Washington, all the north–south streets have number names, and those which go from east to west have a letter (for example: A Street or D Street) or a name. Avenues run diagonally and are named after states. Because a street with the same number or name can be in each of the four sections of the city, in writing an address it is necessary to indicate the section of the city. For example, 415 Fifteenth St., N.W., Washington, D.C.

Because of the way New York and Washington are laid

out, they offer the possibility of holding meetings while walking outdoors. For such a meeting an agent is told not the spot (point) of an area but the location of the route, as a rule a small (short) street along which he is to walk at a given time. In such a case, the intelligence officer can observe the agent to determine whether or not he is under surveillance and can then establish contact at the most convenient place.

In selecting a meeting site, one must consider possible sudden changes in the weather which are quite typical of the climate in the coastal areas of the U.S.A. Sunny weather frequently becomes rainy, and vice versa. Americans listen to the weather forecast and, if bad weather is predicted, they take an umbrella and raincoat; Americans do not wear rubbers. Both men and women use umbrellas. Thus, before going to a meeting, an intelligence officer should listen to the weather forecast and, if necessary, take an umbrella or a raincoat. In addition, he should plan for the possibility of rain by selecting a covered place in the vicinity where a meeting can be held (store entrances, subway stations, movie theaters, museums, libraries, restaurants, drugstores, and others).

The existence of a subway in New York helps in locating different places in the city. It should be borne in mind, however, that the subway system there is quite complicated and should be studied carefully before planning to use it for operational purposes.

In learning the subways and the city, one should make extensive use of directories, guidebooks, and maps.

Parks can serve as meeting places. New York parks are usually grassy fields with only occasional patches of trees and bushes. There are many play areas in the parks. The footpaths are of asphalt. Main roads often cut through the parks.

Washington parks are even more unusual. They are usually full of wooded areas and are dissected by main roads near which there are a number of parking places and picnic areas. In general, there are no footpaths. It is not customary to take strolls through the parks.

All of the parks are free. The people make considerable use of them for resting, sports, and exercise. Walking on the grass is permitted in many parks.

Most athletic clubs are open to the public, including

foreigners. Golf is the most popular sport among the well-to-do. Agent meetings can be held at golf courses as easily as in other athletic clubs. During the week there are very few people at the golf courses. On these days the intelligence officer and his agent can arrive at the golf course (preferably at different times, twenty to thirty minutes apart), each can begin to play alone, and at a previously designated time can meet at, let us say, the sixteenth hole or at some other hole (there is a total of eighteen holes). Saturdays and Sundays are less suitable days for holding agent meetings at golf courses because on these days many players gather, tournaments are held, and single play is not permitted. Golf courses are found on the edges of wooded areas or parks in broken terrain where there are many hidden areas. These hidden areas are the best places for holding meetings. In some cases, meetings can be held in clubhouse restaurants.

To hold successful meetings at golf courses, one should learn the conditions there ahead of time. A basic requirement is to know the game and how to play it. Therefore students should learn this game while still at the academy.

Club membership is rather expensive. Also, not all clubs are equally accessible to our intelligence officers. It is even difficult for local residents, to say nothing of foreigners, to get into some golf clubs, if they do not have a certain position in society.

As a rule, a candidate for membership must be recommended by two or three club members.

New York has golf courses in Pelham Bay Park, Van Cortlandt Park (the Bronx); in Dyker Beach Park (Brooklyn); in Forest Park and Alley Park (Queens); in Latourette Park and Silver Lake Park (Richmond); and others. With club memberships so difficult to obtain it is advisable to use public golf courses.

New York and Washington have numerous restaurants, many of them representing different nationalities. Each restaurant has its own distinctive characteristics. One may specialize in steaks (the most expensive steaks are sirloin and T-bone steak), another in seafood; some restaurants have orchestras, others have not. Before selecting a certain restaurant as a meeting site, one should learn everything about that restaurant; the system of service, the type of customers, whether it has a bad reputation with the police, etc.

It is the practice in all restaurants to tip the waitress 10 per cent of the amount shown on the check.

Depending on the nature of the agent operation, the officer and agent may sit at the same table and hold the meeting during dinner. Or they may sit at separate tables, keeping only visual contact for the purpose of exchanging prearranged signals, and have the meeting later on the street after leaving the restaurant. Restaurants are frequently used as a refuge from bad, rainy weather.

Americans like to spend their time in bars. Many bars have no tables. Customers sit on high round stools next to the bar. As a rule, bars do not provide snacks or hot dishes. One can order only drinks: whisky, gin, beer, etc. In order not to attract undue attention the intelligence officer must know how to order sufficiently well. It is not enough, for example, to ask, "Give me a glass of beer." It is also necessary to name the brand of beer ("Schlitz," "Rheingold," etc.). For the customers' amusement, most proprietors install a television set in a corner above the bar. Customers often sit over a single glass of beer for several hours watching television programs.

It is highly recommended to hold meetings in small restaurants located in the residential area of a city.

The American pharmacy (drugstore) is quite different from European pharmacies. Its assortment of goods is not limited to medicines. In many drugstores one can buy the latest newspapers or magazines, purchase food products, have a cup of coffee, or make a telephone call. American drugstores, especially in the large cities, have almost become department stores. Therefore they are never without customers. Drugstores can be used to hold short meetings, as well as for other agent activities (signaling, clandestine phone calls).

Along the highways between cities and near cities there are many motels. A motel is a small hotel by the highway where people traveling by car can spend the night. Generally there are vacancies. The manager always writes down the license number of the car and the driver's name in a special register. No registration is required of other passengers.

Each motel room has its own entrance. One may leave

the motel at any time. Also, the manager need not be informed in advance of one's departure. As a rule, people
depart from a motel early in the morning. The bill is paid
when the room is rented.

It is easy to hold meetings in a hotel of this type.

It is advisable to use motels in cases in which it is necessary to hold a long meeting with an agent in a closed and
isolated location, e.g., when it is necessary to train an
agent in radio or in the use of operational techniques. The
ability to park the car near one's room or in a nearby
garage facilitates the secret unloading of equipment.

Even American movie theaters are distinctive. Most
movie theaters in large cities are open from 12 noon to
1 A.M. Moviegoers enter as soon as they get their tickets
and they may take any unoccupied seat. The moviegoer
leaves whenever he wishes, but, as a rule, he leaves when
another showing begins. Films are shown continuously.
Americans are not content with only a single feature film.
Therefore, movie-theater proprietors show two films, one
after the other, which lasts three to four hours.

Intelligence officers can make extensive use of movie
theaters when organizing agent communications by spending a certain amount of time in them before a meeting.
The fact is that there are few people in most movie theaters, especially on weekdays during working hours. Movie
theaters located away from the center of the city are often
practically empty. Thus, by arriving at a designated time
at a previously determined movie theater and taking advantage of the many empty seats, the intelligence officer
and agent can hold a meeting right in the theater. As an
alternative, they can use the foyer where there are frequently many vending machines selling cigarettes, cold
drinks, chewing gum, etc.

Agent meetings can also be held in outdoor movie
theaters (drive-in theaters) where one can see the films
from one's car.

In the U.S.A. where the counterintelligence effort is
highly developed, planning and preparation for a meeting
are of the greatest importance. In planning a meeting one
should give the greatest consideration to the above-men-
tioned characteristics of the people and of the country, the
working and family situation of the agent, his capabilities,
etc. Insofar as the intelligence officer himself is concerned,

he should thoroughly work out his own conduct. All his movements, his daily routine, his appearances in the city, and his visits to movie theaters, libraries, and sporting events must be subordinated to one purpose—achieving a more flexible and covert system of agent communications. In this regard, all his activities must be natural and plausible.

In planning a meeting, one must consider the site, the nature of the site, and the time of the previous meeting, so that the next meeting will be held at a different site and, if possible, at a different time. In New York, for example, it is possible to alternate the use of the different "boroughs" —the Bronx, Queens, Brooklyn, Richmond, and Manhattan.

At the same time a meeting site is selected, places must be provided along the route to the meeting site where signals can be posted. Signals can be arranged along this route to cancel a meeting. This is done with the help of radiotechnological means in those cases in which it is established that the officer who is on his way to an agent is under surveillance. Before going to the meeting site, the officer must ascertain that there are no signals which cancel the meeting.

The question of leaving for a meeting must be thoroughly planned. It is particularly important that those officers working in a *rezidentura* under cover know how to leave their offices quite naturally at both a reasonable and required time, how to explain their visits to certain public places, and how to make their "spot checks" along the route. The continuity and regularity of agent communications depends on such planning.

Under present working conditions, one should start for a meeting not later than two to three hours before the scheduled time. During this time one must check along the stipulated route to detect any surveillance by the counter-intelligence service. If surveillance is detected, one must carry out his cover reason for leaving, then return to the point of departure to attempt to make another secure departure. At times the intelligence officer will have to make several tries before he succeeds in evading surveillance. In most cases, therefore, the intelligence officer leaves his office quite early. For example, if on the day of a meeting, while on his way to or from lunch, an intelligence officer notices that he is not being watched, there is no need for him to go home for lunch or to return to work after lunch. He goes to the city, makes another very careful check, spends the rest of his time in a movie theater or some other area which affords security, and appears at the meeting site at the designated time.

Below are several examples which illustrate an intelligence officer's method of departure for a meeting and the nature of an intelligence officer's actions.

An intelligence officer had a Sunday meeting scheduled for the latter part of the day. After breakfast he took his family for a walk in the park. He usually took such a walk every Sunday. On the way he invited a friend. The two families chose some benches in the park and seated themselves in the sun. The adults talked and glanced through newspapers and magazines which they had bought at a stand, while the children played nearby. They all visited the zoo together, and they also looked at some monuments. While passing a movie theater, they looked at the advertising display and decided to see the new film. They all went inside. The intelligence officer who had a meeting scheduled quickly departed through a side door and left for the meeting site along a previously selected route. The meeting was successful. Toward evening the intelligence officer and his family returned home after a restful Sunday.

In another case, a meeting was designated for a Monday evening. After work on Saturday, the intelligence officer left for the house in the country where some families spent all summer and where most of the Soviet officials spent Saturdays and Sundays. As usual on Monday morning he returned to the city in his car. On the way, observing that he was not under surveillance he decided to take advantage of this opportunity. He did not go to work but parked his car instead on a street (some distance from his place of business—and from the meeting site). He then took a subway and went to a different part of the city. He got off the subway at an uncrowded station and confirmed the absence of surveillance; he then bought a newspaper and again boarded the subway. Later the intelligence officer got off at another station and went to an Automat for breakfast. Still there was no surveillance. After breakfast the intelligence officer made several more trips on the subway and fully confirmed the absence of any surveillance. To avoid being detected on the streets by the counterintelligence service, the intelligence officer entered a movie theater. Twenty to thirty minutes before the scheduled meeting, he left the movie theater and proceeded to the meeting site, again checking en route. The meeting took place at the designated time.

The intelligence officer must think through in advance all such problems connected with the planning and conduct of a meeting, including possible variations of departures, and make a report for the *rezident*.

Conduct of a meeting is the basic phase of agent operations. Meetings play an important role in the training of an agent. Therefore they should be conducted in a precise, well-planned manner, with a thorough knowledge of the case and paying attention to all circumstances. During the meeting the intelligence officer must not only describe the order of the meeting with the agent and the cover story for the meeting, review the instructions for the alternate meeting, hear the agent's report, and assign him tasks, but he must also instruct him in various matters, listen to his questions, and give him competent answers. The officer must take a constant interest in the agent's personal affairs and situation so that the agent can be cautioned in advance, if need be, about possible errors in his conduct.

Because meetings should not be too lengthy, the intelligence officer must be well prepared for each meeting. During the meeting he must be alert to catch the most fleeting changes in the agent's mood. To a large extent, an officer's authority depends on his conduct, his discussion of operational matters, the ability to conceal the fatigue which he might be feeling after a long trip and many security checks. Nor should he show any nervousness, whatever the external reasons might be. If the officer exhibits stability and self-control, the agent will acquire confidence in working with our intelligence service.

Despite the fact that very important problems are being discussed at a meeting, the case officer should have a sense of humor, something which is valued highly by American agents, be able to tell appropriate jokes, and enliven the conversation. This aids in establishing good rapport with the agent.

Recommendations for the Conduct of Intelligence Officers
Engaged in Personal Communications

The conduct of an intelligence officer bears directly on his work agents. The people with whom the intelligence officer comes in contact must be convinced that all his actions and his bearing are determined by his job, by the nature of his personal life, and by his cultural tastes. He must accustom those around him to a pattern of activities which naturally includes agent work. To overcome the obstacles of counterintelligence, our intelligence officers, besides following the general rules of intelligence operations, must adopt special measures. The intelligence officers in a *rezidentura* under cover, who are under constant surveillance by the counterintelligence service, are particularly compelled to make considerable use of these measures.

We know that stationary counterintelligence observation posts carefully record the time that all employees of Soviet installations arrive for work and the time they depart. The counterintelligence service can draw up charts on the arrival and departure of our colleagues using them to organize their surveillance. To invalidate such "charts" and make it impossible for the counterintelligence service to establish any kind of regular or recurrent pattern of the length of time our colleagues stay inside an installation, we must explain trips to the city on operational matters by hiding and disguising them. Such trips are made under the pretense of conducting personal business —visits to movie theaters, museums, exhibitions, and athletic events, the purchase of personal articles, etc.

During a trip to the city, the intelligence officer checks for surveillance. If he is sure that he is not under surveillance, the intelligence officer uses this trip to the city to get a better knowledge of the city, to choose new meeting places, dead drops, and locations for posting signals, and to select and confirm routes along which checks can be made for surveillance. If he detects surveillance, the intelligence officer must act according to a previously conceived cover plan: he can act like a person who is very interested in books and, consequently, visit a number of bookstores, or he can pretend to be a devotee of baseball, the most popular sport in the U.S.A. It would be helpful if an intelligence officer could give the impression that he is fond of taking walks about the city. At the same time, he must try to learn the methods of surveillance. Under no circumstances must he reveal that he has detected the surveillance, in order not to show his familiarity with the *modus operandi* of the counterintelligence service. Similarly, an intelligence officer who is under surveillance must not exhibit nervousness or do anything which is unnatural.

The officer should analyze each trip to the city, make conclusions on the operating methods of the counterintelligence service and on the city and public places. These conclusions should be written down in a special notebook. Gradually the intelligence officer will accumulate a collection of very valuable material. The intelligence officer having such notes can adjust more easily to operating conditions. He can select meeting places ahead of time in widely scattered areas, as well as dead drops and places for posting signals. He will be able to develop more plausible cover stories for his actions connected with agent operations.

American stores periodically hold sales of their merchandise at lowered prices. At the beginning of the sale a large number of people usually gather at the store. In their efforts to advertise the sale, the proprietors invite newspaper photographers to the opening of the sale. To avoid being caught by the photographer's lens, our intelligence officers and members of their families should not visit the store during the beginning of the sale.

It is recommended that intelligence officers take more frequent walks about the city at different times. Depending on his work load and the purpose for the walks, he can take walks after work, before work, and during his lunch hour. After he "accustoms" the counterintelligence service to such walks, the intelligence officer can use them later to support agent communications (posting or checking of signals), agent meetings, servicing dead drops, etc.

Every intelligence officer who handles agents must have previously selected and well-learned countersurveillance check routes which afford the most favorable opportunities for the detection of surveillance.

A countersurveillance check route may include travel

by automobile (which can then be parked on a side street or in some city garage); the use of uncrowded streets, especially in those areas where parallel surveillance is impossible; travel by subway with several transfers at quiet stations; visits to large stores and other buildings with numerous elevators, entrances, and exits, and which also have direct access to subways (Pennsylvania Station, Macy's and Saks department stores, Chrysler Building, and others).

At the same time that such routes are being selected, a good cover story should also be developed to explain the intelligence officer's presence in a certain area.

Detecting surveillance, the intelligence officer must not go to meet the agent; but he must spend some time naturally in the city, thereby convincing the counterintelligence agents of his reasons for being in the city, and then return home. Thus, the surveillance agents will have to report that their quarry was not seen committing any clandestine act.

Generally, as we mentioned, there is no particular need for the intelligence officer to return to the *rezidentura* late after an evening meeting. Nevertheless, he must, inform the *rezident* about the meeting by passing or posting a prearranged signal: "Meeting held; all is well," or, "Meeting did not take place," etc. The type of signal will depend on particular conditions: the working and personal relationships between the officer and *rezident*, etc. The signal can be noted by the *rezident* himself, by his chauffeur, or by any other intelligence officer who is free that day. A detailed report on the operation can be made the next day.

The U.S. counterintelligence service regards all Soviet employees as possible intelligence officers and constantly attempts to determine which of them has special work to do. With this in mind, a number of means are employed, the main ones are eavesdropping (in apartments, in automobiles, on the street, etc.), surveillance, and the study and analysis of the conduct of Soviet employees. With this fact in mind, the intelligence officer must not discuss operational matters outside the confines of the specially equipped room in the *rezidentura* and he must conduct himself so as not to arouse the suspicion of those around him. It is vital that he avoid establishing a pattern in his intelligence work.

In organizing agent communications the intelligence officer will often have to make use of the public transportation system. The subway is the primary means of transportation in New York.

There are no ticket collectors on the subway. There are special metal revolving gates at the entrance. The ticket office does not sell tickets but only metal tokens which cost fifteen cents. In passing through the revolving gate, the passenger inserts the token in a special slot.

An intelligence officer should always have several tokens with him, especially on the day of a meeting, so as not to waste any time in buying them at the subway entrance.

It is hard to imagine how an operation for maintaining agent communications can be conducted in New York without using the subway, which, despite its complexity, facilitates one's orientation in the city. It also affords a convenient place to check on the existence or absence of surveillance.

Inadequate knowledge of the city's means of transportation, especially the subway, can sometimes lead to the cancellation of an agent meeting. The following example will underscore this point:

Our officer left for a meeting at the designated time. After carrying out a carefully planned check, he was convinced that he was not under surveillance. Twenty minutes remained before the meeting. During that time he had to go to the meeting site and once more confirm the lack of surveillance. According to his plan, he was required to use the subway for this purpose. At a quiet station he boarded a subway going in the opposite direction from the meeting site, and planned to get off at the next station and take a train back to the meeting site.

There were hardly any passengers in the subway car. A man sat down near him, opened a paper, and began to read.

The officer passed one stop and then got off. The man with the newspaper, apparently recollecting something suddenly, folded his newspaper quickly and also got off the subway. The intelligence officer was alerted. He got on the next train and sat down. The man with the newspaper sat down in the same car and again began to read his paper. The intelligence officer became alarmed—this was obvious surveillance. He rode past his stop. The man with the newspaper did not appear to be paying any attention to him. Finally, the intelligence officer could stand it no longer and got off the subway. The stranger did not even lift his head and rode on. None of the other passengers got off. The intelligence officer went out on the street and made a check—no external surveillance. But by then it was too late to make the meeting. He made another check, confirmed the lack of surveillance, then went home. An important meeting was canceled.

It was later determined that the intelligence officer had at first taken a local train, had passed his stop, and then had taken an express going in the opposite direction. Local residents frequently do the same thing, when they have a long way to go. They get on at the nearest intermediate station and take a train going in the direction of the closest express stop and then transfer to an express. Our officer did not consider this, because he did not know the subway system.

Buses stop at the request of passengers. Before his stop, the passenger must pull a cord overhead which serves as a signal to the driver. The driver also stops the bus when signaled by passengers waiting at a stop, providing, however, that there is room on the bus.

Buses operate without conductors.

One enters a bus through the front door and exits through the rear. By the driver is a small meter similar to a small box into which the passenger drops fifteen cents in New York and twenty cents in Washington. The driver allows the entrance and departure of passengers, makes change, and hands out transfers (at the request of the passenger). He gives change for bills but only up to five dollars. Thus the intelligence officer must always be certain that he has small change or one-dollar bills.

Tickets are not used on buses. The system for streetcars is the same as for buses.

Taxis do not have stands. In addition, they are not allowed to stop on the street for any length of time, because the streets are full of traffic. Taxis move constantly, stopping only for passengers. A taxi can be stopped anywhere; this is done merely by waving the hand or by loudly shouting, "Taxi!" when an empty one passes.

The driver writes in his log the place a fare entered the taxi, the place he got out, and the time. Therefore an intelligence officer must never take a taxi directly to the meeting place. To use taxis properly in operational work, the officer must know several addresses in different areas and be prepared to give the driver a destination at a moment's notice.

In the U.S.A. our intelligence officers make extensive use of personal cars (especially in Washington), not as a site for meeting or talking with an agent, but as a way of going to the meeting area, and of detecting and losing surveillance. The reason is that the counterintelligence service can secretly install in Soviet employees' cars special eavesdropping microphones or devices which emit a signal giving the location of the car.

Automobiles are very widely used as a means of transportation in the U.S.A. An automobile is a necessity in the way of life of the American family. All the streets in the large cities are filled with automobiles. It is difficult to find a free place to park. There are not enough garages and parking lots to meet the demand. Nevertheless, there is always room on parking lots and in garages (old large buildings are often made over into garages). This is because their fees are so high. For example, the cost of parking a car in the center of Manhattan can be as much as seventy-five cents, and even one dollar, for the first hour, up to a maximum of three dollars per day.

The intelligence officer using an automobile in arranging communications should always park his car in a garage or a particular place a considerable distance from the meeting site, even in a different borough. He should continue his mission using public transportation.

There are many companies in the U.S.A. which rent cars. All that is required to rent a car is to present one's driver's license and leave a small deposit. Use of rented cars in the organization of agent communications is recommended, because this has a number of advantages. For instance, an intelligence officer can drive to the city in his own car, check for surveillance, and then leave it in a suitable area or in a parking lot. He can then complete his job in a rented car. This use of automobiles makes the work of the counterintelligence service more difficult.

The largest car rental company is the "Hertz Rent a Car Service."

There are many toll bridges and tunnels in the U.S.A. The toll is collected by a policeman (about twenty to twenty-five cents for a one-way trip). We assume that at these points notice is taken of cars with diplomatic plates, especially of those cars whose drivers are employees of Soviet installations. Therefore we must avoid such places when carrying out intelligence tasks and use, instead, bridges without tolls where it is more difficult to keep track of cars.

[EDITOR'S NOTE: At this point one page is missing from the original document. The missing material evidently includes further discussion of clandestine meetings between intelligence operatives, as well as types of recognition signs and key words ("paroles") for mutual identification of Soviet officers and their agents.]

which can be with initials, with some kind of figure in the form of a stamp or mark, or some kind of special stone. Besides rings, women wear many ornaments around the neck, on the hands, and on their clothing. Depending on the sex of the agent, any of these can be used as a recognition sign.

Americans make widespread use of various wrapping papers with advertisements in the form of writing, photographs, colored pictures, etc. Small objects (a box for vitamins or chewing gum) with a distinctive packaging can also be used as recognition signs.

The best parole is the question, and the countersign, the answer to the question. Both parole and the countersign have predetermined words or phrases. These predetermined words can be the names of museums, movie theaters, libraries, and monuments or the titles of movies, books, newspapers, magazines, etc. Both the question and answer must be short and simple in content and in pronunciation. We know that it is difficult to pronounce some English words. In this regard, additional difficulties may confront our officers who have just arrived in the country.

In arranging for a recognition meeting and, above all, for the recognition signs, parole, and countersign, the intelligence officer has sufficient opportunity to exhibit his initiative, resourcefulness, and creativity, and to solve all problems with originality and with due consideration to local conditions.

Communication Through Cut-outs[4] and Live Drops

In individual cases it becomes necessary to resort to cut-outs and live drops as a means of arranging communications.

In each agent operation, the case officer very carefully trains a cut-out: he instructs and trains him, instills in him the desired qualities, and monitors his fulfillment of tasks. Even when communications are through a cut-out, it is still necessary for the case officer to meet periodically with the agent to determine personally whether the work is going properly and whether the tasks are conveyed to the agent. The officer must take an interest in the relations between the cut-out and the agent in order to influence the entire course of the work.

If the agent lives in another city, the cut-out must have the opportunity of visiting that city. The following people have this opportunity: service personnel of the various types of passenger and freight transportation; representatives and agents of trading and manufacturing firms, insurance companies, and real-estate offices; correspondents, etc.

The cut-out receives (from the agents) only such information as is required for his work. As a rule, the names and addresses of the case officer and agent are not given to the cut-out.

In communications via a live drop there is no personal contact between the agent and the intelligence officer. Operational materials from the agent to the case officer, and vice versa, are passed through a third person who more often than not is the proprietor of a small private business (bookstores, secondhand bookstores, antique stores, drugstores, etc.).

The case officer visits the live drop to receive materials only after a special signal is given. The proprietor of the live drop places the signal after receiving material from the agent.

---

[4] A "cut-out" is an agent or subordinate officer used as an intermediary between the officer and an agent, to make surveillance more difficult.

2. *Impersonal Communications*

Under the complex operating conditions existing in the U.S.A., the primary type of agent communications is impersonal. Experience has shown that this is the most secure type of communication, because there is no direct contact between agent and officer.

Impersonal communication is used to pass operational materials, to assign tasks, and to pass material—technical supplies—to the *rezidentura* and individual agents.

It is used between the Center and a *rezidentura,* as well as within a *rezidentura.*

The basic forms of impersonal communications are radio communications, communications via dead drops, communications via postal-telegraph systems, telephone, press, and communications via signals.

Radio Communications with the Rezidentura

Ultrashortwave (UHF) radio sets are used for communications within a *rezidentura.* These sets greatly improve the efficiency of agent communications. They have a small operating radius. Nevertheless, while on the air, accidental or intentional radio monitoring is possible; and our intelligence service cannot afford to ignore this consideration. The use of specially devised codes, ciphers, signal system, and operating schedule makes the use of this set completely secure. Radio can be used to call the agent for an emergency meeting, to tell him when a dead drop has been loaded or unloaded, to notify him about a change in dead drops, etc. UHF radio can also be used within *rezidenturas* to assign tasks to an agent and to receive intelligence information from an agent. Radio communications over UHF must be short.

There are many different ways of using a portable UHF set. Following are only some of the uses:

. . . when the intelligence officer and the agent are traveling along different streets;

. . . when the intelligence officer and the agent are driving in different parts of the city;

. . . when the intelligence officer is in the city and is transmitting while on the move, and the agent is receiving in his apartment;

. . . when the intelligence officer is on shore, and the agent is in a boat.

To have communications via UHF, one must set up a schedule for radio communications. This schedule provides for a location for each radio station, the precise time to start radio communications (date, hour, and minute), which radio station will begin transmitting first, and other details.

Dead-Drop Communications

Dead drops are extensively used for communication within a *rezidentura,* as well as for communications between the Center and Illegal *rezidenturas,* within agent nets, or with individual agents.

The use of dead drops in communications with agents has several advantages over personal meetings. Some of these advantages are:

. . . dead-drop communications are safer as there is no direct contact between the officer and agent;

. . . they are more secure, because the agent need not know the intelligence officer with whom he is in contact via the dead drop;

. . . by using a dead drop it is unnecessary for the intelligence officer to have a good knowledge of the local language;

. . . when necessary, it is possible to replace or substitute one intelligence officer with another;

. . . there is the possibility of wide flexibility in time.

The use of dead drops, however, is not without its drawbacks. The dead drop is an intermediate link between the officer and agent, and materials placed in a dead drop are outside their control for a certain length of time. Therefore we must reduce to a minimum the length of time during which materials are located in a dead drop.

In practice, stationary, portable, and mobile dead drops are used.

Stationary dead drops are selected or specially prepared in parks and squares, in trees, in the ground, in fences, in benches, in monuments, in public buildings, and beyond populated places such as forests, fields, seashores, riverbanks, etc.

In selecting and preparing a dead drop in a park, one must bear in mind that a number of American parks (for example, Central Park in New York) have many squirrels which can destroy the dead drop (especially in hollow trees) and carry off our material.

As a rule, a dead drop is used only one time, after which a different one is used. In the U.S.A., it is preferable to adopt a system consisting of a series of dead drops for the agent and a certain number for the case officer. One should work out a schedule for using dead drops so that the agent will know the dead drops to be used in January, those to be used in February, etc. The schedule can be prepared for a half year or for a full year, depending on the number available.

The use of portable dead drops is more worthy of consideration because it is considerably easier to find places for them.

We have no particular difficulty in finding places in American cities which contain many discarded objects (boxes, tubes, bottles, cans, match boxes, cigarette packs, paper, and others). Often those objects lie about in plain sight for long periods of time without arousing any interest. Among such objects, which are of no use to anybody, and which can be found in yards, in parks, etc., an intelligence officer may leave a similar object with agent material concealed in it at a preselected place to have it picked up later by another agent.

American household articles, medicines, and many other articles are packaged in all kinds of boxes, cans, tubes, cases, and made of cardboard, metal, and plastic. Hence there is an extremely wide selection of packages which can be used as portable dead drops.

Among the items which can be used as portable dead drops and which can be prepared in advance are pieces of wood, stone, brick, clay, cement, plastic, gypsum, and others.

Wide use can be made of magnetic containers in New York, which has many metallic structures. They can be attached to anything metal.[5]

---

[5] Use of such devices was cited by U.S. authorities in the 1958 spy trial of the Soviet *rezident* Colonel Rudolf Abel.

In communication through a dead drop the agent receives his assignments in written form. These agent assignments must be encoded or enciphered. Also, the material itself must be in a form suitable for passing through a dead drop. Therefore we must train the agent in the use of ciphers, codes, the preparation of soft emulsion film, microdot, and secret writing.

The technical knowledge of the average American is rather high. In his everyday life he makes wide use of machines, equipment, and instruments. Therefore the training of an American agent in operational technology is all the easier.

The types of signals and the places for posting them in connection with dead-drop communications are the same as those which were discussed in the [deleted] section "Characteristics of Other Types of Meetings." Here we need only to emphasize the particular importance and convenience of radio in exchanging signals.

The intelligence officer in the U.S.A. who has initiative and imagination will be able to use dead drops frequently when organizing agent communications.

One or two days prior to loading or unloading a dead drop, the intelligence officer submits his plan for the operation to the *rezident* and receives his approval.

Several hours before the operation (no later than one and a half to two hours) the intelligence officer travels to the city. He uses the time available for a thorough check to determine whether or not he is under surveillance. At the same time, he checks a prearranged place for a danger signal if such arrangements have been made. As a rule, the check for a danger signal is made in an area other than the area where the dead drop is located.

Having determined that he is not under surveillance and that there is no danger signal, the intelligence officer goes to the dead drop. In the immediate vicinity of the dead drop he must once more confirm that conditions are right; then, without losing any time, go to the dead drop, load (unload) it, and proceed on the prescribed course.

On his return trip the intelligence officer can place his signal that the dead drop has been loaded (unloaded).

The Clandestine Use of the Postal and Telegraph Systems

The American postal and telegraph system is highly developed.

The enormous stream of mail sent abroad, as well as that sent inside the country, can be successfully used for intelligence purposes both in peacetime and in war.

The postal and telegraph service is quite efficient, and letters are rarely lost. Thus, we have favorable conditions for using the postal and telegraph system in the interests of intelligence in support of agent communications.

The postal and telegraph system is used to send concealed intelligence messages. Intelligence messages must in no way differ from an ordinary letter, either in superficial appearance or in their overt contents.

To make effective use of the postal and telegraph system in agent communications, we must learn everything concerning the writing and sending of letters and telegrams. All this is especially important for the Illegal intelligence officer.

In the U.S.A. the name of the addressee is written first on the envelope, then the house address and name of the street, and finally the city and state.

Most business letters, and many personal letters as well, are typewritten. Intelligence officers should also type their operational letters in order to conceal the handwriting of the sender.

There is a standard form for business letters. Samples of different letters can be found in the specially issued brochures (letter-writing manual).

When making clandestine use of the postal and telegraph system to send operational messages, we must make full use of ciphers, codes, secret writing, and other means of concealing the message being sent.

Because there is fierce competition among business firms in the U.S.A., it is a usual practice to send enciphered messages addressed both to business enterprises and to private individuals. This helps the work of our intelligence officers in their use of the postal and telegraph system for intelligence purposes.

To have effective agent communications via the postal

and telegraph system even in wartime, we must train the agent in peacetime in the use of ciphers, codes, secret writing, and microphotography, while providing him with accommodation addresses. This is important also because there will be a tightening of the censorship of the postal and telegraph system in time of war.

There are different methods of organizing communications with a *rezidentura*. *Residents* receive correspondence from agents either at their home address or at an accommodation address. Correspondence to the agent can be sent to his home address, to a hotel address, or to a post-office box rented by the agent.

Clandestine Use of the Telephone

The telephone is an integral part of the American way of life. Many business and commercial affairs are transacted by telephone. There are more than four million telephones in New York alone. Besides private (personal) and office telephones, there are also many public telephones. Typical of American public telephones is that they have their own numbers and can receive calls. This can be used in agent communications. For example, on a predetermined date and time the intelligence officer can talk from a public telephone with an agent who goes to another previously specified public telephone at a prearranged time. It is preferable to select a telephone in a sparsely populated area and to use it during working hours when public telephones are not busy. In addition, public telephones can also be used as a signaling means.

The most convenient telephones for an intelligence officer to use are those located in large department stores, subway stations, and drugstores.

One can also call other cities from a public telephone. To make such a call, one dials the operator by depositing ten cents and then gives the city and telephone number of the person being called. In such a case, an additional sum is needed which the operator will indicate; therefore the intelligence officer should have with him one to one and a half dollars in change.

If the circumstances are favorable, it is possible to use an agent's home or office telephone. In both cases the

officer must know the time and the days when the agent
is at home and at work, who might answer the phone,
what the agent usually discusses at that time, etc.

The U.S. counterintelligence service makes extensive use
of telephone tapping; therefore our intelligence officers
under cover rarely use the telephone and when they do,
they do so covertly.

Telephone conversations must be short and well planned.
Special phrases (designating an emergency meeting or
something else) must always be within the context of the
conversation.

Experience shows that individual agents not infrequent-
ly forget the communications arrangements, resulting in
a break of the work routine. It is, therefore, advisable to
check periodically the agent's knowledge of individual
parts of the communications arrangement, including code
words and their meaning.

The following case can serve as an example. A code
phrase had been agreed upon to call an agent to a meeting from another city. When the need arose, the intelligence officer called the agent at work from a public telephone. The intelligence officer identified himself by his
code name and then gave the code phrase. "My wife and
I would like to thank you very much for the gift you
sent us for our family vacation."

The bewildered agent asked, "Who? I? Sent a gift?
What gift?" The intelligence officer realized that the agent
had forgotten the communications arrangements. He then
calmly repeated his name (code name), then asked, "Apparently you didn't recognize me?" He repeated the code
phrase once more. This time the agent understood. He
shouted happily into the receiver, "Excuse me, my dear
friend, I didn't recognize you at first. I'm very glad that
you both were pleased with my modest gift." A week later
the agent appeared for the emergency meeting.

It is an American custom to spell out difficult words,
especially surnames. (In the U.S.A., the word is first
spelled and then, as in England, pronounced.) Our intelligence officer, especially the Illegal intelligence officer,
must be able to spell out loud; he must be able to spell
any word quickly and unhesitatingly. This is perfected
through training. One must prepare a telephone conversa-

tion very carefully so that neither the context of the conversation nor the speaker's accent arouses the suspicions of an outsider.

If one plans to use a telephone when organizing agent communications, he must give serious consideration to the use of a cut-out telephone.

As a rule, a cut-out telephone is called from a public telephone. Such conversations are in code and should correspond to the cut-out telephone owner's work so that they will not vary in the least from the owner's daily telephone conversations. Signals can be given over the telephone (by voice or by rings). In transmitting signals over the telephone, we must pay careful attention to the time set for the signal; the time of day, code phrases, and the number of rings should be changed frequently.

The case officer plans the arrangements for telephone communications, as well as the code, taking into consideration the agent's suggestions.

The Use of the Press and a Signaling System

The U.S.A. has up to two thousand daily newspapers with a circulation of about fifty-seven million, and more than seven thousand magazines. Both newspapers and magazines give considerable space to advertisements and all kinds of announcements. Newspaper companies receive sizable profits from advertisements and announcements and therefore accept them very readily.

For example, in 1958, readers paid a total of one to one and a half billion dollars for newspapers, while representatives of financial and industrial circles paid out more than three billion dollars for advertising. Thus, publishing houses receive several times more in profits from advertisements and announcements than they do from the sale of newspapers.

Advertisements published in American newspapers differ greatly in content and in length. The most common ones deal with the sale and rental of living quarters, the sale of personal effects, employment opportunities, announcements of weddings, divorces, births and deaths, the loss of valuables and pets, etc. Below are several samples of advertisements which could be used in intelligence work. [Following samples appear in English.]

POSITION WANTED

Housework—Mature Colombian maid speaking a little Eng. will give considerable care to children or invalid lady; do efficient general housework. $25–$30 per wk. Exeter 4-0482, 7–10 P.M.

DOMESTIC EMPLOYMENT

Chauffeur, white—wanted. Age 35 married. 12 years exp. Intelligent alert neat. Fordham 4-7457 before noon.

PUBLIC NOTICES AND COMMERCIAL NOTICES

My wife, Jane Smith Doe, has left my bed and board. I am no longer responsible for her debts. John Doe, 17 Leslie Lane, Dobbs Ferry, New York.

LOST AND FOUND

Briefcase left in taxi Wednesday afternoon Jan. 4th traveling Idlewild Airport to 1506 Woodside Avenue, New York. Reward Dunhill 4-0892, ext. 534.

CATS, DOGS AND BIRDS

Poodle tiny white. Lost in Queens, New Year's Day. Answers to the name "Tiny." $250 reward. Humboldt 6-9016.

One can see from these examples that many advertisements can be adapted quite easily to the transmittal of information. Among the code words which can be used are: the names or description of a lost article; a description of the circumstances; the place and time it was lost; the size of the reward for returning the valuable or pet; etc.

Illegal *rezidenturas* have a greater opportunity to make use of the press in arranging agent communications. *Rezidenturas* under cover may use the press on a lesser scale, primarily to transmit information or signals from agent to intelligence officer. On the whole, the U.S.A. presents favorable conditions for the use of the press for intelligence work.

A sum of money is paid to place an advertisement or some kind of announcement in the press. The text of these advertisements will contain a prearranged coded secret message.

In arranging communications involving the use of the press, it is necessary to specify the particular newspaper or magazine in which the coded intelligence information will appear, the approximate dates of publication, and the form of the correspondence (advertisement, announcement, etc.)

Coded announcements in the press can serve as a means of communications not only within a *rezidentura*, but also with the Center. In communicating with the Center, the major newspapers which are sent abroad should be used (*The New York Times*, New York *Herald Tribune*, and others). Within a *rezidentura*, however, it is better to use small local newspapers because there is less likelihood of censorship over them and because it is simpler to place announcements in them.

As a rule, signaling plays an auxiliary role in organizing communications. When using dead drops and when holding personal meetings and recognition meetings, intelligence officers use signaling a great deal.

Signals should be varied as much as possible. We must also make sure that the signals are natural and do not attract the attention of an outsider. They must be sufficiently legible and precise to preclude any misinterpretation.

Agents must exchange signals at a distance while in sight of each other. Various objects may be used for this (handkerchief, gloves, cigarettes), as well as a certain color of clothing and other means.

Signals can also be given by specially constructed technical means. To transmit infrared signals not visible to the eye, a pocket flashlight equipped with a special infrared light filter can be used. Infrared signals are received with the binoculars "B-I-8," which have a special "phosphorus" element for this purpose that changes invisible infrared rays into visible ones.

Signals may be transmitted by an announcement in the local press or by postcard, letter, or telegram.

Lastly, sound signals can be sent by radio or telephone.

Thus, signals can be subdivided into graphic, object, light, sound, and personal signals.

Graphic signals are prearranged marks in the form of geometric figures, lines, letters, ciphers, etc., written in pencil, chalk, nail, or some other sharp object in a specific, prearranged place.

Object signals are various small objects put in a specific, prearranged place. The object itself may serve as a signal; as can its position; or the object and its position together may be a signal.

A thorough study of the specific features of the country enables one to select the most natural signals. For example one of our intelligence officers called an agent for an introductory meeting by sending the newspaper *Washington Daily News* to his apartment. The intelligence officer went to the city, made a careful check, and then called the newspaper office from a public telephone and asked them to start delivery on the next day to the address he gave them (the agent's address). A week after delivery started, the agent appeared at the prearranged meeting place. Signals can also be made by sending the agent books, magazines, or merchandise from self-service stores (markets) where it is the practice to deliver these things to the home.

A large variety of signals allows great diversification in the use of signals and prevents patterns. Certain signals (graphic and object) are used with dead drops; others (light signals, and sound signals transmitted by phone or radio) are used to call an agent for a meeting and to warn of danger. The third group (signals given by radio and signals given through the mails or press) is used for communicating with the Center or with an agent living in another city.

Thus, the selection of signals and the methods for their transmission depend on the circumstances, the tasks, and the operational situation.

*Nature of the Organization of Direct
Agent Communications between the Center and
Intelligence Organs in the U.S.A.*

The U.S.A. is not only a great distance away from the Soviet Union, but it is also located in another hemisphere. This complicates the systematization of direct communica-

tions between the Center and the American *rezidenturas.*
This is the principal characteristic influencing the organization of direct agent communications.

We must, however, maintain regular communications
between the Center and the *rezidenturas* in both peace
and war.

We have three types of direct communications between
the Center and *rezidenturas:* radio communications, courier communications, and communications through the
use of the postal-telegraph system. A brief description
of each type follows below.

Organization and Implementation of Agent Communications in Peacetime

RADIO COMMUNICATIONS: Radio communications provide
the most rapid means for transmitting orders and instructions from the Center to *rezidenturas* and for sending reports from *rezidenturas* to the Center.

Every Illegal *rezidentura* must train a radio operator
and then properly legalize him. It must also get in advance
the latest radio equipment (from the Center) and check its
operation. This must be done even now, in peacetime.

Because of our distance from the U.S.A., should the
need arise, we can set up radio relay stations which can
be located on ships, submarines, and aircraft. We also
must not exclude the possibility that in the not too distant
future we can install a radio station on an earth satellite.

For successful maintenance of radio communications
between the Center and *rezidenturas,* we must work continuously to improve high-speed radio equipment with
long operating ranges.

The broad introduction of radioelectronic equipment
and the large number of specialists in this field facilitate
our work of selecting, training, and legalizing radio operators.

The Center can use our broadcasting stations to transmit instructions to *rezidenturas* by coded signals. Such
signals must be planned in advance and given to *rezidenturas.*

For communications from the Center to Illegal *rezidenturas* widespread use is made of one-way radio com-

munications sent by the Center by way of enciphered radiograms, signals, and prearranged phrases.

The Illegal intelligence officer is given an operational code and a schedule of one-way radio transmissions in which are indicated the date, time, and frequencies of the radio broadcasts.

The intelligence officer may acquire a radio receiver locally with a shortwave band, to receive coded W/T messages. Ownership of such a receiver by the intelligence officer arouses no suspicion whatsoever in the U.S.A. There is no registration of radio and television sets in the U.S.A., nor is there a fee charged for their use. The radio operator receives one-way radio broadcasts from the Center in his own apartment.

Radio-operating conditions in a country may change, depending on internal conditions and international relations. Therefore every intelligence officer must constantly study these conditions carefully and promptly report any changes to the Center.

COURIER COMMUNICATIONS: The great progress in aircraft construction and shipbuilding, and the expanded network of air and sea communication routes between the U.S.A. and other countries of the world, most of all between the U.S.A. and European countries—on which hundreds of thousands of passengers and thousands of tons of freight which are carried yearly, facilitate our organization of Illegal courier communications.

In organizing Illegal courier communications in peacetime between the Center and *rezidenturas* in the U.S.A., great assistance can be furnished by the *rezidenturas* under cover. The Center sends mail (currency, documents, operational equipment, etc.) to the *rezidenturas* under cover by diplomatic pouch. The *rezidenturas* under cover then transfer materials to Illegal *rezidenturas* through the Center's dead drop. Any materials for the Center from Illegal *rezidenturas* are recovered from dead drops by operatives of the *rezidenturas* under cover and are sent to the Center by diplomatic pouch. Such an organization of communications, however, does not guarantee clandestinity and security. This is particularly true of the U.S.A., where our intelligence officers working under cover in

Soviet installations are kept under strict surveillance by the counterintelligence service.

Therefore, even in peacetime we must organize and use Illegal courier communications which are capable of functioning efficiently in wartime.

The quick delivery of materials is vital. Therefore, when organizing courier communications, it is advisable to use the airlines between the U.S.A. and Europe.

The U.S.A. has air communications not only with the NATO countries (Denmark, Norway, England, France, Iceland, Italy, Turkey, the Benelux countries, Portugal, West Germany) but also with the neutral countries (Sweden, Austria, Switzerland). This facilitates the selection of itineraries for the Center's couriers.

The aircrews of the airlines know the operating conditions at the airports well. They should be used as couriers—also ground crew personnel who can deliver material from the U.S.A. to one of the countries of Europe (and from Europe to the U.S.A.) with the help of mobile dead drops in aircraft.

Steamship companies which maintain service between the U.S.A. and Europe can also be used to conduct courier communications between the Center and *rezidenturas* in the U.S.A.

USE OF POSTAL AND TELEGRAPH SYSTEMS: Communications with Illegal intelligence officers are maintained through the use of the postal-telegraph system. All postal correspondence is sent only to specific addresses. Therefore the Illegal intelligence officer is provided with accommodation addresses (primary and alternate) to which he writes letters intended for the Center.

While the Illegal intelligence officer does not have an address, the Center can send letters to him addressed to the hotel where he is planning to stay or where he had stayed. After renting an apartment the Illegal officer is in a position to receive correspondence at his place of residence. He must immediately send his address to the Center, and he must do this in at least two or three letters.

The mails can be used as a way to deliver graphic and object signals. The following can denote signals: sending a certain letter; the color and size of the envelope or paper; the cost or number of stamps; the nature of the letter; the kind of salutation; the signature; etc. The signal must look natural and not attract the attention of postal employees or censors. This is important because the letters containing signals go through the usual postal channels.

Organization and Use of Agent Communications in Wartime

RADIO COMMUNICATIONS: In time of war, the main type of communication between the Center and individual Illegal intelligence officers and *rezidenturas* can be two-way radio communications.

We must remember that in wartime the conditions for maintenance of direct communications between the Center and *rezidenturas* will be considerably more difficult. The search for Illegal radio stations will be intensified; there will be interruptions in the power supply; there will be fewer opportunities to obtain radio spare parts locally; and there will be less power.

To ensure reliable wartime communications during peacetime we must provide for the following:
1) reserves of radio sets and parts (and providing for reliable and long safekeeping);
2) storage batteries for radio sets;
3) selection of alternate apartments for radio operations;
4) timely evacuation of radio equipment from large industrial centers which could be hit by missile strikes;
5) supplying *rezidenturas* with radio operators in case the latter are mobilized or given special assignments.

Modern agent radio communications, with high-speed equipment and separate installations for two-way and one-way communications, reduces to a minimum the operating time of an Illegal radio station. At the same time, this almost completely precludes its being located by counterintelligence direction finding.

In wartime we must conduct continuous monitoring for individual radio-equipped sources, agent nets, and *rezidenturas* on assigned frequencies for high-speed equipment.

COURIER COMMUNICATIONS: In wartime, Illegal couriers cannot be replaced, because they are the only means that can be used to send documents, materials, and technical means. Therefore their organization calls for special preparation.

Experience has shown that in wartime the possibilities for using civilian aviation and ocean liners for courier purposes are reduced; fewer passengers travel to and from Europe; customs inspections are stricter; and it is much more difficult to provide cover stories for travel abroad by a foreign courier (from Europe to the U.S.A., and return).

In the inspection of baggage the customs service in the U.S.A. makes extensive use of the latest achievements in science and technology. Not long ago, the chief of the Federal Bureau of Investigation, Edgar Hoover, proposed the use of X rays to screen baggage transported in aircraft.[6]

For couriers between the Center and Illegal *rezidenturas* in wartime, it is better to use the crews of ships and of civilian and military aircraft. We should therefore try to have agents on steamships (among officers, seamen, stevedores, cooks), on aircraft (among the crew members), at airports, and in the offices of steamship companies.

In the recruitment of agents preference should be given to Americans because they are highly trusted both in the U.S.A. and in the countries of Europe. It is much easier for an American agent to deliver mail for the Center from the U.S.A. to one of the West European countries (neutral countries or an ally of the U.S.A.) and mail to *rezidenturas* in the U.S.A.

We must not exclude the possibility of getting a courier to the American mainland by submarine. It must be remembered, however, that the U.S.A.'s shore defenses are stronger than those of other countries of the American continent. Therefore one should not always attempt to land an agent directly in the U.S.A. At times it is possible to send mail to a third country (for example, Mexico) and then deliver it overland to the U.S.A. Mail sent in this manner can be placed in the Center's dead drops.

To ensure stable courier communications in wartime we must provide in advance for the replacement of couriers

[6] *The New York Times*, April 2, 1960.

who might be called into service and select individuals who for some reason (because of age or health) will not be subject to military mobilization.

Use of the Postal and Telegraph Services

With the outbreak of hostilities, censorship will be tightened and a number of restrictions may be adopted in connection with postal and telegraph correspondence. During World War II the U.S. censor checked practically all correspondence going abroad, making broad use of special chemical reagents to test for secret writing.

Without changing the over-all meaning, the censor is permitted to alter the word order of telegrams and strike out words or entire phrases in letters.

The purpose of all these measures is to hinder the activities of foreign intelligence services. Neither the U.S.A. nor any other country, however, has the censorship capability to subject all postal and telegraph correspondence to control.

In our opinion, business correspondence between American and foreign firms will continue in time of war. Many American firms specialize in selling merchandise imported from other countries. For example, some firms sell British woolens in the U.S.A., others sell West German radios, while still others sell Swiss items, etc. Business, therefore, compels these firms to maintain communications, including postal and telegraph, with their overseas suppliers.

Therefore accommodation addresses should be acquired even in peacetime, based on American organizations and enterprises which will maintain business correspondence with foreign governments even in time of war. They can then be effectively used during wartime.

II. HANDLING AN AGENT NET

In this section we shall examine only some of the problems concerning agent handling; and specifically:
. . . ensuring the completion of the principal intelligence tasks;
. . . ensuring clandestinity of agent net operations;
. . . ensuring a state of readiness in an agent net;
. . . consolidating agents in intelligence nets.

1. *Fulfillment of the Principal Intelligence Tasks*

*Definition of the Basic Intelligence Tasks and Directing
Agent Nets for Their Fulfillment*

Intelligence tasks of strategic agent intelligence are
defined by the General Staff of the Soviet Army.

Under modern conditions, when the U.S.A., as the
principal imperialist power, is preparing to unleash a surprise war with the mass employment of nuclear/missile
weapons, the basic tasks of strategic agent intelligence are
the early warning of U.S. preparations for an armed attack against the U.S.S.R. and other socialist countries and
the report of this to Headquarters.

In view of the probable nature of a future war, an
important task is the systematic collection of the most
complete data on the following questions:
1) the locations of missile bases, depots for nuclear weapons, plants producing atomic weapons and missiles of
various designations, scientific research institutes, and
laboratories developing and perfecting weapons of mass
destruction;
2) information as to the nature and results of scientific
research work in creating new models of nuclear and missile weapons and improving existing ones;
3) the status of antiaircraft defense, including the entire
radar detection and warning system;
4) the plans of U.S. military commanders on the use of
nuclear/missile weapons;
5) U.S. military preparations in the various theaters of
operations.

Strategic agent intelligence in the U.S.A. must learn
of preparations for a surprise attack against the U.S.S.R.
and other countries in the socialist camp and warn Moscow of it. That is its primary task.

To assure the further strengthening of the defensive
power of the Soviet government, we depend to a large
extent on the successful fulfillment of the tasks levied on
the intelligence organs in the U.S.A.

During a crisis period, intelligence efforts must be
directed toward the prompt disclosure of the enemy's im-

mediate preparations for attack and the reporting of his grouping of forces and means, primarily his means of nuclear attack. The most important task of intelligence is the prompt reporting of objectives in the U.S.A. against which we plan to carry out the first strikes.

Assignment of Targets to Agent Nets

We must assign targets to agent nets in accordance with the basic intelligence tasks and the operational capabilities of the agents. First of all, we must have agent nets in those government installations possessing the most complete, authentic information on matters of intelligence interest, primarily data on military planning. The following organs of the supreme military command are in this category:

National Security Council, Department of Defense, Armed Forces Policy Co-ordinating Council, Joint Chiefs of Staff, Departments of the Army, Air Force, and Navy and their staffs, and the Strategic Air Command.

It is vital to introduce agents in those targets where it is possible to obtain data on the work of enterprises producing nuclear and other weapons of mass destruction. Such targets are:

1) Atomic Energy Commission (includes twelve departments and ten operations groups, co-ordinating the majority of atomic plants, laboratories, and testing stations);

2) Joint Congressional Atomic Energy Committee;

3) Specially-created Department for the Construction of Atomic Installations;

4) Military Co-ordinating Committee of the Department of Defense;

5) Bureau of Atomic Energy of the Department of the Navy.

The following centers for the production of nuclear fuel are of great intelligence interest: Oak Ridge (Tennessee), Hanford (Washington), Paducah (Kentucky), and others. One of the largest centers for the production of atomic weapons is Los Alamos (New Mexico).

2. *Establishment of Clandestine Agent Net Operations; Transfer of Agent Nets to Impersonal Types of Communication*

As has been mentioned, in the U.S.A., under conditions of severe counterintelligence activity, impersonal forms of communications constitute the basic method of communication, because they provide the greatest degree of security and clandestinity in the conduct of clandestine operations. The intelligence officer's task is to train his agents properly and to transfer them to impersonal forms of communication promptly. Before converting an agent to working through dead drops, as one of the forms of impersonal communications, the intelligence officer must train the agent in the use of dead drops and in the use of signals.

Initially the agent will not trust the reliability of dead drops and will be reluctant to place classified materials in them. The agent can be convinced of the reliability of dead drops gradually, for example, by first placing money in it for him if he is being paid for his work.

An example proves this point. For a long time Agent S was reluctant to work via dead drops. The intelligence officer's attempts to convince S of the security of working via dead drops were completely unsuccessful. Then the intelligence officer cleverly began placing money in the dead drop for the agent. The first time S came to the dead drop ahead of the case officer and watched him place the money in it. As soon as the case officer had gone a short distance from the dead drop, the agent ran up to the dead drop and removed the money. The second time, the agent removed the money more calmly. Gradually he began to trust the dead drop as a form of clandestine communication and was no longer afraid to place operational materials in it.

Transfer of an agent to impersonal communications requires the case officer to be considerably more careful than when maintaining personal communications. He must instruct the agent thoroughly in such matters as the *modus operandi* of the counterintelligence service, adherence to proper operational techniques in agent operations, etc.

*Briefing of Agents and Indoctrinating
Them in Conspiracy*

Conspiracy in agent operations is directly dependent on
the indoctrination of the agent and on the skill and efficiency with which the officer conducts his briefing. The
officer must brief the agent on specific points, keeping in
mind the main objectives: to provide assistance, to demonstrate how to fulfill his assigned task better and more securely, to help correct mistakes he has committed or
eliminate shortcomings, and to teach him the qualities
required in clandestine operations and in intelligence. It
should be emphasized that the national characteristics of
American agents are such that they are often careless in
their operations and they make poor conspirators. They
therefore need extremely careful briefing.

A good case officer always attempts to be authoritative
in the agent's eyes. Precise, businesslike briefings are very
important in earning respect.

The agent should be briefed very carefully on how to
behave properly in front of his family, at work, and in
public. When necessary, the intelligence officer must brief
the agent on how to smuggle material out of an installation, how to return it undetected, and how to reproduce
the material at home or at work. It is very important that
the agent know how to develop a proper and plausible
cover story for his extra income and for his periodic
absences. Depending on his assignments, the agent is
given certain information on the work of the counterintelligence service. In briefing the agent on this subject,
the officer must not frighten the agent with any exaggera-
tions.

The officer is forbidden to use special Soviet intelligence
terminology in briefing his agents or to reveal intelligence
operating techniques.

3. *Providing a State of Readiness in an Agent Net*

*Training of Agents and Agent Nets for Independent
Communications with the Center*

It is obvious that the operating conditions of a *rezi-*

dentura will change in time of war. From previous experience, the *rezidentura* under cover will stop operations as soon as official Soviet installations are closed. Therefore one of the most important tasks of a *rezidentura* under official cover during peacetime is to train agents and prepare agent nets to maintain independent communications with the Center for operation during wartime. Such training is very complex and includes the following:

Training the agent to operate radio sets; providing him with a radio set; setting up a reserve radio set in case the agent's radio breaks down, and against this eventuality securing an independent power supply; supplying reliable and long-time safekeeping of all radio equipment; renting safe apartments for operational radio communications; carrying out trial runs of radio nets in peacetime in order to keep radio operators in reserve and systematically to check the combat readiness of the equipment.

Arranging special reserves of currency and articles of value; establishing permanent recognition meetings in two or three countries which will permit contact to be made with the Center's couriers; acquiring accommodation addresses, and putting them to use promptly.

Training programs providing for independent communications with the Center must give both the individual agent and principal agent detailed instructions on the problems of organizing and conducting intelligence operations, but only to the degree necessary for them to carry out the work specifically assigned to them. They are made familiar with some of the operating procedures of the counterintelligence service *vis-à-vis* intelligence targets. During training the case officer devotes particular attention to making sure that they are thoroughly briefed and indoctrinated.

The Center makes the decision to transfer an agent or an agent group to a status of independent communications. The intelligence officer handling the agent gives the Center all information necessary to make such a decision. Therefore it is the intelligence officer's responsibility to know the agent and, above all, his operational capabilities, his political orientation, and his feelings toward the U.S.S.R. We should note that some intelligence officers try too hard to learn everything about an agent in one meeting. This immediately puts the agent on his guard. Studying an agent should involve a systematic, planned, and gradual acquisition of information concerning him. In view of the fact that individual agents react very adversely to attempts by the intelligence officer to learn specific pieces of information about them, the officer must prepare very carefully for every meeting with the agent.

Finally, we need to have preliminary talks with every agent scheduled to be assigned to an agent net to get his agreement to continue working under the guidance of a local person (principal agent).

Location of Agent Nets in a Future War

In a future war, despite the irreconcilable contradictions between the capitalist and socialist countries, both sides will pursue the same political and military objectives.

To protect their socialist achievements the Soviet Union and other countries in the socialist camp will be forced to fight for the complete defeat of the enemy's armed forces and the disorganization of his rear area. We anticipate that in order to frustrate the plans of the U.S.A., if it should unleash a war, mass missile strikes will be launched against the most important enemy objectives, including the deep rear. We can assume that in a war which will see the mass employment of the most modern and destructive means of war, including nuclear missiles, the borderline between front and rear disappears.

Under modern conditions, therefore, agent nets must be located in new locations, with consideration given to the nature of a future war. To save valuable agents in wartime, we must disperse the agent net over the entire country, preferably in small cities which do not represent important targets for nuclear/missile strikes. With the advent of a crisis we must take steps for the prompt movement of agents, if this has not been done earlier, away from targets for nuclear strikes. In view of these new conditions *rezidenturas* and agent nets must be small. In special cases, individual agents can be equipped with radios for direct communications with the Center to report on such targets as nuclear weapon depots and missile and other military bases.

4. *Consolidation of Agents in Intelligence Nets*

Methods of Incentive and Coercion

One of the means of consolidating agents in an intelligence net is the proper use of the measures of incentive and coercion. The use of either measure depends on the actions and deeds of the agent. Therefore the case officer's first responsibility is to have a thorough knowledge of the agent, because only in this way can he properly assess the agent's work and skillfully take appropriate measures in order to control the agent. The intelligence officer who knows the national traits of Americans should be able to establish rapport quickly with the agent and positively influence him.

For example, knowing that Americans do not like discipline and are always demonstrating their independence, the intelligence officer must refrain from resorting to obvious pressure on the agent. One should not burden the agent with decisions, but should skillfully encourage and direct intelligent initiative on the part of the agent.

As we know, Americans are distinguished by their efficiency and resourcefulness. Therefore the intelligence officer must exhibit a high degree of precision and efficiency in working with American agents, respond quickly to their reports, and provide intelligent instructions and orders.

Americans have a great love of money and a desire for financial gain. This American trait can be exploited by paying an agent for his work in order to increase his personal interest in working for us. Payments must be prompt and equitable. This disciplines the agent and improves the case officer's authority.

As we know, all measures employed in influencing an agent are divided into those which are moral and those which are material. Material measures are primarily used with agents recruited on a material and financial basis, while moral measures are used with agents recruited on an ideological basis.

A similar distinction is made between incentive and coercive measures.

Among the incentive measures are: praise of the agent's

work by the case officer, statements of appreciation to the agent, gifts to the agent, and the transfer of more valuable and deserving agents from piecework payment to a regular salary.

Among the coercive measures are: noting shortcomings in the agent's work, reducing his salary, suspending his salary for a definite period of time, using threats (employed in extreme cases).

[EDITOR'S NOTE: One page of text is missing here. In the following passage, the lecturer continues his discussion of American living conditions.]

We must bear in mind the standard of living in the country and the agent's ability to provide a cover for the receipt of additional funds. As we know, the standard of living in the U.S.A. is quite high. A qualified industrial worker, for example, earns about four hundred dollars a month, which is several times higher than workers earn in European countries.

In our practice, agents are usually paid by the job, money is paid for each specific piece of material and according to its value. With this system of payment, an agent quickly realizes the necessity for conscientious work.

A system of payments by the month and by the job also induces the agent to make the fullest use of his operational capabilities. Under the system of material inducement an agent who is working poorly can have his monthly payments reduced or stopped. To encourage an agent, monthly payments are increased or bonuses, awards, or valuable gifts are given.

Thus, for example, Agent B, who was on a monthly salary, reduced his production appreciably. His attendance at meetings and visits to dead drops were irregular. Despite rebukes by the intelligence officer, the agent's work did not improve.

The intelligence officer decided that he would have to use material inducement. With the Center's permission he began to pay the agent only for those months during which the agent actually worked and performed his operational activities. Soon B realized that further backsliding would result only in the loss of all his extra income. He began to perform his tasks more efficiently. As a result regular communications with him were now possible.

Payments are used both as an additional inducement to work and as a reinforcement of the ideological motivation of an agent.

How to Use the Basic National Traits and the Customs, Habits, and Way of Life of Americans in Agent Handling

In the U.S.A. people from various strata of society have their own habits, customs, and standards which frequently become unwritten laws.

The intelligence officer who knows all these characteristics well will have a greater understanding of the American agent and his actions. This understanding is vital for effective agent handling and indoctrination.

Realizing that the majority of Americans are open, straightforward, and happy people with a great sense of humor, the intelligence officer can prepare for and conduct a conversation with an agent that is not dull but lively and witty. When preparing for a meeting he must try to anticipate the agent's questions, prepare good answers to them, and at the meeting to answer the agent in such a manner that the agent will feel that the intelligence officer is being frank with him.

During a meeting questions may arise which require a decision by the *rezident*. The officer must know how to evade such questions at the meeting without showing his lack of authority in this.

A proper regard for these American characteristics will help the intelligence officer to win over the agent. As is known, a frank conversation is the best way of learning the agent's political orientation and his biography.

Americans, like other people, are patriots. They are proud of their country's achievements; they honor their national heroes, and value their cultural monuments. Therefore the intelligence officer must be careful not to indiscriminately criticize things American, but must remember that an unfortunate statement, for example, about some popular U.S. President (George Washington, Abraham Lincoln, Thomas Jefferson) might offend the agent. A negative result might also come from an officer's underrating American culture.

The officer can skillfully put to use such American traits as efficiency, resourcefulness, boldness, and perseverance. These will help the agent to carry out operational tasks and to exploit his operational capabilities fully.

Americans, to a larger degree than representatives of many other peoples, have a natural love of freedom and independence, and do not like discipline. The officer must respect this characteristic and not resort to open pressure on the agent. He must not assign tasks rudely but must skillfully direct the agent's work and praise his intelligent initiative. He must not order the agent around. An officious tone of voice by the officer will just antagonize the agent.

An officer, especially a beginner, who does not know English well must be very careful of what he says and not use such unfortunate expressions as, "I order," "You must," etc. Such expressions usually evoke a negative reaction.

As we have said before, Americans have a strong desire to make extra money, to get rich. This characteristic can and must be taken into consideration when carrying out the task of consolidating agents in an agent net.

A thorough understanding of the national characteristics of Americans, as well as other traits, will help the consolidation of agents into agent nets, allow the fuller use of their operational capabilities, permit their thorough indoctrination, and increase the officer's authority.

CONCLUSIONS

The basic principles of organizing agent communications and agent handling, which have been accumulated and verified through many years of experience in Soviet strategic agent intelligence, may be applied to all *rezidenturas* regardless of the country, be it the U.S.A. or some other country.

Therefore, the characteristics of agent communications and handling in the U.S.A., are governed not merely by these principles but also by the proper and thorough regard for the operating conditions in the country and by the consideration of the national traits of Americans, their way of life, their customs and habits. They are also conditioned by the role played by the U.S.A. in aggressive military blocs and by the country's geographic location.

In this training material we have examined only some of the characteristics which exist in the country at the present time. We must keep them constantly in mind in working with agents.

It is necessary, however, to keep something else in mind: each year sees many changes in people's lives. Old buildings and entire city blocks disappear, to be replaced by new buildings and parks. Libraries will be filled with new books, new movies will appear, and people will acquire new customs and different tastes. Technology will develop rapidly. In the U.S.A., a highly industrialized power, these changes will occur to a greater extent than in other countries. Therefore the job of every officer is to seek and consider all such changes which might exert an influence on the organization of agent communications and handling.

The intelligence officer must be prepared to make independent decisions on operational matters during practical work. The degree to which he is able to consider the characteristics of the country, a specific city, the American people, and finally, of a specific person, an agent, will determine the extent to which he learns and acts properly and the extent to which he will be successful in his handling of agents.

The difficult but very absorbing work of organizing agent communications and handling demands that the officer apply all his strength and energy to this task. He must seek constantly new ways of finding solutions to operational questions.

INDEX

R

S

About the Author

OLEG PENKOVSKIY was possibly the greatest spy the West ever had.

FRANK GIBNEY is currently the Vice-Chairman of the Encyclopedia Britannica Board of Editors. Prior to his Board of Editorship, he was President of the Encyclopedia Britannica, Japan, a *Newsweek* Senior Editor, a staff writer for *Life,* and editor and publisher of *Show* magazine. His books include: *The Krushchev Pattern, Frozen Revolution, The Operators,* and *Japan: The Fragile Superpower.*

FOR YOUR EYES ONLY!

True stories of international espionage that read like the best espionage thrillers....

The Ballantine Espionage/Intelligence Library

11